BIG JIM LARKIN

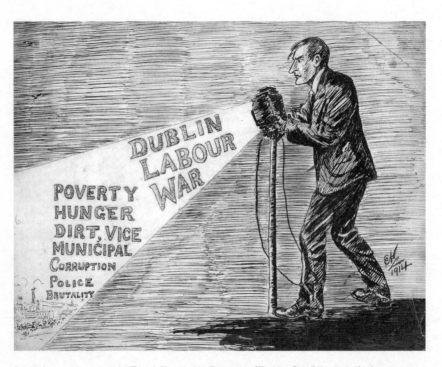

Larkin's struggle, as seen by Ernest Kavanagh. Courtesy of Dublin City Library & Archive.

BIG JIM LARKIN

HERO OR WRECKER?

EMMET O'CONNOR

UNIVERSITY COLLEGE DUBLIN PRESS

PREAS CHOLÁISTE OLLSCOILE BHAILE ÁTHA CLIATH

2015

First published 2015
by University College Dublin Press
UCD Humanities Institute,
Belfield,
Dublin 4
Ireland
www.ucdpress.ie

ISBN 978-1-906359-93-5 *hb*

CIP data available from the British Library

*The right of Emmet O'Connor to be identified as the
author of this work has been asserted by him*

Typeset in Scotland in Adobe Caslon
and Bodoni Oldstyle by Ryan Shiels
Text design by Lyn Davis
Printed in England on acid-free paper by
CPI Antony Rowe, Chippenham, Wilts.

Contents

Illustrations

6a   The WUI Band. The social side of trade unionism was always important to Larkin and a big part of his appeal.

6b   Lying in state with a guard of WUI and Citizen Army veterans. Note his clasped hands, the crucifix, and the Starry Plough.

7a   WUI banner. Larkin as the public history would remember him.

7b   International Brigaders at the Larkin statue in Dublin's O'Connell Street, now a symbol of the city, Labour, and solidarity.

8   Liberty Hall, marking the centenary of the lockout.

Acknowledgements

All biographers of James Larkin should begin with a tribute to the late Emmet Larkin and Donal Nevin, who first placed the study of Larkin on a scholarly basis. I am grateful also to the late and sadly missed Andrew Boyd, John de Courcy Ireland, Tom Crean, and Joe Deasy for sharing their recollections of Big Jim and Young Jim and directing me to sources, to Conor McCabe, Nóirín Greene, Theresa Moriarty, and D. R. O'Connor Lysaght for help with research in Dublin, and to other colleagues of the Labour History Society for inspiration. James Curry regularly offered fresh and unusual angles on Larkin, he and Virginia Hyvarinen generously supplied details on Jack Carney, Jim Monaghan provided ready advice on Irish Trotskyists, John P. Swift kindly clarified references on the 1942 ITUC, Ida Milne assisted with oral history, Gerry Watts alerted me to obscure references, Barry McLoughlin was an indispensable confederate in Moscow, and he and Helga Woggon assisted with queries to German archives and on German history. I am particularly indebted to the staffs of Magee College Library, Derry Central Library, the University libraries at Coleraine and Jordanstown, the Gilbert Library, the National Library, the National Archives, the Labour History Archive, the National Archives of the UK, the Russian State Archives for Social and Political History, UCD Archives Department, the US Federal Bureau of Investigation, and Butte-Silver Bow Public Archives. The British Academy provided financial assistance for research in Moscow, and Ulster University granted sabbatical leave to expedite the writing and paid for translation, photocopying, micro-filming, and off-printing. I am grateful to staff and students at Magee College, and to Gerry Devine, Frank Cassidy, Terry Curran, and Michael Doherty for technical assistance. As before, the anterior debt is to the enlightened directors of UCD Press and their executive editor, Noelle Moran, who is always so supportive and pleasant to work with. And thanks finally to Tom and Teena, Colette, Deaglán, and Laura for everything. None are to blame for what follows.

The book is dedicated to Rosa, a future Rosa sparks, who may read it into the twenty-second century, when she will find me only in the library.

EMMET O'CONNOR

Abbreviations and Note on Terms

ORGANISATIONS, NAMES, PLACES, AND TITLES

ARCOS	All-Russian Co-operative Society
ASRS	Amalgamated Society of Railway Servants
BPA	Belfast Protestant Association
BTUC	British Trades Union Congress
CI	Communist International
CPGB	Communist Party of Great Britain
CPI	Communist Party of Ireland
CPUSA	Communist Party of the United States of America
DMP	Dublin Metropolitan Police
ECCI	Executive Committee of the Communist International
GAA	Gaelic Athletic Association
ICWPA	International Class War Prisoners' Aid
ILP	Independent Labour Party
ILPTUC	Irish Labour Party and Trade Union Congress
IPP	Irish Parliamentary Party
IRA	Irish Republican Army
IRB	Irish Republican Brotherhood
ITGWU	Irish Transport and General Workers' Union
ITUC	Irish Trades Union Congress
IWL	Irish Worker League
IWW	Industrial Workers of the World
IWWU	Irish Women Workers' Union
MP	Member of Parliament
NSFU	National Sailors' and Firemen's Union
NTWF	National Transport Workers' Federation
NUDL	National Union of Dock Labourers
OBU	One Big Union
PC	Parliamentary Committee
RIC	Royal Irish Constabulary
ROP	Russian Oil Products Ltd
RWG	Revolutionary Workers' Groups
SDF	Social Democratic Federation

SIPTU	Services, Industrial, Professional, and Technical Union
SPI	Socialist Party of Ireland
TD	Teachta Dála
UK	United Kingdom
US	United States
USSR	Union of Soviet Socialist Republics
VKP(b)	Vsesoyuznaya Kommunisticheskaya Partiya (bolshevikov) (All-Union Communist Party (Bolsheviks))
WIR	Workers' International Relief
WPI	Workers' Party of Ireland
WUI	Workers' Union of Ireland

SOURCES, ARCHIVES, AND LIBRARIES

DJ	Department of Justice
DT	Department of the Taoiseach
FBI	Federal Bureau of Investigation
ILHA	Irish Labour History Archive
NA	National Archives
NAUK	National Archives of the United Kingdom
NLI	National Library of Ireland
PRONI	Public Record Office of Northern Ireland
RGASPI	Rossiiskii Gosudartsvennyi Arkhiv Sotsial'no-Politischeskoi Istorii (Russian State Archive for Social and Political History)
UCDA	University College Dublin Archives
UUMC	University of Ulster, Magee College
YMCA	Young Men's Christian Association

NOTE ON TERMS

By 'Labour' is meant trade union bodies and related political groups, or officials of these organisations. All other references will be referred to as 'labour'. The Irish Trades Union Congress was founded in 1894, added 'and Labour Party' to its name in 1914, changed the title to the Irish Labour Party and Trade Union Congress in 1918, and to the Irish Trade Union Congress in 1930. Throughout this period it was also known simply as 'Congress'.

The infamous baton charge on Bloody Sunday, 1913 became a stock image of the injustice that fuelled Larkinism. Reproduced courtesy of the RTÉ Stills Library.

INTRODUCTION

Jim Larkin is the greatest figure in Irish Labour mythology. He has of course very human and realistic significance also, but his first association – possibly we ought to say concussion – with the Irish mind in general was distinctly mythological. To many he is non-human and mythological still.

W. P. Ryan[1]

—

'Another book on Ireland's most famous trade unionist needs no defence', began the 2002 biography *James Larkin*. If Larkin is getting better served, he remains understudied. Benchmarking Larkin against James Connolly, and vice versa, is facile, and irresistible. A 'parallel lives' beckons. Some 200 studies of Connolly were available in 1980. Today, the number exceeds 1,000, in languages as diverse as Danish and Catalan.[2] By contrast, relatively little of substance has been written on Larkin, despite his longer, more colourful and controversial life, and greater impact on trade union history. While Connolly has attracted several comprehensive biographies and hundreds of thoughtful interpretations, the typical publication on Larkin is either a short monograph on an aspect of his career, or a semi-popular encomium. Even the centenary of the 1913 Lockout did not change this situation, and gave us more monographs, some indeed very valuable, and more encomiums. While Larkin is referred to in over 700 publications, the only substantial biography is Emmet Larkin's *James Larkin: Irish Labour Leader, 1876–1947* (1965), to which should be added Donal Nevin's edited collection, *James Larkin: Lion of the Fold* (1998), a great, if uneven and repetitive, compendium.

One can understand the reluctance to grapple with a complete wordpicture of Big Jim. He left no private papers, and scarcely bothered with documentation as a union leader. Information on the post 1930 period is particularly inadequate on the Workers' Union of Ireland (WUI). In part this was because of his distaste for paper work. In part it was deliberate, to prevent others knowing his business. The price he paid was that much of the extant comment on his character and motives was penned by his opponents or critics. Personal portraiture, the lifeblood of biography, is even more problematic. Little is known of his domestic life, though pioneering work on his relations with his sister, Delia, and Jack Carney, his sometime familiar, has been done by Moriarty and Curry.[3] Larkin's life, over half of which was spent outside Ireland, has a disjointed, episodic character, and switched back and forth between apparently messianic purpose and languid self-indulgence. The first 30 years were spent in obscurity. For the next seven, from 1907 to 1914, he seems too overwhelming a figure to be condensed in a book. The birth of the Irish Transport and General Workers' Union (ITGWU) was mythic, and the 1913 Lockout an epic. He then spent nine enigmatic years in America, and returned home to a quarrel the trade union movement wished to forget. There followed decades of disappointment, painful for a biographer as well as his subject. Emmet Larkin glossed over the last 25 years in as many pages, pleading: 'To chronicle nearly twenty years of decline is depressing.'[4] Inevitably, all biographers of Larkin are judged on how they handle the darker side of his life. Character flaws and mistakes test the mettle of any writer who wishes to affirm the worth of his subject's work and ideas. As noted, comparison with Connolly is unfortunate and inescapable. Of the two Larkin has come across as the more one-dimensional figure with nothing to offer other than a powerful voice and the simple message of solidarity. In reality, he had plenty of good ideas on trade unionism and on politics, and offered insightful observations on topics as diverse as surviving imprisonment or the commemoration of World War I. They do not deserve to be forgotten just because, unlike Connolly, who obliged historians by collecting his thoughts neatly and clearly, their author scattered his about newspaper articles and speeches or embedded them too implicitly in his activities. And, of course, Larkin's Napoleonic genius for motivation ought to be required study for all would-be leaders of men and women.

My own *James Larkin* (2002) was commissioned as a short, synoptic overview. This did not appear to be a problem initially, given the volume, as distinct from the quality, of writing on the subject, the absence of private papers, and the paucity of sources in Ireland on his activities after 1923. There seemed little more to be said until the archives of the Communist International in Moscow and Larkin's FBI file, not available to previous biographers, presented much more information on the post-lockout years, and – more perplexingly – a radically different picture of the man to that in existing biographies. Now the word limit became a severe hindrance as it was not possible to write comprehensively on the fresh evidence or present *prima facie* the material on which conclusions were based. In consequence, the book's criticism of Larkin was sometimes taken to be unfair, or based on opinion, or an attack on Larkinism. Since 2002, the inadequacy of the book has been increased by the discovery of police files on Larkin in the National Archives of the United Kingdom, and by new intelligence on Delia and Carney. Carney especially, will be an important window on the private Larkin.

Larkin's discrepancy and ego-centrism make him the kind of man who can be understood only through biography. He was no mere reflection of the cause or the organisations he claimed to serve. In consequence of his secretiveness, his private ambitions are not always evident from his public statements. The greatest mistake people make about Larkin is to take him at face value. The coyness has left him open to the charges of inconsistency, hypocrisy, and selfishness. It has also concealed a sophistication in his thinking. Far from being a mindless militant, for example, he appreciated that strikes were usually expensive and often futile. The *Irish Worker*, Liberty Hall, and Croydon Park, were not just a newspaper, a head office, and a recreation centre for the ITGWU. They were alternative methods of class struggle through the weapons of mass media, solidarity, and culture. At a more prosaic level, so many questions about Larkin, such as why he went to America in 1914, why he linked up with Moscow 1924, and why he broke with the Communist International in 1929, can only be answered by painstaking historical archaeology. But they can be answered. Through exhaustive biography it is possible to construct a complete picture and surmount the three supreme challenges posed by Larkinology. The first of these is to be certain that one is dealing with the genuine Larkin, not the public image. The second is to find the evidence that will compensate for the want of records. The third is to do justice to the fact that Larkin's greatness lies not in what he did, but in image and idea; in the image of 1913 and the risen people, and the idea of workers' solidarity as a code of honour. He was unique in inserting an industrial dispute into mainstream Irish history, in creating a positive view of that struggle in an otherwise hostile climate, and in ennobling strike tactics into a morality of struggle. That Larkin has been celebrated more in art and literature than history is appropriate to the extent that we want to capture his relevance to contemporary society.

There are those who would prefer to preserve Big Jim, untarnished, as a legend, and others who think it can do no good to rake over the disruption he caused in the days when he was not so much a black sheep as a raging bull. To these one can only ask: what is it about Larkin that you don't want to know, how is Labour stronger by not squaring up to reality? As Karl Marx argued, the most radical expression of reality is the truth. Aside from the intrinsic fascination of his varied and controversial career, and the complex of motivations behind it, Larkin is far too central to too many events in labour history to leave unscrutinised. Above all, we need to assess his record as a leader. Whether as a political or industrial agitator, trade union general secretary, newspaper editor, or politician, that was the role he aspired to in life. Leadership is a concept which has rarely been examined in Irish labour biography, partly because labour itself is under-researched, and if one does not know the forces, one cannot judge the command. No leader should be evaluated independently of the use he makes of the resources or potential at his disposal. Leadership is the ultimate measure of Larkin. The myth and the legacy are beyond measure.

NOTES

1   W. P. Ryan, *The Irish Labour Movement from the 'Twenties to Our Own Day* (Dublin, 1919), p. 170.
2   See Helga Woggon, 'Landscapes of James Connolly, 1916–2016: from re-interpretation to reconquest?', *Socialist History* (forthcoming, 2016).
3   Theresa Moriarty, 'Delia Larkin: relative obscurity', in Donal Nevin (ed.), *James Larkin: Lion of the Fold* (Dublin, 1998), pp. 428–38; James Curry, 'Delia Larkin: "More harm to the big fellow than any of the employers"?', *Saothar* 36 (2011), pp. 19–25.
4   Emmet Larkin, *James Larkin: Irish Labour Leader, 1876–1947* (London, 1965), p. 294.

ONE

A MAN'S MAN, 1874–1906

*a big boned, large-framed man, broad shoulders held not too high nor too proudly, giving
him an air of stooping over ordinary men when he was speaking to them. Bright blue
eyes flashed from dark heavy brows: a long fleshy nose, hollowed out cheeks, prominent
cheek bones, a long, thick neck, the cords of which stood out when he was angry, a
powerful, stubborn chin, a head longer and a forehead higher than in most men,
suggesting plenty of room for the brain pan. Big Jim was well over six feet tall . . . Long
arms and legs, great hands like shovels, big, rounded shoes, shaped in front like the rear of
a canal boat, completed the picture.*
Bert Wolfe[1]

———

James Larkin was born on 28 January 1874 at 41 Combermere Street, Liverpool,
and baptised on 4 February at Saint Patrick's Church, Park Road, Toxteth. His
birth certificate gave no middle name, though he was married as James Joseph.[2]
The widespread belief that Jim was born in 1876 or later probably owes more to
vanity than genuine confusion on his part. In the 1881 and 1891 censuses, his age
is given, correctly, as seven and 17. But he claimed to be 27 on his marriage
certificate in 1903, 31 in the 1911 census, and 42 in his New York trial in 1920.[3]
Both his parents came of tenant farmer stock from around Newry; his father
from Lower Killeavy, south Armagh, and his mother from Burn or Burren,
south Down. From 1909 at latest, Jim would consistently describe himself as
an Ulsterman, born in the maternal family homestead at Tamnaharry, near
Burren, and Jim's grandson insisted fiercely on the family tradition.[4] Big Jim
too was informed on the topography of his Ulster antecedents.[5] It is possible
that to bond the lad with Ireland – or something better than a Liverpool slum –
Jim's parents brought him up in this belief, but the evidence is against it. In the
1881 census all of their children were listed as Liverpool-born. And Fred Bower,
Jim's boyhood best-friend and future comrade, knew him as 'a tall, raw-boned
Liverpool-born son of an Irishman'.[6] Tellingly, Jim's public insistence on his
Ulster nativity followed his decision to settle in Ireland. Emigration was
sufficiently common a feature of Irish life to make English birth uncontro-
versial, but one with ambition to lead Irish Labour, and about to argue that
Irish workers should be in Irish unions, might have felt it gifted ammunition

to his enemies. This indeed would be the case, and the mud-slinging was not confined to cat's paws of the bosses in the heat of battle in 1913.[7]

The family story was the all too familiar one of flight from a stricken, backward society to the lowest rungs of grimy modernity. Jim's paternal grandfather, Bernard, or Barney, watched his children emigrate one after the other on the boat from Warrenpoint to Liverpool. He too would go, when old age forced him to give up the farm. Liverpool was then the second busiest port in Britain – which itself registered some 40 per cent of the world's shipping – and its vast casual dock labour force made it a magnet for Irish immigrants. Catholics congregated around the north-end docks, and Protestants around the south-end, though there was a sizeable Catholic enclave in Toxteth, near the south-end. Jim's father, James, settled in Toxteth, with his father, his sister, and her husband.

In July 1871, James married Mary Ann McNulty (sometimes spelt McAnulty or McNalty). They met when she was visiting relatives in Liverpool, and Mary Ann did not move to Toxteth until shortly before the wedding. He was 22, she was a year older.[8] There is a family tradition that her parents were farmers, had her destined for life with a businessman in Newry, and that her higher social standing and strong will made her the more assertive partner.[9] However, at the time of the marriage, her father and his were labourers, and both the bride and groom were illiterate. The couple would have three sons and three daughters; Hugh on 21 July 1872; Jim and Agnes, who died at birth; Bridget, to become better known as Delia, on 27 February 1878; Peter on 12 August 1880; and Margaret. Little is known of Margaret other than that she was the youngest.

CHILDHOOD

As with his birth, controversy surrounds Jim's childhood. Friends of his in the British and Irish Labour movements believed he spent some of his early years in Ireland. Jim was the source for his first biography, four articles by George Dallas in the Glasgow socialist paper *Forward* in 1909. Dallas claimed he was

> born in a place with an unmentionable – at least unspellable – name in County Down some 32 years ago. He was taken across to England when a few days old, and sent to school before his third birthday. Returned to Ireland again at six years of age, attended Byrne School, County Down, for some six months – returned to Liverpool at the expiration of the six months referred to, and immediately started work.[10]

W. P. Ryan, assistant editor of the *Daily Herald* during the 1913 Lockout, told a similar story in his pioneering history of Irish Labour.[11] There is a biblical and messianic flavour to the account of R. M. Fox, a friend of the Larkins in Dublin:

> Just after Jim was born, word came to Mary that her father was seriously ill. So when the child was barely a month old she set out with him. The ship ran into a violent storm, and when she landed at Newry she was so ill that she could not continue the journey. Friends looked after her there. Her father died while she was staying in Newry. Her mother relented so far as to send the pony trap from the farm to bring her home. The reconciliation was completed by young Jim, for Mrs McNulty was so pleased with her grandson that when Mary was strong enough to return she left the baby at the farmhouse under his grandmother's care . . . Young Jim did not return to Liverpool until he was about five years old.[12]

The discrepancy in versions of Jim's Irish sojourn itself casts doubt on the story. It is unlikely that he ever left Liverpool. Jim was one of those people who never changed their accent, and that accent was a unique form of Liverpool-Irish.[13] The Irish noted the Lancashire in it, while the English thought it rather Irish. He made no mention of Irish schooling in a statement during his New York trial in 1920:

> I went to school for three and a quarter years altogether, and a great deal of that time I was welcome as a part-timer, in an English school. That is why I drop my 'h's'. It was an English Catholic school too . . . [and] poverty stricken. . .[14]

He may also have inserted gratuitous 'h's'. The *Voice of Labour* caricatured him in 1924 as saying 'h-I've' for 'I've', and 'I h-am' for 'I am'.[15] His school was Our Lady of Mount Carmel, Chipping Street, Liverpool. Bower remembered him as a gang leader at the school, to the fore in battles with Bower's Protestant gang, especially around Saint Patrick's Day and 12 July. Though Bower was two years older, and would grow into a hardy man with a chiselled face, he reckoned Jim as tougher: 'let that tall leader catch me by myself, and I went through it. Two marks I will carry to the grave, where he cut my head open, or rather the skin that covers it.'[16] At the age of seven, Jim became a 'half-timer', a pupil permitted to divide the day between lessons and work. Probably because he suffered from asthma, Jim's father chose to work as a quarryman and foundry labourer rather than a docker; which meant that the money was regular, but there was less of it, and up to the 1880s the family lived in various addresses in the slums. Jim slaved in turn as a help to a milkman, butcher, house painter and decorator, and french polisher. It had an embittering effect. He would

subsequently attribute his 'want of tact' to the crass exploitation involved
and the contrast between the religion imparted at school and the 'Christian'
employers outside.[17]

> I was taught the truth of eternal justice, and I was taught the brotherhood of man
> was a true and living thing, and the fear of God was a thing that ought to cover all
> my days and also control my actions.
>
>   And then I had occasion to go out into the world and found out there was no
> fatherhood of God, and there was no brotherhood of man, but everyman in society
> was compelled to be like a wolf or a hyena, trying to tear down the other man that
> he might gain an advantage either by the other man's suffering, or by the other
> man's sorrow, or, which was more important, the sorrow of his wife, the sorrow of
> his woman, the sorrow of his daughter, the sorrow of his children.[18]

The frustration of dead end jobs also provoked outbursts of egocentrism
and temper. While Jim adored his parents, and appreciated that they needed
the money, he recalled that aged ten – probably he was older – a fight with an
employer caused him to take off for seven weeks on the tramp around Liverpool,
London, and Cardiff.

Meanwhile, his father had risen to become a fitter at 25s per week; giving
him an income just above the poverty line, and enabling the Larkins to move to
a two-story house in Melville Street. This phase of relative comfort was cut
short in February 1888, when James died of tuberculosis. As a gesture, the firm
took on the two eldest boys, Hugh and Jim, as engineering apprentices at 3s per
week, and waived the stiff apprenticeship fee. Jim was now 14, and he may have
already left Chipping Street. The apprenticeship lasted until April 1891 at least,
when Jim was listed in the census as an apprentice fitter, living at 111 Wellington
Road, Toxteth Park. According to himself, he was sacked for refusing to con-
tribute to a sweepstake on the Aintree Grand National. Following a spell of
unemployment, he found work as a seaman, and finally as a docker.

A TYPICAL ILP'ER

Jim's political consciousness was now taking shape. The Larkins was a
political household, and it was easy to stay in touch with Irish politics in the
city. Liverpool's Scotland constituency even had an Irish Nationalist MP, T.
P. O'Connor. Jim's uncles in Killeavy may have been Fenians. After 1908 he
would boast that his father had been a Fenian, and enrolled him in the Irish
National League. Encounters with anti-Irish prejudice was another defining

factor, which may have permanently coloured his attitude to England. Less than four years before his death he recalled:

> In my time at school in England when we came out into the street there would be a gang outside who would shout: 'Hit up these Irish' . . . There was a great deal of hatred throughout England for the Irish. Those who had to travel in England and Wales organising in connection with the trade union movement knew what they had principally to contend with was their Irish faces. They do not hate us any more in England. There is no more of that fanatical hatred for the Irish people, but there is what is even worse, contempt for them.[19]

The sibling closest to Jim was Peter, better known as Pete. Jim recalled Pete's birth in Melville Street, and how delicate he was as a child. Jim's insistence that he take a daily dose of emulsion led Pete to call him 'the Big Fellow' all his life.[20] The pair were two of a kind, in their physical make-up and mentality. 'Was there ever a man with more stentorian tones than Peter?', recalled J. T. Murphy, who first met the Larkins in 1913. 'He was not so big a man as Jim, but nevertheless powerful, a rugged, swarthy dock worker and seaman, who had knocked about the ports of the world.'[21] Pete formed a Catholic Democratic League during anti-Catholic riots in Liverpool in the 1890s, complete with its own fife and drum band, in which Pete was drum major.[22] The title echoed the Irish Democratic League of Great Britain, associated with Michael Davitt. Exile and the absence of a stable home life may also explain why Jim's nationalism acquired a sentimental quality as he matured into middle age. But his collision with the capitalist jungle made the deeper cut, leading to membership of the Social Democratic Federation (SDF) in 1890.[23] Later as a docker he was seriously injured by a machine operated by an apprentice. The boy's father paid him £1 for each of the 19 weeks he took to recover. For Jim it was a 'crowded hour of glorious life'.[24] By day he would read at the Picton Library, and in the evenings listen to the speakers at socialist street meetings.

His restlessness persisted, and perhaps twice Jim stowed away for the Americas. Fox believes that on Jim's first attempt, in 1893, the ship landed in New York, where he was jailed for 'some months' as a stowaway and for shipboard insubordination, and then scampered home a chastened lad. According to Fox, the humiliation had a maturing effect on his personality and politics, while prison converted him to a lifelong reading habit.[25] Certainly, back in Liverpool in 1893 he settled into a more purposeful life.

Jim took to visiting the Clarion club and café at 30 Lord Street. The Clarion movement would have a formative impact on his socialism. Founded as a weekly paper in Manchester in 1891 by Robert Blatchford and Alexander

M. Thompson, the *Clarion*'s ideology and style were encapsulated in the title of Blatchford's best-selling booklet *Merrie England*. Soon there were Clarion vans leafleting the villages of England, Clarion choirs and Clarion scouts, and Clarion drama, cycling, rambling, and handicraft clubs, as well as Clarion cafés. Jim would try to develop a similar socialist culture in Dublin. Unemployment was a regular topic of discussion in the Lord Street café. Often idle himself, Jim joined the socialist demonstrations, and helped his childhood pal, John Wolfe Tone Morrissey, form the Toxteth branch of Keir Hardie's Independent Labour Party (ILP). Some branches of the party, including that in Belfast, were organised in 1892, before the official launch in 1893. It was in the ILP that Jim first met Tom Johnson, a future *bête noire* and then one of its Liverpool branch secretaries.[26] During these years, socialists divided between the Marxist SDF and the non-doctrinaire ILP. Both became foundation groups of the Labour Representation Committee in 1900, but the SDF departed the following year, complaining of the Committee's hostility to Marxism. Though it was not unusual for people to join whichever of the two was foremost in their locality, and he had been in the SDF, Jim was a typical ILP'er, for whom socialism was a humanist religion, rooted in morality rather than science. Throughout his life he was essentially a moralist. In some respects the ILP remained his spiritual home. In 1924 Jim's *Irish Worker* featured a front-page eulogy of Hardie on the ninth anniversary of his death, lauding him as

> a Republican among Republicans: a man above men . . . a rebel all his life against tyranny . . . ever an enemy against all snobbishness, servility, pharisaical respectability . . . the anthithesis of Labour leaders typified by [Ramsay] MacDonald in England, and the [Tom] Johnsonian clique in this country.[27]

It was Jim's self-image too.

Within a few years, Jim was serving his oratorical apprenticeship at ILP meetings around Merseyside. He kept the message simple: capitalism was a moral obscenity, nationalisation of the means of production, distribution, and exchange, would unlock man's capacity to eliminate poverty and exploitation. He also signalled his lifelong loathing of imperialism in organising protests against the Boer War, which was opposed by the British left, and claimed to have helped smuggle David Lloyd George, disguised in a policeman's uniform, through a maddened crowd of jingoes at an anti-war meeting in Birmingham.[28] On another dramatic night, 27 June 1904, Bower decided there ought to be a workers' remembrance in the foundations of Liverpool's Anglican Cathedral and that Jim was the man to help him do it. The pair stole across the site to bury a time-capsule where, three weeks later, King Edward VII and Queen Alexandra would lay the cathedral's foundation stone. The tin capsule contained copies of the *Clarion* and *Labour Leader* and the message:

TO THE FINDERS, HAIL!

We, the wage slaves employed on the erection of this cathedral, to be dedicated to the worship of the unemployed Jewish carpenter, hail ye! Within a stone's throw from here, human beings are housed in slums not fit for swine. This message, written on trust-produced paper with trust-produced ink, is to tell ye how we of to-day are at the mercy of trusts. Building fabrics, clothing, food, fuel, transport, are all in the hands of money-mad, soul-destroying trusts. We can only sell our labour power, as wage slaves, on their terms. The money trusts to-day own us. In your day, you will, thanks to the efforts of past and present agitators for economic freedom, own the trusts. Yours will indeed, compared to ours of to-day, be a happier existence. See to it, therefore, that ye, too, work for the betterment of *all*, and so justify your existence by leaving the world the better for your having lived in it. Thus and thus only shall come about the Kingdom of 'God' or 'Good' on Earth. Hail, Comrades, and – Farewell.[29]

Written by Bower, the message could equally be described as vintage Larkinism.

There were two personal traits in Jim's oratory: a Victorian sense of manly virtue and duty to women and family – he would often select vice to illustrate the evils of capitalism – and a disdain for workers' self-abasement and indifference to their potential. On the quayside, Jim worked in a supremely macho environment. Some 20–25,000 men stood in for work on the Liverpool docks each day, of whom 12–15,000 might be 'put-on' in the summer, and 16–17,000 in the busier winter months, when there would be more coal to move.[30] Injuries were common. There were 89 fatal, and 4,070 non-fatal, accidents reported on docks, wharves, and quays in the United Kingdom in 1898, when the UK had an estimated 74,340 dockers.[31] To social reformers, it was a brutal-ising system of exploitation, which encouraged the violence and drunkenness for which dockers were notorious. Yet most dockers liked the freedom which casualism conferred, and took pride in the survival of the fittest.

In 1901, as work was slack, Jim stowed away again. Daring tramps and salty tales were not unusual among waterfront socialists of the time. The best of them all had their stories. Jim claimed he was discovered en route to Montevideo, was pressed into the crew, defied a tyrannical captain, suffered a harrowing time chained in the brig with the rats eating his nails, jumped ship, and spent a year working his passage around various ports from Valparaiso to Norfolk, Virginia, loafing as a beachcomber, and even joining a revolution in Buenos Aires.[32] Dublin street meetings were entertained to versions of the story in the 1940s, and in 1943, in a speech that was sometimes bizarre, he informed Dáil Éireann that he had a little Spanish.[33]

THE 'COD BOSS'

Returning to Liverpool in 1902, Jim took to a more settled life. By 1903, he had risen to foreman dock-porter with T. & J. Harrison, a permanent post paying £3.10s per week. Harrison's discharged big ships, with six to eight holds, and the foreman docker was a glorified Stakhanovite, whose job was to set the pace for his gang. The dockers called them 'cod bosses' and Jim was bad enough to be nicknamed 'the Rusher'.[34] But he also set a moral standard, by example. He didn't smoke, though he would later take a pipe or a cigar. He didn't gamble. He hated drink. Unlike most foremen, he refused to pay his men in pubs. He never took bribes, which was the major grievance with dockers, and cut pilferage on the ships he handled to a minimum. He came to develop a paternal attitude towards his men, who sometimes looked to him for advice. His free hours were given not only to the ILP, but to charitable work in the slums with the Civic Guild of Liverpool. According to Jack Carney, 'He loved to recite poetry but never got beyond one or two verses. His favourite poets were Francis Adams, P.B. Shelley and William Morris. They were the singers of his discontent.'[35] Through all his days he retained an informed interest in literature, poetry, and drama.

Carney came to know Larkin as few others ever did.[36] Born in Dublin in 1887, Carney was orphaned as a two-year-old and raised in Liverpool by his grandfather. His misfortune continued when his grandfather died and he was forced to abandon a mathematics scholarship to a private school for work in a chemical plant in Widnes. Fifteen miles up the Mersey, Widnes was a major centre of the chemical industry, infamously polluted, and a place of last resort for desperate immigrants from Ireland and eastern Europe. The *Daily Mail* described it as a 'poisonous hell-town'.[37] Carney tried to persevere with his studies at night school until exhaustion forced him to stick with the day job. It seemed the fates had dealt him a death sentence and conspired to ensure there was no escape. Then one day in Widnes, aged 18 and spiritually crushed, he heard Larkin speak. It was a life-changing experience – 'you thrilled me as I have never been thrilled since' – which led Carney from Liverpool to Dublin and Belfast in 1911. Making 'active contact' with Larkin in 1913, he became his closest colleague, and at times a personal secretary, between 1916 and 1937.

In addition to literature, poetry, and drama, soccer is likely to have been another of Larkin's interests. Walking along Clonard Street in west Belfast in 1907 in search of the dockers' champion, Mick McKeown, he stopped and questioned Mick's son, Seán:

'was you playing football today.' Then he told me he had played for Liverpool reserves, and with candour – one of the characteristics of his public life – admitted he didn't make the senior grade because he was too slow and cumbersome. About five years later when playing for Cliftonville against Shelbourne in Dublin, I visited him . . . He was annoyed when I told him I was playing for Cliftonville, and asked could I not play for a working man's team instead of those snobs. I replied that Cliftonville players were all workers like myself, and as I was against professionalism in sport I preferred to play for them.[38]

An incorruptible Corinthian, Seán later became secretary and chairman of the Antrim County Board of the Gaelic Athletic Association and a firm upholder of the ban on 'foreign games'.[39]

MARRIAGE

The picture of Victorian socialist rectitude was complete on 8 September 1903, when Jim married Elizabeth Brown.[40] Elizabeth was 24, tall and russet haired. In the 1901 census she was listed as living at 256 Park Road, Toxteth, with her elder brothers, Thomas and William, and their parents, Robert and Martha. Robert hailed from Croxton in Staffordshire. His wife and children were Liverpool-born. The family had strong dockland connections. Thomas was a warehouseman in the rubber trade, William a shipyard timekeeper, and Robert managed a dockside temperance café which Jim frequented. Robert was also a Baptist lay-preacher, and his daughter was quiet, homely, given to housekeeping and good works, and not known to have an occupation. She showed no interest in politics, but accompanied Jim to ILP meetings. At the time of the marriage, the bride and groom were living in Toxteth Park, he with his mother at 37 Roche Street, she at 58 Ashbourne Road. The couple lived with Jim's mother, and Elizabeth had little contact with her family afterwards. She would eventually have four sons, of whom the eldest, James, was born in Liverpool on 20 August 1904. According to Jim's grandson, it was a marriage of 'chalk and cheese'.[41] As her husband's career became more turbulent, Elizabeth grew to yearn for a quiet life. She may also have felt as neglected by her husband as she would be by historians. Jim later impressed Ellen Grimley, who knew him in Belfast around 1912, as 'a very handsome chap in those days', but no ladies' man; just 'a big thorough going fellow with his pipe in his mouth . . . happy marching with the men . . .' When he and James Connolly got together, 'they would be talking serious matters. I wouldn't be noticed any more than if I didn't exist.' Winnie Carney told her that Jim travelled without a valise, making do with spare paper collars and handkerchiefs.[42] An American secret service agent later noted: 'He is a very shabby dresser.'[43]

The marriage to Elizabeth was a civil ceremony in Liverpool Registry Office. Religion had an importance for Jim, after a fashion. He was born, and died, a Catholic. In adult life he combined a socialist scepticism about the politics and double standards of organised religion with tribal loyalty to the Catholic Church and an ingrained belief in Christian values; which meant he didn't practice, but still identified with mother church. His attitude to religion also depended on context. In Liverpool, where the church was associated with the Irish Nationalist Party and hostile to socialism, he is not known to have quibbled with socialist clashes with the church and Catholic Labourites. Elizabeth may have had a bigger influence on her husband than is appreciated. His speeches had a Protestant complexion in their numerous biblical references and appeals to Christian values rather than Catholic teaching. Yet he claimed to have organised the Catholic Socialist Society in Glasgow with John Wheatley – which is possible, given that it was founded in 1906 and was closely aligned with the ILP – and in Dublin he, the children, and even Elizabeth, were returned as Catholics in the 1911 census.[44] In 1913 he was shocked by the acclaimed and pioneering *Das Mirakel*, a German film based on a medieval legend in which a statue of the Blessed Virgin comes to life to take the place of a nun until the wayward sister, after several spicy adventures, returns to her convent. Jim lambasted it as a blasphemous assault 'on the symbols sacred to me from a child, since the mother that bore me taught me to lisp, Hail Mary, full of grace, and to revere the very name of the Mother of God'.[45] His outrage extended to the very idea that the film should be screened in Catholic Dublin. The *Irish Worker* mourned the death of Pope Pius x in August 1914 with a black-trimmed editorial affirming the eternal power of the Roman Church: 'Long live the Pope . . . The Pope and all he stands for lives.' More usually, Jim deplored the hypocrisy of pharisaic employers and politicians who exploited God in the service of Mammon, and the reactionary clerics who supported them. It was not anti-clericalism but Christianity that made him cynical of Christian tolerance of capitalist greed, and resentful of clerical criticism of Labour. In the United States he would bridle at anti-clericalism on the left, and earn a notoriety for his defensiveness about the church. In Soviet Russia, he would assure the Bolsheviks that God existed.

IN THE 'IRISH UNION'

There was one respect in which Jim was to modify his ideological outlook at this time. James Sexton's contention that initially he shared the hard left view of trade unions as palliatives of capitalism and useless as instruments of political change is plausible. While Jim helped launch a branch of the Workers' Union in Liverpool in 1898, this union for general operatives was intended to be a semi-industrial, semi-political 'Labour League', and was closely identified with ILP'ers before Hardie denounced it as too amorphous to be of service.[46] The Workers' Union would have a rather unfortunate history in Ireland, crossing swords with just about everyone. Jim did not join a union until 1901, when Sexton refused to sit with a 'non' – the polite term for non-unionists – on an unemployed committee on which Jim represented the ILP. Jim joined the National Union of Dock Labourers of Great Britain and Ireland (NUDL).[47] Sexton later claimed he was no more than a token member, but Jim's rise to prominence in 1905 suggests his commitment was more substantial than that.

Sexton's interventions in Ireland from 1907 to 1910 have cast him as a dastardly villain in Larkinite history, which is accurate, but not the whole picture. His early life was as tough as Jim's. Born of Irish itinerant hawkers in Newcastle on Tyne in 1856, his parents subsequently settled in St Helen's on Merseyside and ran a stall in the local market. He would sometimes accompany his father and grandfather on 'missionary' work for the Irish Republican Brotherhood among railway navvies. After primary school he went to sea, and worked in a chemical factory and on the Liverpool docks, where an accident hardened his attitude towards employers. From 1891 he was to the fore in unemployed agitation, and in 1893 became general secretary of the NUDL. Like Jim, he had a literary side, contributed to various newspapers, including the *Clarion*, and wrote stories and two plays.[48]

Founded in Glasgow, as one of the 'new unions' of unskilled workers created during the big strike wave in 1889–90, the NUDL was soon headquartered in Liverpool and known colloquially as 'the Irish union' because of its composition and leadership. One of its rules, number 19, stated:

> No member shall use unbecoming words or references to any other member's religious opinions, or nationality, or antecedents, it being a fundamental principle of the Union that all men are brothers.[49]

It had been a leading 'new union' in Ireland too, spreading south from Belfast in late 1889. By mid-1891 it organised in 15 Irish ports and claimed 2,000 members. The tide was on the turn, however. The railway and shipping companies, widely regarded as the most obdurate employers, had given a lead to their fellows by granting concessions initially. Now they set another example by weeding out activists and replacing them with 'nons'. Strikes were broken in Derry, Sligo, Dundalk, and Waterford, and a heavy defeat followed in Belfast in 1892 after four months of struggle. Decline continued over the next decade, and by 1905 the 'Irish union's' Irish base had dwindled to feeble outposts in Derry and Drogheda.

An able administrator and a good man-manager, Sexton was a popular general secretary. He always pursued a non-confrontational line, arguing that through moderation the NUDL was one of the few 'new unions' to survive. Legal tactics, such as parliamentary enquiries, the extension of the Factory Acts, or the application of safety regulations, were his preferred weapons. However in 1905, he was caught between membership militancy and employer obduracy. Seven of T. & J. Harrison's 35 foremen had let their union membership lapse, and on 27 June 611 dockers struck unofficially to maintain the closed shop. During these years waterfront employers especially used scabs as a standard weapon against strikes. The Shipping Federation operated as a 'free labour' exchange, with the awesome telegraphic address 'Nemesis'. Nine hundred Federation scabs were soon working for Harrison's, though less efficiently than the men they replaced. When Harrison's insisted that the men must return to work as 'free labourers', Sexton decided he had no option but to back the strike, fearing it would become a test case and that victory for Harrison's would encourage other firms to withdraw recognition from the union.

Applying his usual methods, Sexton had Labour MP D. J. Shackleton and the Dublin Labour-Nationalist MP J. P. Nannetti protest in parliament that housing the scabs in dock sheds was in breach of health and safety regulations. The government referred the matter to Liverpool Corporation, and the failure to get the Corporation to take action came as a major blow. By contrast with Sexton's strategy, Jim concentrated on appealing to the men's fighting spirit. Elected to the strike committee, he took an increasingly prominent role as the struggle escalated. This was a new kind of battle for him, one less abstract than politics, and his speeches acquired a more extreme tone. The strikers, he said, 'would chew the grass in Sefton Park' rather than surrender. After 13 weeks, they did surrender. Other employers did not mobilise against the union, but Jim's job with Harrison's was gone and he was unlikely to be taken on anywhere on the waterfront.[50]

The end of one career proved to be the beginning of a lifelong vocation. During the dispute Jim had organised a new branch of the NUDL with 1,200 members, and the union executive appointed him a temporary organiser at a salary of £2.10s per week. Sexton later wrote that he opposed the appointment, feeling that Jim was too self-promotional. Possibly this was hindsight. In November 1905, Jim successfully directed Sexton's campaign for election to Liverpool Corporation. In December, preparatory to the upcoming general election, Jim became Sexton's agent for the Westminster constituency of West Toxteth. It would be a contest of Orange and Green, of shipping magnate and docker. The Liberals withdrew to give the ILP nominated Sexton a straight fight against Robert Houston, a Conservative and a shipowner, who had held the seat since 1892. Since 1904 the big issue for anti-Tories was the Conservative government's introduction of indentured Chinese 'coolies' to alleviate the labour shortage in the South African goldmines caused by the Boer War. Labour feared that a precedent was being set for the importation of cheap labour to Britain, and denounced 'Chinese slavery' as a bitter fruit of the 'blood and treasure' squandered in crushing the Boers. Houston had done well out of the war, leasing his entire fleet to the government, and opening a new shipping line to South Africa. Jim made 'Chinese slavery' his 'battle-cry'. Assisted by Bower, his theatrics included a mock funeral through the main streets, with a brass band, a glass-sided hearse showing a coffin draped in the Union Jack, and a cortège of several cabs trailed by 50 'coolies' in yellow dye, oakum pigtails, and home-made mandarin jackets.[51] It was the stereotypical view of 'John Chinaman' and chimed with the widely held racism of the age, but Jim would later demonstrate repeatedly his respect for men of all races. The election saw the Labour Representation Committee make a break-through, and jump from one to 29 seats. Emboldened, it changed its name to the Labour Party. Though Sexton lost, he acknowledged Jim's efforts:

> Larkin displayed an energy that was almost superhuman. The division was one of the storm centres of religious strife, and the stronghold of the Orange Order, through whom Mr Houston held the seat. My being a Roman Catholic naturally made the situation still more lively. But nothing could frighten Jim. He plunged recklessly into the fray where the fighting was most furious, organised gigantic processions against Chinese labour on the rand, faced hostile mobs saturated with religious bigotry who were howling for our blood, and last but by no means least, competed in the risky game of impersonation then played at almost every election in Liverpool. I am convinced that it was largely owing to Larkin's overwhelming labours that we reduced a Tory majority from four thousand to five hundred, but I would rather not give my opinion on some of the methods he adopted to achieve that highly commendable result.[52]

Here, as elsewhere in his memoir, Sexton was curiously generous to Jim. Houston's majority was 781. The constituency contained about 2,800 trade unionists, and Sexton remarked after the poll: 'The dockers weren't all true to my labour standard.'[53] Sexton also praised Jim's union work in the NUDL executive reports of 1906 and 1907.

Meanwhile, Jim was made a permanent, national organiser. In 1906, he had re-organised the port of Preston in Lancashire for the NUDL, building a branch of 900 members, and negotiating a closed shop and a wage increase. His impact on Scotland, if just a scratch when compared with Irish events, was notable for introducing on some waterfronts a debate between Sexton's moderation and Larkinite militancy, and minor echoes of the big national issues that would engulf Ireland. The Aberdeen branch was re-organised, and Jim frustrated efforts by employers and the National Free Labour Association – formed in 1893 by a disgruntled ex-docker to combat trade unionism – to create a 'free port' in Aberdeen, as they had in Dundee in 1904.[54] After a short, successful stop in Ardrossan, Jim spent nearly six months in Glasgow, ever a troublesome port for the NUDL, recruiting coal-heavers and cranemen. He also worked with 'the most degraded, harassed body of workers I had ever any experience of in my chequered career – the iron ore workers who discharged the boats from Spain on the Govan side of the River'.[55] Many were recruited from Glasgow's 'down and outs', according to Jim they were 'mostly North of Ireland men', and were known as 'the meths drinkers'.[56] It was in a vain attempt to organise them that he met James Fearon. Jim's account of how they met, in an obituary article on Fearon, illustrates Jim at his best: graphic in prose, empathic in spirit, and experiential in method.

Only men who have shovelled Caliened iron ore or Manganese ore can appreciate the labour. They were in a continual state of semi-starvation and drunkenness. These were the first human beings I had ever seen drinking meythalated [*sic*] spirits or, as it's called in Dublin, 'Spunk' . . . A few among them – not lost to all sense of manhood – had tried, time and again, to organise their fellows, but failure had attended their efforts.

I studied the position for some time and then I decided to go and join them, work with them and find out the realities of the situation.

I got a job one night in a limestone boat – one of Robertson's – and among the crowd I noticed a chap who, in the pauses between tubs being hooked on, kept talking – not drink or women, the usual talk, but strange to say, economics. He had a good grip of his subject, but lacked the power of expression. When we knocked off for our 'Morning', a custom followed in all Scottish ports of knocking-off for a quarter of an hour to get a glass of whisky, I noticed this chap did not follow, but went to his coat and took out a bottle filled with tea. I joined him, and started a discussion, and after a few minutes conversation found out he was a Newry man. We compared notes and found out we were neighbours' children. I disclosed my purpose and thus my comrade Jim Fearon and I met and from that hour – we were one in understanding and purpose.[57]

Jim's six months in Glasgow reaped a few rewards. A short-lived branch was formed at Govan, and he overcame 'considerable employer opposition' to talking to Sexton. Arguably, he was already coming to the conclusion that Sexton's reluctance to take action was earning the NUDL no respect from bosses or dockers. Similar to Ireland, he would find the smaller employers more 'amenable' to union pressure, and their willingness to compromise ensured the survival of the union on Clydeside.[58]

It was enough for the NUDL executive. All too well aware of the strength of the Shipping Federation in Glasgow, it was well pleased with Jim's record. With the British Labour Party holding its annual conference in Belfast in January 1907, it seemed timely to attempt the re-organisation of the Irish ports. The Ulsterman was going home.

NOTES

1 Bertram D. Wolfe, *Strange Communists I Have Known* (New York, 1982), p. 52.

2 The most detailed genealogy of Larkin is C. Desmond Greaves, 'Jim Larkin's earliest years', *Irish Democrat*, September 1980; and Donal Nevin, 'Early years in Liverpool', in Donal Nevin (ed.), *James Larkin: Lion of the Fold* (Dublin, 1998), pp. 133–43. See also Emmet Larkin, *James Larkin: Irish Labour Leader, 1876–1947* (London, 1965), pp. 3–22.

3 Nevin, 'Early years in Liverpool', p. 135.

4 Jim Larkin, *In the Footsteps of Big Jim: A Family Biography* (Dublin, 1995), pp. 3–11.

5 *Irish Worker*, 30 May 1931.

6 Fred Bower, *Rolling Stonemason: An Autobiography* (London, 1936), p. 120.

7 A quarter century after the lockout, the following exchange disgraced Dáil Éireann:

> Mr Larkin: I say that it is because of the men who drew the sword on behalf of this nation, few as they were, because of their sacrifice and the blood that was shed, that such as Deputy Dillon is allowed to speak in this House.
> Mr Dillon: And you with a cockney accent.
> Mr Gorey: And an Englishman.
> Mr Larkin: I an Englishman? You are a liar, Sir, as I have had to tell you before.
> Mr Gorey: It is a wise child knows his own father . . .
> Mr Larkin: Go up to Killeavy, County Armagh and trace it. My mother's record can be found in South County Down.

Díosbóireachtaí Páirliminte Dáil Éireann 71, pp. 404–5, 29 April 1938.

8 In the 1881 census they gave their ages as 31 and 32, both born in Ireland.

9 Larkin, *In the Footsteps of Big Jim*, p. 5.

10 Nevin, 'Early years in Liverpool', p. 135.

11 W. P. Ryan, *The Irish Labour Movement from the 'Twenties to Our Own Day* (Dublin, 1919), p. 172.

12 R. M. Fox, *Jim Larkin: The Rise of the Underman* (London, 1957), p. 13. Jim's grandson had a similar story, see Larkin, *In the Footsteps of Big Jim*, p. 7. On Fox see Peter Berresford Ellis, 'An influential historian of Irish labour', *Irish Democrat*, June 2003.

13 See for example the *New York Times*, 23 November 1913.

14 British and Irish Communist Organisation, *The American Trial of Big Jim Larkin, 1920* (Belfast, 1976), p. 75.

15 *Voice of Labour*, 1–15 March 1924.

16 Bower, *Rolling Stonemason*, pp. 120–1.

17   George Dallas, 'Larkin's life history', in Nevin (ed.), *James Larkin*, p. 139.

18   British and Irish Communist Organisation, *The American Trial of Big Jim Larkin*, p. 75.

19   *Díosbóireachtaí Páirliminte Dáil Éireann* 91, p. 965, 22 October 1943.

20   *Irish Worker*, 30 May 1931.

21   J. T. Murphy, *New Horizons* (London, 1941), p. 39.

22   *Irish Worker*, 6 June 1931; Nevin (ed.), *James Larkin*, p. 439.

23   *Irish Worker*, 10 May 1924.

24   Larkin, *James Larkin*, p. 4.

25   Fox, *Jim Larkin*, pp. 15–18.

26   J. Anthony Gaughan, *Thomas Johnson, 1872–1963: First Leader of the Labour Party in Dáil Éireann* (Dublin, 1980), pp. 16–19.

27   *Irish Worker*, 4 October 1924.

28   *New Leader*, 14 August 1943.

29   Bower, *Rolling Stonemason*, pp. 118–22.

30   Eric Taplin, *The Dockers' Union: A Study of the National Union of Dock Labourers, 1889–1922* (Leicester, 1986), pp. 15–16, 20–4.

31   British Parliamentary Papers, *Factories and Workshops. Annual Report of the Chief Inspector of Factories and Workshops for the Year 1899* (Cd.223, 1900), p. 99.

32   Dallas, 'Larkin's life history', pp. 141–3; John de Courcy Ireland, 'As I remember Big Jim', in Nevin (ed.), *James Larkin*, p. 453.

33   Fox, *Jim Larkin*, p. 172; de Courcy Ireland, 'As I remember Big Jim', p. 453; *Díosbóireachtaí Páirliminte Dáil Éireann* 91, 9 November 1943, pp. 1772–9.

34   Taplin, *The Dockers' Union*, p. 68; James Sexton, *Sir James Sexton, Agitator: The Life of the Dockers' M.P. An Autobiography* (London, 1936), p. 201; Aindrias Ó Cathasaigh (ed.), *The Life and Times of Gilbert Lynch* (Dublin, 2011), p. 51.

35   Jack Carney memoir on Larkin, written for Emmet Larkin and kindly passed on to the author; see also a letter from Carney, dated 1 May 1948, 'Larkin and Connolly', in Nevin (ed.), *James Larkin*, pp. 395–400; *Irish Worker*, 21 November 1931; NLI, Seán O'Casey papers, Carney to Larkin, 10 September 1946, 37989. For an account of Carney see Richard Hudelson, 'Jack Carney and the *Truth* in Duluth', *Saothar* 19 (1994), pp. 129–39.

36   See Lawrence William White, 'Jack Carney', in *Dictionary of Irish Biography*, DIB.Cambridge.org.

37   G. E. Diggle, *A History of Widnes* (Widnes, 1961), p. 105.

38   'The autobiography of Seán McKeown', p. 23, emphasis in the original. I am obliged to Neal Garnham for a copy of this unpublished memoir.

39   Ibid., pp. 110–11.

40   For a brief biography of Elizabeth see Donal Nevin, 'On Larkin: a miscellany', in Nevin (ed.), *James Larkin*, pp. 486–7.

41   Larkin, *In the Footsteps of Big Jim*, p. 13.

42   NLI, Ellen Grimley papers, 28871.

43   Federal Bureau of Investigation file, James Larkin, 62–312 Section 1.

44   Emmet Larkin, 'Socialism and Catholicism in Ireland', *Studies* (spring 1985), p. 83; Census, 1911; *Irish Worker*, 1 March 1924.

45   *Irish Worker*, 29 March 1913.

46   Richard Hyman, *The Workers' Union* (Oxford, 1971), pp. 7–10.

47 NLI, Thomas Johnson papers, 17149(1), Sexton to Johnson, 27 April 1925; for the NUDL see Taplin, *The Dockers' Union*, pp. 50–79.

48 G. A. Phillips, 'James Sexton', in *Oxford Dictionary of National Biography*, oxforddnb.com.

49 P. J. Waller, *Democracy and Sectarianism: A Political and Social History of Liverpool 1868–1939* (Liverpool, 1981), p. 97.

50 Eric Taplin, 'Liverpool: the apprenticeship of a revolutionary', in Nevin (ed.), *James Larkin*, pp. 19–21; Waller, *Democracy and Sectarianism*, pp. 214–5.

51 Sexton, *Sir James Sexton, Agitator*, pp. 203–4; Bower, *Rolling Stonemason*, p. 170.

52 Sexton, *Sir James Sexton, Agitator*, pp. 203–4. Waller, *Democracy and Sectarianism*, p. 220.

53 Waller, *Democracy and Sectarianism*, p. 220.

54 William Kenefick, *'Rebellious and Contrary': The Glasgow Dockers, c. 1853 to 1932* (East Linton, 2000), p. 200; Geoffrey Alderman, 'The National Free Labour Association: a case-study of organised strike-breaking in the late nineteenth and early twentieth centuries', *International Review of Social History* 26 (1976), pp. 309–36.

55 *Irish Worker*, 22 November 1924.

56 Kenefick, *'Rebellious and Contrary'*, pp. 92–3.

57 *Irish Worker*, 22 November 1924. See also Bill McCamley, *The Third James: James Fearon, 1874–1924, an Unsung Hero of Our Struggle* (Dublin, 2000).

58 Kenefick, *'Rebellious and Contrary'*, pp. 201–2.

TWO

'PIPING DAYS AND ROARING NIGHTS', 1907[1]

The arrival of Larkin was a godsend to the dockers and carters.
He was the man that gave them the lead.
William Hunter, carter, 1907[2]

—

On Sunday 20 January 1907, Larkin disembarked from a cross-channel ferry at Belfast. For the detectives watching the arrival of delegates to the British Labour Party's annual conference, he was easy to read. What would become a trademark black, broad-brimmed hat provided the bohemian touch affected by socialists of the *fin de siècle*, while his muscular frame, shovel-like hands, worn old great-coat, and thick, droopy moustache, betrayed his 15 years as a docker. Larkin stayed with Tom and Marie Johnson at 2 Frederick Terrace on the affluent Malone Road for a few days while looking for digs. Tom represented commercial travellers on the trades council, and would be a strong admirer of his work in Belfast. They had lost contact since their days in the Liverpool ILP, and Larkin carried a letter of introduction.[3] A new chapter in the history of Irish trade unionism was about to unfold. With astonishing alacrity, Irish industrial relations was about to jump from a staid style reminiscent of mid-Victorian England to one with the violent edginess of new sectors on the economic frontiers of Australia and the US.[4] And in many respects the explanation was that Ireland too was on the periphery, with a high proportion of its labour force in unskilled occupations, a scarcely developed arbitration machinery, and a workforce neglected by British Labour. In search of their explanation, and to make a distinction from what they called 'bona fide trade unionism', to which they pretended to have no objection, employers coined the term 'Larkinism' as a shorthand for militancy, the cult of the agitator, and the sympathetic strike. Larkin would also make transport a leading sector in the Irish Labour movement. So powerful were these innovations, that his setbacks in Belfast would be even more significant than his successes.

BELFAST IN 1907

The northern capital had been transformed in the nineteenth century, from a borough of some 13,000 people in 1800 into a major manufacturing centre of almost 387,000 souls in 1911. With nine per cent of the population, Belfast contained 21 per cent of Ireland's industrial workers, and was pre-eminent in the three major product groups: linen; engineering and shipbuilding; and brewing, distilling, and aerated waters. While Dublin enjoyed a sizeable trade in food, drink, and tobacco, Belfast nearly monopolised other sectors. In 1907, it accounted for £19.1 million of Ireland's £20.9 million worth of manufactured exports, excluding food and drink.[5] Ostensibly, the city was Ireland's Labour as well as its industrial capital, with the island's biggest trades council and strongest left. In some respects Belfast 1907 is a clearer guide to Larkinism than Dublin 1913, when the personalities of Big Jim and William Martin Murphy and the dramatic backdrop of the slums overshadowed the core issues in the struggle. In the public memory, the raw, class solidarity of 1913 came to be understood as a by-product of Dublin's appalling social conditions.[6]

Yet Larkinism began in Belfast, where housing was comparatively good: one per cent of families in the city lived in one room tenements in 1903, compared with 26 per cent in Glasgow, and 35 per cent in Dublin.[7] The root of Larkinism lay in employer hostility to the unionisation of unskilled workers, and Belfast was as difficult a city for unskilled unionism as any other in Ireland. Craftsmen earned above the UK average, and were generally in demand. Labourers' rates were well below average, and many employers believed that the city's prosperity depended on maintaining an abundance of cheap labour. But the employers had an Achilles heel in transport. Transport workers were at the hinge of commercial life, where strikes would have an immediate and widespread effect, and they were becoming more important to the economy. The 1891 census noted 38,231 'persons engaged on railways, roads, rivers, seas, storage, conveyancing messages etc', and by 1911 the number had risen to 62,947. Within transport, coal dockers and carters were more important again. Cities ran on coal, which heated homes, powered ships and trains and factory furnaces, and produced gas for cooking and street lighting. Moving coal was labour intensive work in poor conditions. Between 1907 and 1912 transport accounted for an annual average of 12 per cent of strikers and under four per cent of strikedays in the UK. In Ireland, it accounted for 22 per cent of strikes, 33 per cent of strikers, and 33 per cent of strikedays over the same period.[8]

Larkin had arrived at an exceptional period in Belfast's political history, which enabled him to win some unlikely allies in the great unrest over the summer. His first duty was to attend the Labour Party's annual conference, which opened in the large hall of the Young Men's Christian Association (YMCA) at Wellington Place on Thursday, 24 January. That the conference was held in Belfast reflected the brief and unusual status of the city as a Labour centre. William Walker, an official of the Amalgamated Society of Carpenters and Joiners, and Ireland's best known trade unionist, had persuaded the trades council in 1903 to initiate Ireland's only branch of the Labour Representation Committee. Walker had high hopes of winning the Westminster seat of Belfast North , and British Labour leaders were keen to help him, convinced that one of their few victories before 1906 would come in Belfast. The conference made an impact, however ephemeral, on the city. Three hundred and forty-seven delegates attended. Given that most had to make a winter sea-crossing, the number compared favourably with the 363 in London the previous year.[9] A capacity crowd of 3,000 packed the Ulster Hall for a rally on the opening night. On Friday night the visitors were entertained by Belfast trades council to a social in Saint Mary's Hall. The council was embarrassed to admit that it had not requested the customary civic reception. Much had changed in its relations with the Unionists since Lord Mayor Sir James Henderson extended a hearty welcome to the city's last big Labour convention – the 1898 Irish Trades Union Congress (ITUC) – and the trades council's affiliation to the largely pro-Home Rule Labour Party was probably the cause. Beneath a banner inscribed 'Céad Míle Fáilte', the guests in Saint Mary's Hall enjoyed displays of step-dancing and renditions of Irish and other airs supplied by the Amalgamated Musicians' Union. Keir Hardie commended the evening's 'fine old Gaelic spirit'.[10]

Delegates to the conference were charmed by the prevailing atmosphere, and the absence of loyalist animosity, which had disrupted a parade and rally at the close of the 1893 British Trades Union Congress (BTUC), the last occasion on which British Labour had assembled on the banks of the Lagan. Hardie 'rejoiced . . . that the old order of religious bigotry was passing away from Belfast, and a new era of Labour and Fraternity had begun'. John Hodge, MP, who would become one of the first Labour cabinet ministers in 1916, wrote:

> In the face of the work of the Labour Party, sectarian bigotry is decreasing, the Orange and Green are blending together and making Labour their politics. A policeman voiced to me the opinion that the Labour Party had decreased sectarian rows as nothing else had ever done – and he had been in the force for nearly 20 years.

Bruce Glasier, a veteran of more bruising visits to Ireland, remarked on the 'great change [that had] come over Belfast'.[11] There had been some extra-ordinary developments within Unionism when the Tories were in power and

Home Rule was off the government's agenda. During the 1890s, an ultra-Protestant element led by Arthur Trew had hounded socialist speakers in Belfast. Trew founded the Belfast Protestant Association (BPA) in 1894, and his successor, T. H. 'Tod' Sloan, won a bye-election in 1902 to capture Belfast South from the Unionists and become the city's first working-class MP. Sloan was a semi-skilled shipyard worker, and fought the bye-election for 'Protestantism, Orangeism, total abstinence, and trade unionism'. In 1903 he launched the Independent Loyal Orange Institution of Ireland, more usually called the Independent Orange Order, to combat Dublin Castle's perceived appeasement of nationalists and 'Romanisation' in the Anglican Churches.[12] Belfast trades council had mixed feelings about Sloan. In 1902 it had voted 9–3 against corresponding with the BPA, and in 1905 a motion to endorse Sloan in the next general election was lost 21–18. However, and not for the last time, once dissident loyalists got rolling, they began to pinball about the political table. Under Imperial Grand Master Robert Lindsay Crawford – editor of the *Irish Protestant* – the Independent Orange Order acquired a potted liberalism, and the BPA, serving as its political arm, became a vehicle of working-class criticism of the 'fur coat brigade' in the city's Unionist associations and Orange lodges. To the casual observer, it looked as if the old sectarian mould was starting to crack.

Industrially too, Larkin had arrived at an opportune time. Between 1870 and 1914, the economy was dominated by a cyclical pattern of boom and slump, with each usually lasting three years. An upturn in the trade cycle in 1906 had been generating a resurgence of militancy, especially in Belfast. In May of that year, 17,000 spinners, weavers, and others had struck for wage increases. Then in 1907, retail prices rose by about ten per cent. Thirty-four strikes hit the city in 1907, beginning with a series of stoppages by textile operatives in February, and subsequently affecting engineering, the service trades, navvies, and other labourers.[13] There had also been a favourable change in labour law. In their judgement on the Taff Vale case in 1901, the Law Lords had made unions liable for financial damages caused by strikes. When the Liberals were returned to power in 1906, they introduced the Trades Disputes Act, which was known as 'the Congress Bill' as it was virtually written by the BTUC. The Act restored trade union immunities in lawful strikes and guaranteed the right of peaceful picketing. It was regarded as the cornerstone of trade union rights, and remained the basic statutory instrument in Irish industrial relations until 1990. The Liberal government also approved the development of conciliation and arbitration by the Board of Trade. For all that, what Larkin achieved in Belfast was extraordinary, the moreso as the tide was on the turn. The potential for building a Protestant anti-Unionist coalition had already been undermined by the Liberal victory in 1906, which brought Home Rule back into the realm of possibility. Labour fielded seven candidates for municipal honours in January 1907, its biggest slate to date, and all, including Walker, were defeated.[14]

ORGANISING THE DOCKERS

To find a secretary for his branch, Larkin went to the Falls Road for Michael McKeown. Formerly a Birkenhead docker and vice-president of the NUDL, McKeown had organised for the union in Belfast in 1891–2.[15] The Unionist press exploited McKeown's nationalist politics during the lengthy strike of 1892, and the crippled branch was killed off in the second Home Rule crisis when Protestant dockers withdrew. McKeown was elected to the Corporation as a Nationalist in January 1907. In what may have been a balancing act, Larkin also allied with Alex Boyd, secretary of the Municipal Employees' Association.[16] A local society up to 1905, when it merged with its British namesake, the 600 strong Association included tramwaymen, making it one of the few trades council affiliates with a presence in transport. It had a distinct tradition, embodying an edgy mix of loyalism and Labourism in a sector where discrimination was virtually quantifiable.[17] With 25 per cent of the population, Catholics held 28 per cent of central government and nine per cent of local government jobs in Belfast.[18] Boyd was an Independent Unionist councillor and a prominent Independent Orangeman. At the same time, Alex Bowman, who had been run out of Belfast for supporting Home Rule, had found employment as an organiser of the Association from 1895 to 1901, and the Association was one of the few unions in Belfast to affiliate to the ITUC at the height of the third Home Rule crisis.[19] While he could flip-flop between radicalism and reaction in politics, there was no doubting Boyd's trade unionism or antagonism to 'the fur coat brigade'.

Larkin began his recruitment campaign by holding meetings at places where dockers gathered each morning to seek work. The technique in his greatest talent has never received definitive analysis, and no recording of him exists. But we know that he had an exceptionally loud, booming voice, and usually declaimed in a rapid, forceful manner, using emotion, wit, and body language with sweeping hand gestures. According to Bert Wolfe:

> When Larkin spoke, his blue eyes flashed and sparked. He roared and thundered . . . Sometimes an unruly forelock came down on his forehead as he moved his head in vigorous emphasis. Impulsive, fiery, passionate, swift at repartee, highly personal, provocative, and hot tempered in attack, strong and picturesque of speech, Larkin's language was rich in the turns of Irish poetic imagery sprinkled with neologisms of his own devising.[20]

John Swift, then a young baker in Dublin, recalled:

> There were usually others on the platform, perhaps Connolly, O'Brien, P. T. Daly, Foran, or Farren. But we had eyes, and ears, only for Jem Larkin . . .
>
> Larkin was a fine physical specimen, over six feet tall, broad-shouldered, full-chested, and with large angular features that served as a jutting, mobile lantern to eyes that seemed aflame and ready to burn . . .
>
> But, above all, it was Larkin's speech that enthralled us. I was never to hear a greater orator. Usually when public speakers try to convey impressions of anger or scorn or other strong feelings the effect on their audience is either of good, middling or bad art, of something worked up rather than deeply felt.
>
> With Larkin it was different. With him anger and scorn, and whatever other emotion, were on ready tap, as were the flow of words and cadences that made them poetry and drama to the spell-bound audience.[21]

Desmond MacCarthy made a similar point about his body language:

> Larkin is a fine looking fellow; tall, loose-limbed, he gives that always agreeable, physical impression of great natural strength, which its possessor has not troubled to keep up. His gestures are easy, and about all his movements there is a suggestion of nervous power losing itself, perhaps in a fundamental good-nature . . .[22]

The style was not to everyone's taste. Henry Bolton, inviting him to address miners in County Durham in 1914, asked him not to 'give too much of yourself away', perspire less, and speak more slowly, as some couldn't follow 'your native brogue'.[23] Others thought him longwinded, disconnected, or even raving, and when not dealing with concrete issues, Larkin could be platitudinous. But there are numerous testaments to the power of his presence and oratory. His future *fidus achates*, Jack Carney, offered the best explanation of his effectiveness:

> What impressed me most about Larkin was his ability to translate the feelings of his audience in sympathetic language. One felt that through some mysterious means, he had investigated your personal position and was taking the opportunity of saying for you what you could not say yourself. His language was not the language of tears but the language of hope . . . More than any other man, Jim Larkin taught me that Socialism does not spread by itself because of its own inner beauty or logic or consistency. It spreads when there is something in it that makes it a response to the needs of the hour . . . He had an uncanny insight into the worker's mind.[24]

On first hearing him speak in 1910, Constance Markievicz was also struck by the chemistry between orator and audience.

> Sitting there, listening to Larkin, I realised that I was in the presence of something I had never come across before, some great primeval force rather than a man . . . It seemed as if his personality caught up, assimilated, and threw back on to the vast crowd that surrounded him every emotion that swayed them, every pain and joy that they had ever felt made articulate and sanctified. Only the great elemental force that is in all crowds had passed into his nature forever . . .[25]

By mid-February, Larkin had recruited 400 dockers. In March a branch of the NUDL was formally established. By April, the branch included 2,900 of Belfast's 3,100 dockers.[26] It was impressive progress among workers who were mainly casual, and divided in various ways. About 1,000 were 'constant', and the rest were 'spell-men', casuals paid by the hour. Larkin described the wages system in the port as 'simple chaos', with stevedores sometimes paying different rates for the same job on the same ship.[27] The cross-channel men on the 'high docks', where traffic was more regular, were Protestant. The deep-sea men on the 'low docks' were Catholic. Catholic dockers tended to live close to the waterfront, in 'Sailortown'. The Protestants were more dispersed. There were also about 1,500 carters engaged by the shipping companies or master carriers supplying the docks. Carting was regarded as a superior, more 'Protestant' occupation, though carters and master carriers were drawn from both communities. The caste divisions persisted in the NUDL branch. The cross-channel dockers met in the Municipal Employees' Association's rooms at Victoria Street, and the deep-sea men at Bridge End.[28]

Larkin affiliated his branch to the trades council on 4 April.[29] The union appeared to be winning recognition from employers, and he was happy to let the process mature. Like James Sexton, he wished to avoid confrontation, especially on the issues of recognition or the closed shop, and pursue legal tactics. Like Sexton, he tried to keep the NUDL as a dockers' union; though he welcomed some allied workers, which was more than Sexton would have wanted, he also declined requests for help. And like Sexton in 1905, membership spontaneity and employer militancy would force his hand.

For the moment it seemed that Larkin might make his mark in politics rather than trade unionism. He pushed the council to collaborate with the ILP, and persuaded the trades council secretary, John Murphy, to stand for an aldermanship in the Dock ward with NUDL backing. That same month, he campaigned for Walker in another bye-election in Belfast North, though Walker was famous for his opposition to Home Rule, and infamous for courting the BPA. There must not be a single 'blackleg' at the polls, he told a large meeting in the Painters' Hall on 2 April.[30] Despite his speaking skills, his role in the campaign was overshadowed by the Labour MPs who came to endorse Walker. In May he was in Dublin to represent the NUDL at the annual ITUC and seconded the usual motion commending unions to affiliate to the British Labour Party, a motion opposed regularly by nationalist and republican delegates. He gave further evidence that he was a Labourite first in June and July when he canvassed for Pete Curran, an ILP'er, in a bye-election in Jarrow. In a decision which caused controversy in Irish Labour circles, the United Irish League had decided to contest the seat, threatening to siphon enough votes from Curran to allow a Conservative victory. Curran was an old friend of Larkin's, and won the election comfortably. There was talk of Larkin standing against Joe Devlin, who had recently won Belfast West for the Nationalists.[31]

THE DOCKERS' AND CARTERS' STRIKE

Meanwhile, the industrial war had begun. On 26 April labourers in the Sirocco Engineering Works struck for a pay rise. There is nothing to suggest that Larkin had any influence on the dispute. The men were not unionised, and they had returned to work by 1 May, having signed 'the document', promising not to join a union. Their leaders were blacklisted. But the strike unsettled employers. At Kelly's coal quay, some NUDL men were dismissed on 26 April, and 400 colleagues stopped work in protest. Samuel Kelly said frankly that 'the situation at issue had no reference to wages whatsoever; it was merely as to whether the dockers should associate themselves with a union which he considered should not embrace such a class of employment'.[32] Kelly was not alone. Sometime in late April, the secretary of the Ulster District Office of the Shipping Federation appealed to headquarters for assistance in anticipation of unrest. He was promised the services of 'our general Labour superintendent who will thoroughly investigate the situation, and we shall then be prepared to act immediately should the necessity arise'.[33] Larkin scented trouble, and was anxious to avoid confrontation with the Federation. He opposed the strike at Kelly's. Kelly had contracts with public authorities and would be vulnerable to legal tactics.[34] He was soon using scabs, and Larkin's NUDL members were not so patient.

On 6 May, 70 spell-men with the Belfast Steamship Company walked off the SS *Optic* in protest at the employment and abusive attitude of a non-union man. Again, Larkin tried to defuse the situation. Immediately, he met the legal representative of the Steamship Company, said a mistake had been made, and asked that the men be allowed to return to work. When they reported for

work on 8 May, they found the SS *Caloric* arriving from Liverpool with a
cargo of scabs. Another 140 union men stopped work, and another 100 scabs
arrived the next day. There was a violent response. The locked-out men at
Kelly's assaulted scabs and forced them off the job. They then joined with
other union men and attacked scabs working for the Steamship Company.
Kelly settled on 10 May, recognising the NUDL and granting a pay rise. But
Thomas Gallaher, chairman of the Steamship Company, tobacco factor, and
shareholder in the Belfast Ropeworks, was determined to quash the emerging
organisation of unskilled labour. When, on 13 May, the Lord Mayor proposed
arbitration – to which Larkin was always open – Gallaher refused to negotiate
and called for more police protection.[35]

Larkin now had a major fight on his hands, and it was typical of him to
oppose action initially, and get stuck in once the battle started. As Sexton did
not sanction strike pay until 19 July, the challenge was met in a way that
became part of the Larkin legend. Sexton's memoirs printed the legend:

> Financially Jim had the lives of nine cats, and he lived them all – most of 'em twice.
> He would order a strike as casually as he would ask for bacon for his breakfast,
> trusting to luck for the funds even if he hadn't a copper at this command, and it
> was amazing to see how luck served him . . .[36]

In reality, Larkin grafted hard to make his own luck. He left his digs to sleep
on the floor of the union rooms at Victoria Street and paid his salary into the
strike fund.[37] To sustain the men from street collections, he addressed nightly
meetings and organised parades. His energy and oratory made the fight
peculiarly his. The financial pressure eased a little when the trades council
established a fighting fund on 4 July.

As 'Larkinites' and 'Larkinism' entered the vocabulary, the struggle became
personalised. Larkin was vilified, and, for his part, he lashed back *ad hominem*
when attacked. Indeed, attacked or not, he preferred to go for the man, rather
than the ball. Over the coming weeks, he denounced Gallaher repeatedly.
Violence was always a possibility. A rally on 16 May, which drew over 6,000
people, was followed by clashes with the police. Larkin himself was involved
in a dangerous incident on 31 May. Richard Bamber and a few fellow scabs
boarded on the SS *Caloric* had gone ashore for a drink and Bamber was later
accosted at Victoria Street. Watching from the NUDL rooms, Larkin saw
him draw a knife and stab three men. Dashing to the scene, he hit Bamber
with a stone. Bamber staggered away, before being felled by coal shovel. Both
he and Larkin were charged and eventually acquitted.

For all the excitement, Larkin was still fighting a conventional, sectional
dispute. In a few cases, he had prevented further strikes. That was to change

on 20 June when he demanded a wage increase for all cross-channel dockers, and on 26 June a further 300 men joined the struggle. The trigger of this escalation is unclear. Divers groups of dockers were tendering differing pay demands, and any union official would be anxious to standardise rates. The conflict escalated again the day after when 200 carters struck in sympathy and for their own wage claim. More scabs arrived from the Shipping Federation, and 500 soldiers sealed off the quays from pickets. The carters' dispute centralised another issue; the right to refuse to work with scabs or handle 'tainted goods'. When the majority of carters backed Larkin's insistence on the point, and the master carriers rejected negotiations with the NUDL, a generalised struggle was at hand.

An indication of the pressure on Larkin emerged on 2 July, when he announced that he was handing over the leadership of the strike to 'A Protestant in the person of Mr Alexander Boyd'.[38] In addition to complaints that he was a trouble-maker and a dictator, with the real support of no more than a militant minority, and wild rumours about his background – twice in May he denied being related to one of the Manchester Martyrs – the Unionist press had questioned Larkin's suitability to lead a struggle of largely Protestant workers. Trew, who had split with Sloan after the 1906 general election, denounced Larkin as a nationalist. However, from the outset, there was a firm cross-community solidarity among the 'Larkinites'. Now it was Trew who was driven from the Custom House steps, Belfast's speakers' corner.[39] This was not Larkin's last use of the resignation ploy, and it usually betrayed a personal hesitancy rather than lack of confidence among the workers; in this instance a moment of doubt before confronting the master carriers. After Boyd rejected the resignation offer, Larkin issued a manifesto threatening a general portal strike. Some of the smaller companies settled with the NUDL, but the bigger carriers, and then the coal merchants, retaliated *en bloc*. By 15 July, they had locked out 1,680 carters and porters. Some 2,340 men were now affected, of which only 570 had taken strike action.

Mid July marked the zenith of the struggle and the start of the mythification. As with most myths, those about Larkin simplified a more complex truth. It was said that he led Catholics and Protestants in a 12 July parade. In fact, he spent the day in Liverpool with his mother, who was ill, and went on to Yorkshire, to canvass for Victor Grayson, the ILP candidate in the Colne Valley bye-election.[40] In truth, Larkin forged a brief, triumphant unity across the religious divide, climaxing on 26 July in a grand trades council procession which pointedly wound its way around east Belfast to the Falls and Shankill Roads. One hundred thousand people turned out, led by Larkin, McKeown, Boyd, and Crawford, whose Independent Orange Order had made a collection for the strike on 12th. It was said that Larkin incited the Royal Irish

Constabulary (RIC) mutiny on 24 July, when 2–300 officers, out of 1,000 in the city, assembled to demand better pay and conditions. In fact, he had no direct part in this unrest. In truth, it was a by-product, not only of the burden of strike duties on the force, but of the climate he was generating. The mutiny was instigated by the suspension of Constable William Barrett on 19 July for refusing to sit beside a scab on a motor waggon. Barrett, a Kerryman, made it clear that he objected to the RIC alliance with the masters to crush the carters and dockers. A circular, listing police grievances, was published on 22nd.

The events on 27 July would have been inconceivable without Larkin. Some 600 RIC took over Musgrave Street barracks; Barrett was chaired to the Custom House steps to speak to both workers and police; and, back in the barracks, the RIC were joined in a lengthy conclave by strikers, who advised them to seek redress by petition and return to duties! Sexton later wrote in awe of Larkin conducting this meeting: 'and I still marvel at the power Larkin then revealed.'[41] Actually, Sexton himself was there, but Larkin was in Dublin. Briefly, it looked as if the trouble would spread. Cork RIC sergeants proposed to meet to discuss grievances. Waterford constables telegrammed Belfast: 'Military, Maxims, and Gatlings have no terror for Waterford boys. Ready for any emergency. Wire developments.'[42] By 2 August the mutiny was crushed. Over 270 RIC were transferred from the city and an extra 6,000 troops drafted in. Even the navy was alerted to anchor warships in Belfast Lough.

Sexton arrived in Belfast on 19 July with Alderman Allen Gee and Alderman Isaac Mitchell, vice-chairman and secretary of the General Federation of Trade Unions, in effect a mutual strike fund of some British TUC affiliates. The Federation had rejected a request for aid from the NUDL in June, and Aldermen Gee and Mitchell were concerned primarily with getting a settlement. With an authority gained from promises of desperately needed financial help, Sexton, Gee, and Mitchell first tackled the coal merchants' lockout and a separate ironmoulders' strike. How much the strike cost the NUDL is unclear. It was certainly the longest and most expensive for the union to date. It has been claimed that the NUDL spent almost £5,000 on the dispute, but its annual accounts put total strike pay for 1907 at £921, and its bank reserves were not 'seriously damaged'. What is known is that the strike committee's income amounted to £8,922, of which the General Federation contributed £1,692; dockers still at work were levied, and other local donations were substantial.[43] An end to the coal lockout was negotiated on 25 July. It was a weak settlement, given that Belfast Co-operative Society's importation of several shiploads of coal had made the merchants' anxious to resume normal trading. The men accepted wage rates offered six weeks earlier, and undertook to work with 'nons'. It was not clear whether the union was recognised. Crucially, it was the first sectional settlement, and ended hopes of securing a 'one back, all back' conclusion. With other local labour leaders, Larkin loyally hailed the outcome as a breakthrough. Two weeks later he would complain about his victory plans being spoiled by 'three Englishmen in his absence who knew nothing about the situation'.[44] He was not alone in his disappointment.

By now, Belfast was attracting a stream of visitors from the British left. Since May, Larkin, Boyd, and Walker had been cabling Ramsay MacDonald and other Labour MPs on the conduct of the strike. Larkin was the most persistent, sometimes sending two or three wires a day. He liked telegrams. They were modern, direct, occasionally a theatrical prop, and offered the hope of a *deus ex machina*. Inevitably, the persistence tested patience. A third cable to MacDonald on 28 June asked: 'why wire Boyd, don't you think I know the facts?'[45] From early June, Labour MPs tabled a series of parliamentary questions about the behaviour of strike-breakers, the military, and the authorities. Mostly, this was as much as Larkin requested, but in July he appealed to David Shackleton, MP, and MacDonald to get the House of Commons adjourned.[46] John Maclean was in the city on the weekend of 1–3 August at the invitation of the Belfast Socialist Society, and stayed with Larkin. Belfast made an overwhelming impression on him: 'Addressed strikers at night', he wrote for the SDF paper *Justice*. 'Audience of thousands. Labourers mad to join trade unions . . . Had three monster meetings . . . about 10,000 present, some estimated 15,000.'[47] Then a member of the SDF and sceptical of the political value of trade unions, Maclean acquired an undying admiration for Larkin, and was persuaded that unions could play a radical role in class struggle. He would become best remembered as a leading figure of 'Red Clydeside'. Grayson, who had sensationally won the bye-election at Colne Valley, spoke to a capacity audience in Saint Mary's Hall on 8 August. An over-optimistic Belfast ILP created five new branches in late 1907.[48] Another visiting ILP'er was Bob Morley, a popular orator on the ILP circuit and a leader of the Workers' Union. Morley established two branches of the Workers' Union in Belfast, and appointed Joe Harris, an upholsterer from Dublin, as his Irish agent. Harris raised local membership to 500, before moving south to become a thorn in Larkin's side.[49]

As more troops poured in to protect scab carters, Larkin felt the situation was turning critical. On 6 and 7 August, after talks with Walker and Grayson, he urged MacDonald to summon a joint meeting of the party executive and the BTUC parliamentary committee. He and Walker did secure a meeting with party leaders and warned of 'a religious war' if the army was not withdrawn.[50] As feared, the heavy security presence led to rioting in west Belfast on 10–11 August. Why troops were deployed in a nationalist area far from the docks is unclear, unless, as alleged, it was to provoke the Catholics in a way that would scare the Protestants. On 12 August, soldiers killed two and wounded five others on the Falls Road. McKeown's son was an eye-witness:

One summer evening Bob Bateson, Mick Hamil and myself went down the Falls to the baths where a platoon of military was stationed. From the side streets women were delivering loads of stone-pavors to some dozen or so strikers, or rioters in favour of the strikers, while hundreds lined the side walk on the Baths' side watching the rioters stoning the military, who were standing to attention with their backs to the walk on the opposite side. The pavers bounced round the soldiers who had to duck sometimes to save their heads. The corporal in change maintained a steady, stoical stance, but eventually winced when struck by a stone. He ordered and led a charge on the rioters. Leader of the rioters was a well-known character named 'Covey' Cochrane who was well fortified. He never flinched as the soldiers came for him at the double, the leader well ahead of his troops. As he approached Cochrane, the latter advanced staggering to meet him and flung a heavy pavor that caught the plucky Corporal in the midriff and doubled him up. He turned and fled after his already retreating companions. Cochrane and his comrades were not long in possession of the field, a more deadly enemy appeared in quick time to end the mimic battle in tragedy for several onlookers. A Major down near Albert St. read the riot act while soldiers dropped on their knees with rifles at the ready and before the spectators were aware of what was about to happen a volley of shots rang out. My pals and I ran up the road to get out of the danger zone, as we passed, a man named Sinn Féin Nolan standing on the kerb shouted, 'yellow-bellies! Running away from British blank shot.' 'You stay them Billy,' said one of our boys, 'we're for Conway St, they haven't made bullets yet to go round corners'. Some two hundred yards up the road from the scene of the riot several people were shot – one was shot near the scene – two were killed.[51]

In the wake of the RIC mutiny, and increasing nationalist criticism of the authorities, the riots were enough to convince some working-class Protestants of claims that the strike masked nationalist sedition, and brought the Falls– Shankill interface to the brink of sectarian violence. Larkin hurried back from Dublin, and with Boyd, Walker, and Catholic priests, arranged for picketing of the affected area after the military were withdrawn. Handbills were distributed urging workers not to play 'the employers' game of dividing Catholic and Protestant'.[52] On 13 August, Larkin telegrammed Augustine Birrell, the Chief Secretary for Ireland, saying that the press had turned the conflict from a trade union into a 'political or religious' dispute, and appealing for arbitration. Trade unionists enroled 'a special police force' to patrol areas of tension.[53]

That same day, the British government did intervene, in the person of the Board of Trade's newly appointed conciliator, George Askwith, who would become the government's chief industrial troubleshooter and one of the 'secret masters' of the age of agitation. Askwith decided that the first thing to be done was to interview Larkin. Askwith's recollections of events, published in

1920, were confused with subsequent history – he mentions James Connolly, then in America, as 'the brain' behind the dockers – and his memory of Larkin was of a volatile bohemian: 'a tall, thin man, with long dark hair and blue-grey mobile eyes, at that time wearing a very heavy black and drooping moustache, a large black sombrero hat, and a kind of black toga.'[54] In fact, Larkin's hair was short and the 'toga' was probably his great-coat. Despite Askwith's bourgeois sensibilities, he thought Larkin 'an interesting man', admired his 'zest', and, like others of his class, was amazed at his ability to be as critical of workers as he was of employers and take no nonsense from the more curmudgeonly of his men. Again, a sectional approach was adopted, with the carters' strike being dealt with first. Sexton left it to the General Federation of Trade Unions to represent the strikers in the negotiations until 14 August when, alarmed by the violence, he 'left a sick bed contrary to doctors' orders' to hasten to Belfast.[55] On 15th, in Saint Mary's Hall, with two revolvers in his pockets, he persuaded the carters to accept the terms. Larkin listened in silence. Employers conceded a wage increase, and shorter hours. There would be no victimisation, but no guarantee of re-employment, or union recognition. Eager to wrap up the crisis, Labour Party headquarters sent Larkin and Walker the patronising cable: 'Labour Party congratulate you on success of your peaceful efforts. Authorities must be compelled to defend themselves by public enquiry.'[56]

True to form, Larkin would not admit defeat. On Sunday 25 August he joined 10,000 workers in London's East End, marching behind a banner inscribed: 'in memory and sympathy with our comrades in Belfast killed in the interests of capitalism. Workers remember Trafalgar-square, 1887; Mitchelstown, 1887; Featherstone, 1893; Belfast, 1907'. Violently denouncing the Shipping Federation, he declared that the strike was not yet over.[57] But now isolated, the dockers' fate was worse again. The Board of Trade failed to get agreements with the employers, and the strikes collapsed piecemeal in late August and early September. In some cases, wages were improved, but there were many instances of victimisation, and in all cases, dockers were obliged to work with 'nons', or even the scabs who had taken their mates' jobs. Labour was on the defensive, so much so that the trades council investigated ludicrous accusations in the *Belfast Evening Telegraph* that Catholics had received higher strike pay than Protestants, and that the strike had targeted companies employing Protestants. Though the *Telegraph* was a standing joke in Labour circles for its trenchant Toryism, the council decided it had better be seen to take the allegations seriously. Larkin concurred, and offered to submit the evidence to a jury of three Protestants.[58]

Larkin faced one further round of battle in Belfast. In mid September the masters moved to divide and conquer by sponsoring a company union for

Protestants, which became the Belfast Coal Workers' and Carters' Benefit Society. Five hundred coal-heavers struck on 14 November rather than work with members of the Society.[59] Thirty carters and all 50 cranemen in the port came out in sympathy, and coal boats were blacked in Newry, Drogheda, and Dundalk. On 25 November, the cranemen tendered an abject apology to get their jobs back, and some of the coal heavers followed suit. It looked as if the strike was collapsing from scabbing and lack of support from an exhausted Labour movement. Then Sexton made a cynical intervention, designed simply to check Larkin. The two were scarcely on speaking terms, and Sexton later complained that Larkin had not consulted him about the progress of the dispute, repudiated his authority, and said on platforms in Belfast, in Sexton's presence, that 'he recognised no boss but himself'. Whatever the truth of the matter, Larkin commanded the trust of the men; Sexton did not. On Sexton's arrival in Belfast on 26 November, the NUDL branch insisted that Larkin be present in settlement talks. Instead, Sexton met the employers alone, instructed the men to resume work, with an assurance that 'no advantage would be taken of any man', and that Board of Trade arbitration would follow, and left with the Liverpool boat that evening. The following day, the majority of men were informed that their jobs had been filled. Board of Trade arbitration never came.[60]

OVATIONS IN DERRY, ROUND THE RING IN NEWRY AND DUNDALK

Larkin had visited Derry before the Belfast strikes, and contributed to a revival of Labour in that resolutely non-militant city. From May onwards, Derry trades council supported various campaigns to organise girls in the shirt factories, municipal employees, and general workers.[61] But while the city's employers extended a grudging toleration to trade union membership, they usually met workers' demands with lockouts. Derry dockers had a longer history of organisation than most other sectors in the city, and were all too familiar with the consequences of defeat. Saint Columb's Quay Labourers' Society had enjoyed a quasi-guild status until crushed in a strike in 1891. The Quay Labourers then re-formed as no 16 branch of the union, as the NUDL was disintegrating in other Irish ports.[62] Following the loss of another strike in 1896, the chastened dockers pledged unanimously to obey union rules, and the branch was henceforth committed to a policy of non-militancy.[63] Quietly, so quietly that Sexton and Larkin behaved as if it didn't exist, the Derry NUDL survived, and recovered its closed shop on the docks. When, on 17 May 1907, dockers refused to unload a steamer for reduced rates, they were replaced by 'nons'. The NUDL quickly disowned the strike and confined its response to attempts to win public sympathy. There is no doubt about Larkin's personal popularity in the city. He received an enthusiastic welcome at a large NUDL meeting in Saint Columb's Hall on 5 July, and a 'deafening ovation' at a packed rally in the Guildhall on 22 August. September would see a strike of local newsboys, a class of employees destined to become the mascots of Larkinism.[64] But the NUDL branch continued a policy of opposition to strikes. The dockers' secretary, W. J. McNulty, was firmly on Sexton's side.

The last action of the year centred on Newry. A relatively big branch of the NUDL, no 24 with 209 paid up members, had existed in Newry in 1891.[65] A successor was established on 27 September 1907 after a meeting in the Town Hall, addressed by McKeown. Larkin's friend and 'fellow' Newryman, James Fearon, was appointed branch secretary for Newry and Dundalk. The locals knew Fearon as 'Round the ring' for his declaration that he would fight the bosses 'in the ring, out of the ring, and round the ring'. The action in sympathy with the Belfast strike on 19 November quickly escalated into a series of strikes and lockouts of 350 workers in Newry, Warrenpoint, and Dundalk.[66] Employers tried to carry on with blacklegs, and the leading Newry coal merchants, F. Fisher and F. Ferris, warned that if work was not resumed they would apply to the Shipping Federation for free labour and appeal to the authorities for troops. Without consulting the NUDL, the Catholic Bishop of Dromore drafted an agreement. Employers were to be free to engage whom they liked, but equally to appoint a fair person to hire staff and not to be biased in recruitment on grounds of religion or political beliefs or membership of a union; and a conciliation board was to be established, comprised of representatives of the Harbour Board, two employers, and two dockers. If the conciliation board could not resolve a dispute it was to be referred to a mutually agreed arbitrator. The arrangement was to run for 12 months. Despite Fearon's opposition, the men accepted the deal on 12 December. Three days later a conflict broke out over the wages to be paid for discharging a collier which had unloaded some of its coal during the dispute. Sensing disaster, Fearon and Larkin urged a resumption of work. The men were divided and financial help would not be forthcoming from Liverpool. It was too late. Nearly 20 Newry employers signed a notice saying that 'no man connected with the union will receive employment' in their yards. Resistance to the lockout collapsed in January, and the Newry branch with it. Larkin fared better in Dundalk. He and Fearon met the Dundalk Harbour Board on 23 December and secured an agreement that future disputes should be dealt with through conciliation.[67] Larkin subsequently reported that the Dundalk branch had secured recognition and improvements in wages and conditions, but was not yet willing to affiliate to Liverpool, which would not have re-assured Sexton.[68]

After November 1907, Larkin had upped sticks for Dublin, and had little further to do with Belfast, where he was getting tepid support from an embittered and demoralised movement. Some colleagues were embarrassed at his continuing presence. His followers did not fault his leadership or doubt his integrity. He received an illuminated address from the NUDL branch in July 1908, and Boyd affirmed that they would gladly stand with him again.[69] But the stuff of Larkinism was too marginal to mount another assault on the hurdles of sectionalism and sectarianism. In Dublin and other cities of the de-industrialised south, Labour recognised that the alliance of 'transport and general' was the key to the revival of trade unionism; despite setbacks, they would return to it again and again. Industrialised Belfast had a well-estab-lished craft unionism, and its most powerful sector, the metal trades unions, constituted a movement onto themselves, which had minimal contact with the trades council. Larkin turned south, and what happened in Belfast and Newry would be repeated in Cork, Wexford, Galway, Sligo, and ultimately in Dublin in 1913.

NOTES

1   Sexton's description of that summer in Belfast; James Sexton, *Sir James Sexton, Agitator: The Life of the Dockers' MP. An Autobiography* (London, 1936), p. 284.

2   PRONI, Belfast, interviews of Sam Hanna Bell with veterans of the 1907 strikes in the 1950s, D3358/1.

3   J. Anthony Gaughan, *Thomas Johnson, 1872–1963: First Leader of the Labour Party in Dáil Éireann* (Dublin, 1980), pp. 16–19.

4   For a contemporary study see Fred S. Hall, PhD, 'Sympathetic strikes and sympathetic lockouts', *Studies in History, Economics and Public Law* (New York, 1898–9). I am obliged to Gerry Watts for this reference.

5   See L. A. Clarkson, 'Population change and urbanization, 1821–1911', in Liam Kennedy and Philip Ollerenshaw (eds), *An Economic History of Ulster, 1820–1939* (Manchester, 1985), pp. 137–54; Michael Farrell, *Northern Ireland: The Orange State* (London, 1976), p. 18; L. M. Cullen, *An Economic History of Ireland Since 1660* (London, 1987), pp. 16–62.

6   For example, Curriculum Development Unit, *Dublin 1913: A Divided City* (Dublin, 1984), a text for secondary schools, said little about trade unionism and much about the city's social divisions.

7   W. Coe, 'The economic history of the engineering industry in the north of Ireland' (PhD, Queen's University, Belfast, 1961), pp. 325–62. This is not to deny that Belfast had its poor housing and serious public health problems. The Public Health Committee estimated that 3,000 dwellings in the city had no water closets. *Northern Whig*, 26 January 1907.

8   NAUK, Ministry of Labour reports on strikes and lockouts, 1907–12, LAB 34/7-12, LAB 34/25-30; British Parliamentary Papers, *Reports on Strikes and Lockouts*, 1907-12, Cd.4254,

Cd.4680, Cd.5325, Cd.5850, Cd.6472, Cd.7089. Figures for 1913 have been excluded as statistics for the lockout were not broken down by sector.

9   Campaign for Labour Representation in Northern Ireland, *The Forgotten Conference* (Belfast, 1982).

10   *Irish News and Belfast Morning News*, 24–26 January 1907; Austen Morgan, *Labour and Partition: The Belfast Working Class, 1905–23* (London, 1991), p. 80.

11   From reports in *Labour Leader*, cited in Campaign for Labour Representation in Northern Ireland, *The Forgotten Conference*.

12   UUMC, Belfast trades council minutes, 20 February 1904. On Sloanism see J. W. Boyle, 'The Belfast Protestant Association and the Independent Orange Order, 1901–10', *Irish Historical Studies* 13:50 (1962), pp. 117–52; and Henry Patterson, 'Independent Orangeism and class conflict in Edwardian Belfast', *Proceedings of the Royal Irish Academy* 80, section C, 1 (1980), pp. 1–27.

13   Emmet O'Connor, *A Labour History of Ireland, 1824–2000* (Dublin, 2011), p. 77.

14   John W. Boyle, *The Irish Labor Movement in the Nineteenth Century* (Washington, DC, 1989), pp. 281–5.

15   C. Desmond Greaves, *The Irish Transport and General Workers' Union: The Formative Years, 1909–1923* (Dublin, 1982), p. 5, 12; Eric Taplin, *The Dockers' Union: A Study of the National Union of Dock Labourers, 1889–1922* (Leicester, 1986), p. 36, 45; Morgan, *Labour and Partition*, pp. 93–4.

16   For Boyd see Boyle, 'The Belfast Protestant Association and the Independent Orange Order, 1901–10', pp. 117–52.

17   Peter Gerard Collins, 'Belfast trades council, 1881–1921' (DPhil, University of Ulster, 1988), appendices. For loyalism and the Municipal Employees, see Emmet O'Connor and Trevor Parkhill (eds), *Loyalism and Labour in Belfast: The Autobiography of Robert McElborough, 1884–1952* (Cork, 2002).

18   See A. C. Hepburn, 'Work, class, and religion in Belfast, 1871–1911', *Irish Economic and Social History* 10 (1983), p. 34, 50.

19   See Terence Bowman, *People's Champion: The Life of Alexander Bowman, Pioneer of Labour Politics in Ireland* (Belfast, 1997), pp. 106, 121–56; UUMC, ITUC, *Annual Report* (1914), p. 107.

20   Bertram D. Wolfe, *Strange Communists I Have Known* (New York, 1982), p. 53.

21   *Irish Socialist*, May 1984.

22   *New Witness*, 27 November 1913.

23   NLI, William O'Brien papers, Bolton to Larkin, 19 July 1914, 15679(1). Bolton was the main Socialist Sunday School organiser in Chopwell, Durham, in 1914. I am obliged to Lewis Mates for details on Bolton.

24   Cited in Patrick Lynch, 'Larkin in history', in Donal Nevin (ed.), *James Larkin: Lion of the Fold* (Dublin, 1998), p. 118.

25   Cited in Anne Haverty, *Constance Markievicz: An Independent Life* (London, 1988), p. 95.

26   Morgan, *Labour and Partition*, p. 94.

27   Emmet Larkin, *James Larkin: Irish Labour Leader, 1876–1947* (London, 1965), p. 20.

28   Morgan, *Labour and Partition*, pp. 94–5; Greaves, *The Irish Transport and General Workers' Union*, pp. 12–13.

29   UUMC, Belfast trades council minutes, 4 April 1907.

30   *Irish News and Belfast Morning News*, 3 April 1907.

31 UUMC, Dublin trades council minutes, 2 July 1907; ITUC, *Annual Report* (1907), p. 27; Morgan, *Labour and Partition*, p. 94; John Gray, *City in Revolt: James Larkin and the Belfast Dock Strike of 1907* (Belfast, 1985), pp. 56–7.

32 Cited in Gray, *City in Revolt*, p. 59.

33 Ibid.

34 Greaves, *The Irish Transport and General Workers' Union*, p. 13.

35 Gray, *City in Revolt*, pp. 60–4.

36 Sexton, *Sir James Sexton, Agitator*, p. 205.

37 'The autobiography of Seán McKeown', p. 24. I am obliged to Neal Garnham for a copy of this unpublished memoir.

38 Gray, *City in Revolt*, p. 79.

39 Patrick Maume, 'Arthur Trew', *Dictionary of Irish Biography* 9 (Cambridge, 2009), pp. 488–9.

40 Sexton, *Sir James Sexton, Agitator*, p. 207.

41 Ibid., p. 204.

42 *Derry Journal*, 2 August 1907.

43 Gray, *City in Revolt*, p. 110; Taplin, *The Dockers' Union*, p. 73; Ken Coates and Tony Topham, *The History of the Transport and General Workers' Union: Vol. I, Part I, 1870–1911: From Forerunners to Federation* (Oxford, 1991), p. 374.

44 Gray, *City in Revolt*, p. 107.

45 Daniel V. McDermott, 'The British Labour movement and Ireland, 1905–25' (MA, University College, Galway, 1979), p. 86.

46 Ibid., p. 87.

47 B. J. Ripley and J. McHugh, *John Maclean* (Manchester, 1989), pp. 30–2.

48 Gray, *City in Revolt*, p. 150; Henry Patterson, *Class Conflict and Sectarianism: The Protestant Working Class and the Belfast Labour Movement, 1868–1920* (Belfast, 1980), p. 76.

49 Richard Hyman, *The Workers' Union* (Oxford, 1971), pp. 29–30.

50 McDermott, 'The British Labour movement and Ireland, 1905–25', pp. 87–8.

51 'The autobiography of Seán McKeown', p. 24.

52 Larkin, *James Larkin*, p. 35.

53 *Derry Journal*, 14 August 1907.

54 Lord Askwith, *Industrial Problems and Disputes* (Brighton, 1974), pp. 109–11.

55 *Freeman's Journal*, 14 August 1907.

56 McDermott, 'The British Labour movement and Ireland, 1905–25', p. 88.

57 *Londonderry Sentinel*, 27 August 1907.

58 UUMC, Belfast trades council minutes, 5–12 September 1907.

59 NAUK, Ministry of Labour reports on strikes and lockouts, 1907, LAB 34/7.

60 Gray, *City in Revolt*, pp. 183–7.

61 *Derry Journal*, 20, 22 May 1907.

62 Ibid., 23 November 1891; Taplin, *The Dockers' Union*, pp. 168–9.

63 *Derry Journal*, 26 August 1896.

64 Ibid., 9, 20, 22 May, 8, 29 July, 23 August, 11, 20 September, 20 December 1907.

65 Taplin, *The Dockers' Union*, p. 168.

66   NAUK, Ministry of Labour reports on strikes and lockouts, 1907, LAB 34/7. For Larkin and Newry, see the conflicting accounts of Bill McCamley, *The Third James: James Fearon, 1874–1924, an Unsung Hero of Our Struggle* (Dublin, 2000), pp. 11–15, and Dermot Keogh, *The Rise of the Irish Working Class: The Dublin Trade Union Movement and Labour Leadership, 1890–1914* (Belfast, 1982), pp. 113–6.

67   McCamley, *The Third James*, p. 14, 16.

68   NLI, William O'Brien papers, 15679(1).

69   Gray, *City in Revolt*, p. 188, 192.

THREE

THE LEAVING OF LIVERPOOL, 1908

. . . he had cut his boat adrift from the other side, and if he [could] fight out an existence in
Ireland he intended to do so . . .
Irish Independent, 1 December 1908

———

So James Larkin defined his position, as he squared up to the loss of his job with the NUDL. It was not stirring stuff, and it was the real Larkin, thinking aloud as he concluded on options he had mulled over throughout the transitional year of 1908. While the south was free of the politics that made agitation in the north so tortuous, it posed an enormous challenge to an organiser of unskilled men. Its manufacturing base was small and weak, and trade unionism, being confined largely to about 50,000 craftsmen and a scattering of shop assistants, clerks, public sector employees, and a few labourers, could be similarly described. According to the 1911 census, of some 900,000 employees, 348,670 were classed as agricultural or general labourers, 170,749 were in domestic or related service, and 201,717 worked in textiles and dressmaking. Thus, over seven out of every nine employees were to be found in largely unorganised, subsistence-waged employment. But if the problem of organisation was surmounted, then unskilled unionism could lead the Labour movement in a way that was not possible anywhere else in the UK. Discontent was there to be tapped: wages had risen very slightly since 1890, and lagged behind rising prices after 1906.[1] So too was a feeling that Labour needed a fundamental redirection. Trade unions had been in decline since the Great Famine, as the economy and population declined. Despite splintering from the BTUC to form their own Congress in 1894 on the grounds that Irish problems needed an Irish voice, trade unionists continued to seek safety in the shelter of the big battalions of British Labour. Some 75 per cent of them now belonged to the amalgamateds, the euphemism for cross-channel unions in Ireland as so many were prefixed 'Amalgamated Society of . . .'[2] Coping with the contradiction and the imperative of sloughing off nationalism generated an ideological commitment to 'internationalism'. Calls from advanced nationalists in fringe groups like Sinn Féin and Cumann na nGaedheal for a completely separate Irish Labour movement were easily dismissed by the ITUC as green advice from green people.[3] But the amalgamateds had not managed to reverse trade union decline, and Labour radicals too were wondering whether it was time to develop an Irish general union. If Larkin were to take that road, he would have significant supporters. Equally, he would meet outraged opposition from numerous union officials who were passionately attached to the links with Britain and would take any intrusion of the national question into Labour affairs very personally as a despicable aspersion on their patriotism. More fundamentally, the future of an Irish general union would depend on its ability to build a bargaining power for unskilled, easily replaced workers in the teeth of employer militancy. Sympathetic action in Belfast had shown that that could be done, and that there was a man to do it. Larkin knew he could do it. Whether he could do it and sustain an Irish union simultaneously he was not so sure. He dithered, until James Sexton made his mind up for him.

TURNING SOUTH

Larkin had visited Dublin on 18 July 1907 to raise funds for Belfast, and sound out the potential for an NUDL branch.[4] The branch was inaugurated on 11 August in the Trades Hall, Capel Street. Familiar with the worst of Liverpool and Glasgow, Larkin was shocked by the Dublin slums and the open prostitution on O'Connell Street. His pitch combined perfectly the personal and the political, and included a typically Larkinite challenge to manly virtue.

> no man in that room could guarantee that tomorrow night he would be in his job. Four out of every eleven men in that room were going to die in the workhouse, asylum or jail unless they altered the laws and they could only alter them if they combined . . . If Dublin men were so proud of their city why did they not look after the little children who were running about the streets hungry, dirty and badly clothed and why did they not put a stop to the disgraceful scenes in O'Connell Street when fellows from the slums of London in red uniform were coming along with Irish girls on their arms who they would ruin in body and soul. Let them join the union – either put up or shut up.[5]

By September, on the strength of a few short visits from Belfast, he had recruited 2,000 men. In October, the branch applied for affiliation to Dublin trades council, and on 26 October, with less than a dozen comrades, Larkin formed a Dublin branch of the ILP at 87 Marlborough Street.[6] As his telegrams to Labour MPs over the summer made obvious, he regarded the British parties as useful to an organiser.

Larkin moved gradually towards a break with Liverpool in 1908. Up to May, his duties required a heavy cross-channel commitment, and he did an enormous amount of travelling, which he always enjoyed. From January to mid-March 1908, he was in London every Thursday as a member of a government commission on dock wages.[7] On 19–21 April he represented the Dublin branch at the ILP annual conference in Huddersfield, where he complained of his non-election to the party's National Administrative Council and the Council's failure to send speakers to Dublin; symptoms, he said, of the neglect of Ireland. Military intervention in the Belfast strike had led numerous ILP, Labour, and union branches to express their solidarity with Larkin, but also generated trenchant criticism of the Labour leadership on the far left, and Larkin did not help his case at Huddersfield with an oblique criticism of some ILP organisers as 'blacklegs'.[8] The gruelling travel went on. Submitting his annual report to the NUDL from 169 Finnieston Street, Glasgow on 22 May, Larkin recorded visits to Cork, Limerick, and Dundee, and spent a considerable amount of time in Glasgow since the new year.[9] But Ireland had already acquired a special significance for him, and he was clearly thinking of making it his home. Elizabeth and Young Jim were now in Rostrevor, County Down, where Delia had managed a boarding house, 'Chislehurst' on Killowen Terrace, since the Belfast strike, and Elizabeth was expecting his second son.[10] Denis was born in Rostrevor on 18 June, and James Fearon became his Godfather.[11]

The NUDL annual conference in May further strained relations between Larkin and Sexton, and a breach was broached. Calls for a native trade unionism were starting to come from Irish-Ireland groups, probably under the influence of the ubiquitous P. T. Daly. Born in 1870 and a little older than Larkin, Daly survived on a portfolio of jobs and contacts, and managed to be an activist in the Dublin Typographical Provident Society and a regular delegate to Dublin trades council and the ITUC, a councillor on Dublin Corporation from 1903 to 1909, a member of the Irish Republican Brotherhood (IRB), sometime secretary of divers small unions – such as the 24-member Dublin Corporation Pavoirs' Society – and an organiser for Cumann na nGaedheal. Larkin claimed he was the only Dublin union leader to come to his aid in Belfast in 1907.[12] In 1905 the manifesto of the Dungannon Clubs, another republican forum, proposed that trade unionism be 'reorganised and nationalised' instead of 'a mean tail to an English democracy'.[13] Cumann na nGaedheal made a similar demand at its annual convention in 1906. An indignant ITUC Parliamentary Committee resolved unanimously:

> That this Committee . . . refutes the reference to amalgamated trades contained in the resolution of Cumann na nGaedheal; resents the attempts of Irish political societies to create division among trade unionists; and emphatically declares that while the employing and capitalist classes, irrespective of politics, creed, or nationality, continue to form associations, trusts, and combines for the protection of

vested interests and the exploitation of wage-workers, it is imperative that the
trade unionists of Ireland and Great Britain should draw closer together . . .[14]

Larkin did not see the options as straightforward, and may have imagined
parallels between himself and Joe Harris of the Workers' Union. Like most
officials of unskilled unions in Ireland, Harris found himself living on scraps
and casting about for a more secure membership base. He was new to the work,
and meeting all the obstacles. During the Belfast unrest he had recruited hundreds of builders' labourers, and lost them again. He then turned his attention
to the linen industry, only to find Mary Galway objecting to the Workers'
Union's affiliation to Belfast trades council on the grounds that it was poaching from her Textile Operatives' Society.[15] Poaching wrangles would dog the
Workers' Union in Ireland because of its readiness to recruit any unorganised
workers rather than concentrating on unorganised sectors. Moving to his
native Dublin, Harris formed a local branch on 1 March 1908 and enlisted
William O'Brien as secretary. A tailor and left-wing activist since the days of
James Connolly's Irish Socialist Republican Party, O'Brien was despondent
about the prospects for his own party, the Socialist Party of Ireland, and keen
to switch to union work.

On 5 April the Workers' Union held a recruitment meeting for 'general
labourers and semi-skilled men in all classes of employment' in the Trades
Hall in Capel Street. One of the speakers was to be 'Jem Larkin, Dockers'
Organiser'.[16] Despite reports of a successful meeting, Harris told O'Brien that
the union wouldn't make progress because it was British. It was a lame excuse,
given the dominance of English unions, and Harris would actually denounce
the formation of Irish unions at the 1909 ITUC.[17] But in April 1908 he reckoned
an Irish general union might be the bait to enlist Larkin. 'He[Larkin] would
be heart and soul with it', Harris assured O'Brien, possibly because Larkin had
backed him in his dispute with Mary Galway and the Dublin ILP appeared to
favour the Harris/O'Brien initiative.[18] Sinn Féin too was interested, and Daly
published an outline of Harris's scheme in the nationalist weekly, the *Peasant*.[19]
Discussions dragged on until May, when Larkin scuppered the project with a
bombshell to O'Brien: 'I might accept the view that there was a case for an
Irish Socialist Party, but I would never agree to divide the workers on the
industrial field.'[20] Judging from Larkin's stance in the winter of 1908–9, it is
likely that a lack of faith in the economy of an Irish general union weighed
more heavily with him, and that he was reluctant to get involved with a breakaway not totally under his control.

What was really on Larkin's wily mind is revealed in his report to the
NUDL for its annul conference in May, which included a veiled suggestion that
he stick with the union in return for some measure of financial autonomy.

Workers in Cork and Limerick, he claimed, were willing to join up, but not to forward all money to Liverpool, an arrangement worth 'earnest consideration'. He hazarded guarded criticisms of headquarters, saying that victory in Belfast had been thrown away by representatives of the General Federation of Trade Unions and negotiations should have been left to local officials, and that the Newry branch was lost 'principally from want of a little timely support'. The report ended on an ambiguous note, vaguely threatening a split and vaguely pleading for an accommodation:

> Before closing I desire to call your attention to the reports of the Executive and resolutions embodied therein, especially those concerning Belfast. *Ex parte* statements have been accepted, and conclusions arrived at which are neither honest or true. I have had the doubtful honour of having to appear before a packed jury, during the last few months, but if I had my choice of being dealt with, either by a capitalist jury or the late Executive, I would undoubtedly prefer the packed jury. They at least would allow you to state your case, whereas, on the contrary, I have on more than one occasion been tried in my absence, and found guilty. My connection with you, as an official, will very possibly come to an end consequent upon a recommendation made by some persons who are not satisfied with my work – a recommendation which they have reasons for, and which they can, I hope, justify. As I opened I close this report. I meet you with every confidence, prepared to accept the responsibility of all my actions, and to justify same, feeling assured that the men who compose this Congress will not allow personal animosity, jealousy, or rancour to warp their judgment.[21]

Whatever about the NUDL executive, it was always unlikely that Sexton would agree to autonomy for the Irish branches. He had a higher strategy of centralisation, and co-operation with other unions and with employers. In his own report, Sexton protested that 'Newry and Dundalk and every other port that could be influenced by Messrs Larkin and Fearon were called out on strike and without the slightest consultation with us in Liverpool, the only place where the money of the union exists to any great extent'.[22] At the conference, Larkin escaped narrowly a censure for insubordination, according to Sexton. Sexton believed that developments in Ireland were encouraging his own critics in the union and the wider movement. Belfast had made Larkin a hero to militants, and the union was being transformed. Since 1905, NUDL membership had risen from a stable 13,500 or so to some 22,000. It was not all due to Larkin of course, but he had been a big inspiration. Sexton found himself 'the target for every delegate with a bee in his bonnet' at the 1908 conference, and failed to get re-elected to the BTUC Parliamentary Committee that year, for which he blamed Larkin. By the end of 1909 the membership tally was back to 13,500.[23]

Over the summer of 1908 Larkin got more involved with the Irish scene. On 8 June he was in Belfast's Ulster Hall for the ITUC's annual Congress with two other NUDL delegates, both from Belfast. In contrast with his limited interventions at the 1907 Congress, he made a point of speaking on various topics, and signalled an ambition by standing for the Parliamentary Committee. With 32 votes, he secured the last place available, a good showing for a controversial *parvenu*.[24] He also became a regular voice in the fortnightly meetings of Dublin trades council. The council was usually associated with artisans at this time, but it represented divers other employees – shop assistants, postmen, telephonists, mineral water operatives, stone cutters, papers cutters, pavoirs, carriers, and labourers – and devoted much of its time to lobbying public authorities for recognition or improvements in wages and conditions. Larkin volunteered for several deputations and sub-committees and got the council to establish a 'Right to Work Committee'.[25]

Another field of activity close to his heart, and to which the council was sympathetic, was the temperance movement. Larkin was chief speaker at a Fr Mathew commemoration in August, where he led contingents of 400 Dublin and 300 Dundalk NUDL men.[26] Larkin was equally temperate on the industrial front, and worked patiently to secure recognition. When some NUDL coal dockers were victimised in June, he and Fearon applied the standard union tactic of lobbying public bodies, and Dublin trades council agreed to send deputations to the Corporation, the poor law unions, and Richmond Asylum board.[27] There was a touch of insubordination about Fearon's involvement. He had been hospitalised for chronic stomach trouble after the Newry dispute and was no longer an official of the union.[28] As the employers continued to refuse to meet union officials and to hire non-union men, Larkin informed the Dublin Coal Masters' Association on 4 July that his members would no longer work with 'nons' after 20 July. It may have been an opening bid: he denied that he was seeking a closed shop and adopted a moderate tone.

Events began to escalate. The Coal Masters, Tedcastles, and the Dublin Steam Packet Company replied that no NUDL members would be employed after Friday 11th. One hundred and twenty men were locked out by four firms and police were drafted in to patrol the quays. Larkin convened a public meeting on Sunday 12th, and had a broad range of speakers on the platform, including Councillor Lorcan Sherlock, a leading figure in the local United Irish League and friendly with moderates on the trades council, William Field, Labour-Nationalist MP for the Dublin constituency of Saint Patrick's, and Frank Kilkelly, president of the NUDL, who said that Sexton was detained by duties in England and promised full support. Field affirmed that they could fight in Dublin 'as well as the men of Belfast'. Anxious to prevent another Belfast, the newly ennobled Lord MacDonnell, Permanent Under-Secretary to the Lord Lieutenant, intervened to secure a resumption of work on 13th pending talks. Arriving in Dublin on 18 July, Sexton arranged a conference with the employers, who were still refusing to treat with Larkin. A settlement on 30th provided for union recognition and a conciliation board to resolve further disputes. In return, Sexton conceded employer demands that they not have to deal with Larkin and that members should not display the badge during working hours, contrary to NUDL rules. He was pleased that a repetition of events in Belfast had been avoided. Larkin said nothing as Sexton explained the terms to the men. Privately, he told O'Brien that the NUDL was 'not prepared to fight', and O'Brien agreed that the settlement was a surrender.[29]

A split was now inevitable, though neither of the two adversaries wished to appear to provoke it. Larkin would often decline to embrace new departures, preferring to stick to his way of doing things and allow events take their course. After July, he became increasingly insubordinate, and financially unaccountable. He subsequently testified in court that he could not explain his expenditure for the last months of 1908. When told by Sexton to organise the port of Cork in August, he despatched Fearon. In October, Larkin was reprimanded by the NUDL executive and told to inform them of any ports he intended to visit. Two of his expense claims were not approved. On 11 October, Sexton refused to sanction a proposed visit to Cork. Larkin went anyway.

Larkin's reception in Waterford on 15 October explains his growing bravado. Three bands marched to meet himself and Fearon, who was travelling incognito as 'Mr Phelan', and a huge crowd escorted a torchlight parade to the City Hall. In the Assembly Room, the High Sheriff presided, and six other members of the Corporation sat on the platform, together with Bernard Dalton, President of the Waterford Federated Trades and Labour Union, a one-time trades council which had superannuated into a social club. A large number of businessmen and politicians occupied the front seats, all eager to see this much talked about man at first hand. The coal merchants were not so equable. Shortly after Larkin rose to speak, there were loud protests against 'an English union'. Violence erupted in one corner of the room. Chairs were smashed and used as weapons. One man sustained serious injury before police and firemen restored order. A coal merchant had hired a gang to disrupt the meeting. The attempted sabotage failed. Cross-channel coal-fillers were signed up that night, and a small branch of the NUDL was founded subsequently. The fillip given by the visit led directly to the revival of Waterford trades council in May 1909.[30]

By November 1908, Fearon had recruited 800 men in Cork, and on 9 November he led a strike of 200 coal dockers. The following day, 150 men from the Shipping Federation arrived to take their place. Larkin visited Cork on 11th and brought out the City of Cork Steam Packet Company dockers. Carters then refused to handle goods unloaded by the scabs, pickets were dispersed by an RIC baton charge, and union leaders were arrested. Larkin left Fearon in charge, and would always insist that it was Fearon, an old Connaught Ranger, who first organised the Citizen Army, or at least a picket-militia with long staffs and red armbands; though whether Fearon's army first appeared in November 1908 or in the big strike of 1909 is not certain.[31] After four days both sides agreed to suspend the dispute, pending a conference to be held in early December. In the interim, there were further dismissals for refusals to handle tainted goods, and a resumption of picketing and arrests. Larkin was back in Cork on 8 December to finalise negotiations in the conference, through the mediation of a local curate, Fr Patrick O'Leary. That evening he announced that full recognition and a satisfactory settlement had been reached for what he called 'the Cork Dock Labourers' Union'. Sexton had disowned the strike, refused an appeal for funds, and suspended Larkin from his job the day before.[32] He had grounds for complaint: Larkin had not applied to Liverpool for membership cards for Cork.[33]

Meanwhile, Larkin was directing an extraordinary struggle of carters in Dublin. On 30 September, he had circularised the leading master carriers with the first of a series of letters requesting a new wage scale. The employers simply ignored him.[34] On 16 November, 150 carters struck four firms. On the following day, the strike extended to 320 men, and a day later canalmen came out in a separate dispute. Over the next five weeks, the two strikes would escalate to involve over 1,000 workers, and on 12 December a third dispute of 400 malsters broke out. Larkin had been in Derry on 16 November, and quickly came under union orders not to return to Dublin, but to move on to Aberdeen. When he ignored the executive, Sexton felt justified in refusing any help for Dublin. This was the first big dispute in which Larkin could fight as he wanted. Initially, his stance was moderate. He tried to discourage incidents of violence, and was happy to effect a return to work, pending negotiations, on 20 November. It seemed that he had secured his basic goal: recognition. However, when the employers broke off negotiations on 26 November, he adopted a more militant strategy, determined to counter the employers' two weapons – starvation and scabs – by broadening the battlefield. He extended picketing and 'black-ing', let strikers join the union with no requirements for being 'in benefit', emphasised the class nature of the struggle, defied the police, and dared the authorities to use the army.[35] This was both a reprise and an extension of 'new unionism'; a risky way of fighting, which trusted to local subscriptions and the weapons of solidarity, sympathetic action, and the numerical capacity of the working class to overstretch the police and the employers. Ultimately, it was dependent on the employers' inability to deploy a sufficient number of scabs, or unwillingness to suffer a protracted battle that would starve the men into submission.

The decision to escalate militancy reflected Larkin's tendency to lose his temper in struggle, and he was not as surefooted as Sexton imagined. Addressing the strikers in Beresford Place on 29 November, he made a series of threats that any informed observer would know to be empty. Telling the men that they must 'crush the masters out' or else be crushed, he warned Dubliners of a general transport strike. Condemning the behaviour of the Dublin Metropolitan Police (DMP), he told British Labour MPs not to vote for the Irish Police bill, which was to improve police pay, or he would denounce the party throughout England. Playing the Belfast card, he said he had received a letter, 'written on foolscap', from 'A Constable', stating that 'a large number of the DMP with some members of the RIC' were ready to join the strike. The letter was generally regarded as a hoax.[36]

At the same time, the mood in Dublin was with Larkin. The biggest crowd yet to assemble for the strikers gathered in Lower Abbey Street on 30 November where a convoy of over 70 carts was in progress. As the people began to hustle the DMP, the authorities feared the congestion was escalating beyond their control and directed mounted police to disperse them.[37] After explaining his difficulties with Sexton, Dublin trades council offered Larkin every assistance. The press, clergy, and public opinion disapproved of the employers' obduracy, especially following their termination of peace talks on 11 December, and the Lord Mayor contributed to the strike fund. Crucially, the workers were determined. On 3 December, Larkin announced that posses of strikers would be formed to police districts from which the DMP had been withdrawn, and a colleague urged workers to acquire sticks for defence against the police; Larkin himself was ambiguous on the issue of weapons.[38] The fear of major unrest in the lucrative Christmas season discouraged the importation of scabs, and without them an employers' victory would be slow and costly. A lasting truce was agreed on 21 December.[39] Larkin thought the eventual arbitration award a disappointment, but he honoured his word, and the outcome was reasonably good in the context of high unemployment and Sexton's hostility.[40]

THE FATEFUL STEP

The Cork and Dublin strikes precipitated the inevitable. Sexton had warned Larkin on 28 November that the union executive had strongly condemned him for 'acting contrary to instructions', and given Sexton the power to suspend him.[41] Larkin's response was public defiance. On 30 November, he told a meeting of carters in Beresford Place:

There was a movement on foot for organising the whole of unskilled labour in Ireland. He was in favour of the international federation of labour, but it was a question whether the first step was not to organise the Irish workers as Irishmen, separately, and then to federate. He was seriously considering whether he should take up this project.[42]

On 7 December, Sexton notified all NUDL branches of Larkin's suspension, leaving his antagonist with no alternative.[43]

Larkin gave no indication of considering a link with another union. Clearly, he wanted to be his own boss, and the public justification for the breakaway had to be the need for an Irish union. It was an exaggeration to say that there was a 'movement on foot' for an Irish general union, but the idea was in the air and there were at least a few Labour separatists such as O'Brien, Daly, and Michael O'Lehane, who were sanguine about it, and with whom Larkin consulted. Sexton's behaviour suggests he was resigned to the loss of Ireland if it meant he would be rid of Larkin, whom he feared as a potential threat to his own job. He had no plans to fight for the retention of the Irish branches, though he would be drawn into some quarrels. Within the NUDL, he sought to move cautiously and quietly. Larkin had been suspended rather than dismissed, and was not replaced as national organiser until 1909, in circumstances which remain unclear and were described cursorily in the union's annual report. Larkin's successor was James O'Connor Kessack, a Scot who was expected to concentrate on Scotland. Kessack had covered the Belfast dock strike for *Forward* and spoken with Larkin.[44] But his organising experience was in the ILP rather than trade unionism, he had never been a docker, and looked more like a bank clerk. In a union where that was a serious handicap, he was unlikely to become a challenge to Sexton. Like Sexton, Kessack hadn't heard the last of Big Jim.[45]

On Monday 27 December Larkin conferred with some of his leading NUDL men in the home of John O'Neill in Townsend Street, Dublin. O'Neill would soon be secretary of the no 1 branch of the new venture. Seán O'Casey later romanticised the occasion, mistakenly dating it after Larkin's imprisonment in 1910:

> So Jim came out of jail, and in a room of a tenement in Townsend Street, with a candle in a bottle for a torch and a billycan of tea, with a few buns for a banquet, the Church militant here on earth of the Irish workers, called the Irish Transport and General Workers' Union, was founded . . .[46]

It was not exactly the foundation. Even Larkin had to observe some decorum. The most fateful step in the history of Irish Labour occurred the following day, at a meeting of what was styled 'the Irish executive' of the NUDL. No such body existed, and Larkin may have simply summoned a few picked men. 'Delegates' from Belfast, Cork, Dublin, Dundalk, and Waterford were present. Michael McKeown 'represented' Belfast, without a mandate. Whoever 'represented' Cork – Fearon was in court that day on a charge of intimidating a director of the Cork Steam Packet Company – the Cork branch did not leave the NUDL until 23 January 1909, when a show of hands was called in the presence of Larkin and Fearon. Nothing is known of procedures elsewhere. The 'executive' duly met on 28 December 1908 in the Trades Hall, Capel Street, Dublin, and agreed to found the ITGWU.[47]

NOTES

1 Séamus Cody, John O'Dowd, and Peter Rigney, *The Parliament of Labour: 100 Years of the Dublin Council of Trade Unions* (Dublin, 1986), pp. 49–50.

2 John W. Boyle, *The Irish Labor Movement in the Nineteenth Century* (Washington, DC, 1989), pp. 125–6.

3 UUMC, ITUC, *Annual Report* (1907), pp. 14–15.

4 C. Desmond Greaves, *The Irish Transport and General Workers' Union: The Formative Years, 1909–1923* (Dublin, 1982), p. 17.

5 *Freeman's Journal*, 12 August 1907, cited in Cody, O'Dowd, and Rigney, *The Parliament of Labour*, p. 54.

6 John Gray, *City in Revolt: James Larkin and the Belfast Dock Strike of 1907* (Belfast, 1985), p. 191; Emmet Larkin, *James Larkin: Irish Labour Leader, 1876–1947* (London, 1965), pp. 49–51; UUMC, Dublin trades council minutes, 28 October 1907; *Labour Leader*, 24 April 1908.

7 Larkin, *James Larkin*, pp. 50–1.

8 Daniel V. McDermott, 'The British Labour movement and Ireland, 1905–25' (MA, University College, Galway, 1979), pp. 88–103; Independent Labour Party, *Report of the Sixteenth Annual Conference* (London, 1908), p. 42.

9 NLI, William O'Brien papers, 15679(1).

10 *Harp*, March 1910; Theresa Moriarty, 'Delia Larkin: relative obscurity', in Donal Nevin (ed.), *James Larkin: Lion of the Fold* (Dublin, 1998), p. 429; NLI, William O'Brien papers, 15676(2), part 2.

11 Jim Larkin, *In the Footsteps of Big Jim: A Family Biography* (Dublin, 1995), p. x, 24; Bill McCamley, *The Third James: James Fearon, 1874–1924, an Unsung Hero of Our Struggle* (Dublin, 2000), p. 32.

12 Séamus Cody, 'The remarkable Patrick Daly', *Obair* 2 (1985), pp. 10–11; Donal Nevin (ed.), *Between Comrades: James Connolly, Letters and Correspondence 1889–1916* (Dublin, 2007), p. 579.

13 *Belfast Labour Chronicle*, 7–14 October 1905.

14 UUMC, ITUC, *Annual Report* (1907), pp. 14–15.

15 Richard Hyman, *The Workers' Union* (Oxford, 1971), p. 30; UUMC, Belfast trades council minutes, 5 September 1907.

16 NLI, William O'Brien papers, LoP108, handbill; and *Evening Telegraph*, 11 April 1908.

17 UUMC, ITUC, *Annual Report* (1909), p. 51.

18 William O'Brien, *Forth the Banners Go: The Reminiscences of William O'Brien as Told to Edward MacLysaght, D.Litt* (Dublin, 1969), p. 55.

19 *Peasant*, May 1908, cited in the *Harp*, June 1910.

20 O'Brien, *Forth the Banners Go*, p. 55; see also Dermot Keogh, *The Rise of the Irish Working Class: The Dublin Trade Union Movement and Labour Leadership, 1890–1914* (Belfast, 1982), pp. 136–7; Greaves, *The Irish Transport and General Workers' Union*, p. 20.

21 NLI, William O'Brien papers, 15679(1).

22 McCamley, *The Third James*, p. 14, 16.

23 Eric Taplin, *The Dockers' Union: A Study of the National Union of Dock Labourers, 1889–1922* (Leicester, 1986), pp. 73–4, 77.

24 UUMC, ITUC, *Annual Report* (1908), pp. 56–7.

25 UUMC, Dublin trades council minutes, 14 September 1908.

26 Larkin, *James Larkin*, p. 54.

27 UUMC, Dublin trades council executive minutes, 9 June 1909.

28 McCamley, *The Third James*, pp. 14–15.

29 Taplin, *The Dockers' Union*, p. 74; Cody, O'Dowd, and Rigney, *The Parliament of Labour*, pp. 54–5; Larkin, *James Larkin*, p. 52; for the terms of the settlement see Arnold Wright, *Disturbed Dublin: The Story of the Great Strike of 1913–14, with a Description of the Industries of the Irish Capital* (London, 1914), pp. 305–7.

30 *Waterford News*, 16–23 October 1908; Emmet O'Connor, *A Labour History of Waterford* (Waterford, 1989), pp. 117–20.

31 *Irish Worker*, 15–22 November 1924; McCamley, *The Third James*, pp. 22–3.

32 NAUK, Ministry of Labour reports on strikes and lockouts, 1907, LAB 34/7; ITGWU, *Fifty Years of Liberty Hall: The Golden Jubilee of the Irish Transport and General Workers' Union, 1909–1959* (Dublin, 1959), p. 21; Greaves, *The Irish Transport and General Workers' Union*, pp. 22–3; *Irish Times*, 9 December 1908.

33 McCamley, *The Third James*, p. 15.

34 *Irish Times*, 27 November 1908.

35 Keogh, *The Rise of the Irish Working Class*, pp. 125–30.

36 *Irish Times*, 30 November 1908.

37 Ibid., 1 December 1908.

38 Ibid., 4–5 December 1908.

39 Keogh, *The Rise of the Irish Working Class*, pp. 130–3.

40 Larkin, *James Larkin*, pp. 58–60.

41 Gray, *City in Revolt*, p. 192.

42 *Freeman's Journal*, 1 December 1908.

43 Keogh, *The Rise of the Irish Working Class*, p. 133.

44 Gray, *City in Revolt*, pp. 104–5; Donal Nevin (ed.), *Trade Union Century* (Cork, 1994), plate 16.

45 Taplin, *The Dockers' Union*, pp. 76–8.

46 Hugh Geraghty, *William Patrick Partridge and His Times (1874–1917)* (Dublin, 2003), p. 114; Seán O'Casey, *Autobiography Book 3: Drums under the Windows* (London, 1972), p. 190.

47 Greaves, *The Irish Transport and General Workers' Union*, p. 25, 32; on Fearon see Larkin, *James Larkin*, pp. 69–71; and McCamley, *The Third James*, pp. 17–19.

FOUR

THE LIVERPOOL LEFTOVERS, 1909–10

We do not deny that in most cases the cause of Labour is the same the world over; but that we should confess our inability to grapple with such problems by placing our headquarters in London or Glasgow, and sending Irish money to those centres, and seeking instruction from foreigners, is not the way to prove our ability to govern ourselves. This is a clear national issue, and one that deserves a clear and distinct answer. The national forces of Ireland were ever composed mainly of workingmen, and if there is a future for Ireland it is the workingmen who will achieve it. To Irishise everything from Dunleary to Ceann Leime is our object, and to do this we want the workingman – and we should cut a sorry figure trying to Irishise Ireland with a man acknowledging as his headquarters London or Glasgow. Our metropolis is Dublin – bad as it is . . .
Irish Worker, 4 January 1913

———

The leaving of Liverpool turned a rebellious prince into an insecure king, in a barren kingdom. A union of casual men, who might or might not have the dues in any one week, and based on a handful of ports, could only be insecure. And Larkin was not sure that the ITGWU could profitably expand much beyond Dublin dockland, and was unwilling to take risks. By mid-1909, after initial uncertainty about how to project the ITGWU, Larkin had decided that it would be assertively nationalist and vaguely socialist, and had too an outline plan for the re-organisation of the Labour movement, in which it would be brought under Irish control, united in a federation, and represented by its own political party. But he was slow to make progress. Economic circumstances were not favourable. He was dogged by the consequences of his breach with Liverpool. And some unforeseen deficiencies were exposed once he assumed supreme command. Despite his aspirations, he had no strategy for the union, showed no ability to manage branch development, and jealousy discouraged him from creating a chain of command; leaving the ITGWU excessively centred on him, and he on the capital. After 1908, he never led a strike outside Dublin. Indeed, now that he was his own boss, he displayed surprisingly little interest in organisation. For all that, he was plainly the most dynamic personality in trade unionism. The Irish-based, militant movement he was seen to embody attracted ever increasing interest.

54

WHAT KIND OF UNION?

The ITGWU was formally registered as a union on 4 January 1909. Larkin's immediate concern was to carry with him as much of the Irish NUDL as he could. With one nasty exception, it was a clean break. Drogheda stayed with Liverpool, and the Derry branch 'strongly condemn[ed] the action of the late organiser and other branch officials of Belfast in their efforts to create a division in the ranks of the union by the formation of an opposition organisation . . .'[1] Dublin, Cork, Dundalk, and Waterford defected. James Sexton responded reactively. He made no effort to repossess the union's Dublin offices at 10 Beresford Place, but accepted Alex Boyd's invitation to intervene in Belfast.

On 6 January, Boyd rallied the cross-channel men behind the old union, describing the ITGWU as a 'Sinn Féin organisation that not even a decent nationalist in Belfast would have anything to do with'.[2] Two days later, at Michael McKeown's invitation, Larkin spoke to 400 deep-sea dockers, who resolved to join the ITGWU. Sexton arrived in Belfast on Tuesday 12th to attend a meeting chaired by Boyd. W. J. McNulty, secretary of the Derry branch, was also there in support. The ITGWU branch had begun formal enrolment that day, and ITGWU men disrupted the meeting. The following day McNulty accompanied Sexton to Derry, where he 'answered the charges against him by Larkin'. Thanks mainly to McNulty's popularity, the Derry branch gave him 'a fine reception' and unanimous backing. For McNulty, it was a choice between 'the old union' or Larkin and strikes, and 'he never yet knew of a strike which benefited the worker'.[3] Back in Belfast on 14th, Sexton spoke at the York Street hall. There was a heavy RIC presence, and hecklers were ejected. Belfast trades council offered to mediate in the dispute, but Sexton refused to meet Larkin, saying it was a waste of time to deal with a man who was 'not even a good liar'.[4] On the following day, the NUDL started court action to repossess union books and head offices from McKeown and the ITGWU. One week later, McKeown agreed to surrender the books. Recriminations now surfaced over the conduct of Larkin and Sexton during the 1907 strike, and in part the schism reflected secular differences arising from that year. Dispirited by the defeats of 1907, the cross-channel sections were more inclined to moderation; whereas the deep-sea dockers were still awaiting militancy on their behalf. Nonetheless, the net effect was to divide the dockers along sectarian lines. The split also allowed the employers to play one side off against the other. In late 1908 they had established a Labour Bureau, which Larkin denounced as a scab clearing house. On 8 February 1909, membership of the Bureau was made a requirement for employment on the deep-sea docks. The

NUDL accepted this arrangement, and ITGWU members watched helplessly as their workmates and non-unionists took their livelihood. Within weeks, to Sexton's delight, the ITGWU branch had collapsed. But the employers were soon squeezing out the NUDL men too, and by May their branch was inactive.

Larkin's idea of the ITGWU was not quite settled. In Dublin he spoke of the union as a radical departure; in Cork, as the NUDL by another name.[5] He played down its nationalist rationale in the north, claiming that he had not been validly suspended from the NUDL, and challenging Sexton to resign and let them both contest an election for general secretary. In Dundalk, he told men in the railway workshops that his union would not be confined to Ireland, but 'affiliated with England and Scotland'.[6] Almost certainly, this was tactical rhetoric. He made no attempt to fight within the NUDL or in Britain. He could be under no illusions that Ireland would be his bailiwick.

It is unlikely that he was having second thoughts, and more likely that he was making a pitch to the railwaymen, who might be presumed to value the link with Britain, their main union being the London-based Amalgamated Society of Railway Servants (ASRS). He was particularly keen to recruit on the railway, where men in steady employment would have regular money for regular union dues. The first union badges were marked 'ITWU', suggesting that he intended originally to found a transport union, unconvinced that a general union could be sustained, and doubtful if railwaymen would want to be bracketed with general workers. By 4 January, he had changed his mind to the extent of registering the union as the ITGWU. William O'Brien claimed he pressed for the inclusion of 'and General', and Larkin agreed reluctantly.[7] But on 24 January, Larkin told Joe Harris that he wanted to organise transport before tackling general workers, adding that he had 'sacrificed £4.7s 6d a week in order to stand by the Dublin men'.[8] According to James O'Connor Kessack, he had been the highest paid organiser in the NUDL.[9] As general secretary of the ITGWU he took a weekly salary of £2.10s, his starting pay in the NUDL.[10]

Other than a pipe, the odd cigar, and a few books, Larkin had little use for life's luxuries, and was renowned for being an easy touch for hard luck cases; so much so that around 1912 it was arranged for the ITGWU to pay his wages to Elizabeth directly.[11] But he worried about money – his own at least – and had reason for apprehension. In February 1909 he was judged a bankrupt on the petition of Belfast Harbour Commissioners. The Commissioners had had him prosecuted for addressing workers on their property during the 1907 strike, and Larkin had failed to pay the costs of litigation. He told the Court of Bankruptcy that his last paypacket from the NUDL had arrived on 25 November 1908, and his only income since then came from £5 from the sale of some of his deceased mother's furniture in Liverpool, and collections made for him in Dublin which went to pay his board at 14 Saint Benedict's Terrace,

Drumcondra. He claimed he didn't own 'even a watch'. Asked about if he had an agreement for remuneration from the ITGWU, he replied: 'None at present. The whole thing is in a sort of flux at present. There is no executive. A sort of temporary committee carries on the work.'[12] Elizabeth was soon to move to Dublin and give birth to a third child, named Fintan Lalor, on 20 January 1910. The family rented a house at 27 Auburn Street, which was to be home until the 1913 Lockout.[13] Despite the financial insecurity, Jim was determined to be his own boss. When Harris offered to transfer Workers' Union branches to the ITGWU in return for a leading post in the union, Larkin replied that he would 'sink or swim alone'.[14]

By May Larkin was more ebullient. The preamble to the ITGWU rules registered on 6 May confirmed that the union would be not Irish merely, but nationalist as well:

> Are we going to continue the policy of grafting ourselves on the English Trades Union movement, losing our identity as a nation in the great world of organised labour? We say emphatically, No. Ireland has politically reached her manhood.

The rulebook described its target constituency as the 'so-called unskilled', and said that 'the old system of sectional unions amongst unskilled workers is practically useless for modern conditions'. Yet no provision was made for an industrial unionist structure. In a further anomaly, the rules defined the ITGWU moderately as a medium to improve wages and conditions by negotiation, arbitration, or, in the last resort, strikes. Its 'immediate programme' demanded 'legal eight hours' day provision of work for all unemployed, and pensions for all workers at 60 years of age. Compulsory Arbitration Courts, adult suffrage, nationalisation of canals, railways and all means of transport. The land of Ireland for the people of Ireland'. Its ultimate ideal was an 'industrial commonwealth', which would 'obliterate poverty, and help to realise the glorious time spoken of and sung by the Thinkers, Prophets and the Poets...'[15] The rules reflected Larkin's lack of confidence in dealing with theory. He had stumbled across two key ideas since coming to Ireland, sympathetic action and industrial unionism, but he was unable to integrate them into a strategy. He found it easier to relate Labour to a third idea, separatism.

In a further advance in his thinking, Larkin gave his thoughts a general application on 3 July in the *Irish Labour Journal*, 'The organ of the workers of Ireland, under the auspices of the Dublin Trades' Council', edited by P. T. Daly. After years of deliberation, the council had issued the weekly paper in June. It would run to September. It offered in-depth, lengthy articles but was dry and limited in range, and too much the house journal of the trades council regulars to acquire a popular appeal. In an article entitled 'The Labour problem in Ireland', Larkin set out a personal manifesto that encapsulated his vision for trade unionism in Ireland. After declaring the 'root cause' of the deplorable state of the workers to be 'private property in land and capital', he went on to identify three difficulties more amenable to resolution: poor education; weak union organisation and dependency 'on the experience and initiative of people from other countries in managing their trade organisations'; and lack of political representation. These problems should be addressed in three steps. The first was to 'combine in trades unions organised by Irishmen and controlled by Irishmen . . . with headquarters in the metropolis'. The second step heralded what would be an abiding and unfulfilled ambition of Larkin, and a source of endless frustration: the use of union funds for commercial projects. Sectionalism, he argued, ought to be replaced with a federation of all workers, skilled and unskilled, for tactical reasons and so that instead of sending money to England, it might be used by the federation to stimulate 'present industries' and start others on a co-operative basis. The third step was to create a Labour party, and its immediate demands should be: adult suffrage, an eight-hour day, compulsory wages and arbitration boards, provision of work for all unemployed, pensions for all at 60, compulsory tillage, direct labour, municipal housing, municipal control of public utilities, nationalisation of transport, socialisation of land, and free education at all levels. The article was signed 'Seamus O Lorcain'.

Unfortunately for Larkin, his jealousy and impatience with structures and procedure would repeatedly hamstring the pursuit of these aims. The problem was evident in the governance of the ITGWU. In drawing up a rulebook, Larkin simply copied what seemed appropriate from other union manuals, so that the political values of the union were not embedded in its structures or *modus operandi*, even in theory.[16] In practice, he had no time for regulations, and it was always his intention that the administration of the union would amount to one man rule. Even the process of adopting the rules was high-handed, according to a witness at Larkin's court hearings in Cork:

> They went to business on Sunday evening in the Transport Hall in Beresford Place. Mr Larkin took the chair, and there were present Mr Green, witness and Mr Fearon, and from nine to twelve more. The rule books of other unions were produced, and Mr Larkin read them, and each rule that would suit the new rule book they were going to form would be marked off, and it would be sanctioned by the meeting for the transport union.[17]

While the rules provided for a General Executive Council, comprising the president, secretary, and treasurer, together with district and branch committees, there was *de facto* no executive, and a proposed annual national convention of delegates never met. Up to 1917, the two general officers, the president and secretary, who were supposed to be chosen by the members biennially, were elected annually by the no 1 branch, and the no 1 branch committee, in theory, supervised all union affairs.[18] Larkin's writ extended to everything, and the no 1 branch committee would not decide on so much as the buttons on the uniform of the union band or the allocation of a brush to the caretaker of Liberty Hall without his approval.[19] But increasingly, he left financial management to the committee.

PROGRESS IN UNION POLITICS

Over the next two years, Larkin pursued his agenda and ITGWU interests through Dublin trades council and the ITUC rather than developing union organisation. Fortuitously, the trades council was evolving in a like-minded direction, and starting to support causes like votes for women, the Irish language, action on unemployment, the revival of May Day celebrations, and independent Labour representation. The council made no issue of the ITGWU's displacement of the NUDL, and on 1 March 1909 Larkin and key confederates Daly and O'Brien were elected to the 16-man council executive. Daly topped the poll with 45 votes, and Larkin came third with 37.[20] The executive usually convened weekly, with 53 meetings over the next 12 months. Larkin was present at 30, an impressive record given his unavoidable absences between July and September.[21] Constrained as an NUDL official, Larkin was now becoming increasingly careless in making personal attacks. He also revealed an inordinate sensitivity to criticism, and assumed that an injury to Jim was the concern of all. On 10 May he challenged the credentials of renegade socialist E. W. Stewart and moved the suspension of standing orders so that the council could discuss a hostile statement by P. J. McIntyre, secretary of the Workers' Union in Dublin. The delegates backed Larkin.[22]

The council could be a bear-pit of personality conflicts or inter-union disputes, and for all his foibles, Larkin was a dutiful and effective colleague, serving the council well on numerous sub-committees and deputations. While some became increasingly estranged from what Stewart called 'the socialist element', Larkin enjoyed a growing reputation with the majority, who were not as socialist as Stewart made out. In July 1910, the council declined, by 21–14 votes, to hear a lecture from James Connolly, just returned from America and hoping to earn a living by organising for the Socialist Party of Ireland. By contrast, Larkin's practical work earned respect. The council was prepared to back his industrial tactics, and be persuaded by his more political interventions, such as his motion for the nationalisation of the railways.[23] His next challenge was to win over the ITUC. Given the weakness of the ITGWU, the trades council's backing would be important.

On 13 February Larkin joined the ITUC's Parliamentary Committee in a lobby of John Redmond and other leaders of the Irish Parliamentary Party (IPP) in Dublin's Mansion House. It was a rare occasion. The Committee had met Redmond only twice before, in 1902 and 1904. Each member of the Committee raised their particular concerns. Larkin protested at the behaviour of the police towards workers and their failure to uphold the Trades Disputes Act, called for compensation for relatives of those shot in the Belfast riots, and urged the IPP to support the nationalisation of canals, railways, and shipping. In a discordant remark, he said that while 'he believed in using any weapon that was in their hand', he did not regard the IPP as a labour party. Redmond seemed stung and devoted much of his response to the IPP's friendly relations with the British Labour Party and record on social legislation, insisting that 'we are the Labour Party, as far as Ireland is concerned'.[24]

That same day the Parliamentary Committee received a letter from Michael McKeown asking it to investigate the dispute between the ITGWU and NUDL in Belfast and blacklegging by members of the NUDL on members of the ITGWU. The Committee decided to refer the matter to Belfast trades council and, with Larkin alone dissenting, to exclude the ITGWU from Congress pending a resolution of the dispute. Sexton weighed in on 1 March, with a letter to the Committee asking it to follow BTUC policy in debarring the ITGWU as a splinter union, and requesting Larkin's removal from the Committee on the ground that he had been elected to it as an NUDL official. When the Committee met on the eve of the annual Congress, Stewart successfully moved a motion of expulsion.[25]

The Congress opened on 31 May in Limerick's Athenaeum. Determined to fight his corner, Larkin took the train from Kingsbridge. The ITUC's Standing Orders Committee agreed to the ITGWU's admission following representations from branches in Dublin, Cork, Waterford, and Dundalk. But the Congress president, Michael Egan, a coachmaker from Cork, ruled that the Parliamentary Committee's report took precedence. The report finally came up for discussion on the second day of the Congress, after luncheon. Daly moved an amendment which would lift the proscriptions on Larkin and the ITGWU. The debate quickly evolved into an argument on Larkin and his style: the radical young guard of Dublin trades council citing his achievements and contrasting his zeal with Sexton's dilatoriness, while the old Congress stalwarts depicted him as a disruptive force. The Ulster delegates in particular scented a threat to the amalgamateds and raised the spectre of a split between Irish and British unions. 'Mr Larkin was a great organiser,' said John Murphy, secretary of Belfast trades council, 'but he must be boss, or all the fact would be in the fire. If the delegates voted against the Parliamentary Committee, then the Congress would cease to represent Trades Unionism in Ireland'. On his feet in the gallery, Larkin vainly demanded the right to defend himself. According to O'Brien, he was 'very high' and roared 'traitor, skunk, betrayer, tools of England'. Disorder ensued as several delegates appealed to the chair. Daly's amendment was defeated, 39–49. All was not lost. Congress agreed to appoint a committee of seven, including three of the Parliamentary Committee, to investigate the dispute in the NUDL and the formation of the ITGWU.[26]

The committee met in July in the Dublin Trades Hall, Capel Street and, after two lengthy sittings and consideration of evidence from both sides, reached a judicious conclusion which offered something for everyone: that there was no 'real' justification for the ITGWU's secession from the NUDL, that no objection should be made to the formation of 'purely Irish trade unions', and that the ITGWU was a *bona fide* union, entitled to recognition.[27] Essentially, it was a good result for Larkin. But the findings still had to be endorsed by the next annual Congress, which assembled in Dundalk on 16–18 May 1910. Stewart opened for the old guard, arguing that admission of the ITGWU should be postponed pending the resolution of its dispute with the NUDL over 'the ownership of a large sum of money'. The NUDL's two delegates, from Derry and Drogheda, went further, and moved an amendment to the committee's report, deleting the reference to the ITGWU's *bona fide* status.[28] Fortunately for Larkin, attitudes in Congress had softened since 1909. Possibly because of the ITGWU's lack-lustre performance on the industrial front, there was now much less anxiety about its implications for the amalgamateds. To 'loud cheers', the NUDL amendment was defeated by 38–32 votes. Further assistance came from an unexpected quarter. William Walker intervened, saying that continued opposition to Larkin was simply turning him into 'a martyr'. His amendment for the affiliation of the ITGWU was carried, 42–10. It was a bitter moment for the chairman, Councillor James McCarron, an old Congress mugwump and Labour-Nationalist from Derry. His ruling that the matter would have to be ratified by the Parliamentary Committee after lunch was too much for Larkin. Storming from the gallery to the floor, and speaking 'in a very excited manner', he denounced some of the delegates of 'notorious blacklegs' and enemies of trade unionism. After interventions, McCarron relented, and agreed that Larkin and the five ITGWU delegates – all from Dublin – be admitted immediately. Larkin too relented, apologising for his remarks, promising the ITGWU would not discredit the movement, and affirming that he belonged to no party but Labour. Ominously, he promised 'he would deal with [his critics] at another time'. It was still too much for McCarron, who announced his retirement from the Parliamentary Committee at the close of the Congress.[29]

Once admitted, Larkin took an active part in proceedings, and would assume a leading role in debate on structural reform. Proposals for federation came before Congress in two waves, 1895–1900, and 1909–12, coinciding with cognate discussions in Britain in the 1890s, and the growth of Larkinism after 1909. Most were essentially pious, and often included reference to organisation in Britain, to accommodate the amalgamateds, who were unable to reconcile reform of Irish Labour with their cross-channel links. Larkin was determined to replace the pieties with practical plans to transform Labour, and sweep away the amalgamateds if necessary. He opposed a motion for a merger of the ITUC and British TUC, and it was defeated 23–15 votes. He then seconded Michael O'Lehane's resolution for a 'closer union [of] the various trade and labour bodies in Ireland' leading to an 'Irish Federation of Labour'. 'It was nonsense,' said Larkin, 'to talk of internationalism in Ireland until they had made them first realise their responsibility to their own nation.' Ultimately, the proposal was rejected in favour of a spoiling amendment for a federation of all workers in 'Ireland, England, and Scotland'. The amalgamateds still held sway in Congress, accounting for 40 delegates, against 34 from Irish unions. Hugh MacManus, Irish organiser of the Typographical Association and a friend of Larkin's, encapsulated the negativity of their provincial mindset:

> [H]e had been trying to federate the workers in his own craft before some of them were born (laughter). It could not be done in Ireland then, and would not be done now. They were only 'gasing' (laughter). Were they going to start a small weak body in Ireland when they could be members of a strong body that was already in existence (applause).[30]

Larkin also proposed that Congress create an Irish Labour Party. It too was rejected. Larkin himself was narrowly defeated in the elections to the Parliamentary Committee, just missing out on a seat with 30 votes.[31] It had been a Congress of mixed fortunes for him. He had made progress in surmounting the dispute with the NUDL and getting the ITGWU affiliated, but these victories had as much to do with his perceived weakness as his strength. On the strategic questions, the amalgamateds were as arrogant as ever. It seemed, in 1910, that Big Jim was not quite the threat he had been.

ANTI-CLIMAX ON THE INDUSTRIAL FRONT

Larkin had marked time in industrial relations. There was no recruitment drive or wages offensive to fanfare the birth of the union. Larkin was never a strike-happy wildcat. The ITGWU rules advocated compulsory arbitration, and as late as 1912, he declared his opposition to strikes, while defending sympathetic action.[32] In Dublin, the ITGWU had inherited disputes of carters and malsters which had begun in November 1908 and were now in arbitration. At a meeting in the Trades Hall on 18 February, Larkin welcomed the arbitration award as 'a glorious victory'. In fact, as he admitted, the award for the malsters was very disappointing – 'the worst he had ever known', in his own words – but the union was recognised and employer attempts to exclude him from negotiations had been defeated.[33] With a meagre war chest and a trade recession in 1908–9, he had good reason for caution. Yet those factors hadn't stopped him in 1908. The capital, at least, had his constant attention. The provinces, he neglected. One after another the branches disintegrated, in Belfast, Cork, Waterford, and Dundalk. In Dublin, some 50 per cent of NUDL members had not re-enrolled in the ITGWU. Over 1,500 workers joined up in 1910, the bulk of them in the latter half of the year, bringing ITGWU membership to about 3,000, but this was scarcely more than the NUDL total for Dublin two years earlier.[34] Larkin seemed intent on expanding at the expense of existing unions. Where the opportunity arose, he challenged the credentials of delegates to the trades council or the *bona fides* of their unions, and ITGWU recruitment involved the council in regular poaching disputes. Even when trade improved and prices increased in 1909–10, the caution persisted.

Lax management of the ITGWU in the provinces had terrible conse-quences in Cork in the summer of 1909.[35] A recovery of local Labour confidence had been underway for over a year, boosted by Larkin's intervention in 1908. Tramwaymen had struck in April 1909, and builders' labourers in May. On 16 May, Larkin spoke at Cork's first Labour Day demonstration in many years. With over 40 societies and 6,000 workers in affiliation, Cork United Trades and Labour Council was buoyant.[36] Relations on the quayside remained tense in the wake of the 1908 unrest. In April a riot had erupted after James Fearon had been threatened by hostile dockers and then led a counter-attack of ITGWU dockers.[37] Now there were rumours of plans to introduce steam winches. When Harris established a section of the Workers' Union for coal-porters on Morrison's Island, there were fears that he was being brought in by stevedores to facilitate the mechanisation.

There were many echoes of Belfast 1907 in what followed. On 10 June, ITGWU coalporters struck for the dismissal of Workers' Union men without seeking head office approval or waiting to negotiate with management. They were promptly joined by carters and storemen. Fearon and three others were arrested, following clashes with the RIC. Days later, 140 ITGWU men with the City of Cork Steam Packet Company came out in sympathy. As workers were dismissed for refusing to handle 'tainted goods', and replaced by scabs, the strike spread to railwaymen and carters. On 16 June, the Cork Employers' Federation was formed, and it pledged to replace any man who refused orders out of sympathy with the strike, leading to lockouts of mineral water workers, flour millers, bacon salters, building workers, and railwaymen. An employers' statement on 6 July set out four demands, making it plain that they opposed the unionisation of unskilled men, and did indeed have plans for mechanisation:

1. That in case of unskilled workers, employers shall be free to employ either members of Union[*sic*] or non-Unionists . . .
2. That unskilled workmen, desiring employment, must make application direct to their late employers . . .
3. That all such workmen applying for re-employment, and who may be re-instated, shall undertake to obey all lawful orders, under all conditions in future, and not to leave their employment again without giving legal notice.
4. That employers my adopt any conditions necessary for the conduct of particular businesses (including the use of machinery) and that workmen shall agree to same.[38]

By now, over 2,000 men were affected.[39]

This was the first real example of Larkinism without Larkin. Workers were spontaneously adopting the method of conflict that he had used in Belfast and Dublin. The big difference in Cork was Larkin's absence. Initially, he hurried to Cork to address a mass meeting in Parnell Place. Obviously not on top of events and more concerned with the politics of the ITGWU, he declared that the issue was the conflict between an Irish and a British union. After failing to persuade the Steam Packet Company to settle, or Harris to get his members not to blackleg, he returned to Dublin. Had he led the fight, in person, he might have generated the same degree of public and Board of Trade concern which prevented Dublin employers from smashing the struggles of 1908 with scabs. In Dublin, Labour closed ranks behind Larkin. Dublin trades council reckoned that 'Capitalism is trying to destroy combination amongst the workers now', and, significantly, endorsed sympathetic action: 'we are convinced that the spread of the dispute from a trades' union standpoint was unavoidable.'[40] In Cork, the trades council adopted an apologetic stance, pleading with employers that the strike 'was the result of a blunder, and that would happen to anyone'.[41]

Without Larkin's presence in Cork, the financial miracles of Belfast and Dublin were not forthcoming. The ITGWU men received 3s 6d a week strike pay up to 11 July, and 1s 5d afterwards. Already, a drift back to work was underway. The defeat had a devastating impact on Cork Labour, reversing the promising revival of 1908–9. On 12 August the Typographical Association led other craft unions out of the United Trades and Labour Council to form the Cork District Trades Association. In part the split was motivated by the friction in local IPP politics that followed the formation of the breakaway All For Ireland League by William O'Brien, MP, earlier that year. But it also reflected a desire to get away from militancy. There were complaints, on the Trades and Labour Council, that 'the "class" argument was responsible for what happened'.[42] Fearon was attacked in the council, and asked what kind of a union was it that couldn't support its members on strike? Only the coal-porters remained out, unwilling to accept employers' terms for mechanisation, but railwaymen and others continued to be blacklisted. Larkin had shown that he was psychologically unable to cope with defeat. Despite emotive pleas for a morale boosting visit, he declined either to go to Cork or call off the strike at the Steam Packet Company, and let it disintegrate. The ITGWU branch collapsed with it. It would not be revived for another four years. In Dublin, the trades council and the *Irish Labour Journal* continued to stand by Larkin, and blamed the Cork debacle on the Workers' Union. An 'immense concourse of people' rallied in Beresford Place on 15 August to hear Larkin deal with 'the mendacious statements' of Harris and others of the Workers' Union. Larkin opened with the observation that the absence of Harris 'was like playing Faust without Mephistopheles'. The crowd 'hugely enjoyed' his performance.[43]

'AN OUTRAGEOUS CONSPIRACY'[44]

More immediate trouble materialised on 18 August. As Larkin left Beresford Place for home that evening, he was arrested.[45] The following day he was taken to Cork and charged, along with Fearon, Denis Sullivan, and Daniel Coveney, members of the Cork branch, with 'conspiracy to defraud'. Ostensibly, the case arose from information given by stevedore Simon Punch that he had been swindled out of 1s 3d paid to the NUDL.[46] After a few days, Larkin was out on bail, but the preliminary hearings continued from 24 August to 21 September. The crown's case was that there had never been an NUDL branch in Cork, and therefore £167 in dues taken from the Cork dockers in the name of the NUDL, and £147 sent from Cork for the Dublin strikes in 1908, amount-ed to defraud. The crown's belated concern for the financial welfare of Cork dockers did not impress impartial observers. That the crown prosecutor was also legal adviser to the Cork Employers' Federation signposted the origins of the vindictiveness.

The court hearings cast a damaging light on Larkin's ability to manage things beyond his immediate reach. Sexton was subpoenaed to give evidence and travelled to Cork, as he had to Belfast in 1907, clutching the butt of a revolver in his coat pocket. 'More than once,' he claimed, 'I had to reveal the fact that I was armed to men who shadowed me wherever I chanced to go.'[47] Sexton claimed that the NUDL had not ratified the Cork branch or received so much 'as the stroke of a pen' from Fearon. His executive affirmed that strikes had been started and settled in Cork without its knowledge, and it had been embarrassed to receive letters from Cork asking why no dispute pay was forthcoming.[48] And a queue of local dockers represented Fearon as a petty-tyrant who ran the branch with an iron fist. The crown also released letters found on Larkin, which exposed the difficulties of the ITGWU in Cork. Larkin's defence rested on his moral character. No account books were produced. The magistrate decided that Larkin should be returned for trial at the winter assizes in Cork, and face 24 charges, including criminal conspiracy to deception and misappropriation of funds. Larkin did at least succeed in having the trial moved to Dublin, on the grounds that he could not get a fair hearing in Cork. He remained buoyant and confident of acquittal.[49]

The crown 'conspiracy' boosted not only Larkin's reputation, but Larkin*ism*. By the tenets of Sexton's trade unionism, Larkin had flouted the rules. Just the same, he had acted, and put workers first. And many decided that that was more important. Dublin trades council formed a Larkin defence fund in September.[50] There were serious consequences for the NUDL in Scotland. Sexton's willingness to be chief witness for the crown shocked his colleagues. George Dallas accused Sexton of trying to excuse 'his own inaction' in Cork. Kessack joined Dallas and other comrades from the Glasgow socialist paper *Forward* on a Larkin defence committee, and Larkin received a 'rousing reception' at a support meeting in Glasgow City Hall on 15 November.[51] Kessack went so far as to resign from the NUDL, but was persuaded to reconsider by Sexton. Sexton was unpopular with Glasgow dockers – 60 per cent of whom were Irish Catholics – for his opposition to 'shipside arbitration', and his testimony against Larkin was the final straw.[52] In June 1910 Glasgow trades council denounced 'the attempt to crush Mr Jim Larkin', and in January 1911 the Glasgow branch was formally dissolved by Sexton. Five months later the local dockers were re-organised in the Scottish Union of Dock Labourers following a visit from Larkin.[53]

THE HARP THAT ONCE

In January 1910, Larkin acquired another string to his bow: a set, indeed, of *Harp* strings. Few could resist wordplays on the title. The paper belonged to Connolly, a man whose posthumous critics liked to measure him against Larkin. Before Easter Week, no one had any doubt that Larkin was the big man. The two had much in common. Connolly too was born in Britain (Edinburgh in 1868), of working-class parents from south-east Ulster (Monaghan), and raised in an Irish enclave; leaving school as soon as he could, he went through a succession of dead-end jobs, became active on the left, and settled in Dublin relatively late in life (1896) to work as an organiser (for the Irish Socialist Republican Party). Despairing of the tiny party, and anxious to find a better future for his six daughters – he was an ardent feminist – he emigrated to the US in 1903 to soldier with the Socialist Labor Party.

From 1907 he began to gravitate back towards Ireland and the Irish. When the Socialist Labor Party decided to set up language federations for non-anglophone members, Connolly insisted that the Irish too needed a dedicated appeal, founded the Irish Socialist Federation, and launched the *Harp* as its monthly organ in January 1908.[54] Largely written and sustained by Connolly himself, the *Harp* relied heavily on articles about socialism, Irish history, nationalism, and Catholicism, pitched at an Irish-American readership. Membership of the New York-based Irish Socialist Federation was less than 100, but Connolly's engagements on speaking tours enabled him to boost subscriptions to the *Harp* to 3,000.[55] In March 1909, the *Harp*, which rarely featured news of events in Ireland, gave a front-page welcome to the formation of the ITGWU and its activities in Cork, reprinting items from the *Irish Nation* and the Dublin *Evening Telegraph*. Connolly was obviously delighted that it was to be an Irish union and heartened by Larkin's work in Belfast and Cork. Tired of the notoriously factionalist American left, he was keen to come home, provided he could get a decent stipend as a party organiser. Larkin's impact suggested that Irish Labour was astir. Stirring too was the Dublin left. Encouraged by Connolly, O'Brien convened a socialist unity conference in June 1909, out of which emerged the second Socialist Party of Ireland (SPI) with a Connollyite platform. Larkin loitered on the fringe. He had abandoned the ILP after founding the ITGWU, and begun cultivating advanced nation-alists. In May 1909, he spoke to the Drumcondra branch of Sinn Féin, in favour of an Irish Labour Party. Though he and Arthur Griffith would develop a mutual animosity – Griffith liked the idea of an Irish based union while deploring its association with an 'English' agitator – Larkin insisted that Griffith was not Sinn Féin.[56] Another group on the fringe of the SPI included J. W. O'Beirne and W. P. Ryan, who ran the *Irish Nation*, an Irish-Ireland weekly, eager to nudge republicans to the left, but reluctant to endorse socialism for fear of provoking a split with Sinn Féin.

By the autumn of 1909, Connolly was corresponding with O'Brien about returning to organise for the SPI and, meanwhile, moving the *Harp* to Dublin. O'Brien was doubtful about the wisdom of transferring the paper, but Connolly was determined to have it sold in Ireland and in Britain, hoping that it would revive his reputation and attract speaking engagements on his return. O'Beirne too was sanguine, thinking he would have a good manager in Larkin, who was eager for the job. O'Brien met O'Beirne on 8 January 1910 and Larkin on 15th. It was agreed that the *Harp* would be published from the office of the *Nation*, with Ryan as technical supervisor, Larkin as manager and sub-editor, and Connolly as nominal editor. O'Brien noted in his diary: 'C. will find L. won't be a cypher . . .'[57]

Larkin's first issue of the *Harp* appeared in February. It was now sub-titled 'a monthly progressive Irish review', and the mast-head retained flanking quotes from James Fintan Lalor ('The principle I state and mean to stand upon is this: that the entire ownership of Ireland, moral and material, up to the sun and down to the centre, is vested of right in the people of Ireland'), and Wolfe Tone ('Our Independence must be had at all hazards. If the men of property will not help us they must fall: we will free ourselves by the aid of that large and respectable class of the community – the men of no property'). It made a terrible impression on the SPI. Much of the lengthy stuff on socialism and nationalism was replaced with features of trade union interest. The shift in focus was a good idea. Connolly's *Harp* could be tedious in its endless re-working of the same theme. But some of the new material, such as a reprinting of the Labour Exchanges Act (1909), was dull, and Larkin's editorial was simply a vulgar tirade against the Unionists, the IPP, the All-For-Ireland League, and Sinn Féin, who were variously denounced as 'sycophants', 'place-hunters', 'carrion crows', and 'more concerned about the price of whiskey'. It brought six threats of libel action.[58]

O'Brien noted astutely: 'In America the paper was "too much Connolly" to be a success, and I hope it's not going to be "too much Larkin" here.'[59] For once, Larkin did not want 'too much Larkin'. He was embarrassed by the issue and took the criticism from the SPI to heart, explaining to O'Brien that Connolly told him he was too busy to send copy and to get 'as many SPI men as possible to write for the paper'.[60] Things got a little better. The March number featured a lengthy article from Ryan, and chapter 12 of Connolly's 'Labour in Irish History'. Larkin's editorial was more composed. He made a point of thanking comrades for their 'injunctions', and claimed progress in building a 'Bardic circle' or fellowship of support for the paper: a concept developed by the *Clarion*, and later by the *Daily Herald* League and Larkin's own *Irish Worker* League. He also proposed a conference of potential contributors 'in Ireland and the island adjacent', and explained: 'This paper does not pretend to be a literary magazine. We desire to articulate working class opinion. What is wanted in Ireland . . . is an honest expression of dissatisfaction . . .' The March *Harp* also featured the following advertisement for Delia's boarding house, in old Irish script: 'A Ghaedheala! Nuair a bhéas sibh i gCaisleáin Ruadhrí (Roistreibheor) badh cheart dóibh fanamhaind ag "Chislehurst". Tá gach rud thar bárr ann. SPECIAL THANKS TO BRITISH AND AMERICAN COMRADES.' The April issue relied more heavily on Connolly, who contributed 'Notes from America', another excerpt from 'Labour in Irish History', and the editorial, calling for a Labour party in Ireland. Larkin agreed too with Connolly's concern to address religion, and included repeated references to John Wheatley and his Glasgow-based Catholic Socialist Society. At the same time, there were differences of emphases between them. Connolly was uncomfortable equally with confessional socialism and with irreligious propaganda.[61] Larkin was happier to mix the two, and combine appeals to Christian values with a streak of anti-clericalism.

Difficulties persisted. A special May Day number was abandoned for want of copy, and in the June issue Larkin made good his threat to 'deal with' his critics at the ITUC in Dundalk with a controversial report on the heated debate surrounding his admission to Congress. O'Beirne informed O'Brien that more libel suits were threatened, from McCarron, Stewart, Harris, and P. J. McIntyre, secretary of the Dublin branch of the Workers' Union. O'Brien advised him to suspend production until Connolly's arrival. Aside from the libel actions, subscriptions collected in 1909 were exhausted, Connolly was complaining that he had sent $128 to Dublin without receiving receipts or copies of the paper, and Larkin was headed for Mountjoy.[62]

HARD LABOUR AND TRIUMPH

The court case over the NUDL monies concluded on 17 June 1910, with the judge handing down 12 months hard labour. There was little surprise at the verdict, but the sentence, for a trumped-up charge, was a bombshell. However Larkin received it, he recovered bravely to interrupt the judge before sentence was passed on his co-defendant, Coveney, pleading that he, Larkin, should bear all responsibility. Coveney was released. Connolly wrote to O'Brien, just before embarking for Ireland: 'It completely unnerves me. Poor fellow, he has to suffer hard for his cause. What will become of the Union? Has it men enough to fill the breach? Is he married and with a family?'[63] It was curious that Connolly and Larkin were aware of each other's importance, were almost identical in outlook, and yet knew very little about each other. Walker raised the issue on the British Labour Party's executive committee on 30 June. The executive deputed Hardie, Walker, and J. R. Clynes to interview the Irish attorney-general.[64]

Few could have expected how difficult prison would be for Larkin. Confinement always seemed to suck the life out of such a naturally hyper-active man. Although the Mountjoy authorities gave him light work, O'Brien found him, in early July, 'in good spirits but [looking] worn out and haggard' and swearing revenge on Sexton.[65] On his release, Larkin would say he had been treated 'with every courtesy' by the acting-governor and warders, but condemn the prison system: 'It is not reformative at all, but tends to deteriorate a man's character.'[66] No preparation had been made for a regency in the ITGWU. It was at a meeting in Beresford Place to protest against Larkin's sentence that Councillor Lorcan Sherlock proposed his late fellow councillor for acting general secretary. Daly agreed reluctantly, and spent most of his time nursing the branch in Belfast. He confessed to O'Brien that he was not up to the job and that the union was 'sinking fast'.[67] In reality, the situation was not so bad, and Larkin would say it had improved by his release; a self-serving remark to excuse his absence but not likely to be made if the union was falling apart.[68] The saturnine O'Brien liked to note his rivals' weaknesses. And, of course, the general secretary had not designed the ITGWU to function without him.

Connolly returned to Ireland on Tuesday 26 July, sailing into Lough Foyle on the liner *Furnissia*, a day behind schedule. He immediately entrained for Dublin, arriving at 1 pm, and went straight to Mountjoy.[69] O'Brien had urged him to be in Dublin by Tuesday as Larkin was anxious for 'a long interview' to clear up any misunderstandings, and was due in court on the Wednesday to appeal for a re-trial. Were the appeal to fail, as it did, Larkin would lose remand status and have more restricted visiting rights. For the moment, Connolly was too pleased to be home to be awkward about the *Harp*. He would later write privately that 'the whole thing had been mismanaged' and describe the Dublin edition as 'somewhat painful'.[70]

Larkin had the consolation that the harsh sentence gifted him a propaganda windfall, winning him the admiration of his fellows and even the sympathy of his opponents. Daniel Corkery published one of his first tributes from the literati, and pioneered a theme attractive to intellectuals: that Larkin was just too great an idealist for his own good:

> he had raised himself so much above his fellows that he deceived himself if he believed he could find lieutenants in their ranks. Here is a drama for any Ibsen that cares to write it – the failure of a leader of the democracy to find lieutenants.[71]

Corkery himself would eventually write it in his play *The Labour Leader*. On 20 June Dublin trades council passed a motion of confidence in Larkin's 'honesty and integrity of character' and 'protest[ed] in the strongest manner against the unwarrantable sentence which has been passed against him'.[72] The council later presented *James Larkin's Ordeals: A Plea for Justice, Release Memorials* to the Lord Lieutenant, signed *inter alia* by the Lords Mayor of Dublin and Cork, and the four Dublin and two Cork MPs.[73] The sentence was commuted, and at 8.30 on the morning of Saturday 1 October hundreds assembled outside Mountjoy to escort Larkin to Auburn Street. That evening, some 7,000 joined a torchlight procession to Beresford Place. Afterwards, Larkin celebrated by taking Elizabeth to the Abbey Theatre.[74] The day after, on a scorching afternoon, it was the turn of union leaders and city councillors to eulogise him from four platforms before a crowd of 10,000 and eight bands packed into Beresford Place. On behalf of the ITGWU, John Simmons, secretary of Dublin trades council, presented him with an illuminated address costing £30, and expressed 'their determination now and in the future to march forward under his leadership by the principles of industrial organisation (not sectional organisation), and by the methods Larkin had proved successful, not only in Belfast but in all the ports of Ireland'. From the SPI there was a purse of gold, which Larkin generously donated to the party for propaganda and for a fund to keep Connolly 'at home in Ireland'.[75] One of those curious to see the great man in person was Constance Markievicz. 'Hot and weary' after cycling in to town, she was offered a seat on the lorry drawn up as a platform, and invited to speak before Larkin. He dissented from her remarks about England being the cause of all the trouble and pointedly thanked friends across the channel for their solidarity. She was nonetheless overwhelmed by his oratory, and penned one of the great descriptions of its power, adding, 'From that day I looked on Larkin as a friend and was out to do any little thing I could to help him.'[76]

'That day' was a turning point for Larkin too. There had been a series of disappointments since his break with Liverpool. Aside from the setbacks in Cork and with the *Harp*, he had struggled to adjust to his new economic status. Employment had given him securities and constraints. Self-employment made him less secure and less constrained. He was taking no risks with the ITGWU, but he was freer to lash out at his enemies, and indulge a preference for agitation rather than the more mundane work of organisation. But he had soaked up the worst his enemies could throw at him, and, as the winter of 1910 approached, he could claim to have won acceptance for the ITGWU, from Dublin employers and the ITUC, and to have made solid progress in building support on Dublin trades council. He was also attracting interest in advanced nationalist circles, having moved from being a British to an Irish socialist, and reached the same conclusions as Connolly on the way ahead. The reception on his release from prison and the restoration of his reputation as a fighter was important to him. Adulation was the fuel of his self-confidence. With the Liverpool leftovers behind him, he could now shape his own future for the union. It would feature a newspaper, and, more surprisingly, a positive re-engagement with Britain.

NOTES

1   *Derry Journal*, 15 January 1909.

2   On the Belfast debacle, see John Gray, *City in Revolt: James Larkin and the Belfast Dock Strike of 1907* (Belfast, 1985), pp. 198–203; and C. Desmond Greaves, *The Irish Transport and General Workers' Union: The Formative Years, 1909–1923* (Dublin, 1982), pp. 29–31.

3   *Derry Journal*, 15 January 1909.

4   Gray, *City in Revolt*, p. 199.

5   Emmet Larkin, *James Larkin: Irish Labour Leader, 1876–1947* (London, 1965), p. 70.

6   Greaves, *The Irish Transport and General Workers' Union*, p. 29.

7   NLI, William O'Brien papers, 15679(20).

8   Greaves, *The Irish Transport and General Workers' Union*, pp. 27–8, 32.

9   Pádraig Yeates, *Lockout: Dublin 1913* (Dublin, 2000), p. 470.

10 ITGWU, *The Attempt to Smash the Irish Transport and General Workers' Union* (Dublin, 1924), p. xix.

11 James Plunkett, 'Big Jim: a loaf on the table, a flower in the vase', in Donal Nevin (ed.), *James Larkin: Lion of the Fold* (Dublin, 1998), p. 114.

12 NLI, William O'Brien papers, 15679(16).

13 Ibid., 15679(16), 15679(20).

14 Greaves, *The Irish Transport and General Workers' Union*, p. 32.

15 Dermot Keogh, *The Rise of the Irish Working Class: The Dublin Trade Union Movement and Labour Leadership, 1890–1914* (Belfast, 1982), pp. 139–40; Larkin, *James Larkin*, p. 63. According to Greaves, *The Irish Transport and General Workers' Union*, p. 327, the rulebook did not survive in Ireland, but copies are held privately elsewhere.

16 Keogh, *The Rise of the Irish Working Class*, pp. 139–40.

17 *Cork Examiner*, 10 September 1909, cited in Keogh, *The Rise of the Irish Working Class*, p. 140.

18 Francis Devine, *Organising History: A Centenary of SIPTU, 1909–2009* (Dublin, 2009), p. 18; ITGWU, *The Attempt to Smash the Irish Transport and General Workers' Union* (Dublin, 1924), p. xii.

19 Aindrias Ó Cathasaigh (ed.), *The Life and Times of Gilbert Lynch* (Dublin, 2011), p. 149.

20 UUMC, Dublin trades council minutes, 1 March 1909.

21 Ibid., 10 March 1910.

22 Ibid., 10 May 1909.

23 Ibid., 18 July, 24 October 1910.

24 UUMC, ITUC, *Annual Report* (1909), pp. 8–10.

25 Greaves, *The Irish Transport and General Workers' Union*, p. 37.

26 Thomas J. Morrissey, SJ, *William O'Brien, 1881–1968: Socialist, Republican, Dáil Deputy, Editor and Trade Union Leader* (Dublin, 2007); UUMC, ITUC, *Annual Report* (1909), pp. 40–2; *Irish Labour Journal*, 19 June 1909.

27 *Irish Labour Journal*, 7 August 1909.

28 UUMC, ITUC, *Annual Report* (1910), pp. 23–5.

29 Ibid., pp. 28–30, 61.

30 Ibid., pp. 47; *Irish Worker*, 27 May 1911.

31 UUMC, ITUC, *Annual Report* (1910), pp. 47–8, 57.

32 Larkin, *James Larkin*, p. 94.

33 Devine, *Organising History*, pp. 22–3.

34 Greaves, *The Irish Transport and General Workers' Union*, p. 55.

35 For the Cork disputes see ibid., pp. 39–42, 69; Larkin, *James Larkin*, pp. 64–6, except where stated.

36 *Irish Labour Journal*, 10 July 1909.

37 Bill McCamley, *The Third James: James Fearon, 1874–1924, an Unsung Hero of Our Struggle* (Dublin, 2000), p. 25.

38 *Irish Labour Journal*, 10 July 1909.

39 NAUK, London, Ministry of Labour reports on strikes and lockouts, 1909, LAB 34/9.

40 *Irish Labour Journal*, 10 July 1909.

41 Ibid.

42 Ibid., 28 August 1909.

43 Ibid.

44 George Dallas, 'The crushing of Jim Larkin. An outrageous conspiracy. Funds wanted immediately', *Irish Labour Journal*, 25 September 1909, reprinted from *Forward*.

45 On the arrest and trial see Greaves, *The Irish Transport and General Workers' Union*, pp. 52–4, and Larkin, *James Larkin*, pp. 68–74.

46 *Irish Labour Journal*, 25 September 1909.

47 James Sexton, *Sir James Sexton, Agitator: The Life of the Dockers' M.P. An Autobiography* (London, 1936), p. 206.

48 NLI, William O'Brien papers, 15679(1).

49 Keogh, *The Rise of the Irish Working Class*, pp. 146–8.

50 UUMC, Dublin trades council minutes, 13 September 1909.

51 Kenneth G. Dallas, correspondence, *Saothar* 6 (1980), p. 7; *Irish Labour Journal*, 25 September 1909.

52 I am obliged to William Kenefick for this detail.

53 William Kenefick, 'James O'Connor Kessack', in *Oxford Dictionary of National Biography*, oxforddnb.com; *Irish Worker*, 3 June 1911.

54 Austen Morgan, *James Connolly: A Political Biography* (Manchester, 1988), pp. 67–8.

55 Donal Nevin, *James Connolly: 'A Full Life'* (Dublin, 2006), pp. 281–2.

56 Keogh, *The Rise of the Irish Working Class*, pp. 148–9.

57 Nevin, *James Connolly*, pp. 310–11, 319; C. Desmond Greaves, *The Life and Times of James Connolly* (London, 1961), p. 189.

58 Greaves, *The Life and Times of James Connolly*, p. 189.

59 Nevin, *James Connolly*, p. 312.

60 Ibid., pp. 312–3.

61 Donal Nevin (ed.), *Between Comrades: James Connolly, Letters and Correspondence 1889–1916* (Dublin, 2007), p. 40.

62 Nevin, *James Connolly*, p. 313; Nevin (ed.), *Between Comrades*, pp. 423, 427–8.

63 Nevin, *James Connolly*, p. 321.

64 I am obliged to Mike Mecham for this reference.

65 Keogh, *The Rise of the Irish Working Class*, p. 151.

66 *Evening Telegraph*, 1 October 1910.

67 Devine, *Organising History*, p. 31; Greaves, *The Irish Transport and General Workers' Union*, p. 52.

68 Devine, *Organising History*, p. 72.

69 Nevin, *James Connolly*, p. 379.

70 Nevin (ed.), *Between Comrades*, p. 45, 427.

71 *Leader*, 1 July 1910.

72 UUMC, Dublin trades council minutes, 20 June 1910.

73 NLI, William O'Brien papers, 15679(22).

74 *Evening Telegraph*, 1 October 1910; William O'Brien, *Forth the Banners Go: The Reminiscences of William O'Brien as Told to Edward MacLysaght, D.Litt* (Dublin, 1969), p. 65.

75 *Forward*, 15 October 1910.

76 Ibid.; Larkin, *James Larkin*, p. 74; Anne Haverty, *Constance Markievicz: An Independent Life* (London, 1988), p. 95.

FIVE

WRATH AND HOPE AND WONDER, 1910–11

Reader, have you ever known what it is to get up on a box or chair, physically and mentally tired, perhaps suffering from want of food; amongst strangers, say a mass of tired workers released from their bastilles of workshop or factory... The life all around seems to stagnate; everything seems miserable and depressing... And then suddenly when things seem blackest and dark night enshrouds abroad, lo! the Sun, and lo! thereunder rises wrath and hope and wonder, and the worker comes marching on. Friends there is hope for the future. The mouse of industrial unionism has cut through the net of sectional trade unions... Hurrah for the Social Revolution!

Editorial, *Irish Worker*, 12 August 1911

———

1911 to 1913 were James Larkin's greatest years, when he became the most famous man in Ireland: to Labour, the rousing hero of a risen people; to employers, the agitator who adulterated 'bona fide' trade unionism with the syndicalist sympathetic strike. It is unlikely that he would have moved so far so fast without the aid of events in Britain. Syndicalism took root in Britain between mid-1910 and mid-1911, having originated in France in the 1880s from disillusionment with the performance of socialist parties. The idea that workers should look instead to trade unions and industrial conflict as the primary instruments of class struggle and ultimately effect the revolution through a general strike was well established in the French Confédération Générale du Travail. Whether British or Irish workers embraced syndicalism *in toto* is questionable, but it is also to miss the point. Syndicalism, in the words of Big Bill Haywood, co-founder of the Industrial Workers of the World, was socialism in its working clothes.[1] Uniquely among socialist ideologies, it offered a practical toolkit from which one could pick and choose à la carte. Tactical strength through sympathetic action, unity of all grades through industrial unionism, the use of culture as a forge of solidarity, and power to the rank and file were especially attractive items on the menu. In Liverpool, Jim's brother Pete became prominent among waterfront syndicalists, and Jim kept a weather eye on cross-channel developments, keen to see what he might take from them, and what he should resist. What Jim wanted were tactics which would enable him to apply the ambitions he had outlined in the preamble to the

ITGWU rules and his article in the *Irish Labour Journal* in July 1909. What he didn't want was to be brushed aside by a new invasion of British unions, or overwhelmed by militancy beyond his control.

Since Belfast in 1907, Larkin had repeatedly stressed the importance of sympathetic action. Since 1909 he had advocated industrial unionism. He would soon become interested in the syndicalist idea of building the embryo of the new society within the unions by promoting commercial, social, and cultural projects. At the same time, he differed from the syndicalists in some respects. He believed in the value of party political work, a Labour party having a particular significance in Ireland as it entailed a rejection of Irish allegiance to the British Labour Party. He didn't want strikes, if he could help it; though if he couldn't, he would be to the fore. Unless and until consumed by the red mist of the battle, he hated the expense of strikes, partly because of his insecurity about finance, and partly because he reckoned he had better uses for his money. Once the ITGWU was on an even keel, he put his time and cash into a newspaper rather than building branches or a fighting fund. The paper was to be his voice. He also hoped it would be a substitute for strikes. Similarly, he welcomed the National Insurance bill, knowing it would boost union membership, though British syndicalists condemned it as a device to discipline Labour and a step towards 'the servile state', and Irish trade unionists were concerned that it would operate mainly to the benefit of conservative friendly societies like the Ancient Order of Hibernians, as indeed it did.[2]

Only with the spread of unrest from Britain did Larkin adopt a more aggressive industrial policy. The spirit of revolt in the hot summer of 1911 was unique in British labour history. Having averaged 2.7 million from 1900 to 1907, the number of strike days jumped to ten million in 1911, with big strikes of railwaymen and dockers. It was not the scale alone, but the character of action that seemed extraordinary. Union leaders who had been stoking the fire for months were nevertheless astonished at the response, and spoke of a 'blaze spread rapidly', 'a bolt from the blue', a 'great magic wave'. Historians would label it 'mysterious', 'inexplicable', a 'spontaneous combustion'. History would remember it as 'the great unrest'.[3] Ireland too was, literally, hungry for protest. The cost of food on which workers lived – tea, sugar, milk, white bread, butter, potatoes, bacon, and eggs – had risen by about 15 per cent since 1900, with sharp increases in 1906–7 without a general improvement in wages.[4] Larkin's role was more reactive than pro-active. It was workers who pushed for action; gradually he met the challenge. Nonetheless, it was important that there was in Ireland a leader willing to respond, and a union committed to do or die at home.

RE-ENGAGING WITH BRITAIN

Larkin's court case in 1909–10 had become a cause for emergent militants in Britain. Larkin had lobbied Keir Hardie, and his imprisonment drew protests from *Justice*, the *Clarion*, and the Industrial Workers of Liverpool.[5] The Larkin Defence Committee, featuring quite a few Glaswegians, published a 68-page pamphlet *Labour War in Ireland: Story of a Great Betrayal, Larkin versus Cork Employers, Simon Punch, James Sexton, the Alleged Labour Leader, and Others*. Liverpool's Larkin Release Committee issued the 20-page *James Larkin, a Labour Leader and an Honest Man*. Frank Pearce, secretary of the Release Committee, was also secretary of Liverpool's International Club.[6] Dubbing Larkin 'the stormy petrel of the labour movement', Pearce's pamphlet hailed the ITGWU as a new development for Britain:

> The Irish Transport Workers' Union is but the forerunner of the English, the British, and the International Union. There is a place for James Larkin in an organisation which shall express the hopes and attain the aims of all transport workers.
>
> Tom Mann; Ben Tillett; James Larkin . . . What a delectable trinity!![7]

Soon after his release from Mountjoy, on 6 October, Larkin was in Liverpool. When he stepped onto the platform in Picton Lecture Hall, after speeches by Victor Grayson and Tom Mann, 'the vast meeting simply went mad cheering for a full five minutes.'[8] The NUDL executive was so concerned about the impact of the pro-Larkin pamphlets in Britain that it subvented Sexton to sue Pearce for alleging that he had conspired with employers to have Larkin prosecuted. Larkin himself testified at the Liverpool assizes, and received a reprimand from the judge. Sexton won £200 damages for libel. The NUDL's Larkinites then took the union to court, pleading that its subvention to Sexton ought to be repaid.[9] Sexton had little to say in his annual report for 1910, and union officials reckoned he was still smarting from the 'Larkin affair'.[10]

In other respects, things were moving in England, and Larkin was drawn into them. As trade improved in 1910, the problem of how to deal with employer militancy acquired a fresh urgency. Mann had returned to England on 10 May after a nine-year stay in Australia, where his experience of the miners' defeat at Broken Hill convinced him that sectional trade unionism was a curse and indus-trial unionism the answer. Coevally, James Connolly sent him his pamphlets *Socialism Made Easy* and *The Axe to the Root*, where Mann found conclusions 'identical' with his own. Larkin's stumbling syndicalism in the ITGWU rules failed to register like Connolly's clarity, though Mann wrote later that the formation of the ITGWU 'gave more hope for drastic and beneficial economic and social change than anything that had ever been tried before'.[11]

On 30 May Mann was in Paris for a tutorial from the Confédération Générale du Travail. In July he launched the monthly *Industrial Syndicalist*. The second issue was devoted entirely to transport. Britain, he argued, flagged half the world's ships, carried half its oceanic cargo, and processed a huge import-export trade in its several ports. Employers were profiting from speed-up and the introduction of labour-saving mechanisation, but there had been no commensurate improvement in wages and conditions. An obvious first step was to surmount the sectionalism and multiplicity intrinsic to the divisions between the 20 odd unions in transport. Through the London-based Dock, Wharf, Riverside, and General Labourers' Union, Mann invited all transport unions to federate. Fifteen answered the call and in September the National Transport Workers' Federation (NTWF) was formed provisionally.[12] One of its functions was to co-ordinate disputes. Though not a syndicalist organisation, it was undoubtedly water to the mill.

Larkin was one of 198 delegates from over 70 union branches and radical societies at the first conference of the Industrial Syndicalist Education League on 26 November in Manchester's Corn Exchange. Others present included Pete Larkin, currently a coal-heaver in Liverpool, and delegate of the anarcho-syndicalist Revolutionary Industrialists, Pearce from the Liverpool International Club, and Jim's boyhood pal Fred Bower. The League aimed to promote syndicalism within existing unions, and Mann proposed the main resolution, calling for the merger of all unions into industrial unions 'throughout the British Isles'. Jim told them to leave Ireland out of it. 'They had made enough hash of their own affairs – they must not interfere with Ireland.' He then upheld industrial unionism with one of his garbled speeches, rambling over his time in Belfast and in prison before concluding: 'his union was formed on the industrial basis, and took in all workers in the transport industry. The transport industry held the key, for they could stop the whole of the rest of the trades.'[13]

The ITGWU also had a presence at the formal inauguration conference of the NTWF in March 1911, but when it applied for affiliation, the NUDL had it blackballed.[14] Larkin continued to pursue a link with the Federation, and while he demanded it be on an international basis, he was willing to trim his separatism if need be.[15] There were compelling reasons. The Federation's message of industrial unity chimed with his own. Havelock Wilson, leader of the National Sailors' and Firemen's Union (NSFU), and a prominent figure in the Federation, had launched a campaign for an ambitious programme of demands, including a conciliation board, a national minimum wage, and fixed working hours: precisely the demands that Larkin wanted to secure for all waterfront workers, and which would be of huge financial benefit to his union. There was also the prize of winning the railwaymen to the ITGWU. The ASRS had joined the Federation initially, though it subsequently withdrew. Furthermore, the Federation's leaders were obviously preparing for a major industrial offensive which was likely to impact on Ireland. In 1889, new unionism had swept across the channel and rolled Irish Labour into British Labour. If the ITGWU was to hold its own, it had to be both a part of the British offensive, and jealously guard its own patch, a manoeuvre that Larkin executed superbly.

Larkin was also in demand in Glasgow in May 1911. He spoke at a May Day rally, and then helped to organise the Scottish Union of Dock Labourers.[16]

THE IRISH(ISING) WORKER

At home, the big event that May was the publication of the *Irish Worker and People's Advocate* – commonly known as the *Worker* – on Saturday 27th. It ran to four pages – apart from a Christmas number in 1912 – and cost 1d. It sold about 5,000 copies. The second issue sold 8,000 copies, and the third 15,000.[17] Larkin claimed that sales were about 20,000 a week, and if he was given to exaggerating these matters, others have accepted that the figure was close to 20,000, and limited only by the poor printing facilities available, and the typically Larkinite concentration on Dublin.[18] Readership would have extended to the bulk of the Dublin working class. For a political weekly, this was phenomenal; the moreso as wholesalers and many newsagents refused to handle it. For distribution, Larkin relied on his mascots, the newsboys, who received a commission 75 per cent above the going rate. The large circulation made it an attractive outlet for publicity, and Larkin gave a sizeable chunk of the paper to advertisements from shops and small businesses in Dublin. Some tailored their pitch, with straplines like: 'Strike against big profit!! Try R. W. Sholedice for Watch and Clock Repairs'; 'Manley's, The Workers' Provisions Store'; 'Made by Trade Union bakers, Eat Farrington's Bread'; or 'T. P. Roche, The Workers' Hairdresser . . . Success to the Workers' Cause!' Where possible, advertisers commonly made an appeal to buy Irish, and even to patronising 'The Only Picture House in Dublin Owned by an Irishman: The Irish Cinema'. In a paper pitched at manual workers, there was a chilling touch in the slogan for Dr King's hair restorer: 'You Can't Afford to Look Old.' Curiously, the 1913 Lockout had no adverse effect on the advertising.

Initially the *Irish Worker* was managed by a co-operative printing company, with Mícheál Ó Maoláin, a radical Irish-Irelander from the Aran Islands, as secretary. In March 1912 Larkin set up the Irish Co-operative Labour Press

Ltd. The co-op had a formal structure of committee and officers, with William O'Brien as chairman, but its stated position was that 'policy of the paper was to be left entirely in the hands of the Editor, Jim Larkin'. The co-op intended to issue 8,000 shares at 5s each. Only £1,000 was raised, and plans to treble the size of the paper were abandoned. The money subscribed was not returned, which generated some controversy.[19] The paper remained profitable, and Larkin claimed it was earning a gross income of around £18.10s per week for the ITGWU in August 1913.[20]

The *Irish Worker* was the paper that Larkin had intended the *Harp* to be: a mixture of news and views of working-class interest in short, punchy articles, laced with humour, poetry, songs, sport, and the visual appeal of photographs and cartoons. This time, he was better prepared, and had been planning the production for months. As the paper progressed, he recruited correspondents from Belfast, Limerick, Cork, Dundalk, Sligo, and Waterford, though the content remained Dublin-centric, and the challenge of creating an effective distribution network in the provinces was never surmounted. Talented contributors included George Russell, G. K. Chesterton, W. B. Yeats, Stephen Gwynn, James Stephens, poetess Maeve Cavanagh, Maud Gonne, S. C. Harrison, Constance Markievicz, Dora Montefiore, and Francis and Hanna Sheehy Skeffington, as well as regulars like Delia, Connolly, William Partridge, Seán O'Casey, cartoonist Ernest Kavanagh, and playwright A. Patrick Wilson. Wilson, who later managed the Abbey Theatre, served as a sub-editor and contributed under the pseudonym 'Euchan', the name of a burn in his native Scotland.[21] Larkin's love of literature was reflected in the reprinting of poems by Browning, Tennyson, and Whitman, and essays by Mark Twain and George Bernard Shaw. He also encouraged new literary voices like Patrick MacGill. Political features included a serialisation of *Labour in Irish History*, and articles by Liverpool syndicalists. In every way, it was Larkin's triumph. Over 41 months and 189 issues, he edited about 170 – Connolly deputised for him when necessary during the 1913 Lockout – and wrote the editorials and almost 400 articles in total. It was obviously a labour of love, and neither the editor nor the contributors received any payment.

Larkin bothered little with drafting, and wrote as he spoke, in a descriptive, *ad hominem*, colloquial, almost conversational, style. In editorials especially, he would address readers personally. He liked humour, and used irony, self-deprecation, sarcasm, or ridicule as the mood took him. Seán McKeown recalled a visit as he worked on the paper, and the editor lecturing him on soccer in Belfast while simultaneously dictating to a typist.[22] Lowery argues that his articles 'reveal a fairly modest person', as he rarely wrote of 'his own achievements'.[23] The praise has some validity. He was usually the central figure in the editorials, but their aim was to challenge and change mentalities.

He tended to boast only in defence of his record, on which he was sensitive, and was not so concerned with adulation as long as he got his own way. His absolute control of the paper made it a comfort zone, which in turn brought out his better side. As an editor, he was tolerant, and happy to publish those with whom he disagreed or material critical of himself. If jealous of Connolly, he still printed over 60 of his articles. The *Irish Worker* was less of a mouth-piece for Larkin than the *Harp* had been for Connolly. Neither was it so constrained by an editorial line, as the *Belfast Labour Chronicle* had been by William Walker's anxiety not to be seen as a nationalist, much less a staid gazette like P. T. Daly's *Irish Labour Journal*. Yet it was unmistakeably Larkin's. He was the editorial board, wrote what he wanted, and gave the paper an obvious slant. Inevitably its success would foster his brash personality cult. By 1913, references to Larkin and Larkinism were becoming ubiquitous in the paper, and ITGWU men were being dubbed 'Larkinites'. In the aftermath of the lockout, it featured an unsettling amount of copy on Larkin, and started to acquire the tone of injured innocence that became all too characteristic of its unfortunate post-1923 successor.

The *Irish Worker* is remembered as a thundering, inchoate hammer against social oppression, in the style described by Bert Wolfe:

> [Larkin] had no taste for theory at all, but made up for that by a strong sense of justice, and a belief in his personal mission to lead men in combat, in all manner of struggles for a better life, a little more dignity, a little more freedom. He made no appeal to reason, advanced no theories, only recited wrongs and outrages in angry tones, labor's wrongs and Ireland's together. When men fought him, he lashed out not at their ideas but at their persons. When a single symbolic name could not be selected, he still knew how to make the contempt and hatred and anger seem personal. He never excoriated 'the capitalist press' only a particular newspaper owner or editor who was the target of his wrath. For their part, his opponents and the hostile newspapers paid him in kind.[24]

Dublin was ripe for this type of moral offensive. The Belfast bourgeoisie derived a moral confidence from the city's housing record, its industrial prowess, and the wage rates of its skilled elite. In Dublin, there was widespread embarrassment about the capital's social conditions. Out of a population of 300,000, 87,000 people lived in the slums. Twenty thousand families lived in one-room flats. Sanitation in the tenements was usually confined to a few toilets and water taps in the yard. Residents and visitors would never forget the smell of the buildings. Larkin would find some unexpected allies among intellectuals and Irish-Irelanders, for whom the social decay was a grotesque reflection of the nation's strumpet soul.

The slums bulked large in literary and guilt-ridden liberal perceptions of Larkinism. For Larkin himself, they were a symptom, not a cause, to which the antidote was decent wages. As leader of a small, struggling union, his primary concern lay with recruitment, and that was evident in the *Irish Worker*. Numerous items simply cited the conditions in particular employments. One read, in part:

SWEATING!

Dublin Window Cleaners' Present Conditions of Work
Working Hours from 6.45 am to 6 pm. No time allowed for meals.

Men are subject to broken time, half and three quarter days.

Men pay their own insurance and laundry. Men are fined for breaking rules made by the Companies, such as a man going to his breakfast after finishing his morning's work consisting of between 10 and 15 shops.

Men are not paid for Bank Holidays, although the companies are paid by the shops and other contract work.

Men are not paid for overtime, although they have to work it. A man's wage for a full week's work is from 12s to 15s, less fines, insurance, and laundry money deducted.[25]

'Unvarnished statements' such as this, according to Larkin, had rectified 'grave abuses', and been responsible for pay increases 'in many instances of from 25 to 40 per cent'.[26] 'Unvarnished statements' were a lot cheaper than strikes. When successful, Larkin could be almost ingratiating. One 'unvarnished statement' on 'Sweating in the Brewery Trade' led to Watkins, Jameson, Pim & Co. inviting himself and Michael McKeown to talks. After 'a most pleasant and informal discussion', according to the *Irish Worker*, the management agreed to pay increases. Concluding a report so gushing that he felt obliged to say he was not actually telling readers to consume the products of Watkins, Jameson, Pim & Co. – though if they had to drink, they could do worse – Larkin lavished praise on the master brewer,

who has gained the affection of his men . . . the thanks of [their] women and children . . . and [of] I personally, a man who has more enemies than any other man in this country – a man who totally disagrees with the present system, and lives for the day when there will be no employee or employer, when we will all be workers, working together like brothers believing in the brotherhood of man, and fulfilling the fatherhood of God.[27]

Another theme of the *Irish Worker* was that the working class must awaken to its own strength and dignity, and an intrinsic part of its method was to show that the greatness of the rich and powerful was based on subjugation, exploitation, and hypocrisy. It reflected Larkin's most and least attractive traits. He empathised with the oppressed. They were his audience and his plinth, but he felt for their humanity in a way that most Labour leaders could not. To say that he offered workers no defined socialist prescriptions is to miss the point. As a syndicalist, he wanted to be a guide at their side, not a sage on the stage, even if his demagoguery contradicted it. The flip side of the coin was the vituperation and nihilism. While there was a political rationale to ridiculing 'the great', Larkin needed personal enemies to stoke his outrage. He needed to destroy, in order to raise up. The *Irish Worker* would become notorious for appalling attacks on individuals. Larkin boasted of being in seven libel actions during its first 12 months, and never to have lost a case, a record that O'Brien would dispute.[28]

The third theme in the *Irish Worker* was socialist republicanism. The mast-head retained the *Harp*'s quote from Fintan Lalor. Wolfe Tone was replaced with:

> Who is it speaks of defeat? I tell you a cause like ours is greater than defeat can know. It is the power of powers. As surely as the earth rolls round, as surely as the glorious sun Brings the great world moon-wave, Must our cause be won.

The front page of the first issue set out 'Our platform and principles'. The manifesto was similar, in content if more refined in style, to Larkin's first editorial in the *Harp*. He began by addressing himself to the working class, and urging it to secure its freedom. He then reviewed the concepts of freedom held by the nationalists and 'Official Sinn Féin', deliberately isolating the Arthur Griffith element of advanced nationalism, and contrasted them with his own:

> By Freedom we mean that we, Irishmen in Ireland, shall be free to govern this land called Ireland by Irish people in the interest of all the Irish people . . . We owe no allegiance to any other nation, nor the king, governors, or representatives of any other nation . . . we are determined to accomplish not only National Freedom, but a greater thing – Individual Freedom – Freedom from military and political slavery, such as we suffer at present, but also from a more degraded slavery, economic or wage slavery! How then are we to achieve Freedom and Liberty?
>
> To accomplish political and economic freedom we must have our own party!

It lacked the sophistication of Connolly, but the basics were the same. The *Irish Worker* would frequently invoke the memory of the patriot dead, like the Manchester Martyrs, and its many articles on republicanism would emphasise the difference between socialist republicanism and bourgeois nationalism.

If anything, Larkin was more of a nationalist than Connolly, and undoubtedly more of an enthusiast for cultural nationalism. Since 1909 he had taken to Irish, though his use of the language never went beyond a few expressions like 'mar dhea' or 'ná bac leis', to which he was partial at this time, or signing letters as 'Seumas' or 'Seamus'. His limited command may explain the paucity of Irish in the *Irish Worker*. Ó Maoláin, who sometimes wrote for the paper on Gaelic games and Conradh na Gaeilge, helped the Larkin household complete its census form for 1911 in old-script Irish. With a tenuous grasp of the spelling and grammar, Jim returned himself as 'Séamus O'Lorcáin', 'Fear an Tighe', 'Rúnaire Cummann na bhFhear Céardhithe', born 'Co. Dúin', and able to speak 'Beurla agus Gaedilge'. Elizabeth was returned as 'Éilís Ní Lorcáin', 'A bean', 'Saghasanach'. Under 'Religious profession', the entire family was described as 'Catoilicigh'. Jim also sent his three eldest sons to the Pearses' Scoil Éanna, which they heartily disliked for its spartan regime.[29] In 1911 the *Irish Worker* gave extensive coverage to Gaelic football in Dublin, constantly emphasising the level of working-class support for the GAA, and the GAA's duty to uphold trade unionism against scabs or employers in dispute. The level of sports coverage was squeezed by industrial issues in 1912, but the regular 'Irish-Ireland notes' column continued. As the *Irish Worker* declared in 1913: 'To Irishise everything from Dunleary to Ceann Leime is our object . . .'[30]

LABOUR AND LIQUOR AND 9D FOR 4D

Larkin continued his intense involvement with Dublin trades council in 1911, and enlisted O'Brien to help him canvass for the vice-presidency, the vice-president being customarily appointed president the following year. In March he lost the contest to Christopher Timmins, a printer and council veteran. Three ITGWU delegates had failed to turn up. If Larkin was 'sore' over the defeat, as O'Brien claimed, it didn't affect his commitment.[31] He stood for re-election to the council's executive, coming second in the poll with 42 votes. Over the course of the year he spoke at 20 of the council's 28 fortnightly meetings, and attended 27 of the executive's 49 meetings. He also volunteered to serve on the Trades Hall Club Committee, the board of the Richmond Asylum – a valued source of employment and of coal contracts – and the Labour Representation Committee. When the Richmond Asylum board refused to accept his nomination – E. W. Stewart had protested to the Corporation that

Larkin was an undischarged bankrupt – the ITGWU pledged to liquidate all his liabilities to enable him to take his seat. The council established a steering group for the Labour Representation Committee in January 1911, and had it launched in April.[32] To avoid the personality wrangles that had bedevilled the Labour Electoral Association created by the trades council for the first democratic local elections in 1899, the Committee had no individual membership and consisted of delegates from the trades council and its affiliates. Its object was simply to secure independent Labour representation in parliament and local government. Sinn Féin had decided to withdraw from elections in favour of propaganda work the previous year, partly because Larkin had alienated trade unionists from Griffith, and Labour was positioned to fill the vacuum.[33] All its six candidates, including Thomas Greene, ITGWU, were successful in the forthcoming hustings for the Poor Law Guardians, bodies dominated by 'the organised forces of reaction and the liquor interest' according to the *Irish Worker*. Larkin, of course, was enthusiastic about the fight between Labour and liquor and spoke 'at considerable length' at Greene's eve of poll rally on 28 May, giving his opinions 'freely' on publicans and on socialism. Greene topped the poll in the South Dock ward, well ahead of two publicans.[34]

One week later Larkin led a six-man team of ITGWU delegates to the annual ITUC, which opened in Galway Town Hall on Monday 5 June. Connolly had hoped to be among them. His family had returned to Ireland in November 1910, settling first in Dublin, and then moving to Belfast, where it was easier for the eldest girls to find work. On joining them in May 1911, he immediately enrolled in the local ITGWU with a view to getting a nomination for Congress. To Connolly's disgust, Larkin privately favoured Michael McKeown, a Nationalist councillor, over a comrade who had intended to plead for an Irish Labour party. For months past, Connolly and Larkin had been circling around each other like tigers. O'Brien had wanted Connolly to seek a job with the ITGWU from the outset, knowing the SPI would struggle to pay his wages. Initially, Connolly was determined to concentrate on political work or return to the US, but he was gradually drawn into extensive speaking engagements in Ireland and Britain, and his resolve was worn down by the chronic problems of raising finance. For his part, Larkin had no desire to share the stage with another big name. McKeown's nomination confirmed Connolly's mounting suspicion of Larkin, and he made his feelings plain in a letter to O'Brien on 24 May:

> Do not pay any attention to what Larkin says. He is simply stringing you. He knows perfectly well that McKeown is going to Galway, and he himself wrote a personal letter to McKeown urging him to get the nomination for delegate. As to what he says about me not taking part in the Union in Dublin you know that he

organised a dozen demonstrations in Dublin while I was there, and invited all sorts
of hybrids to speak for him, but never invited me at any time. Did you notice that
while in Glasgow, he claimed at the May Day Demonstration, to be a member of
the SPI? The man is utterly unreliable – and dangerous because unreliable.[35]

But Connolly knew too that Larkin was the main man, and he couldn't afford
to cross him.

It was Larkin's most successful Congress to date. His antagonism to Joe
Harris and P. J. McIntyre had not been assuaged by their conspicuous lack of
success. The Workers' Union's membership had climbed from 4,500 in 1910
to 18,000, and would jump to 143,000 by 1914. The great majority were in
England, but the union had expanded its corps of organisers from six to 40
and was infamous for recruiting anyone, anywhere.[36] It remained a potential
rival. No sooner had the Congress opened than Larkin, shouting at the top of
his voice, demanded that the Workers' Union delegates withdraw.[37] The chair
refused to comply, but the next day Larkin had the satisfaction of seeing the
outgoing Parliamentary Committee's report uphold complaints of the Brush-
makers, Dublin Corporation Workmen's Society, and the ITGWU against
the Workers' Union, and agree that it had been guilty of acts detrimental to
trade unionism and should not be recognised by Congress. Larkin spoke for
the motion calling for an Irish Labour party, which was narrowly rejected in
favour of William Walker's amendment that affiliates support the British
Labour Party.

He was evidently keeping abreast of the related Connolly-Walker dispute
which had opened in *Forward* on 27 May and would run until 8 July. During
the debate he was accused by Patrick Lynch, a Cork tailor, of having 'preached
allegiance to the British Labour Party on the streets of Cork' as a salaried
agent of the NUDL. The sensible thing would have been to explain why he
had changed his mind on that score. Instead, he snapped 'That is a deliberate
lie'. As Lynch persisted he shouted 'You dirty cur . . . You are a liar' and started
to unbutton his coat. A 'heated scene' ensued, with Larkin squaring up to Lynch
with clenched fists, delegates holding him back, and the chairman vigorously
ringing his bell, before the antagonists were persuaded to withdraw their
accusations. Triumph came in the elections to the Parliamentary Committee.
The incoming Committee was largely Larkinite, with Michael O'Lehane as
chairman, Daly as secretary, and Larkin, O'Brien, and Councillor Richard
O'Carroll, Brick and Stonelayers, holding three of the remaining seven seats.[38]
In towns where Labour was weak, Congress normally included a public rally
to promote organisation, and Larkin was among the speakers at a well-attended
meeting in Eyre Square on the Tuesday evening. To the surprise of the

Connacht Tribune, he returned to Dublin without attempting to form a branch of the ITGWU.[39]

For Labour, and Larkin, the most important piece of legislation that year was the National Insurance bill, the centrepiece of the Liberal government's programme of social reform.[40] Part one of the bill provided for medical benefits. Each employee earning under £160 per annum would be required to pay 4d per week to the scheme, to which the employer would add 3d and the state 2d. David Lloyd George, the Chancellor of the Exchequer, called it the '9d for 4d'. In return, contributants would receive free medical treatment and be eligible for up to 15 weeks sick pay. Part two provided for unemployment benefit for up to 15 weeks in a year for those in certain occupations. In this case the worker and employer each contributed 2 1/2d per week, and the state 3d. To avoid displacing their benefit functions, trade unions were allowed to become 'approved societies' under the state system. It proved to be an incentive to join unions and was the major factor behind the 60 per cent surge in British TUC affiliation over the next two years.[41] Dublin trades council welcomed the bill at a special meeting on 31 May, and at the Galway Congress Larkin seconded a detailed motion from Walker listing proposed amendments.[42]

To Labour's consternation, the *Irish Independent*, the Catholic hierarchy, and sections of the medical profession condemned the bill as an unnecessary expense, and the IPP, while upholding it in principle, as it was obliged to do under its pact with the Liberals, opposed the extension of the bill's medical provisions to Ireland. The ITUC feared that without the medical provisions, unions in Ireland would not be able to establish attractive insurance sections. There were too, other disturbing instances of Ireland's exclusion, from legislation such as the Sweated Industries bill and the Feeding of Necessitous School Children bill; issues which Larkin, O'Brien, and the SPI had raised with Dublin trades council.[43] Trade unionists suspected that with an Irish government and exchequer in the pipeline, the IPP was revising its hitherto indulgent attitude towards public spending, and that here was 'a foretaste of what they were going to get in the future under Home Rule'.[44] The *Irish Independent* said as much in editorials, welcoming 'A great scheme' on 5 May, and then saying on 10 May: 'While approving heartily of the principle of the Bill, we cannot disguise from ourselves that, in view of Home Rule, it raises a problem of enormous importance . . .'[45] The bill spurred Congress into more vigorous lobbying of the IPP and British Labour. The 1911 Congress would herald the beginning of regular engagement with the IPP throughout the third Home Rule crisis. At one level it was a paradoxical development in that it coincided with the ascendancy of Larkin, who, with Connolly, was utterly hostile to the IPP. Yet Larkin was practical enough to make use of the IPP and collaborate with its more progressive MPs. In January 1910 he had appealed on Dublin trades council for the withdrawal of opposition to a motion of support for J. P. Nannetti, the leading Labour-Nationalist MP, in the upcoming general election.[46]

The Parliamentary Committee convened specially on 1 July 1911 to digest submissions from affiliates on the Insurance bill, and drew up a memorandum of amendments.[47] On 9 July Larkin spoke at a Dublin trades council public rally on the bill at Smithfield, accompanied by an ITGWU band. Describing the bill as the most beneficial legislation ever to come before parliament, he implied that more could be achieved through politics than strikes, and urged workers to lobby 'the Abrahams, the Fields, the Devlins, and the advanced section' of the IPP. MPs William Abraham and William Field had spoken earlier, and Joe Devlin had been scheduled to attend.[48] A meeting with Redmond followed on 16 July, with Michael McKeown representing the ITGWU. Redmond sought to accommodate the ITUC by promising that the IPP would introduce amending legislation to have medical benefits extended to Ireland if it could be shown that the demand existed, by facilitating Congress lobbying at Westminster, and by appointing Devlin to the IPP's committee on the bill. 'Wee Joe' favoured the bill *in toto*, partly because the Ancient Order of Hibernians, in which he was prominent, stood to make substantial gains from becoming an approved society.[49] When Lloyd George declined to meet a Congress delegation, an interview was secured, on 17 July, through Redmond and Devlin. Larkin later joined a Congress deputation which met the IPP committee on the bill in the United Irish League's Central Office, and introduced Dr Seymour Stritch to put the case for the extension of the bill's medical benefits to Ireland.[50] Ultimately, the Act did not extend medical benefits to Ireland. The bulk of employees continued to be treated under the dispensary system, which O'Lehane described as 'congested . . . inadequate [with] a general air of contamination about it that is most objectionable to the ordinary worker'.[51] The eventual shape of the Act was as negative for the development of Irish health services as it was positive for the evolution of the British welfare state.

'STRIKE! STRIKE! STRIKE!'[52]

The anticipated industrial conflict exploded in June. First to move were porters who refused to coal the SS *Olympic*, the largest liner afloat, as she lay at Southampton on Saturday 3 June 1911. They were demanding a standard rate of £6 a month. The following day, Whit Sunday, Larkin bade farewell to an ITGWU excursion to Cork, Queenstown, and Blarney. The attention he gave to the social side of belonging to a union was very much a part of his appeal. An advertisement for the trip invited readers to 'Visit sweet Cork, where your Soggarth was born . . .'[53] The 'Soggarth' was Fr Patrick O'Leary, who had helped Larkin resolve disputes in Cork and said mass for the excursionists. Daly also entrained, and was to stay in Cork as 'southern organiser'; it was Larkin's first industrial offensive since 1909.[54] Larkin then headed to Galway for the ITUC. That same day, the International Seamen's Strike committee met in London to consider 'universal' action. On 12 June, Havelock Wilson made a final appeal to the Shipowners' Association. He also commissioned the ITGWU as his union's agent in Ireland, which was exactly the kind of relationship that Larkin wanted with the British unions. On 14th, with rockets and naval flags signalling 'war', the NSFU took up the general clamour for wage movements with a strike at all ports for a uniform pay scale.[55] Unrest spread to dockers and carters. In Belfast, J. H. Bennett, Irish organiser of the NSFU, pushed for the appointment of Connolly to the ITGWU staff. Larkin accepted that he needed an experienced official in Belfast if the ITGWU was to retain credibility with the NSFU. Reluctantly, Connolly took the job of northern organiser.[56]

Larkin ran the Dublin end of the seamen's strike, which hit deep-sea rather than cross-channel routes. His strategy was clear: support, don't extend, and keep control. Stressing that ITGWU men 'should take no action until they got advice from headquarters', he tried to have the ITGWU black ships with scab crews or 'tainted' cargoes while discouraging sympathetic strikes.[57] The distinction was wasted on the Coal Merchants' Association, and on 14 July they locked out 800 men for standing by colleagues who refused to unload a boat crewed by scabs. Within days, the dispute affected 2,000 men. On Monday 17 July Larkin rushed out a 'special lockout edition' of the *Irish Worker* featuring a 'black list' and a 'union list' of coal and shipping companies, and had Dublin trades council suspend standing orders to hear an upbeat Mann announce that 'fully 98 per cent of the shipping of the British isles was being settled on lines satisfactory to all concerned (hear, hear)'.[58] Mann was also scheduled to speak at a rally that evening along with Connolly, Daly, Larkin, and Luella Twining of Denver, Colorado and the Western Federation of Miners. Twining had also been a delegate to the founding convention of the Industrial Workers of the World.[59]

By 21 July Larkin was becoming sufficiently worried about the financial position of the ITGWU to summon a special meeting of the trades council. At the same time, he insisted absolutely on the necessity of sympathetic action. The *Irish Worker* of 29 July was the first to publish the famous *Don't Shoot* leaflet, written by Bower for soldiers deployed against strikers. Larkin had asked Bower to write 'something' for the paper. He got 'something' alright.

The leaflet was translated into half a dozen languages, and its republication in the Industrial Syndicalist Education League's monthly, the *Syndicalist*, would lead to the prosecution of the printers and publishers, including Mann.[60] On 31 July Larkin had good news for the trades council. The success of the strikes in Britain, together with Dublin Castle intervention, had led to a resumption of work, union recognition, and wage increases. The ITGWU had won its first strike.[61]

In England, sectional stoppages on the railway led to a second big strike wave in August. On 17 August, in response to mounting pressure from its members over the inadequacy of conciliation machinery and the tardiness of the railway companies in dealing with grievances, the ASRS called a UK strike for the following day. Larkin had been critical of the railwaymen for not standing together with other transport sectors, but they would soon be responsible for Ireland's first nation-wide sympathetic action. At 8 pm on 18 August Larkin and Walter Halls, Irish national organiser of the ASRS, addressed a mass meeting of Transport and railwaymen in Beresford Place. Larkin was included in the rail strike committee, on which he signed himself 'Jim Larkin, Irish Transport Union, Sailors' and Firemen's Union', pointedly including the cross-channel union to impress members of the British-based ASRS.[62] The intervention of Lloyd George, who appealed for national unity at a time when the Agadir crisis threatened to bring Britain into war with Germany, bought a quick settlement. The day after, a Sunday, the satisfactory conclusion was hailed with an 'immense' parade to the Phoenix Park, preceded by a banner saying: 'All Grades. All Creeds. No Distinction.' Noting some trouble with the police during his speech, Larkin asked:

> Why do the police beat the crowd? Not because they are better men or stronger men. Not at all. They do it because they are a disciplined body. They have to act on the orders of their superior officers, otherwise their clothes would be taken and they would be sacked. We have to act in a similar way. We must be an army of disciplined men – not a mob. We have to show to the employing class that the docker, the coal heaver, the railway man, the sailor and the fireman are all of one class and if one section is struck at all the others will say 'out we go'.[63]

The employers decided to test this resolve. During the rail strike ITGWU men had refused to handle 'tainted goods'. Dublin timber merchants retaliated with a lockout on 19 August. When the rail strike ended, the timbermen would not go back without a pay rise. Four loads of timber consigned to the Great Southern and Western Railway were 'blacked' and returned to the companies. In September, the railway companies invited the timber merchants to try again. On 15 September, a timber consignment was 'blacked' at

Kingsbridge, headquarters of the Great Southern and Western, the largest of the railway companies. Two porters were singled out for dismissal. On 18th the chairman of the Great Southern and Western, Sir William Goulding, met the Permanent Under-Secretary for Ireland, and secured guarantees of state protection. As dismissals and walk-outs extended along the railway, the ASRS executive hastened from London. Failing to get its members re-instated, the executive called a national strike for 21 September. Larkin gave the ASRS his total support, inserting its call to arms at the head of an editorial of the *Irish Worker*.[64] He met his match in Goulding. The Great Southern and Western locked out all employees, including 1,600 not on strike, and imported labour from England. Police patrolled the railway installations and troops were deployed to protect the lines. In Waterford, the cavalry were called out to disperse strikers.[65] The conflict diffused Larkinism as never before, almost wherever the railway extended. As it generated further instances of 'tainted' goods being blacked, it revealed a remarkably wide degree of support for Larkin's doctrine among workers.

Nowhere was that more evident than in Wexford, which was added to Belfast, Newry, and Cork in the roll call of centres overwhelmed by Larkinite industrial conflict. In August, the Pierce company had locked out all its employees because some of them were being recruited into the ITGWU. Within a week, two smaller ironworks had joined the pre-emptive lockout, and 680 men were affected. There followed the familiar pattern of blacking, scabs, police, and violence. Larkin spoke in Wexford town on 9 September, but generally left the dispute to Daly, though it looked as if Wexford would be a hopeless drain on union resources and eventually go the way of Belfast, Newry, and Cork.[66] According to J. M. MacDonnell:

> During the Wexford strike every penny that could be raised in Dublin was sent to support the strikers, and when Jim came to look for his wages all that could be found was £1. Walter Carpenter and he split it between them, but even Jim shrunk from offering Mrs Larkin 10s for her weekly housekeeping, and begged Carpenter to call round and leave the money with her.[67]

Carpenter's engagement with the ITGWU may have been another act of charity on Larkin's part. Secretary of the SPI, Carpenter had been imprisoned for distributing a manifesto against the King during the royal visit to Ireland in July. His release was marked with a rally in Beresford Place on 27 August, chaired by Connolly, who had written the offending manifesto. Larkin was not scheduled to be present, but arrived late in the proceedings, and when, inevitably, called to address the meeting, ignored the occasion and spoke on the newsboys strike. It was typical of his angular relationship with the SPI.[68]

The unrest differentiated nationalists. The mainstream press and constitu-
tionalists responded with a torrent of criticism against the import of 'foreign'
ideas into Irish industrial relations. Advanced nationalists pooh-poohed the
hysteria and thought it all boiled down to the question of whether unskilled
workers were to have the union recognition already conceded to craftsmen.
The Leinster council of the GAA organised benefit matches to raise funds for
the locked out men in Wexford. The Dublin GAA would act similarly during
the 1913 Lockout.[69] *Saoirse na hÉireann: Irish Freedom*, organ of the Wolfe
Tone Clubs, reminded readers:

> A vast amount of unmitigated rubbish has appeared in papers that ought to
> know much better about the horrors of Socialism and syndicalism and the blood
> red flag . . . The label 'Syndicalism' was not invented in the early eighties, but the
> thing itself was alive and kicking in Ireland. Parnell's favourite maxim, which 'Sinn
> Féin', if we mistake not, has hailed as an adaptation of its principles, that the battle
> would not be in the House of Commons but on the rack-rented holdings of Ireland
> was the pure gospel of syndicalism. The 'No Rent campaign', inaugurated as a protest
> against his imprisonment in Kilmainham, went further than the Irish Transport
> Workers' Union has gone in its wildest dreams, and the sympathetic strike had its
> parallels in the refusal of railway servants, dockers and cattle-men to handle the
> beasts seized by the sheriffs for non-payment of rent during the Land War.[70]

The rail strike revitalised employer attempts at counter-mobilisation.
Dublin employers had met on 30 June to discuss the formation of an Employers'
Federation modelled on the Cork namesake that had smashed the 1909 dock
strike. On 21 September, Dublin Chamber of Commerce met in emergency
session to consider ways of assisting the railway companies. One week later, a
general meeting of the Chamber urged resistance to what one termed 'not a
strike in the ordinary sense of the word . . . but the beginning of a social war . . .'[71]
In October, delegates of various Chambers of Commerce gathered in Dublin
to consider founding an association 'which shall advise its members on labour
troubles as they may arise and make effective preparation to protect the trade
and commerce of the company'. Within weeks, local employers' federations
were being formed throughout the country.[72] The vice-president of the
Dublin Chamber, one William Martin Murphy, was particularly impressed
with Goulding's handling of the crisis. On 28 September the ASRS admitted
defeat. Larkin offered more sympathetic action, but the ASRS decided to concentrate on getting the men back their jobs and pension rights. The railway
directors would not be denied their revenge. When the strike collapsed on 4
October, the Great Southern and Western refused to re-employ ten per cent
of the strikers, and re-engaged others at reduced rates; men recruited during

the strike were retained, and those who had stayed at work were rewarded with bonuses. So pleased were the Great Southern and Western directors with crushing Larkinism on the railway, that they marked the occasion with the gift of a clock to each of the 121 station masters.[73] It was a big setback for Larkin's hope of winning over the railwaymen.

THE IRISH WOMEN WORKERS' UNION

Larkin availed of the unrest to form a second union, the Irish Women Workers' Union (IWWU). There was a good case for a female union. The historic difficulties of organising women workers suggested that they might be more amenable to a different kind of trade unionism. Belfast trades council had created the almost entirely female Textile Operatives' Society of Ireland in 1893, Derry trades council launched the City of Derry Textile Operatives' Association for girls in the shirt factories in 1906, and Mary Macarthur founded the British-based National Federation of Women Workers that same year. Britain was currently experiencing a major movement for female emancipation, and its spirit had washed over both British Labour and Ireland: the IWWU would engage with the feminism emerging from the campaigns for the vote and an Irish-Ireland. Equally, one could argue for male separatism, and contend that manliness was part of the ITGWU ethos and it was better to retain it. Big Jim liked to appeal to his members as men, to be men, do the manly thing etc. Instead, according to O'Brien, who would always resent the move, Jim ignored the many rational excuses he might have called on, and justified the IWWU on the ground that 'persons' in rule five of the ITGWU rulebook referred to males.[74] Is there a significance to the fact that Jim cited his occupation in the 1911 census as 'Rúnaire Cummann na *bhFhear* Céardhithe'? Or was rule five a flimsy pretext which occurred to him after the summer of discontent got underway. He had advertised the union in the *Irish Worker* of 27 May as 'Open to all section [*sic*] of workers except skilled men'. In all likelihood he wanted to create a suitably grand role for his sister Delia, who would run the IWWU as her personal fiefdom, without the inconvenience of an executive.[75] Strict and school-mistressy, she was a formidable personality in her own right and, though four years younger, she both hero-worshipped and dominated her big brother. Jim had a weakness for nepotism, but he may have been a trifle embarrassed by it, and where he had a private motive he was often clumsy in explanation. Neither did he consider the position of the union in Belfast, where Connolly had the potential to recruit among a sizeable female workforce. O'Brien claimed that Connolly, a fervent feminist, was disgusted by the initiative, and when approached by spinners in October, he organised them into a third union, the Irish Textile Workers. Larkin promptly directed him to turn it into a branch of the IWWU.[76]

Delia had left Rostrevor, and, since April at least, was living with Jim, Elizabeth, and the three boys in Auburn Street. Whether she had a regular job is unclear. In the 1911 census she was returned as 'Bridhe Ní Lorcáin', able to speak 'Béurla agus Gaedilge', and her occupation was given as 'muinteóir', a profession that required no qualification. For whatever reason she did not join Hanna Sheehy Skeffington and others in the suffragist boycott of the census. Delia was probably involved with the *Irish Worker* from the outset. Her first signed item in the paper was a poem, 'Rouse up, ye workers', on 8 July. On 12 August she began a regular 'Women workers' column', which would run for over two years. Like her brother she was an ardent separatist, keen to develop a cultural agenda, and a socialist progressive on women's issues rather than one who prioritised feminism. Her opening column appealed to women for contributions on the home and its comforts, cookery hints, dress and dress reform, women workers' grievances, and the 'mission and work' of women in the world, or anything which would 'benefit the cause of labour, lighten the burden of the toiler, or help build an Irish-Ireland'.

The *Irish Worker* heralded the union on 19 August, and it was launched on 5 September at the Antient Concert Rooms, with addresses from Countess Markievicz, James Nolan, Dublin trades council, Hanna Sheehy Skeffington, and Jim as the star turn. Appealing to women workers to stand united, Jim dwelt on the civilising role of women:

> On them principally depends the efficiency and welfare of the race. Good or bad, the men are what the women made them. If the women are not healthy, the men will degenerate. If the women are ignorant, the men will be beasts.[77]

He gave no indication of why a specifically female union was needed. Delia became general secretary, Jim, incongruously, became president, and the ITGWU provided the IWWU with rooms in its headquarters and paid its staff.[78]

THE BALANCE SHEET

When Daly was arrested for 'incitement' in Wexford in January 1912, Larkin despatched Connolly to replace him. Connolly's negotiation of a reasonably good settlement to the lockout in February marked the end of the strike wave. It had been an extraordinary year, and, clearly, the British unrest was the trigger. The 18 strikes in the traditional industries of the north east in 1911 were distributed evenly throughout the year. By contrast, 32 of the 36 disputes in other sectors took place after mid June. The large number of 'miscellaneous' militants included newsboys and golf-caddies, sandwichmen and bill-posters.[79] By the end of 1911, the ITGWU had about 8,000 members and branches in Dublin, Kingstown, Bray, Belfast, Dundalk, Sligo, Waterford, and Wexford.[80] It was not a spectacular performance. Certainly, Irish employers remained formidable opponents. Some 43 per cent of strikes, accounting for almost 60 per cent of strikers, were completely unsuccessful in 1911.[81] But Larkin could have done better had he shown a personal interest in the provinces, or engaged more organisers. In Dublin, however, he did rise to the occasion, as an editor, an agitator, and a tactician, and in a hectic year of tireless commitment he consolidated his reputation in Ireland and Britain. Most of all, he established sympathetic action as a principle of trade unionism. His next step was to broaden the concept of trade unionism and advance the cause of industrial unionism.

NOTES

1   William D. Haywood, *Bill Haywood's Book: The Autobiography of William D. Haywood* (New York, 1929), p. 158.

2   Bob Holton, *British Syndicalism, 1900–1914: Myth and Realities* (London, 1976), pp. 137–8; Mel Cousins, 'The creation of association: the National Insurance Act, 1911 and approved societies in Ireland', in Jennifer Kelly and R. V. Comerford (eds), *Associational Culture in Ireland and Abroad* (Dublin, 2010), pp. 155–64.

3   Ken Brown, *The English Labour Movement, 1700–1951* (Dublin, 1982), p. 208; Ken Coates and Tony Topham, *The History of the Transport and General Workers' Union: Vol. I, Part I, 1870–1911: From Forerunners to Federation* (Oxford, 1991), pp. 336–7, 344–5.

4   Séamus Cody, John O'Dowd, and Peter Rigney, *The Parliament of Labour: 100 Years of the Dublin Council of Trade Unions* (Dublin, 1986), pp. 49–50.

5   *Harp*, March 1910; Dermot Keogh, *The Rise of the Irish Working Class: The Dublin Trade Union Movement and Labour Leadership, 1890–1914* (Belfast, 1982), p. 151.

6   NLI, William O'Brien papers, 15679(22).

7   Ibid., LOp92; Larkin Release Committee, *James Larkin: A Labour Leader and an Honest Man* (Liverpool, 1910), p. 20.

8   *Forward*, 15 October 1910.

9   Eric Taplin, *The Dockers' Union: A Study of the National Union of Dock Labourers, 1889–1922* (Leicester, 1986), p. 75; James Sexton, *Sir James Sexton, Agitator: The Life of the Dockers' MP. An Autobiography* (London, 1936), pp. 206–7.

10   Coates and Topham, *The History of the Transport and General Workers' Union: Vol. I, Part I*, p. 340.

11   Tom Mann, *Tom Mann's Memoirs* (London, 1923), p. 240, 281.

12   Coates and Topham, *The History of the Transport and General Workers' Union: Vol. I, Part I*, pp. 324–9. For unrest in Britain see also Henry Pelling, *A History of British Trade Unionism* (Harmondsworth, 1974), pp. 123–48.

13 *Industrial Syndicalist*, December 1910, reprinted in *The Industrial Syndicalist* (Nottingham, 1974), pp. 166, 187–8.

14 Coates and Topham, *The History of the Transport and General Workers' Union: Vol. I, Part I*, p. 329.

15 Ken Coates and Tony Topham, *The History of the Transport and General Workers' Union: Vol. I, Part II, 1912–1922: From Federation to Amalgamation* (Oxford, 1991), pp. 523, 536–40.

16 Donal Nevin (ed.), *Between Comrades: James Connolly, Letters and Correspondence 1889–1916* (Dublin, 2007), p. 461; *Irish Worker*, 3 June 1911.

17 For studies of the paper see Donal Nevin, 'The *Irish Worker*, 1911–1914', in Donal Nevin (ed.), *James Larkin: Lion of the Fold* (Dublin, 1998), pp. 152–8; R. G. Lowery, 'Seán O'Casey and the *Irish Worker*', in R. G. Lowery (ed.), *O'Casey Annual No. 3* (London, 1984), pp. 33–114; John Newsinger, 'A lamp to guide your feet: Jim Larkin, the *Irish Worker*, and the Dublin working class', *European History Quarterly* 20 (1990), pp. 63–99; and James Curry and Francis Devine (eds), '*Merry May Your Xmas be & 1913 Free From Care': The* Irish Worker *1912 Christmas Number* (Dublin, 2012).

18 *Irish Worker*, 9 March 1912.

19 *Irish Times*, 4 October 1912.

20 Nevin, 'The *Irish Worker*, 1911–1914', p. 155; *Irish Worker*, 9 March 1912; Francis Devine, *Organising History: A Centenary of SIPTU, 1909–2009* (Dublin, 2009), p. 48.

21 Steven Dedalus Burch, *Andrew P. Wilson and the Early Irish and Scottish National Theatres, 1911–1950* (New York, 2008), p. 13.

22 'The autobiography of Seán McKeown', p. 23. I am obliged to Neal Garnham for a copy of this unpublished memoir.

23 Lowery, 'Seán O'Casey and the *Irish Worker*', p. 43.

24 Bertram D. Wolfe, *Strange Communists I Have Known* (New York, 1982), pp. 60–1.

25 *Irish Worker*, 15 July 1911.

26 Ibid., 9 March 1912.

27 Ibid., 10 June 1911.

28 Ibid., 11 May 1912; O'Brien claimed that one plaintiff, at least, got damages. NLI, William O'Brien papers, 15679(20).

29 Jim Larkin, *In the Footsteps of Big Jim: A Family Biography* (Dublin, 1995), p. 113, 122.

30 *Irish Worker*, 4 January 1913.

31 William O'Brien, *Forth the Banners Go: The Reminiscences of William O'Brien as Told to Edward MacLysaght, D.Litt* (Dublin, 1969), pp. 57–9.

32 NLI, William O'Brien papers, 15709(4); UUMC, Dublin trades council minutes, 30 January, 13 February, 13 March, 10 April, 8 May 1911.

33 See Peter Murray, 'Electoral politics and the Dublin working class before the First World War', *Saothar* 6 (1980), pp. 15–16.

34 *Irish Worker*, 3 June 1911.

35 Joe Deasy, 'As I remember Big Jim', in Nevin (ed.), *James Larkin*, p. 461.

36 Coates and Topham, *The History of the Transport and General Workers' Union: Vol. I, Part I*, p. 384.

37 *Derry Journal*, 7 June 1911.

38 UUMC, ITUC, *Annual Report* (1911), pp. 20–1, 39–42; *Irish Times*, 8 June 2011.

39 John Cunningham, *Labour in the West of Ireland: Working Life and Struggle, 1890–1914* (Belfast, 1995), p. 151; *Connacht Tribune*, 10 June 1911.

40 The most detailed discussion of the National Insurance Act and Ireland is in Ruth Barrington, *Health, Medicine, and Politics in Ireland, 1900–1970* (Dublin, 1987), pp. 39–66, and says remarkable little on trade union objections.

41 Pelling, *A History of British Trade Unionism*, pp. 128–33.

42 UUMC, Dublin trades council minutes, 31 May 1911; UUMC, ITUC, *Annual Report* (1911), pp. 29–31.

43 UUMC, Dublin trades council minutes, 31 May 1911.

44 UUMC, Belfast trades council minutes, 7 December 1911.

45 Between May and July 1911 the *Irish Independent* published 15 editorials against the bill. *Irish Independent*, 10–12, 15, 25, 30 May, 1–2, 6, 12, 29 June, 7, 14–15, 18 July 1911.

46 UUMC, Dublin trades council minutes, 17 January 1910.

47 UUMC, ITUC, *Annual Report* (1912), p. 21.

48 *Irish Worker*, 8–15 July 1911.

49 A. C. Hepburn, *Catholic Belfast and Nationalist Ireland in the Era of Joe Devlin, 1871–1934* (Oxford, 2008), pp. 132–3.

50 UUMC, ITUC, *Annual Report* (1912), pp. 21–35.

51 Barrington, *Health, Medicine, and Politics in Ireland*, p. 41, 59, 65.

52 Leader in the *Irish Worker*, 24 June 1911.

53 Ibid., 27 May 1911.

54 C. Desmond Greaves, *The Irish Transport and General Workers' Union: The Formative Years, 1909–1923* (Dublin, 1982), p. 58.

55 *Irish Independent*, 15 June 1911.

56 Austen Morgan, *James Connolly: A Political Biography* (Manchester, 1988), p. 89.

57 *Irish Worker*, 24 June 1911.

58 UUMC, Dublin trades council minutes, 17 July 1911.

59 *Irish Worker*, 17 July 1911; William D. Haywood, *Bill Haywood's Book: The Autobiography of William D. Haywood* (New York, 1929, 1983 edn), p. 227.

60 Fred Bower, *Rolling Stonemason: An Autobiography* (London, 1936), pp. 179–80; Mann, *Tom Mann's Memoirs*, pp. 282–314.

61 UUMC, Dublin trades council minutes, 21, 31 July 1911; Emmet Larkin, *James Larkin: Irish Labour Leader, 1876–1947* (London, 1965), p. 90.

62 *Irish Worker*, 19 August 1911.

63 Ibid., 26 August 1911. For the rail strikes see also Conor McCabe, 'The context and course of the Irish railway disputes of 1911', *Saothar* 30 (2005), pp. 21–31.

64 *Irish Worker*, 23 September 1911.

65 Emmet O'Connor, *A Labour History of Waterford* (Waterford, 1989), p. 123.

66 NAUK, Ministry of Labour reports on strikes and lockouts, 1911, LAB 34/11, 34/29; Michael Enright, *Men of Iron: Wexford Foundry Disputes 1890 & 1911* (Wexford, 1987).

67 J. M. MacDonnell, *The Story of Irish Labour* (1921, Cork Workers' Club reprint), p. 26.

68 *Irish Worker*, 2 September 1911; Nevin (ed.), *Between Comrades*, p. 469.

69 Enright, *Men of Iron*, p. 31; *Irish Worker*, 11 October 1913.

70 *Saoirse na h-Éireann: Irish Freedom*, October 1911.

71   Thomas J. Morrissey, SJ, *William Martin Murphy* (Dundalk, 1997), pp. 44–5.

72   Emmet O'Connor, *A Labour History of Ireland, 1824–2000* (Dublin, 2011), p. 85; Waterford Chamber of Commerce, minutes, 30 October, 14 November 1911.

73   Irish Railway Record Society Archive, Dublin, Great Southern and Western Railway, files 1019, 1069. I am obliged to Conor McCabe for these references.

74   NLI, William O'Brien papers, 15676(1), part 1; see also Mary Jones, *These Obstreperous Lassies: A History of the Irish Women Workers' Union* (Dublin, 1988), p. 4.

75   See *Evening Herald*, 16 November, *Irish Times*, 17 November 1914. I am obliged to James Curry for drawing my attention to these references. On Delia and her influence on Jim, see Larkin, *In the Footsteps of Big Jim*, pp. 100–1; Frank Robbins, *Under the Starry Plough: Recollections of the Irish Citizen Army* (Dublin, 1977), p. 20.

76   NLI, William O'Brien papers, 15676(1), part 1; Donal Nevin, *James Connolly: 'A Full Life'* (Dublin, 2006), pp. 398–9.

77   *Irish Worker*, 9 September 1911.

78   Devine, *Organising History*, p. 33.

79   NAUK, Ministry of Labour reports on strikes and lockouts, 1911, LAB 34/11, 34/29.

80   Estimates of ITGWU membership during these years vary enormously. There is broad agreement that the union had under 5,000 members in mid-1911. Based on returns to the Registry of Friendly Societies, and a presumptuous multiplication of known recruitment to the no 1 branch, Greaves puts membership at 18,000 by the end of 1911, rising to close on 30,000 by mid-1913. Greaves, *The Irish Transport and General Workers' Union*, pp. 70, 82–3, 91. Emmet Larkin rejects the Registry of Friendly Society returns in favour of the ITUC affiliation figure for 1912: 8,000, and the number of contributors under the National Insurance Act in 1913: 9,580. Larkin, *James Larkin*, pp. 108–9. Insured membership figures are probably the most reliable indicator, as they were less likely to be exaggerated. O'Brien claimed that insured membership was close to total membership, though the union would have had a few more members than contributors to the insurance scheme. In November 1913 there were 12,829 ITGWU men in receipt of support from the British TUC lockout fund. Pádraig Yeates, *Lockout: Dublin 1913* (Dublin, 2000), p. 459.

81   NAUK, Ministry of Labour reports on strikes and lockouts, 1911, LAB 34/11, LAB 34/29; British Parliamentary Papers, *Report on Strikes and Lockouts* (Cd. 6472, 1911).

SIX

LARKIN'S NEXT STEP, 1912–13

Trade unionism in Ireland has arrived at a certain stage of growth when this question
confronts us – What is to be our next step in fostering its future development?
ITGWU rules, 1912[1]

———

On 10 October 1912 the ITGWU registered a second rulebook. Certain amendments were needed to comply with the National Insurance Act, and the rules were otherwise largely the same. The opening sentence was exactly the same. Yet that phrase 'next step' had acquired a resonance since James Larkin coined it in May 1909. In early 1912 syndicalists in south Wales had issued a best-selling pamphlet *The Miners' Next Step: Being a Suggested Scheme for the Re-Organization of the Federation*, arguing for militancy and industrial unionism. It marked the high tide of British syndicalism and, arguably, was a factor in precipitating a national coal strike for a minimum wage in February. While industrial conflict eased a little in Ireland, the continuing 'great unrest' in Britain, where the number of days lost in strikes jumped to 40 million in 1912, sustained an atmosphere of militancy. And whereas syndicalists were mainly on the periphery in Britain, Larkinites were in the driving seat in Ireland. Larkin himself was well positioned to effect a step change, not just for the ITGWU, but for 'trade unionism in Ireland'.

The slackening of industrial conflict provided Larkin with a welcome respite, and allowed him to spread his wings and devote more of his time to matters political, cultural, and social. It ought to have been a year of steady progress. In January 1912, Larkin was elected to Dublin Corporation. In February, he acquired Liberty Hall. In March, the ITGWU moved in, Larkin announced big plans for the *Irish Worker*, and placed a large ad for the paper over the entrance.[2] In April, the Home Rule bill was introduced to parliament, making the case for an Irish Labour party virtually unanswerable and for turning the ITUC into 'One Big Union' a little stronger. In May, Larkin became chairman of the ITUC's Parliamentary Committee and the closest thing that Irish Labour had to a leader. In July, the National Insurance Act came into force; with it a big incentive to join the ITGWU and expand union services to the social sphere.

Then, in August, Larkin resigned from the chair of the Parliamentary Committee. It was not of great consequence to his own standing. Congress was much less important than the ITGWU. But Larkin could have turned it from an annual talking-shop into a real movement. In fact his failure to do just that prompted William O'Brien and James Connolly to demand a revision of the ITUC constitution. The resignation was the first sign of a perverse tendency to self-destruct on the cusp of higher achievement. Was it that Larkin could never lead where leadership had to be conciliar and procedural, or was he coincidentally unbalanced by the pressure of work? He was starting to over-reach himself with an arduous range of responsibilities. Reluctant to delegate, he maintained his intense involvement with Dublin trades council, speaking at 21 of its 25 meetings in 1912, and every one of its 13 meetings in the first half of 1913. In the union and the *Irish Worker* he indulged a shameless personality cult. It was one way of keeping the adrenalin going. It also drew the fire of all anti-Labour elements, and the strain on his health began to tell.

MORE THAN A UNION

Despite a mild recession, the ITGWU marched on. Larkin started to take a greater interest in the provinces, and not without fresh controversy. Arriving in Sligo on Sunday 24 March at 5.50 am on the 'scabby' train from Broadstone – as befitted a transport man he liked to take the train and rate the quality of the service – he attended mass in the Priory at 11 am only to hear a letter from John Clancy, Bishop of Elphin, read at all masses, denouncing him as 'a noted leader of the Socialistic movement', and warning Catholics not to attend his meeting at 4 pm that day. An erstwhile supporter of Labour organisation, Clancy was one of those who distinguished between Larkinism and 'bona fide' trade union-ism, and had issued a 'remarkable denunciation' of socialism and the recent establishment of a local ITGWU branch a year previously.[3] The episcopal words carried little weight. Larkin was led through the town by a band, and drew a big audience. Making his own distinctions, he said Clancy was entitled to his politics and called for three cheers for the bishop. That evening he spoke to Sligo Trades Club, the occasion concluding with an impromptu concert and 'some rousing National songs and recitations'. The *Irish Worker* brassily reprinted Clancy's letter in full, and asked why the bishop had recently raised rents in houses he owned.[4]

By April, the ITGWU's Kingstown branch had opened a new premises; the Newry branch was reactivated; a Storemen's and Carmen's Union was incor-porated as a branch in Cork; and the Wexford fight had led to the formation of branches in Enniscorthy and New Ross. Larkin was back in Wexford on Sunday 14 April to celebrate P. T. Daly's release from Ballybricken gaol and triumphant return to the town. On 5 May he spoke at Waterford's biggest

May Day rally to date – the parade was grand enough to be cinematographed by Theatre Royal Pictures – and on 26th he led 300 union members to Wexford on the ITGWU's annual excursion. That evening, no train being available, he motored to Clonmel for the ITUC's annual congress on the following day.[5] In June, Daly and Michael McKeown handled a dock strike in Sligo, which ended in victory. Later that month Larkin was instrumental in detaching Dublin stevedores from their employers by persuading them to form their own association. One who refused to join found himself blacked by union members. Larkin then negotiated a much improved schedule of wages and conditions for dockers.[6]

The texture of Larkin's syndicalism became clearer in 1912, though it required close reading. He was a defender of the sympathetic strike who didn't like strikes, an agitator who hoped the consolidation of the ITGWU would lead to a stabilisation of industrial relations through compulsory arbitration, and a revolutionary who made a clean distinction between the immediate, incremental objectives of trade unionism and the long-term goal of building an industrial commonwealth. Machinery for the resolution of disputes by boards of conciliation and arbitration was more advanced in Britain than in Ireland's comparatively primitive industrial relations environment. The Conciliation Act (1896) had encouraged a movement for arbitration, and the Board of Trade's arbitration machinery was augmented in 1908, and again in 1911, in response to the 'great unrest', when an Industrial Council, comprised of representatives of employers and workers was created within the Board of Trade.[7] There were 293 conciliation boards in operation in Britain by the end of 1911, and 325 by the end of 1913, and the Industrial Council reckoned the system was working quite well.[8] On 30 July 1912 Larkin and P. T. Daly, as president and secretary of the Congress, appeared before the Council's 'enquiry into industrial agreements'. Larkin again called for compulsory arbitration, explaining: 'I do not approve of strikes at all. I have been through too many. I have been through 33 of them both as a striker and a leader of strikers.' It was a point he had often made before. At the same time, he defended the sympathetic strike as a logical riposte to the employers.

> We follow the same lines of organisation as the Shipping Federation. Whenever an individual shipowner is affected they are affected everywhere, and they take up the fight. Whenever we find one of our friends attacked anywhere we take up the fight, too.

Equally, he upheld the doctrine of 'tainted goods'. 'The principle I have been working on always is that when the cabinet workers are on strike I am on strike, and if that stuff is made under unfair conditions I have no right to handle it.' On arbitration, he insisted that the voluntary mode was useless.[9] It was, of course, a time when Irish employers were more militant than unions and less amenable to arbitration, and strikes were likely to be unsuccessful.

Larkin was equally nuanced on the 'great unrest'. An editorial in the *Irish Worker* of 25 May commended the *Daily Herald*, new organ of the British left, and syndicalist leaders Tom Mann and Guy Bowman, and deplored the ILP's *Labour Leader* and Ramsay MacDonald. Yet what prompted the editorial was a sense of being forgotten by his British comrades and resentment at the *Herald* taking credit that ought to have gone to the *Irish Worker* for championing Mann in 1911. The same editorial included a savage attack on James 'Slimy' Sexton for endorsing a new dock registration scheme intended to phase out casualism. Many dockers liked the freedom that went with casualism, and feared that registration would be used to victimise militants and control the workforce. Ostensibly, Jim was identifying with the Merseyside syndicalists, and critics of the scheme, who included Pete Larkin, had excerpts from the editorial reprinted in the handbill *What's This* and distributed in Liverpool. Sexton sued the author, John T. Mitchell, for libel.[10] But what provoked the attack on Sexton was the fact that the NUDL had recently held its annual congress in Drogheda, uncomfortably close to Jim's patch. In reality, Jim was less engaged with British syndicalists. In contrast with 1911, the *Irish Worker*'s coverage of the 'great unrest' was relatively subdued, a little quizzical and querulous, and intent on keeping it at arm's length. In May the Port of London Authority took on the NTWF over the right to employ non-unionists. There was talk of a national dock strike. 'To those gentlemen who know everything,' counselled the *Irish Worker*, 'may we say that the General Strike is not coming off. When things are ready for a General Strike, there will be no need for a General Strike. There is a partial or local strike in London, and, in the words of Asquith, "wait and see".' The national strike began in June, and ended in disaster in August. The *Irish Worker* offered a terse and sober obituary: 'Let their defeat be a warning and an inspiration to the workers here in Ireland.'[11]

Larkin's preference for means other than strikes, and spending money on things other than strikes, explains his preoccupation with the National Insurance Act. Though he complained that 'without Medical Benefits [it] was practically of no use to them in Ireland', the Act provided for a time-limited dole and insurance in the event of sickness, disablement, maternity, or confinement to a sanitorium to those in approved societies. The ITGWU was one of only nine trade unions in Ireland to establish an approved society and another official, W. P. Partridge, was engaged to work in the insurance section. Some were bemused that the dangerous syndicalist went to inordinate lengths to advertise the benefits of the Act in union recruitment.[12] By contrast, Larkin was amused, and the *Irish Worker* published a parody of the 'Charge of the Light Brigade', entitled 'Charge of the 'sick' hundred'.

> Homeward those sick ones went, with money to pay the rent, Which Lloyd George had kindly lent, Happy Sick Hundred! And tho' they're badly crushed, Into the pub, they rushed, later with faces flushed, Homeward they went.[13]

He saw no contradiction. State insurance complimented his ambition to make the ITGWU a social power, and he hoped the union might develop its own health services. Coincidentally, Georges Sorel, the French theorist of syndicalism, commended the British dockers' unions for introducing mortality benefits on the grounds that it was difficult for them to flourish on the basis of wage militancy alone.[14] Connolly too defended Larkin's position against objections from British socialists. The ITGWU's second rulebook was another opportunity missed to apply industrial unionism within the union, and confirmed Larkin's aversion to internal democracy. It differed politically from the first only in that the reference to compulsory arbitration was deleted at Connolly's suggestion, though Larkin would hardly have agreed had he not been confident in the ITGWU's better bargaining position.[15]

From 1911 Larkin took a serious interest in the idea of building a working-class counter-culture in the unions, and making the unions the embryo of a new society. The provenance of his thinking in this respect is not certain, though the possibilities are obvious. Embedding politics in a social and cultural project had attracted him since his days with the Clarion fellowship, his opposition to capitalism was always fundamentally moral, and syndicalists attached an importance to moral transformation. For Sorel, it was of supreme relevance: 'it is inexact to say that the social question is a moral question [but] economic transformations cannot be realised if the workers have not acquired a superior level of moral culture.'[16] Syndicalists sought to nurture a culture that would counter capitalist individualism, bond workers and their families with trade unions, and foster self-reliance, solidarity, fraternity, and caring. Larkin believed that small, ordinary things could make a big difference, open a window on life under socialism, and demonstrate that socialism was sensible and practical. In addition to the *Irish Worker*'s coverage of sport, he organised two football teams and a boxing club.[17] His own moral outlook had a puritanical streak. He invoked God, condemned vice, and excoriated William Martin 'Ananias' Murphy's papers for their titillating coverage of divorce cases, 'immoral literature', and 'filth'.[18] One intriguing ad in the *Irish Worker* promoted 'a lecture [to be] delivered by a woman who is able to deal with matters concerning human relationships. All wives and daughters of the readers, and those women who read 'The Worker', are earnestly invited to attend. Music, song and the truth'.[19] Temperance made him very popular with workers' wives; O'Brien noted that the ITGWU's participation in a temperance parade on 4 October 1911 was the 'talk of the town'. That Christmas, the union laid on a breakfast for 80 sandwichmen, and dinner and toys for 500 children. Greaves commented cryptically: 'It would be a cynic who would suggest that these good deeds were performed in view of the municipal elections in January' in which Larkin was to be a candidate.[20] In the 1930s Larkin would become adept at combining union benefaction and his political career. But there is no doubt about his genuine ambition to broaden the ambit of trade unionism, and his workerism was all the more impressive for his refusal to romanticise workers. Daniel Corkery 'never heard him speak to the class for which he stood that he did not half offend them by dwelling on the failings which kept them powerless and timid'.[21] He could be equally impatient with bad workmanship.

After 1911, Larkin had the resources to act in earnest. In February 1912, he took the unusual step for a small, unskilled union of moving the ITGWU's head office from two 'sparsely furnished' rented rooms at 10 Beresford Place to the former Northumberland Hotel, 18 Beresford Place. The Hall was opened formally on Sunday 3 March.[22] Who christened it Liberty Hall is unclear. Greaves suggests that Larkin lifted the name from a passing reference in Captain Marryat's popular tale of the British navy in the Napoleonic wars, *Mr Midshipman Easy*, which sounds plausible, given Larkin's English boyhood and maritime associations, but the term featured also in a variety of plays, operas, novels and history books as a synonym for a place of equality and freedom, and was given to quite a few American institutes of public service. In addition to housing the ITGWU, the IWWU, and the local NSFU, Liberty Hall was intended to be a cultural power-house and social centre, open seven days a week, 10 am to 10 pm, and offered rooms for the ITGWU's two bands, Irish classes, the Irish Workers' Choir, the Juvenile and Adult Dancers, and the Workers' Dramatic Society. Football clubs and 'any other working-class societies requiring rooms' were invited to call on the caretaker. Delia had formed the choir in February and coached the players in her Workers' Dramatic Society, which made its debut on 26 December with four one-act plays, directed by Patrick Wilson.[23] 'With the exception, perhaps, of the Maison du Peuple in Brussels', editorialised the *Manchester Guardian*, 'no Labour head-quarters in Europe has contributed so valuably to the brightening of the lives of the hard-driven workers around it . . . It is a hive of social life . . .'[24] 'Two well-known seats of learning', quipped Connolly when the London *Times* mentioned Liberty Hall and Trinity College in the same breath.[25]

Similar use was made of a headquarters for the Inchicore branch, which Larkin acquired in October 1912 and christened 'Emmet Hall'. Partridge was appointed manager, with instructions to open the hall to all unions and trade unionists and their families only. Partridge established a temperance association, and inaugurated classes in typing and book-keeping, concerts, céilís, aeríochtaí, and sports activities. From 1914 to 1916, the hall was used for drilling by the Citizen Army.[26] Along with the union's annual excursion, a summer camp was introduced, and the idea inspired Croydon Park. Renting Croydon Park house and three acres of grounds in Fairview as a 'pleasure home of the workers', at £20 per month, was one of Larkin's most imaginative ventures.[27] The festivities started on Sunday 3 August 1913 with a cavalcade of 'side-cars and common cars, drags, four-in-hands, and coal lorries' from Liberty Hall to a picnic in Blanchardstown. Croydon Park centre was opened officially the next day with a 'Grand temperance fête and children's carnival'.[28] Larkin explained the idea to a Liverpool audience:

> We have our own park of 162 acres [*sic*], our own vinery [*sic?*] and gardens, and we bring our women and men down there on Sunday or Saturday afternoon and teach the boys and girls how to cultivate the garden, and show them the beauty of life in its full expression. They play football too [he was in Liverpool] and no-one is allowed to come who is not either in the union or the wife of a worker . . . We make our family life focus around the union . . .[29]

The way in which Larkin envisaged little, everyday things making a big change was captured by 'Euchan', Wilson's pseudonym, in the *Irish Worker*:

> To watch a dock labourer walk into a mansion, saunter into the dining-room and proceed to put a tuppence doorstep sandwich and a penny bottle of minerals out of sight without the slightest air of surprise at his surroundings struck me as the most revolutionary sight I ever saw in my life . . .[30]

Larkin made his own contribution to the revolution by appearing without a collar. The project was very dear to his heart.

HOME RULE FOR LABOUR AND ONE BIG UNION

In January 1912, Larkin was one of seven candidates of the 'Dublin Labour Party', as the trades council's Labour Representation Committee was now called, to contest the elections to the 80-member Dublin Corporation. The party's manifesto demanded the employment of direct labour and municipal workshops for the manufacture of clothing; improvements in housing; mental and physical improvement through the provision of recreational amenities;

admission of the public to meetings of all public boards and evening sittings of
the Corporation; municipal ownership of gas and tramways; and the enforce-
ment of regulations concerning public health, weights and measures, and
inspection of food and factories. Larkin was one of five Labour men to be
elected, with a resounding 1,190 votes in the North Dock ward, a majority of
789 over the outgoing Nationalist, C. L. Ryan.[31] The triumph was cut short by
a legal challenge involving Ryan's personation agent. E. W. Stewart, who continued to snap at Larkin's heels and went so far as to publish what he considered
an expose, *The History of Larkinism in Ireland*, in 1912. The courts eventually
ruled that the 1910 conviction debarred Larkin from sitting on the Corporation
for seven years and fined him £5, and he lost his Corporation seat in late
March. Larkin blamed William Martin Murphy for instigating and financing
the petition against him.[32] Murphy's *Irish Independent* had run a scurrilous
campaign against 'the socialists' during the hustings. Despite this setback
Larkin took an assertive position on Home Rule and continued to push his
two strategic objectives, an Irish Labour party and industrial unionism.

The Government of Ireland bill was introduced to parliament on 11 April.
The *Irish Worker* greeted it on 13 April, before quoting Parnell's *dictum*: 'No
man! has the right to fix the Boundary to the March of a Nation', and listing a
series of misgivings about its proposed parliament. Larkin described it as 'unjust
and inadequate and . . . refused to accept it as final' at a meeting of Dublin
trades council on 22 April, and got the council to reject a motion of protest at
its exclusion from a Home Rule convention sponsored by the United Irish
League. While welcoming devolution as a step in the right direction, he took
particular exception to the suggestion of 'guarantees for Ulster', and a nominated senate. He also condemned the exclusion of women from the franchise
in the bill.[33]

The ITUC got its first opportunity to respond to the bill at its annual
congress in Clonmel Town Hall on 27–29 May. The apparent imminence of
Home Rule promised a profound change in the political landscape and there
was a giddy sense of history in the making about the delegates. The weather
too was exceptionally summery, though not matched by the mood of the
manageress at Magner's Hotel as Larkin checked in on Sunday night. 'I am
nervous about taking you in,' she told him. After breakfast, Larkin found that
rumours were prevalent of a riot at the Congress rally on Tuesday evening.[34]
The preliminary speeches in the Town Hall were careful to echo the nationalist proclivities of most delegates without endorsing the principle of the Home
Rule bill. The prospect of Home Rule was probably the major factor in tipping
the scales in favour of an Irish Labour party. On the first day of the proceedings,
Connolly moved a carefully worded proposal 'That the independent representation of Labour upon all public boards be, and is hereby, included amongst

the objects of this Congress . . .' With Home Rule in the bag, as it seemed, he didn't need to polemicise against the Walkerite policy of backing the British Labour Party and simply stressed the need to have worker representation in the College Green parliament. At Connolly's request, O'Brien stood aside to give a colleague from Belfast the honour of seconding the motion.[35] Larkin was third on his feet: 'They were not humbugged in the least,' he said, 'by people who said that Home Rule meant the millenium, but they believed that Home Rule would give them an opportunity of expressing themselves physically and mentally (applause). They should be ready to do their own work . . . [It] would be too late,' he concluded, 'to prepare when the battle note was struck (applause).' Some old Walkerites agreed, and it was a feeble opposition that came from other Ulster and amalgamated delegates. The only controversy arose from the customary personal attack on Larkin, which sidetracked the debate. After the discussion resumed on Tuesday, the motion was passed by 49–18 votes.[36]

It was unfortunate for Larkin's place in history that it was Connolly's motion, as it created the historical impression that Connolly founded the Labour Party. It was Connolly's first Congress, and he was there as one of Larkin's lieutenants, albeit one with a good reputation as a socialist propagandist. Larkin had called for an Irish party at the Congresses of 1910 and 1911. He had made the movement that breasted the tape in 1912. It was unfortunate too for the symmetry of Labour myth that it was not the two giants who had jointly proposed the motion. Connolly had not read the script of history.

Later in the day, Larkin opened the debate on the Home Rule bill. Formally, Congress confined itself to specifics, chiefly the schedules for constituency representation. The bill envisaged a 40-member Senate and a 164-member House of Commons, elected from constituencies based on Dublin University, the six-county boroughs, and the 32 counties, subdivided in most cases on a geographical basis. Some divisions in Dublin city, Belfast, and Cork city would return three, four, or five MPs, and the others one or two, giving a total of two university seats, 34 urban seats, and 128 rural seats.[37] Larkin proposed that urban areas be grouped in separate constituencies to ensure representation for industrial workers. After excoriating farmers and how 'Having got the land they turned round and dealt out farmers' justice to the men who had helped them', he declared:

> If the towns did not get adequate representation in the new Parliament they would be far worse off under a nominal Home Rule than under an alien Government because they would be under a few people ruling the country in a more vicious manner than it had been ruled. He said that as one who was a Home Ruler by birth, training and conviction (applause).

He caught the mood of the delegates perfectly, in most of whose hearts the expectation that Home Rule would strengthen Labour was qualified by fear of a farmer-dominated parliament. It set the tone for the Congress response to the bill. Larkin went on to propose a second motion, calling for the franchise to apply to men and women equally, and for the state to pay elected members, candidates' expenses, and returning officers' fees.[38] That evening, Larkin was the star speaker at the public rally, and delighted with the reception. No riot materialised, and the only trouble came from a few hecklers who asked about 'the money we stole in Cork'. At the close of the meeting, preceded by a pipe band, Larkin was carried on the shoulders of two local stalwarts to the Workingmen's Boat Club, where a sing-song – he liked these 'real Irish nights' – continued into the small hours.[39]

Larkin may have left the Labour Party business to Connolly because he had a bigger plan. Disturbed at the mobilisation of his 'native' Ulster against Home Rule, he saw it not merely as a means of uniting all grades of worker, but of binding the north and south. Two days earlier, he had informed ITGWU excursionists at the Faythe in Wexford:

> He was going to Clonmel, if God willed it, to do what he believed was God's work. They were going to light a torch in Clonmel which would set fire every thinking man in the country and make him unite with his fellows so that Ireland would be theirs in very few years . . . Tomorrow they were going to advocate one society for Ireland for skilled and unskilled workers, so that when a skilled man is struck at, out comes every unskilled man, and when an unskilled worker is struck at, he will be supported by the skilled tradesmen (cheers).[40]

And on the third day of the Congress he rose to move that 'a closer union should exist between the various trades and labour bodies in Ireland', and to this end the Parliamentary Committee should be instructed to draw up a constitution for 'an Irish Federation of Trades'. 'It was,' he said, 'true industrial unionism. The body he spoke of should be the one to rule trade unionism in Ireland.'[41] J. H. Bennett was the seconder. Bennett's union, the NSFU, was British, but the Dublin branch was 'subject absolutely to the control of James Larkin', in the reproving words of its general secretary, Havelock Wilson.[42] Other British unions were not so accommodating, and, as usual, provided the opposition. 'The employers were organised in a world-wide organisation (hear, hear), and Mr Larkin now wanted the workers to confine themselves to Ireland alone,' said James McCarron. 'If this resolution was passed his Society or any other amalgamated Society would not send their delegates to any future Irish Trades Congress (hear, hear).' The scheme was rejected by 29–23 votes. The amalgamateds still had a majority in Congress, accounting for 46 delegates, compared to 26 from Irish unions – including eight from the ITGWU and Delia from the IWWU – and 15 from trades councils. Larkin had better luck in the hustings for the Parliamentary Committee, and was elected chairman of a committee which was entirely Larkinite, with the exception of Mary Galway. His buoyancy at the close of proceedings was reflected in his proposal that the Congress accept an invitation to meet in Cork in 1913. Knowing his opponents associated Cork with the rout of 1909, he struck a defiant note: 'He, personally, would be very glad to renew acquaintance with the men of Cork. They had been beaten there once, but they could not expect to win every time, and they would win there again (hear, hear).'[43]

CHAIRMAN OF THE PARLIAMENTARY COMMITTEE

Traditionally, the role of chairman of the Parliamentary Committee was to preside over the Committee's quarterly meetings, and ensure that Congress resolutions were pursued with the relevant cabinet ministers, MPs, and public bodies. Larkin was more pro-active, leading deputations to the IPP, Westminster, and the British Labour Party's annual conference. He was unfortunate that it was not a good year – when was it ever? – for the ITUC's legislative programme. The Parliamentary Committee ultimately reported 'many and serious disappointments', notably in relation to the National Insurance Act and the Osborne Judgment.[44] The latter, given by the Law Lords in 1909, prevented unions from funding political parties. The unions – in Britain, and by extension in Ireland – deplored the judgement as an unwarranted intrusion in their affairs, and wanted it completely reversed, as the Taff Vale decision had been. The government offered legislation to enable unions to maintain political funds, provided members approved in a ballot and dissentients were allowed to 'contract out'. Eventually the government had its way in the Trade Union Act (1913). Ironically, Larkin would invoke the Act in his legal action against the ITGWU in 1923–4. Larkin was unfortunate too that history has highlighted Connolly's disgust with his failure to advance the development of the Irish Labour Party. And it is true that Larkin was given to prioritise his own interests, and that his bull-headed style was sometimes counterproductive.

Larkin's major legislative concern was with the National Insurance Act; the failure of the government to extend its medical provisions to Ireland and give Irish trade unions representation on the commission supervising the operation of the Act; the anomaly that Irish-based members of amalgamated societies were not entitled to the same medical benefits as their brothers in Britain; the possibility – and threat from an Irish union perspective – that Irish-based members of amalgamateds might become eligible for medical benefits; and the fear that 'interested persons', such as the Ancient Order of Hibernians or employers' provident funds, would form approved societies to 'cripple' the unions. In July 1912 he led the Parliamentary Committee to meet John Redmond, Joe Devlin, and John Dillon, in Dublin's Gresham Hotel. Opening the discussion with the Insurance Act, he went on to urge amendments to the Government of Ireland bill to ensure fair representation for Labour and full adult suffrage, demand protection for workers recently expelled from their employments by loyalists in Belfast, and, in the light of the recent *Titanic* disaster, appeal for adequate life-saving apparatus on ships. Other Committee members spoke on the railway bill, wage rates, government contracts in Ireland, reforms to the Truck Act and the Shop Act, and the extension of the Feeding of Necessitous School Children Act to Ireland. Redmond promised favourable consideration on all points except the Insurance Act.

Larkin and P. T. Daly, as secretary of the Parliamentary Committee, then went to London to seek an interview with the Prime Minister, H. H. Asquith, on the Insurance Act, but got no further than the Financial Secretary to the Treasury. They then discussed the Congress legislative agenda with the committee of the British Labour Party. The British promised assistance and agreed to raise the Belfast expulsions in the House of Commons. But the outcome was marred by a dispute in the letters page of the *Freeman's Journal* when the British Labour Party challenged the veracity of Daly's report of the discussion. Relations between the ITUC and the British party became testy over the next 12 months. In August, Daly reiterated the ITUC's grievances in a letter to Redmond. Subsequently, a parliamentary question on the schedules of the Government of Ireland bill was put to the Chief Secretary for Ireland, Augustine Birrell, who replied that he had received the resolutions of the ITUC and could not agree to any change.[45]

Chairing the Parliamentary Committee did not come easily to Larkin. He made a terrible start at the first quarterly meeting in August in Dublin's Trades Hall when he resigned after O'Brien challenged a ruling from the chair with the backing of the rest of the Committee. O'Brien implies that the dispute was motivated by Larkin's wish to obstruct the creation of a Labour party. The incident was covered up.[46] The Committee pretended that Larkin was still chairman, and so too did Larkin when it suited him. Already dismayed that nothing had been done since the Clonmel Congress, Connolly was appalled at the implications for the proposed Labour Party, and urged O'Brien to call a public meeting in Dublin. Larkin supported O'Brien's call on Dublin trades council on 12 August, and then refused to be on the platform.[47] So too did Connolly, for very different reasons. In a letter to O'Brien on 13 September he poured out his resentment of Larkin, and offered astute advice on how to handle a man who had become so indispensable:

Your very distressing letter just arrived. I begin to fear that our friend Jim has arrived at his highest elevation, and that he will pull us all down with him in his fall. He does not seem to want a democratic Labour movement; he seems to want a Larkinite movement only. The situation will require the most delicate handling. I would have been in favour of cancelling the Antient Concert [Rooms] fixture, of informing Larkin that as he will not attend, you do not see your way to go on with it, and that pending and awaiting his co-operation you feel it unwise to go forward with the movement. This seems tame and slavish advice, and it is, I fear, the only way to get him on the move again. He must rule, or will not work, and in the present stage of the labour movement he has us at this mercy. And he knows it, and is using his power unscrupulously, I regret to say. We can but bow our head, and try and avert the storm.

It is impossible that I should be there. He would have too much of a grip on me, as he would be able to appeal to my own members against me, on the plea that I neglected my duty to go there against his wish . . .

I am sick of all this playing to one man, but am prepared to advise it for the sake of the movement.[48]

Connolly did not exaggerate how petty and jealous Larkin could be, though neither did he concede that his own record in politics and trade unionism bore no comparison with Big Jim's. On 16 September Larkin arrived late at the Antient Concert Rooms, pointedly wearing an anonymous flat cap rather than his trademark 'wide-awake', and sat with a group of dockers near the door. When called on to speak, he confounded the audience with an irrelevant denunciation of the Union Jack. Some anti-Larkinites were intent on causing trouble of their own, and one James Farrell accused Larkin of grabbing him by the throat and throwing him out of the meeting. The dispute went to court in October. Farrell admitted to being a friend of the right-wing Labourite E. L. Richardson, and to having a long-standing beef against Larkin for having subscribed to the expansion of the *Irish Worker* and not receiving his money back. Daly and others testified that Larkin had never taken his hands out of his pockets. The judge sent the case to a jury trial.[49]

Trades councils were advised of the party project, but little progress was made until the 1914 Congress. Stress may explain Larkin's contrariness. Unusually, he later claimed to have been ill, and apologised.[50] It may be too that disbarment from public office had soured his interest in politics. But it's more likely that jealousy and an inability to be conciliar made him slyly intent on playing the wrecker. He continued to emphasise the value of politics in the *Irish Worker*, promote candidates of the Dublin Labour Party in local elections, and, through the Parliamentary Committee, address the question of new relations with the British Labour Party, which were transformed by the decision to create an Irish Labour party. But it was one thing to help lesser men onto Dublin Corporation. It was another to assist those greater in some respects than himself to create a national structure to which he would be made accountable.

Larkin and Daly encountered another embarrassment when they sought to address the British Labour Party's annual conference in London in January 1913, hoping to speak for the ITUC on representation under the Government of Ireland bill, and the National Insurance Act and the Feeding of Necessitous School Children Act. Denied a hearing, they leafleted delegates to attend a public meeting where they put their case. The British pleaded that they had not followed due process with the Standing Orders Committee. An indignant Parliamentary Committee thought its chairman and secretary ought to have been shown more respect.[51]

The frustration began to take its toll. On 22 March O'Brien sent another gloomy post to Connolly on the recent meeting of the Parliamentary Committee;

> Things are in a very bad way still. We requested Larkin to reconsider his decision to resign the Chairmanship, but he flatly refuses to do so, and moveover he states that he will not even be a delegate to the Congress. We believe he means this too. All his principal supporters here have appealed to him to give way and consent to go, but he is adamant and won[']t budge an inch. He says he'll go to Cork to [the] Transport Union Conference and hold a public meeting, but won[']t touch the Congress . . .
>
> We hear that there is to be a big fight put up against us in Cork. We are told that a record number of delegates will attend from Cork City, and that there is to be a whip up of all the 'old gang' from all parts of the country. [D. R.] Campbell, Daly, Larkin, and myself are at all cost to be removed from the PC [Parliamentary Committee]. [James] McCarron, I have reason to believe, will be one of the big guns against us. He was a member of the PC from its inception to 1910, and up to that year always come out on top. If Larkin does not attend we must run you for the PC, and then there will be some hope of getting work done. The whole year has been wasted and absolutely nothing to show for it.[52]

The damning verdict on Larkin's tenure may have been the source of O'Brien's initiative to get the Parliamentary Committee revamped at the next Congress.

In the heel of the hunt, Larkin did attend the Congress, which opened in Cork City Hall on 12 May. Travelling south on the train, endlessly relighting his pipe – there is no doubt about his love of strikes in that respect – he fretted about the residue of animosity among local trade unionists, willingly sustained in the Crosbie press, and talk of how he'd be 'kicked through the streets'. He had declined to sign the Parliamentary Committee's annual report and shrank from delivering the chairman's address, passing the buck to a nervous O'Brien.

It was probably guilt about the 1909 debacle that induced the anxiety; one couldn't accuse Larkin of cowardice. Public meetings on Grand Parade and in Queenstown went ahead and Jim and Pete spoke with little of the anticipated disruption. Nonetheless Jim found it bruising, and complained subsequently of 'a rather severe campaign carrying the truth [to] the misguided men of Cork'.[53] The Congress itself went well, and put him in better form. Proposing the vote of thanks for O'Brien's address, he lauded his future nemesis as 'heart and soul with the labour movement . . . as thorough an Irishman as could be found the world over, and for courage, honour and honesty he was well worthy of the great name he bore (loud applause)'.[54] He also seconded O'Brien's motion to give greater effect and continuity to the Parliamentary Committee. The incoming Committee was instructed to draft a new constitution and pursue, among other things, the creation of a Labour party. Larkin suggested Ulster be guaranteed representation on the Committee, but did not press the point.[55] He spoke frequently, was again returned to a Larkinite Parliamentary Committee, and received the rare honour of a second term in the chair. Delia too had put her name forward for the Parliamentary Committee, but withdrew it. As O'Brien predicted, there was a bigger Cork contingent at the Congress. Two Corkmen won seats on the Committee, but the 'old gang' fared badly at the hustings, and it seemed that the ITUC was more Larkinite than ever. When W. J. McNulty, NUDL branch secretary in Derry, sarcastically congratulated the delegates on choosing a 'scab' Committee, he was unanimously expelled from the Congress at Connolly's request.[56]

The Parliamentary Committee was directed to pursue its grievances with the British Labour Party and, at a meeting in the House of Commons on 15 July, Larkin finally got to put his complaints to senior Labour MPs on the schedules of the Government of Ireland bill, and the failure to extend the Feeding of Necessitous School Children Act and the medical sections of the National Insurance Act to Ireland. The British party, he claimed, was reluctant to act for the ITUC and happy to take counsel on Ireland from the IPP. The criticisms were valid. MacDonald had separately conceded to Belfast trades council that Labour's hands on legislation were tied by 'a firm bargain' between the IPP and the government, and implied that if the Irish voted for the IPP, they had to accept the consequences.[57]

But Larkin's blunt, curmudgeonly style won him no favours, and he was offering the British nothing in return for assistance. Arthur Henderson, who would lead his party from 1914 to 1922, repudiated the allegations. MacDonald and Keir Hardie were more conciliatory, saying these misunderstandings showed the need for closer liaison between them.[58] That the British wanted a quid pro quo is evident in relation to the thorny problem of the finances of the Irish Labour Party. The Irish demanded the remittance of monies paid by Irish members of British-based unions. It was agreed to defer the matter to a second conference, held in the library of the Trades Hall, Dublin on 6 September. Larkin's absence on this occasion made a resolution no easier, and indicated the extent to which his separatist mentality had become widespread. The British cited various difficulties about the remittance of monies, but Henderson – revealing his national pride – made it plain that were the Irish party to accept a subordinate status to the British party on matters pertaining to the UK as a whole, then 'it would be quite easy to find a solution to the money question'.[59] The Irish replied that their party would be absolutely independent. The issue remained unresolved.

STRIKES AND STRESS

The strain began to tell on Larkin in 1913. An improvement of trade and rising prices contributed to a growth of strikes, with 30 in Dublin alone between January and August. The ITGWU itself was involved in only two major disputes, one with the City of Dublin Steam Packet Company beginning in January, and a violent, generalised strike in Sligo beginning in March.[60] But almost any militancy had become synonymous with Larkin, and he was vilified in the press as its instigator. Though he dished out worse himself, he found abuse distressful, especially from his own kind, and a curiosity of anti-Larkinism was the procession of renegade Labourites who lined up to traduce him. Even O'Brien was moved to pity:

> The misrepresentation in the press is cruel and has a very bad effect on [Larkin's] members, I greatly fear. Scarcely a day passes but the *Independent* contains an attack of some kind, and the *Telegraph*, which up to 9 months ago was not so bad, is even worse because it has ten times the influence of Murphy's rag. How it will all end 'tis hard to say. Larkin is looking and feeling bad lately and if the strain is not eased soon I fear he will break down mentally and physically. He must be made of iron to stand it so long.[61]

The pressure may account for Larkin's editorial in the *Irish Worker* of 26 April, which was headed 'Open letter to the people: how to stop strikes', though his sentiments were entirely consistent with previous appeals, and with his view of strikes as 'a damnable but necessary evil at present'. Beginning with an acceptance that employers want profits and workers need employment, he urged that readers consider his letter impartially, without 'personal antagonism'. His scheme proposed that if workers' demands were rejected by an employer, they be submitted to a Trade Wages board, made up of an equal number of representatives from employers and workers. If the Trade Wages Board could not find a solution, the issue would be referred to a City Wages board, comprised of five employers and five workers. An employer or union which refused to accept the arbitration of the City Wages Board was to receive no help from other employers or unions. He also proposed a right to a closed shop in cases where unions recruited 80 per cent of the workforce. Concluding, he asked employers to weigh up the scheme as a commercial proposition, 'forgetting the proposer', and promised to elaborate on the cause and effect of strikes in the following week. His mood must have changed, as the next editorial was a 'Manifesto to Dublin labourers' on how to raise their hourly rate from 4 1/2d to 6d.

May brought a succession of good news. On 6th, the ITGWU secured an excellent settlement in Sligo. On 26th, the shipping strike ended with an agreement with the City of Dublin Steam Packet Company and five other firms providing for improved wages, a conciliation board, and one month's notice of future strikes.[62] The implicit concession of sympathetic action in return for recognition of the ITGWU promised a new equilibrium in industrial relations. In July, on the suggestion of Archbishop Walsh, the Lord Mayor convened talks with Dublin Chamber of Commerce and Dublin trades council to set up a conciliation board.[63]

Nonetheless, Larkin's health continued to deteriorate. One day he would be despondent, the next exhilarated. Speaking at the Dublin Labour Day demonstration on 22 May, he explained that his voice would not carry so well as he was 'under adverse difficulties' and had yet to recover from his campaign in Cork.[64] O'Brien finally persuaded him to see a doctor, who found his constitution 'very much run down' and prescribed a rest from speaking.[65] It was a paradoxical condition, and not physical alone. Larkin's stress and energy fed on each other. Success merely exacerbated his insecurity. He had a narrow escape from injury in a tragic incident on 1 July. Leaving the Trades Hall – though it was after midnight, he had been working – he was drawn to a crowd gathered before a blaze at 29 Capel Street. When he spotted a tenant, the 64-year-old George Fields, still in the building, he broke into the premises and rushed to the top of the stairs, where old Mr Fields stood in his nightshirt: 'All right Jim,' he said calmly, 'wait till I get some clothes on'. 'Damn your clothes, come with me,' said Larkin. As Larkin descended, the stairs gave way. Fortunately, he was picked up and able to walk into the street. He then tried to scale a ladder to the top story. Firemen eventually recovered the body of Fields, suffocated by smoke.[66]

The consequences of Larkin's condition for union administration could be exasperating. As he was berating Labour MPs at Westminster on 15 July, Connolly was writing him a curt letter threatening to resign unless something was done about arrears of his clerks' salaries and monies due for insurance benefits.[67] Squeezing funds out of Liberty Hall was a chronic problem for the union's Ulster organiser and, if Connolly is to be believed, his general secretary was a bullying, tight-fisted slave-driver, querulous, demanding, and happy to take advantage of the socialist commitment of his subordinates. The pair had a stand-up row in Dublin on Larkin's return from London. Larkin's attitudes to others were often as contrary as his condition. Sitting in 'the dirt and filth of Liberty Hall . . . just for the interest of watching the man', William Orpen was struck by his modesty in handling union members. In a sketch admired by Larkinites – flattered perhaps by the attention of the distinguished portrait artist – Orpen has Larkin looking like a devoted bloodhound, serving grotesquely miserable supplicants.[68] But if the faithful hound scented a rival, he would growl, as Connolly confided to O'Brien on 29 July:

> I don't think I can stand Larkin as boss much longer. He is simply unbearable. He is forever snarling at me and drawing comparisons between what he accomplished in Belfast in 1907, and what I have done . . . He is consumed with jealousy and hatred of anyone who will not cringe to him and beslaver him all over.[69]

In fairness, it is Connolly's side of the story that was preserved, carefully, by O'Brien. Another perspective is given in Jack Carney's fiercely partisan and often unreliable memoir. Like Seán O'Casey, Carney could not avoid traducing Connolly when exalting his hero. Working with the ITGWU in Belfast, Carney alleged that the branch accumulated a debt of £800 'due to Connolly spending more time concerning himself with political issues . . .'

> . . . Larkin came and addressed an emergency meeting of the Belfast branch. He made a bitter attack on the Belfast members for allowing the Dublin members to carry them on their backs. The members complained that they were being neglected and Larkin turned on Connolly and told him to attend his Union duties first. Larkin then ordered a levy of 6d a month on all members of the Belfast branch until their debt to the Union was settled. I never saw a man so abused as was Connolly on this occasion . . .[70]

For all that, Larkin does seem to have had a particular problem with Connolly, who clearly had a problem with him. Sources other than Connolly and O'Brien attest that Larkin was insecure, volatile, jealous, and stressed, and knew of only one coping strategy. On 8 June, he had launched a campaign for the recruitment of farm labourers in County Dublin.[71] The tramwaymen were next.

NOTES

1　Cited in Francis Devine, *Organising History: A Centenary of SIPTU, 1909–2009* (Dublin, 2009), p. 888.

2　See ITGWU, *Fifty Years of Liberty Hall: The Golden Jubilee of the Irish Transport and General Workers' Union, 1909–1959* (Dublin, 1959), photo facing p. 24.

3　*Derry Journal*, 30 May 1911.

4　*Irish Worker*, 30 March 1912; John Cunningham, *Labour in the West of Ireland: Working Life and Struggle, 1890–1914* (Belfast, 1995), pp. 156–8; Denis Carroll, *They Have Fooled You Again: Michael O'Flanagan (1876–1942), Priest, Republican, Social Critic* (Dublin, 1993), pp. 22–3.

5　*Irish Worker*, 23 March, 6 April, 4 May, 8 June 1912; Michael Enright, *Men of Iron: Wexford Foundry Disputes 1890 & 1911* (Wexford, 1987), pp. 38–40; C. Desmond Greaves, *The Irish Transport and General Workers' Union: The Formative Years, 1909–1923* (Dublin, 1982), p. 72.

6　Greaves, *The Irish Transport and General Workers' Union*, pp. 78–9. The recalcitrant stevedore, Matthew Long, won compensation against Larkin for the blacking. See *Irish Independent*, 3 December 1912, 24–25 April 1913.

7　Industrial Council, *Report of the Industrial Council of the British Board of Trade on Its Inquiry into Industrial Agreements: August 18, 1913* (1913, reprinted Memphis, TN, 2010), pp. 1–2.

8　Elie Halevy, *A History of the English People in the Nineteenth Century, VI: The Rule of Democracy, 1905–1914 (Book II)* (London, 1952), p. 477.

9　British Parliamentary Papers, 'Minutes of evidence taken before the Industrial Council in connection with their enquiry into industrial agreements' (Cd.6953, 1913), pp. 245–8.

10　Eric Taplin, *The Dockers' Union: A Study of the National Union of Dock Labourers, 1889–1922* (Leicester, 1986), pp. 112–14.

11　*Irish Worker*, 25 May, 10 August 1912.

12　UUMC, ITUC, *Annual Report* (1913), p. 4; *Irish Worker*, 24 February 1912; Mel Cousins, 'The creation of association: the National Insurance Act, 1911 and approved societies in Ireland', in Jennifer Kelly and R. V. Comerford (eds), *Associational Culture in Ireland and Abroad* (Dublin, 2010), p. 160; George Dangerfield, *The Strange Death of Liberal England* (London, 1983 edn), pp. 279–80.

13　*Irish Worker*, 26 April 1913.

14　John L. Stanley, *From Georges Sorel: Essays in Socialism and Philosophy* (New Brunswick, NJ, 1987), p. 84.

15　Donal Nevin (ed.), *Between Comrades: James Connolly, Letters and Correspondence 1889–1916* (Dublin, 2007), p. 492; Greaves, *The Irish Transport and General Workers' Union*, pp. 82–3; NLI, William O'Brien papers, 15679(18).

16　Cited in Stanley, *From Georges Sorel*, p. 90.

17　Emmet Larkin, 'James Larkin, Labour leader', in Donal Nevin (ed.), *James Larkin: Lion of the Fold* (Dublin, 1998), p. 5.

18　*Irish Worker*, 21 October, 11 November 1911, 17 August 1912.

19　Ibid., 29 March 1913.

20　Greaves, *The Irish Transport and General Workers' Union*, p. 70.

21　Donal Nevin, 'Writers on Larkin', in Nevin (ed.), *James Larkin*, p. 391.

22　*Irish Worker*, 2 March 1912.

23   Greaves, *The Irish Transport and General Workers' Union*, pp. 72, 82, 343–4; ITGWU, *Fifty Years of Liberty Hall*, p. 16; *Irish Worker*, 1 June 1912; Theresa Moriarty, 'Delia Larkin: relative obscurity', in Nevin (ed.), *James Larkin*, pp. 431–2.

24   Reprinted in the *Irish Worker*, 22 November 1913.

25   William O'Brien, *Forth the Banners Go: The Reminiscences of William O'Brien as Told to Edward MacLysaght, D.Litt* (Dublin, 1969), p. 255.

26   Hugh Geraghty, *William Patrick Partridge and His Times* (Dublin, 2003), pp. 147, 153–4.

27   The rent is cited in NLI, William O'Brien papers, 15676(2), part 2.

28   *Irish Worker*, 9 August 1913.

29   *Liverpool Daily Post and Mercury*, 2 December 1913, cited in Bob Holton, *British Syndicalism, 1900–1914: Myth and Realities* (London, 1976), p. 188.

30   *Irish Worker*, 9 August 1913.

31   Ibid., 22 December 1911, 20 January 1912.

32   Greaves, *The Irish Transport and General Workers' Union*, p. 71; Séamus Cody, John O'Dowd, and Peter Rigney, *The Parliament of Labour: 100 Years of the Dublin Council of Trade Unions* (Dublin, 1986), pp. 90–1.

33   UUMC, Dublin trades council minutes, 22 April, 3, 17 June 1912.

34   *Irish Worker*, 1 June 1912.

35   Letter from James Connolly to Heron, *Irish Times*, 22 June 2012.

36   UUMC, ITUC, *Annual Report* (1912), pp. 12–19.

37   UUMC, ITUC, *Annual Report* (1914), pp. 27–30.

38   UUMC, ITUC, *Annual Report* (1912), pp. 51–3.

39   *Irish Worker*, 1 June 1912.

40   Ibid., 8 June 1912.

41   UUMC, ITUC, *Annual Report* (1912), p. 61.

42   Statement of Havelock Wilson, November 1913, quoted in Halevy, *A History of the English People in the Nineteenth Century, VI: The Rule of Democracy, 1905–1914 (Book II)*, p. 485.

43   UUMC, ITUC, *Annual Report* (1912), pp. 61, 69–70, 77–9.

44   UUMC, ITUC, *Annual Report* (1913), p. 3.

45   Ibid., pp. 3–13.

46   O'Brien, *Forth the Banners Go*, pp. 47–8.

47   UUMC, Dublin trades council minutes, 12 August 1912.

48   ITGWU, *The Attempt to Smash the Irish Transport and General Workers' Union* (Dublin, 1924), p. 163.

49   *Freeman's Journal*, 17 September 1912; *Irish Times*, 17 September, 4 October 1912.

50   Emmet Larkin, *James Larkin: Irish Labour Leader, 1876–1947* (London, 1965), pp. 99–104.

51   UUMC, ITUC, *Annual Report* (1913), pp. 22–3, 35.

52   UUMC, William O'Brien papers, 13908(iii).

53   *Irish Worker*, 17, 31 May 1913.

54   UUMC, ITUC, *Annual Report* (1913), p. 33.

55   Ibid., pp. 38–40, 48.

56   Ibid., p. 51, 66.

57   UUMC, Belfast trades council minutes, 7 December 1911.

58   UUMC, ITUC, *Annual Report* (1914), pp. 1–4.

59   Ibid., pp. 5–6.

60 Greaves, *The Irish Transport and General Workers' Union*, pp. 84–7; on Sligo see Cunningham, *Labour in the West of Ireland*, pp. 156–72.

61 UUMC, William O'Brien papers, 13908(iii), O'Brien to Connolly, 22 March 1913,

62 Larkin, *James Larkin*, p. 115.

63 Dermot Keogh, *The Rise of the Irish Working Class: The Dublin Trade Union Movement and Labour Leadership, 1890–1914* (Belfast, 1982), p. 180.

64 *Irish Worker*, 31 May 1913.

65 Nevin (ed.), *Between Comrades*, p. 490.

66 *Dublin Saturday Post*, 5 July 1913.

67 NLI, William O'Brien papers, 15678(2), Connolly to Larkin, 15 July 1913.

68 Sir William Orpen, 'Larkin at Liberty Hall', in Nevin (ed.), *James Larkin*, p. 203; the sketch is in Larkin, *James Larkin*, facing p. 110; and WUI, *1913: Jim Larkin and the Dublin Lock-Out* (Dublin, 1964), frontispiece.

69 Nevin (ed.), *Between Comrades*, p. 494.

70 Jack Carney memoir on Larkin, written for Emmet Larkin and kindly passed on to the author; see also a letter from Carney, dated 1 May 1948, in Donal Nevin, 'Larkin and Connolly', in Nevin (ed.), *James Larkin*, pp. 395–400.

71 Greaves, *The Irish Transport and General Workers' Union*, pp. 89–90.

SEVEN

CRUSHING LARKIN, 1913

Crushing Larkin: the tycoon who saved Dublin from anarchy
Lead headline, celebrating William Martin Murphy, *Business Plus*, September 2013

—

The ITGWU first canvassed the tramwaymen in August 1911. James Larkin returned to the theme, developing an obsession with William Martin Murphy. As a hard, anti-union employer, President of Dublin Chamber of Commerce, proprietor of Independent Newspapers, the *Irish Catholic*, the Imperial Hotel, and Clery's drapery store, chairman of the Dublin United Tramway Company, and director of several railway companies, Murphy served Larkin's compulsion to put a face on the enemy. The *Irish Worker* pilloried him as a 'blood-sucking vampire', 'a soulless, money-grubbing tyrant', a 'whited sepulchre'.[1] On 26 July 1913, the paper thundered:

> You have been driven from public life as a toady, a renegade, an untruthful and dishonest politician; a false friend, a sweating employer, a weak tyrant . . . Larkin has tamed better, braver, cleaner, and honester foes than you. The gage of battle is accepted. We will drive you to defeat, or we will break your heart . . .

For all the personal spite, Larkin's motivation was to consolidate the ITGWU financially by pushing into steady employment sectors. With the end of the Dublin shipping strike, conditions seemed ripe for a qualitative leap in recruitment. Guinness's and the trams were the obvious targets. Guinness's wages and philanthropy kept general unionism at bay until the 1940s. On Murphy's splendid tramway system, on the other hand, pay was poor, and conditions worse. Larkin envisaged a standard, limited struggle. Murphy had other ideas.

Public perceptions of the dispute have followed Larkin in focussing on the personal, the social, and the moral. Larkin was scarcely on the boat to America when the first play on the lockout, *The Slough*, was presented at the Abbey Theatre. Written and produced by Patrick Wilson, with Wilson playing the Larkin-type union secretary Jake Allen, the play depicts Allen as a towering moral force, browbeating the union committee to take a firm line against a drunken scab from the slums.[2] William O'Brien thought it too close to the bone, 'show[ing] Jim up rather badly'.[3] The more usual image of the lockout, as a clash of Big Jim and William 'Murder' Murphy in the shadow of the slums, has been powerfully reinforced by literary admirers of Larkin, especially Seán O'Casey and James Plunkett. O'Casey recalled being under the great man's spell in his autobiographies, notably *Drums under the Windows*. O'Casey and Larkin are conflated as 'Ayamonn Breydon' in the play *Red Roses for Me*, which is based on the 1911 rail strike and the 1913 Lockout. Plunkett, who became one of Larkin's union officials in 1946, developed a radio play *Big Jim* into a stage play of the lockout, *The Risen People*, and his best-selling novel of Dublin before and during the lockout, *Strumpet City*, was serialised for television with Larkin played by Peter O'Toole.[4] Writers have commonly used the image of Larkin as an Old Testament prophet or a Messiah of the oppressed. George Dangerfield reported one employer saying of Larkin: 'You cannot argue with the prophet Isaiah,' and added himself, with a nod to the slums: 'but if ever a social Isaiah was needed, surely he was needed here.'[5] 'The Kingdom of Heaven is within us,' wrote W. P. Ryan, 'we know from the Gospel; but who had sought for it hitherto amongst the slums and "unskilled" slaves of Dublin?'[6] Fifty years on from the lockout, Donagh MacDonagh's ballad 'Dublin 1913' included the line 'God sent Larkin in 1913, a labour man with a union tongue'. The collision of big house and slumdom is central to *Strumpet City* and the raw, class solidarity of the ITGWU came to be understood as a by-product of Dublin's appalling social conditions. The perspective was given a scholarly gloss in *Dublin 1913: A Divided City*: produced primarily for schools, it says little about trade unionism and much about the city's stark social divisions.[7] Today, trade unions would like to celebrate 1913 as a noble fight against what even the official history of the Federation of Irish Employers called 'the notorious William Martin Murphy' for the right to join a union.[8] According to the ITGWU's official history: 'The point at issue . . . was a simple one. It was the right of a worker to join the trade union of his choice. Whatever the remoter calculations of those who assailed this right, that is the ground they choose.'[9]

For Murphy too it was personal. At 68 years of age, he was too much a gentleman of the old school to appear upset by one he called 'a mean thief'.[10] But Murphy was a proud and arrogant man, who must have found the *Irish Worker* revolting; after August 1913, the Employers' Federation complained repeatedly about its content. The *Irish Independent* regularly attacked Larkin, and on 29 July, Murphy informed his staff that his objection was not to their forming a 'legitimate union', but to a 'disreputable organisation' which would place them under one who used men 'as tools to make him the labour dictator of Dublin'.[11] Asked later what he thought of Larkin, Murphy replied: 'I have never set eyes on him but I am told that he is a big man, wearing a slouch hat and with a swaggering style, throwing downstairs any smaller man than himself and giving the impression of great physical courage.' He expressed surprise that craftsmen should associate with 'scum like Larkin and his followers' or be deceived by his 'claptrap'.[12] Yet whereas Larkin's vendetta was merely a compulsive *modus operandi* concealing a standard industrial relations objective, Murphy's was a rational extension of a considered grand plan. 'I have seen for a long time,' he told employers,

> that the head of this labour agitation in Dublin has been aiming for a position that was occupied some time ago in Paris by man who was called 'King' Pataud, who was able to hold up the whole business of the city by raising his little finger. That man was driven out of Paris, and the other man will be driven out of Dublin shortly.[13]

Emile Pataud, syndicalist leader of French electricians, was famous for spectacular industrial action. Following the disruption of a gala for the King of Portugal at the Paris Opera, he fled to Belgium rather than face imprisonment. Murphy made no secret of the fact that his dispute with Liberty Hall was not about wages or conditions. Business could not survive the 'system known as "syndicalism" or "sympathetic strikes",' he argued.[14] He also wished to scupper the Lord Mayor's proposed conciliation board, or at least the ITGWU presence in his employment before it came into effect. Impressed by the speedy defeat of the September 1911 rail strike, he thought the ITGWU could be similarly despatched. In his simple, ruthless conflict analysis, provided the police and military maintained order, the company could carry on, and the union would be bankrupted. Whatever happened, the workers would starve before the shareholders.

Protagonists had no doubt that syndicalism lurked at the heart of the matter. Sir George Askwith recalled that while British strikes of the period were 'chiefly based upon economic issues, the serious riots in Dublin, although founded on poverty, low wages and bad conditions, included the determination to establish the transport workers' union as "the one big union" in Ireland and put into practice the doctrines of syndicalism'.[15] Arnold Wright, the employers' historian, represented his patrons as defending the protocols of responsible labour-management against the impossible Mr Larkin and his reckless syndicalist belief in the sympathetic strike, and stressed the influence of the government's failure to contain industrial unrest in England.[16] More surprisingly perhaps, it is easy to find Labour voices in agreement with Askwith. Ryan, a former member of the SPI and a champion of Larkin's efforts to rally support in Britain as assistant editor of the *Daily Herald*, also placed the syndicalist 'menace to the industrial order' at the kernel of the dispute, adding that the employers 'were quite correct from their point of view'.[17] Robert Williams, editor of the NTWF's *Weekly Record*, wrote in October:

The methods adopted by Larkin challenge the very constitution of wagery and capitalism. The measure of the employers' vehement antagonism is the measure of Larkin's success. It may be said in passing that capitalism sets a limit to purely trade union activities, and that the limit has to some extent been reached in Dublin ... We are seeing more and more that the workers are clamouring to be considered human factors in present-day wealth production and distribution, and that in spite of all documents signed, agreements, made, and contracts entered into, there will be a steadily-growing reluctance to refrain from the use of the sympathetic strike.[18]

And while 'rebels' like Ryan and Williams might be expected to emphasise the political dimension, their sentiments were shared by O'Brien, secretary of the ITGWU's lockout committee:

For some years in Dublin, Belfast, Cork, and a few other centres, the [ITGWU] had been developing a new and militant defensive and offensive policy with its slogan: 'An injury to one is the concern of all.' It had from time to time used the weapon of the sympathetic strike . . . Recognising that sooner or later an organisation with a policy like this would become master on the industrial field, the leading employers of Dublin made up their minds to crush the [ITGWU] before it could be strong enough to reach its goal.[19]

The first academic history of Irish Labour, written in 1925, offered a very similar analysis.[20]

Understanding the essence of the conflict is vital to an evaluation of Larkinism. The lockout was not a conventional dispute about wages, conditions, or even union recognition. It was about the balance of power in industrial relations. Yes, that had political and social ramifications, and yes, Murphy was determined to smash the ITGWU, while Larkin was willing to compromise on the sympathetic strike. But the lockout arose from a collision of union strategy and employer policy: it was a product of Larkinism in the framework of industrial relations, not social misery. The slums were a red herring. Undoubtedly they affected Larkin, reinforced his moral offensive, and generated graphic propaganda for the Labour cause. But Larkin had already shaken Belfast, where housing was relatively good, and the Dublin slums became an explanation of working-class behaviour only after the riots that followed the start of the dispute.

OPENING

Murphy's dismissals of suspected trade unionists forced Larkin's hand.[21] Forty workers in the despatch department of the *Irish Independent* were paid off on Friday 15 August, 200 tramwaymen on 17th, and 100 in the parcels service on 21st. As victimised men were put on strike pay, time was not on the union's side. To add to Larkin's headaches, he was assaulted at 6 pm on 21st as he walked home. The assailant, Peter Sheridan, was an unemployed clerk, associated with anti-Larkin Labour elements. After following Larkin from O'Connell Street, shouting repeatedly, he attacked him with a walking stick in North Frederick Street. The former docker overpowered the former clerk before the DMP arrived. Each accused the other, and both were summonsed to appear in court on 23rd. Witnesses verified Larkin's account, and the magistrate sentenced Sheridan to six weeks in gaol. Larkin appealed for clemency, saying he was used to being harassed.[22] On 22nd, the tramwaymen made formal demands for improvements in wages and conditions. As Murphy would not accept communications from Liberty Hall, it made no difference. Following a ballot in the small hours of Sunday 24th, Larkin was mandated to strike when opportune. He delayed in vain hopes of enlisting the power-house men, who could stop all trams with the flick of a switch, and finally – with a touch of Pataud's flair – signalled immediate action at 9.40 am on Tuesday 26th, the first day of the annual Dublin Horse Show. Most crews left the trams where they were. The ensuing traffic chaos not only made an impact, but concealed the weakness of the strike. Liberty Hall claimed that 7–800 men, of 1,700, were out. The company put the figures as low as 200 conductors and motor men, and 140 in the parcel service.

The first inkling that this was to be a different kind of struggle came in the vigour of the political response. Since the Belfast troubles in 1907, the authorities had been afraid of confronting Larkinism in Dublin. Murphy visited Dublin Castle on 19 August, and emerged with assurances. When attacks started on the trams, RIC and special constables were quickly deployed to supplement the DMP. On 30th, the police fatally injured John Byrne and James Nolan, and wounded 200 others in street clashes.[23] The police themselves suffered 30 casualties. On 28 and 29 August, Larkin, O'Brien, P. T. Daly, Councillor Thomas Lawlor, James Connolly, and W. P. Partridge were arrested for sedition. Freed on an undertaking of good behaviour, Larkin announced a big demonstration in O'Connell Street for Sunday 31 August and, when the meeting was proscribed, promised to be there 'dead or alive'. He was giving an interview to the German socialist paper *Vorwarts*, when told that another warrant had been issued for his arrest. This time he slipped away to Countess Markievicz's house in Rathmines. O'Brien switched the Sunday meeting to Croydon Park, but 3–400 people gathered around the General Post Office on Sunday morning, not knowing what to expect. Some 300 police deployed along the street. At 10 am, an elderly, bearded man, wearing Count Markievicz's frock-coat, had checked into the Imperial Hotel with his 'niece'. Around 1.30 pm, he walked into the smoking room, stepped onto the balcony, and shouted 'I'm Larkin'. He spoke briefly, saying that he had kept his word, and then retired. As Larkin was being led into custody, the crowd surged forward repeatedly against a police cordon. After a stone went through Clery's window, the police charged across the street, and from O'Connell Bridge, swinging their batons indiscriminately as people scattered in panic. When riots erupted along the tramway lines and in working-class areas, the police entered the tenements, ransacking homes and assaulting the residents. Rioting continued the following day. The disturbances resulted in over 400 civilian injuries. Hundreds more were arrested. Tom Clarke, the Fenian veteran of many a riot, told the *Irish Worker*:

> nothing I know of during my whole career can match the downright inhuman savagery that was witnessed recently in the streets and some of the homes of our city, when the police were let lose to run amok and indiscriminately bludgeon every man, women and child they came across.[24]

The employers were unmoved, and would remain so. On the day after the strike began, Murphy told the *Irish Independent*, 'I think I have broken the malign influence of Mr Larkin and set him on the run. It is now up to the employers to keep him going . . .' This they did. Some subvented a crude propaganda campaign in the *Liberator*, a scurrilous anti-Larkin paper which appeared on 28 August, and was joined by the *Toiler* on 13 September. The first major sympathetic lockout came at Jacob's on 1 September. The following day, two tenements collapsed in Dublin's Church Street, killing seven people and leaving 11 families homeless. Employers were stung by the resultant bad publicity, but there were not going to accept responsibility for the slums, any more than for the police riot.[25] On 3 September, as Nolan was being buried, Murphy presided over a meeting of 404 employers, who agreed to serve their employees with 'the document', a paper requesting a worker to renounce the ITGWU on pain of dismissal. The Lord Mayor convened a peace conference on 5 September, but talks broke down on 8th over the re-instatement of ITGWU men, and guarantees against future strikes. While Murphy expected a short campaign, he and other employers were determined to seize the moment to crush Larkinism. By 22 September, 25,000 workers were locked out, for refusing to handle 'tainted goods', or for not signing 'the document'.

THE DIVINE MISSION

As the masters trusted in starvation, Larkin had turned to Britain. Up to early December, his energies would be devoted chiefly to getting British unions to 'black' Dublin goods. Connolly, when not in jail, deputised in Liberty Hall. The ITGWU had done as much as it could in Dublin, where trams were still running. A national labour movement had yet to be forged, and Ireland remained dependent on British militancy. Apart from County Dublin, the Belfast docks, and Sligo, provincial workers limited their solidarity to finance; and in some instances, clerical hostility made solidarity extremely tentative. Though Larkin was chairman of the Parliamentary Committee, he made no attempt to mobilise the ITUC, a sad reflection on its continuing inefficacy. The Committee's report on the dispute confined its acknowledgments of help to the 'munificent contributions' of Limerick Pork Butchers and Limerick Carters and Storemen, and to British Labour.[26] Aside from these considerations, Britain was not foreign to Larkin. He had been instrumental in organising sympathetic action in Dublin for the British transport strikes of 1911, and he thought it only natural that the British should reciprocate.

What came to be known as 'Bloody Sunday' had generated enormous sympathy in Britain, and, fortuitously, the BTUC's annual conference had opened in Manchester on 1 September. The greatest parliament of labour in the world suspended standing orders on 2nd to hear a delegation despatched by O'Brien and Daly. As Harry Gosling recalled, 'the day's set work was dead. Ireland was in all our minds.' In the spirit of the moment, James Sexton put aside the old feud to call for an enquiry into 'Bloody Sunday', and it was agreed to send a six-man embassy to Dublin at once.[27] The BTUC and its affiliates, the *Daily Herald* and the rebels associated with its auxiliary *Daily Herald* Leagues, the Labour Party, the Co-operative Wholesale Society, and divers British radicals and liberals were to be integral to the shape of the struggle. While Larkin was fortunate that the lockout intersected with the topical debate on the British left, the level of British involvement would have been inconceivable without him, his oratorical ability, and the admiration for him across the channel. He was unfortunate that one British heavyweight was missing: Tom Mann was on a speaking tour in the United States.

Released from prison on bail on Friday 12 September, Larkin left immediately for England, and commenced a hectic round of travelling. On 14th he was a 'surprise' guest at a rally in Alexandra Park, Manchester, where the trades council had planned a protest about Dublin. With his showman's instinct, he had circulated rumours of his attendance, turned up in the crowd, without his moustache, and was invited onto the platform. In fighting form he denounced the brutality of the DMP, held up a truncheon broken over the head of a

Dubliner, and delivered his celebrated epigram: 'I care for no man or men. I have got a divine mission, I believe, to make men and women discontented ... No Murphy or [Lord] Aberdeen ... can stop me carrying on the work I was born for ...' That went for Labour men too. 'Our whole trade union movement is absolutely rotten', he added, alluding to the 'great unrest' and mounting frustration with trade union and Labour Party efforts to contain it.[28] On 16 September, Liverpool railwaymen 'blacked' Dublin goods, leading to the usual spiral of suspensions and walk-outs. The trouble extended to over 13,000 railwaymen in Liverpool and the midlands before J. H. Thomas, general secretary of the National Union of Railwaymen, got the men back to work. Thomas was a resolute opponent of sympathetic action, arguing that it would have his members permanently out of work. Larkin was back in Dublin on 15th, and was informed on 16th that the BTUC had voted £5,000 for the ITGWU and promised a weekly subvention. O'Brien suggested he take the assistance in kind. Spending the money in Dublin would have won friends and influence with local retailers, but the sight of food ships sailing up the Liffey to break the boom of starvation made for irresistible propaganda. Larkin was in Glasgow on 21st, met the NTWF executive in London on 22nd, and BTUC officials on 23rd. He then left for Manchester, where the first foodship, *Hare*, was provisioned by the Co-operative Wholesale Society in Balloon Street.[29] For Gosling and J. A. Seddon of the BTUC Parliamentary Committee, the *Hare*'s arrival in Dublin at 12.45 pm on 27 September was one of those unforgettable moments when solidarity becomes flesh:

> We went up the Liffey in the greatest triumph, with cheers and blowing of whistles from every side ...
>
> As we approached, Seddon and I were preparing to make great speeches to the folks assembled, for the quay was crowded. Larkin was there with a great body of men who had volunteered their services to unload the ship. But instead of talking we could only stand dumb, with tears in our eyes. It was the most wonderful sight I had ever seen![30]

Delia and Constance Markievicz turned Liberty Hall into an efficient commissariat, distributing clothes, food, and welfare for the duration of the lockout.

There was further relief for the ITGWU on 24 September when Augustine Birrell announced that the Board of Trade, in the person of Askwith, would attempt to broker a settlement. Pessimistic about the chances of 'a single Englishman' resolving the dispute, Askwith decided to lead a three-man team with Sir Thomas Ratcliffe-Ellis, legal adviser to the Mining Association of Great Britain, and Labour MP J. R. Clynes. The enquiry opened in Dublin Castle on Monday 29 September. T. M. Healy, KC, MP, made a three-hour presentation of the employers' case and called several prominent employers to the witness box. Larkin cross-examined most of them, firing detailed questions to elicit inaccuracies in their statements. On 3 October, the public enjoyed the fascinating spectacle of Larkin cross-examining Murphy. It was their first meeting. A Dublin literatus recalled 'his tall ungainly figure, craning forward as he bellowed forth his arraignment; and opposite him the calm handsome face of Murphy, with trim white beard, speaking just above his breath and glancing occasionally at his angry foe'.[31] Murphy's only concession to his own emotions was to stand throughout the interrogation. Employers were infuriated by Larkin's performance throughout, seeing it as rude, digressive, and theatrical. He was given considerable leeway by Askwith, possibly because Askwith believed that he was the real target of the lockout, and that Murphy was a villain of the piece. By contrast, and in contrast too with his often unrestrained speeches in Britain, the substance of Larkin's case was measured, and complimented Askwith's conviction in compromise as the basis of industrial peace. The British union observers, who might have been resentful of the way Larkin displaced Gosling, formally the workers' counsel, were impressed with his command of facts and ability to match Healy's court-room cunning.[32]

The next day, the union leaders made their concluding statements. Larkin spoke after Gosling, Williams, and Tom MacPartlin, president of Dublin trades council. There were high expectations of another oratorical gem, and they were not disappointed. Delivered, as usual, without notes, the speech is a fine example of Larkin's style:

> I hope you will bear with me in putting before you as plainly as possible a reply somewhat of a personal character, but which I think will cover the matters dealt with during the last few days. The first point I want to make is that the employers in this city, and throughout Ireland generally, have put forward a claim that they have a right to deal with their own; that they have a right to use and exploit individuals as they please; that they have duties which they limit, and they have responsibilities which they also limit, in their operation. They take to themselves that they have all the rights that are given to men and to societies of men, but they deny the right of the men to claim that they also have a substantial claim on the share of the produce they produce, and they further say that they want no third party interference.
>
> They want to deal with their workingmen individually. They say that they are men of such paramount intelligence and so able in their organising ability as captains of industry, who can always carry on their business in their own way, and they deny the right of the men and women who work for them to combine and try to assist one another in trying to improve their conditions of life . . .

There must be fair play between man and man. There are rights on both sides, but these men opposite assume to themselves certain privileges, and they deny to the workingmen, who make their wealth and keep them in affluence, their rights. Shakespeare it was, who said that: 'He who holds the means whereby I live, holds my life and controls me.' That is not the exact quotation, but I can give it. 'You take my house when you do take the prop that doth sustain my house, you take my life, when you doth take the means whereby I live.'

It means that the men who hold the means of life control our lives, and, because we workingmen have tried to get some measure of justice, some measure of betterment, they deny the right of the human being to associate with his fellow. Why, the very law of nature was mutual co-operation. Man must be associated with his fellows. The employers were not able to make their own case. Let him help them. They had had all the technique and the craftsmanship, but they have not been able to put their case in proper focus. What was the position of affairs in connection with life in industrial Ireland? Let them take the statement made by their own apologist. Take Dr Cameron's statement that there are 21,000 families – four and a half persons to a family living in single rooms. Who are responsible? The gentlemen opposite would have to accept the responsibility. Of course they must. They said they control the means of life; then the responsibility rests upon them. Twenty-one thousand people multiplied by five, over 100,000 people huddled together in the putrid slums of Dublin, five in a room in cubic space less than 1,000 feet, though the law lays it down that every human being should have 300 cubic feet.

We are determined that this shall no longer go on; we are determined the system shall stop; we are determined that Christ will not be crucified in Dublin by these men. Mr Waldron was good enough to say yesterday that Larkin had done what was right and just in getting facilities for the workers on the Canal to be enabled to get to Mass on Sundays. Let them go further with the argument and add a little more to the picture. There were phases of the subject that he was not going to enter into in a mixed audience.

The argument was used that Larkin came from Liverpool. Well, if that was so, it was time that someone came from some place in order to teach those whom he addressed their responsibilities. What about the gentlemen on the other side? Were they to be asked to produce their birth certificates? Could they all speak as men who represented the Irish race? These men had no feeling of respect for the Dublin workman or for its development. The only purpose and desire they had was to grind out wealth from the poor men, their wives and children.

Let people who desire to know the truth go to the factories and see the maimed girls, the weak and sickly, whose eyes are being put out and their bodies scarred and their souls seared and when they were no longer able to be useful enough to gain their £1 a week, or whatever wage they earned, were thrown into the human scrap heap. These things were to be found in their midst, and yet the people who caused these conditions of wretchedness described workingmen as loafers.

True it was that Mr Murphy said that the Dublin workman was a decent man; but he would deny the right of the Dublin workmen to work in their city on terms of decency, on the streets or on the quays. He would deny their right to develop their activities and to receive proper and living wages. He was an instrument to bring down the wages. The souls of these men were steeped in the grime of profitmaking. This dispute would do one thing and had already done something in that directions – it would arouse the social conscience . . .

Mr Murphy was absolutely unable to state his own case. He admitted he had no knowledge of the details of his own business. He admitted he had no strikes at any moment during his connection with industry concerns, but had proved that his life had been one continuous struggle against the working classes. I give him credit, too, that in a great many cases he came out on top, because he had never been faced by a man who was able to deal with him; he had never been faced by a social conscience such as now existed, and according to which the working classes could combine to alter the present conditions of labour . . .

I am concerned in something greater, something better, and something holier – a mutual relation between those carrying on industry in Ireland . . .

These men with their limited intelligence cannot see that. I cannot help that. I cannot compel them to look at the thing from my point of view. Surely they have a right to realise the work in which I am engaged. It is not to our interest to have men locked-out or on strike. We don't get double wages. They say 'Larkin is making £8 a week', and has made more than £18 a week, but he never got it unfortunately . . .

I am called an anti-Christ and an atheist. If I were an atheist I would not deny it. I am a Socialist and have always claimed to be a Socialist . . .

Can anyone say one word against me as a man? Can they make any disparagement of my character? Have I lessened the standard of life? Have I demoralised anyone? Is there anything in my private life or my public life of which I should feel ashamed? These men denounced me from the pulpit, and say I am making £18 a week and that I have a mansion in Dublin. The men who are described as Larkin's dupes are asked to go back. All this is done two thousand years after Christ appeared in Galilee. Why, these men are making people atheists – they are making them godless. But we are going to stop that.

When the position of the workers in Dublin was taken into consideration, was it any wonder that there was necessity for a Larkin to arise . . . My suggestion to the employers is that if they want peace we are prepared to meet them, but if they want war, then war they will have.[33]

Askwith's report on 6 October proposed that in return for withdrawal of 'the document' and re-instatement of the workers, the ITGWU would renounce the use of sympathetic action against employers willing to submit to Board of Trade arbitration, and no strike or lockout would take place before conciliation. Larkin agreed to restrict sympathetic strikes if the report was accepted. Contrary to their claim that sympathetic action was the bone of contention, the employers said they would not recognise the ITGWU until it was 'reorganised on proper lines' with 'new officials' acceptable to the British Joint Labour Board. Meanwhile, the lockout of workers refusing to sign 'the document' would continue.[34] Public opinion shifted. More than that, Larkin's heroic leadership ennobled the struggle, raising it to an Olympian plain. To the side of the workers was drawn, as Connolly put it:

> all the intellect, the soul and the spirit of the nation, all those who have learned to esteem the higher things of life, to value the spirit more than the matter. Publicists of all kinds, philanthropists, literary men, lovers of their kind, poets, brilliant writers, artists, have all been conquered by the valiant heroism of the Dublin workers.[35]

George Russell, alias AE, expressed their indignation in his famous open letter 'To the masters of Dublin' on 7 October. Remembered as a writer and artist, Russell was too an advocate of the co-operative commonwealth. His *Irish Homestead* was the only Irish paper to have been commended in a recent English translation of the syndicalist classic *Comment Nous Férons la Revolution*.[36]

Employer intransigence reinforced Larkin's conviction that action, not 'charity', was the only thing that would win. It was a possibility, but there was a fine line to be walked. Rank and file pressure alone would compel British Labour leaders to sanction 'blacking'. Arguably, Larkin should have concentrated on building a rank and file movement within the unions, rather than trying to force the hand of their leaders, who were never going to sanction sympathetic action unless pushed into it.[37] On the other hand, he hadn't the time, resources or patience to do so, the ITGWU needed the financial aid of the BTUC, and if action for Dublin became synonymous with 'rebellion' against officialdom, a threatened leadership would never countenance it. It is also forgotten that Larkin himself was an official. By profession, he had more in common with fellow union bosses than shopfloor militants. His egregious error was to make the struggle dependent on the leaders and to alienate them all at once. He slipped naturally into personalising the conflict, and was incapable of restraint in the heat of battle.

In early October, he spoke at a series of rallies convened by the *Daily Herald*, thus openly identifying with the rebels. His attacks on other union leaders became increasingly personal, and included those who regarded themselves as his allies.[38] He was careless too in not saying precisely or consistently what was expected of British unions. Dublin demanded 'blacking', but at times Larkin and the rebels called for a general strike. Critics were quick to exploit the confusion. If union officials agreed with sympathetic action in certain circumstances, they feared its elevation into a principle. It had proved a winner in the 1911 strikes. In the big dock strike of 1912, the NTWF was defeated by the failure of other ports to come out in solidarity with London.[39] More generally, it meant that any group of workers could be caught up in a fight without reference to themselves or their officials. Havelock Wilson complained that the NSFU's Dublin branch had been 'involved continuously in disputes' without consultation with his executive.[40] Sexton even wrote a play, *The Riot Act*, to expose the folly of sympathetic action as a principle.[41]

The zenith of the divine mission came on 10 October at a star-studded rally in London's Memorial Hall, organised by the *Daily Herald* League. After the crowd received Larkin with a rendition of 'For he's a jolly good fellow', London dockers' leader Ben Tillett, MP, asked for another verse with the words 'For he's a jolly good rebel'. Larkin was in no mood for niceties. He began with an attack on union officials, 'as useful as mummies in a museum', for restraining rank and file sympathetic action, and went on: 'The officials of the Railwaymen's Union plead that there are agreements and contracts. To hell with contracts! The men are far in advance of their leaders. They will tell their leaders to get in front or get out.'[42] Just as his claim to have a 'divine mission' was seized on by opponents to depict him as a manic zealot, so 'To hell with contracts' would be used by employers to corroborate their claim that he was utterly untrustworthy and the real obstacle to a settlement. After listening to 'his appalling story' of Dublin, Mrs Dora Montefiore slipped him a note asking if he would approve a scheme to give the children of distressed workers a holiday with families in England. She knew of similar schemes adopted in the United States and Belgium.[43] It was a common enough tactic. Connolly had raised the idea during the Wexford Lockout of 1911–12. On this occasion, Connolly anticipated anglophobia, and may have shared it. When the clergy generated a furore about proselytism to cripple the project, Connolly was happy to have it wound up. In November, Daly told an ITGWU rally in Waterford City Hall that the initiative had been a blunder.[44] Larkin had less patience for fears of being misunderstood, and said it was a poor religion that couldn't survive a fortnight's holiday in England. The *Irish Worker* later printed a front-page article by James Stephens entitled 'Come off that fence'. 'Tell the clergy,' he urged, 'to come down off that fence, and, if it is necessary, pull them down. It is as necessary for their own good as it is for yours that they be honest. Teach them that their business is not Mammon but God.' The article provoked a hammer attack on the *Irish Worker*'s type and printing material by a young man 'well known in Dublin Catholic circles'.[45] Undaunted, the paper took a more explicitly critical view of clerical influence in the new year, challenging the Lenten pastorals of 1914, which focussed on the labour question and were normally published verbatim in the provincial press, and launching a series of broadsides against the Ancient Order of Hibernians.[46]

The divine mission was halted by a trial for sedition and incitement to riot and robbery in a speech made before Bloody Sunday. On 27 October, Larkin received seven months hard labour for sedition. He was acquitted of the incitement charges. The popular indignation was enormous. Forty thousand people applied for a ticket to a protest rally in London's Royal Albert Hall, at which the speakers included Delia, Connolly, Montefiore, Russell, Tillett, and George Bernard Shaw. Sylvia Pankhurst's East End Federation of the Women's Social and Political Union had been prominent in organising the event. For Dangerfield, it encapsulated the irrationality that inflicted a 'strange death' on liberal England.

> on the speakers' platform sat, in serried ranks, the united grievances of England. For the first and last time Irish Nationalism, Militant Suffrage, and the Labour Unrest were met together . . . for what? Simply to demand the release from prison of a messianic strike-leader whose mind – to say the least – was a trifle unbalanced, and whose methods were definitely not sanctioned by the Trade Union leadership? Or was Trade Union leadership itself under fire? One thing, at least, is certain; the vigorous and passionate oratory [was not] merely the irritable expulsion of reformist steam. It resembled rather the gathering of a heavy cloud, caught up out of some teeming sea; for its strength was drawn from every factory, every workshop, mine, wharf and slum throughout the length and breadth of England.[47]

The audience pledged to heckle every meeting addressed by a government minister until Larkin was free. Following a poor bye-election result in Reading on 9 November, government intervention secured his release from Mountjoy at 7 am on 13th. After calling home, he was at Liberty Hall by 10.30 am, and addressed a growing crowd of well-wishers at noon. His speech was defiant, but his voice didn't carry, and he retired early.[48] Elizabeth, described as 'well-featured, and with a mass of red-gold hair', by a *Daily Sketch* reporter, took his place that evening. According to the *Sketch*:

> While Liberty Hall was celebrating the release by fireworks, processions and speeches, Jim Larkin himself was at home minding the babies. Severe pains in his head had driven him to his modest little house in Auburn-street, and as he was too

unwell to risk the strain of speaking, his wife came down to explain his absence, and herself walked in the parade round the city. 'I don't often get the chance to go down,' Mrs Larkin told me on her doorstep, 'because I don't like to leave the children in bed; so last night I thought I would take the chance when Jim had to be at home.'

She seems to feel the strain of being a rebel's wife, although she herself is keenly enthusiastic for the cause of labour. She has three children, the eldest boy at school, but smilingly declared they were too young to be rebels yet.[49]

When the parade concluded outside Liberty Hall, Connolly invited his audience to form an army, the Transport Union Citizen Army as it was first called. The concept and name had long been suggested in Britain by the SDF, but it had too an Irish pedigree, in Cork. Larkin had alluded to something similar during the Dublin carters' dispute of 1908, and it was spoken of also in the Wexford Lockout. During the riots in August 1913, Larkin invited workers to take their cue from the Ulster Volunteer Force. On 14 November Captain Jack White made his way to Croydon Park and offered his services. A hero of the Boer War turned anarchist and pacifist, White reckoned, as old soldiers do, that drilling would be good for the discipline and morale of men without work. His memoirs recalled his bitter disappointment with the number and quality of recruits, and the claim of 1,200 members by 27 November might include Larkinite exaggeration.[50] However, the *Irish Times* was impressed by its first parade through Dublin that day, when nearly 3,000 ITGWU men turned out. What is certain, from fluctuating numbers, is that commitment was a problem. There were 'regulars' and 'casuals'. And without rifles or uniforms – they carried staves and wore armlets – their role in the lockout was largely confined to protecting meetings, and opposing evictions.[51] Coincidentally, the foundation of the Irish Volunteers took place in the Rotunda on 25 November. Four thousand men joined up immediately. From the outset, Citizen Army men resented being overshadowed by the bigger force, and complained of the presence in the Volunteers of anti-Larkinites, and worse, fellow trade unionists. An ITGWU contingent attended the Rotunda meeting to heckle Larry Kettle, a strike-breaking farmer in north Dublin. When Kettle was invited to read the manifesto of the Volunteers, a picture of Larkin was held up, accompanied by shouts of 'Cheers for Larkin' and the singing of 'God save Larkin'. Detonators were thrown and scuffles broke out before the bulk of the union men left for a meeting at Liberty Hall.[52]

THE 'FIERY CROSS'

Though not in good health, Larkin had returned to England, to launch a second crusade, which he christened, with characteristic literary flair, the 'Fiery Cross'. The burning cross was a traditional call to war of the Scots clans, popularised in modern England by Sir Walter Scott's narrative poem 'The Lady of the Lake'. Larkin's punishing schedule opened on 16 November in Manchester. A galaxy of agitators – including Larkin, Connolly, Williams, Tillett, and 'Big Bill' Haywood – assembled in the Clarion Café on Market Street and walked to the Free Trade Hall, where a capacity crowd of 4,000 were within, and 20,000 more milled about outside. As Larkin took the stage '[t]he whole audience as one mass leapt to their feet and stood cheering and shouting "Hurrah" for some minutes. "England arise" sang the Clarion Choir, and the whole audience joined in the refrain with great heartiness'.[53] He spoke at further rallies in Bow on 19 November, the Albert Hall on 20th, Bristol on 25th, Sheffield on 26th, Mile End on 27th, Liverpool on 1st, and Leeds on 8 December.[54] The Fiery Cross brought Larkin international renown. Haywood had joined the campaign from Paris at the request of the *Daily Herald*. One of America's leading agitators, he wrote of the Albert Hall rally: 'I have never spoken at any meeting with more satisfaction.' He also noted Larkin spending his free time reading Rabelais, and went on to review the Citizen Army at Croydon Park.[55]

Together with the importation of scabs to Dublin, the Fiery Cross triggered a second wave of sympathetic action, involving 30,000 railwaymen in south Wales and Liverpool. Union agents strained to keep the lid on the pot. One London official reported:

> In all my experience I have never known a time when there has been manifested a desire to help any union in dispute as there is among dockers both in London and the provincial ports towards Dublin ... We have had to rearrange the whole of our paid officials in London, placing them in certain centres with the express purpose of preventing any disorganised move ...[56]

For others, the position was not so clear-cut. Some of the sympathetic action by railwaymen was 'secondary, secondary', in strikes for the reinstatement of men dismissed for 'blacking' Dublin goods. The *Daily Herald* noted that action was more likely in sectors with ties to Ireland. Separate grievances over pay and conditions were also a factor.[57] The BTUC Parliamentary Committee concluded that a definitive response was needed. On 18 November, it met a Dublin delegation which requested steps to prevent the transit of scabs and 'tainted goods' to Dublin. On 19th, the Committee agreed to summon a special conference on Dublin. In reality, the BTUC was preparing an authoritative 'No', and, to add insult to injury, the conference would not assemble until 9 December. Larkin's relations with the BTUC were already acrimonious, and fresh attacks on labour leaders probably made little difference. On 22 November he published a manifesto in the *Daily Herald* urging the rank and file to press for action for Dublin, but also making a typically rebel critique of the leadership:

> Comrades in the British Labour Movement,
> Giving every credit to your leaders of the best of intentions with reference to the accomplishment of our work in Dublin, I feel that something more might have been done . . . I have suggested to those in command that you have only got to be asked the question, 'Are you workers, you of the common people, prepared to stand by your brothers in Dublin in the truest sense, that you do not intend to mislead us, that you are always with us, and that we are one and indivisible as a class?' . . . We intend to carry out to its fullest and highest the spirit of trade unionism which is embodied in the well-worn phrase, 'An injury to one is an injury to all.' We say that your leaders have come far short of this gospel of human brotherhood. They seem to have no vision. They seem to think, speak and act as though trade unionism was meant to be used as a salve for the sore of poverty . . . We say trade unionism is a root remedy and by industrial action we can accomplish great things. We are not willing to say that trade unionism shall be used either by industrial commissioners, Conciliation Boards or by Cabinets to chloroform the workers, to persuade them to remain as dumb, driven dogs. Some of your leaders have forgotten that they worked at the bench, in or out of the factory, on the socks, or in the stokehole. They have forgotten the footplate and the engine; they have forgotten the laborious work of the goods yard; they seem to think that round tables, conferences, nice language, beautiful phrases, that fall trippingly from the tongue, conciliation boards, and agreements are the be-all and the end-all of life.

Union leaders now started to go public with their private dislike of Larkin and the increasingly common belief that he was the obstacle to a settlement. They were after all sustaining a phenomenal financial lifeline for Dublin, for which Larkin showed little gratitude. More tension arose from rumours that a British Labour Party and BTUC deputation to the Archbishop of Dublin's peace conference on 4 December had pressured the ITGWU to yield on the final sticking point, and accept a return to work without guarantees of re-instatement.

The BTUC special conference met in the Memorial Hall, London on Tuesday 9 December. Connolly, O'Brien, and MacPartlin travelled from Dublin, embarrassingly and unavoidably on a scab-crewed ferry. No elections were held for the 600 delegates. Elections might have worked to the advantage of the rebels, though the case is not certain. In fairness to the BTUC there was no precedent for the conference and the simplest thing to do was to recall that year's annual Congress. Less fairly, Williams, a key supporter of Larkin, was excluded on the spurious grounds that he represented a federation rather than a union. It gradually became apparent that the British leaders had been irretrievably alienated by Larkin, and were concerned primarily with upholding their reputations. Arthur Henderson opened the proceedings with a defence of the British representatives to the Dublin peace conference. Connolly smoothed the ruffled feathers a little with an appeal for an end to recriminations. After that, things turned openly partisan. Tillett, who was regarded as close to the rebels, moved a motion deploring attacks on British union officials. Thomas declared he would not be slandered 'for fifty Larkins (cheers)'. Havelock Wilson protested that he had been called 'a scab and a renegade because I have tried to impress privately a little common sense into the heads of those who have been mismanaging the business in Dublin (cheers)'. By the time he rose to speak, Larkin had written off his audience. 'He was,' he said, 'an Ishmael, and bound to be attacked by the [BTUC] leaders' who wanted him 'out of the road'. Amidst noisy heckling, pacing restlessly, 'eyes flashing and a stray wisp of hair falling over his brow', 'perspiration streaming down his face', he delivered a defiant, taunting address, his booming voice drowning out the constant dissent that would have fazed a lesser man.[58] After reviewing old quarrels with Wilson and Sexton, he got to the nub.

> Your money is useful but money never won a strike. (Cheers). Discipline, solidarity, knowledge of the position, and the strength to carry out your will – these are the things [with which] you could win in Dublin tomorrow if you mean to. If you do not mean to you should shut up . . . Larkin will keep on fighting, and go down fighting.[59]

When he finished, the air was so charged that the chairman adjourned the meeting to let tempers cool. On resumption, Tillett's motion passed with only six votes against: on a card vote the figures were 2,280,000 in favour, and 203,000 against.[60] The conference agreed to continue the search for a settlement and financial support, but a rebel amendment that if employers rejected a reasonable offer by a fixed date, goods from Dublin be 'blacked', was defeated heavily.

The conference signalled the beginning of the end. The *Daily Telegraph* reckoned that Larkin had no chance of recovery, as Larkinism itself had been repudiated by British Labour.

The rights and wrongs, however, of the Dublin strike had little to do with yesterday's meeting. What was really at issue was the character of British trade unionism. If Larkin had been victor instead of vanquished, the stability and discipline of trade unionism would have been shattered.

Yesterday's result was a striking vindication of the trade union leaders who stand for a sense of responsibility, observance of contracts, fulfilment of obligations, and reasonable dealing.[61]

ENDGAME

Larkin insisted the game was not up. The day after the conference he was in Glasgow, addressing a crowd of 4,000, and the following day he spoke in Edinburgh to almost twice as many.[62] On 14 December, the ITGWU executive, convened by Connolly, decided to advise members to resume work without signing 'the document'. Larkin overruled the decision on his return. On 18th, British Labour made its final peace initiative. The BTUC delegation to Dublin met the same response as before. By January, men were drifting back to work and the BTUC was warning of compassion fatigue in Britain. The last card was snatched from the ITGWU's hand when its desperate hopes of a good showing in the municipal elections on 15 January were dashed. 'Vote for Labour and sweep away the slums' was the Dublin Labour Party's slogan, but the press portrayed the elections as a plebiscite on Larkinism and, unusually, a special election edition of the *Irish Worker* appeared on the eve of polling. Labour polled well, taking 42 per cent of the vote, but won just two of the 13 seats it contested. Labour blamed the arcane franchise qualifications and corrupted registration system. Prospective electors were obliged to appeal to Registration Courts, where party agents sought to maximise the registration of those deemed sympathetic and advance every conceivable objection to others, and Labour minds were elsewhere during the revision sessions of 1913. In the one ward where Labour had devoted serious attention to registration, its 'several hundred' objections were dismissed on a technicality.

The outcome was nonetheless depicted as a 'Larkinite rout', and Larkin lashed out in an editorial both vicious and pathetic: 'They beat Larkinism by votes: but they can never beat Larkinism by reason, by facts, by principles.'[63] Pressure in the ITGWU resulted in a general assembly at Croydon Park on 17 January. Larkin did not turn up, and affirmed that evening that the struggle continued. The next day, there was another assembly.[64] MacPartlin proposed the return of all who could go back to work without signing 'the document'. Larkin arrived late and denounced the motion, saying they could hold out for another year if necessary. He was received in silence. Two hours later, it was agreed to make the policy known publicly. On 22 January Larkin and O'Brien made a vain appeal in person to the BTUC Parliamentary Committee, and one week later Larkin and Connolly travelled to Glasgow for the British Labour Party's annual conference. They were denied a hearing.[65] The BTUC relief fund closed on 10 February. The BTUC had contributed two thirds of the £150,000 subscribed for Dublin, with the remainder coming from other British groups and workers in Europe, America, Australia, and Africa.[66] Strike pay ended on 15 February. There were still 5,000 locked out.

The lockout was a turning point in Larkin's life, in his personality and his relations with Elizabeth and the ITGWU. As always, defeat had a devastating effect on him, and the scale of this defeat left him shaken to the core. Inevitably, it had been an ordeal for Elizabeth and the boys too. Evictions of families unable to meet rent payments had begun in October, and Jim advocated a rent strike. An unpleasant round of summonses, court hearings, and visits from the bailiffs with furniture carried out onto the street and taken back again, followed for possession of 27 Auburn Street. On 23 December bailiffs forced an entry through an upstairs window after Elizabeth had barred the front door.[67] The union's solicitors hurriedly lodged an appeal. When eventually ejected, with no landlord willing to accommodate them, the family squatted in an empty house in the North Strand, only to find it rat infested. On 17 January, they moved into the servants' quarters at Croydon Park, which they shared with Delia.[68] Elizabeth was now pregnant again. Aside from anything else, she preferred the quiet life, and the boys were growing up seeing little of their father. She and Jim were drifting apart. The ITGWU continued to have confidence in his leadership, but not in his ability to manage union affairs. Its *de facto* executive, the no 1 branch committee, began to function independently of the general secretary, and conceal information from him. Larkin was losing his wife and his union, and he didn't know it.

NOTES

1   Arnold Wright, *Disturbed Dublin: The Story of the Great Strike of 1913–14, with a Description of the Industries of the Irish Capital* (London, 1914), p. 71; for Murphy see Thomas J. Morrissey, SJ, *William Martin Murphy* (Dundalk, 1997), p. 47.

2   Dedalus Burch, *Andrew P. Wilson and the Early Irish and Scottish National Theatres, 1911–1950* (New York, 2008), pp. 37–51.

3   William O'Brien, *Forth the Banners Go: The Reminiscences of William O'Brien as Told to Edward MacLysaght, D.Litt* (Dublin, 1969), p. 260.

4   See Theo Dorgan, 'Larkin through the eyes of writers', in Donal Nevin (ed.), *James Larkin: Lion of the Fold* (Dublin: 1998), pp. 102–9.

5   'Historians on Larkin', in Donal Nevin (ed.), *James Larkin: Lion of the Fold* (Dublin, 1998), p. 380.

6   W. P. Ryan, *The Irish Labour Movement from the 'Twenties to Our Own Day* (Dublin, 1919), p. 201.

7   Curriculum Development Unit, *Dublin 1913: A Divided City* (Dublin, 1984).

8   Basil Chubb (ed.), *Federation of Irish Employers, 1942–1992* (Dublin, 1992), p. 3.

9   C. Desmond Greaves, *The Irish Transport and General Workers' Union: The Formative Years, 1909–1923* (Dublin, 1982), p. 95.

10   R. M. Fox, *Jim Larkin: The Rise of the Underman* (London, 1957), p. 81.

11   Donal Nevin, 'The battle opens', in Nevin (ed.), *James Larkin*, p. 163.

12   Fox, *Jim Larkin*, p. 81; Morrissey, *William Martin Murphy*, p. 57.

13   Cited in Nevin (ed.), *James Larkin*, p. 467.

14   Morrissey, *William Martin Murphy*, p. 56.

15   Quoted in John Newsinger, *Rebel City: Larkin, Connolly, and the Dublin Labour Movement* (London, 2003), p. 16.

16   Wright, *Disturbed Dublin*, p. 29, 94.

17   W. P. Ryan, 'The struggle of 1913', in WUI, *1913: Jim Larkin and the Dublin Lock-Out* (Dublin, 1964), p. 7.

18   *Weekly Record*, 11 October 1913.

19   ITGWU, *Fifty Years of Liberty Hall: The Golden Jubilee of the Irish Transport and General Workers' Union, 1909–1959* (Dublin, 1959), p. 35.

20   J. D. Clarkson, *Labour and Nationalism in Ireland* (New York, 1970, first edn New York, 1926), pp. 241–4.

21   The definitive history of the lockout is Pádraig Yeates, *Lockout: Dublin 1913* (Dublin, 2000); see also Greaves, *The Irish Transport and General Workers' Union*, pp. 95–121; Dermot Keogh, *The Rise of the Irish Working Class: The Dublin Trade Union Movement and Labour Leadership, 1890–1914* (Belfast, 1982), pp. 180–238; and, for a most succinct account, Conor McCabe, '"Your only God is profit": Irish class relations and the 1913 lockout', in David Convery (ed.), *Locked Out: A Century of Irish Working-Class Life* (Dublin, 2013), pp. 9–21.

22   Yeates, *Lockout*, p. 10, 12.

23   Ibid., pp. 51–3.

24   *Irish Worker*, 27 September 1913; British Parliamentary Papers, *Report of the Dublin Disturbances Commission* (Cd.7269, 1914).

25   Yeates, *Lockout*, pp. 106–9; Wright, *Disturbed Dublin*, pp. 150–2.

26   UUMC, ITUC, *Annual Report* (1914), p. 24.

27   Harry Gosling, *Up and down Stream* (London, 1927), p. 120; Ken Coates and Tony Topham, *The History of the Transport and General Workers' Union: Vol. I, Part II, 1912–1922: From Federation to Amalgamation* (Oxford, 1991), p. 473.

28   Michael Herbert, *The Wearing of the Green: A Political History of the Irish in Manchester* (London, 1991), p. 89; *Manchester Guardian*, 15 September 1913.

29   Coates and Topham, *The History of the Transport and General Workers' Union: Vol. I, Part II*, p. 475; Greaves, *The Irish Transport and General Workers' Union*, pp. 102–3.

30   Gosling, *Up and down Stream*, p. 125.

31   John Eglington, *A Memoir of AE, George William Russell* (London, 1937), p. 86.

32 Wright, *Disturbed Dublin*, pp. 190–204; Coates and Topham, *The History of the Transport and General Workers' Union: Vol. I, Part II*, pp. 476–8; Lord Askwith, *Industrial Problems and Disputes* (Brighton, 1974), p. 267.

33 *Irish Times*, 6 October 1913.

34 Morrissey, *William Martin Murphy*, pp. 53–4; Askwith, *Industrial Problems and Disputes*, pp. 262–70.

35 *Irish Worker*, 20 December 1913.

36 Emile Pataud and Emile Pouget, *How Shall We Bring about the Revolution: Syndicalism and the Co-operative Commonwealth* (London, 1990, first edn France, 1909, British edn 1913), p. 237; Leann Lane, 'George Russell and James Stephens: class and cultural discourse, Dublin 1913', in Francis Devine (ed.), *A Capital in Conflict: Dublin City and the 1913 Lockout* (Dublin, 2013), pp. 333–52.

37 This point is made in Newsinger, *Rebel City*, pp. 97–8.

38 *Daily Herald*, 13 October 1913.

39 David Howell, *A Lost Left: Three Studies in Socialism and Nationalism* (Manchester, 1986), p. 119.

40 Statement of Havelock Wilson, November 1913, quoted in Elie Halevy, *A History of the English People in the Nineteenth Century, VI: The Rule of Democracy, 1905–1914 (Book II)* (London, 1952), p. 485.

41 James Sexton, *The Riot Act: A Play in Three Acts* (London, 1915). The play strongly reflected Sexton's experience in dealing with militants as general secretary of the NUDL.

42 Yeates, *Lockout*, pp. 247–8.

43 Dora B. Montefiore, *From a Victorian to a Modern* (London, 1917), p. 156.

44 Emmet O'Connor, *A Labour History of Waterford* (Waterford, 1989), p. 128.

45 *Irish Worker*, 13 December 1913; *Ottawa Journal*, 24 January 1914.

46 For the pastorals see the *Derry Journal*, 23 February 1914; for the wider context see Joseph A. MacMahon, OFM, 'The Catholic clergy and the social question in Ireland, 1891–1916', *Studies* 70:280 (winter 1981), pp. 263–88.

47 George Dangerfield, *The Strange Death of Liberal England* (London, 1983 edn), p. 195.

48 Yeates, *Lockout*, p. 393.

49 Quoted in Nevin (ed.), *James Larkin*, pp. 469–70.

50 Jack White, *Misfit* (London, 1930), pp. 263–4.

51 *Irish Times*, 4–5 December 1908; Donal Nevin, 'The Irish Citizen Army, 1913–1916', in Nevin (ed.), *James Larkin*, p. 257; Francis Devine, *Organising History: A Centenary of SIPTU, 1909–2009* (Dublin, 2009), p. 62.

52 Yeates, *Lockout*, pp. 437–9; *Freeman's Journal*, 26 November 1913.

53 *Liverpool Daily Post and Mercury*, 17 November 1913, cited in Bob Holton, *British Syndicalism, 1900–1914: Myth and Realities* (London, 1976), p. 195.

54 Holton, *British Syndicalism*, pp. 225–6, fn. 17; see *New Witness*, 27 November 1913 for a description of Larkin at the Albert Hall.

55 *Irish Worker*, 29 November 1913; William D. Haywood, *Bill Haywood's Book: The Autobiography of William D. Haywood* (New York, 1929), pp. 272–4.

56 Holton, *British Syndicalism*, p. 193.

57 Howell, *A Lost Left*, p. 117.

58   *New York Times*, 10 December 1913.

59   Cited in Yeates, *Lockout*, p. 470.

60   *New York Times*, 10 December 1913.

61   Cited in ibid.

62   Holton, *British Syndicalism*, pp. 196–7.

63   Peter Murray, 'Electoral politics and the Dublin working class before the First World War', *Saothar* 6 (1980), pp. 8–22; *Irish Worker*, 3–24 January 1914.

64   *The Times*, 19 January 1914.

65   Greaves, *The Irish Transport and General Workers' Union*, p. 119.

66   ITGWU, *Fifty Years of Liberty Hall*, p. 37.

67   Yeates, *Lockout*, p. 492.

68   James Plunkett, 'Big Jim: a loaf on the table, a flower in the vase', in Nevin (ed.), *James Larkin*, pp. 113–14; Greaves, *The Irish Transport and General Workers' Union*, p. 120.

EIGHT

MERCURY TAKES FLIGHT, 1914

Ireland must no longer be Niobe but Mercury among the Nations.
James Larkin, June 1914[1]

—

This mixture of Greek and Roman mythology, which James Larkin addressed to the ITUC, might equally have been applied to his own situation after the lockout. Should he stay in Ireland, bereaved and brooding over his sorrows like the lachrymose Niobe, or fix wings on his heels like the messenger of the gods, and spread the divine gospel of discontent across the globe? Mercurial was Larkin's mood after the lockout, and while the rank and file begged him to stay, his ever greater mood swings tried the patience of his colleagues and eroded his authority in the higher echelons of the ITGWU and ITUC. In the summer of 1914 there were suggestions that a trip to America might do him good, and there were some, William O'Brien certainly, who wanted rid of him.

Why did Larkin tarry? A speaking tour of the new world had been suggested to him by 'Big Bill' Haywood when they met in Manchester in November 1913. One month later, it looked all the more alluring to one who couldn't bear the burden of defeat. On Christmas eve, Larkin told workers in Kilmainham that he would carry the Fiery Cross to American workers and raise funds for the union, prompting the *New York Times* to publish an editorial piece entitled 'Larkin is coming', and the US Secretary of Labor to say his admission would be for the inspectors on Ellis Island. According to the *Daily Telegraph*, the *New York Times* view of Larkin as the latest European celebrity to seek fame and fortune in the US caused 'much interest' and dismay in Dublin, obliging Larkin to deny that he had any intention of going away without the consent of the ITGWU.[2] Privately, he continued to explore the possibilities of a global speaking tour, and his 'New Campaign' in England in February and March turned into something of a test-run. The campaign was promoted in the *Irish Worker* as an effort to revitalise the union, but for Larkin personally it stretched on into the summer, and gradually evolved from fund-raising for Dublin to roving agitation for the British rebels, leaving the ITGWU feeling neglected. Rumours of his departure gradually became known. By June 1914 there was a wider appreciation of his stressed condition, and an acceptance that he needed a break. No one would have begrudged him a few months holiday, the more so if he raised funds on the way. But his natural aversion to others knowing his business made him secretive about his plans, and he had a guilty secret: he would not go to fulfil anyone else's agenda or fund-raise for the union, and would have an open mind about coming back. How much his youngest child weighed in his calculations is unclear. Bernard, or Barney as he would be known, was born in Croydon Park on 11 August. There was a cursory character about the birth certificate. Barney received no middle name, and the father gave his profession simply as 'secretary'.[3]

What *is* clear is that Larkin became more militantly republican and anti-Redmondite and took a greater interest in the Citizen Army and the IRB as the year progressed. The lockout, of course, had accentuated the differentiation of nationalists on the social question: republicans had generally sided with the ITGWU, while Redmondites were silent, at best. It is also possible that his deepening engagement with Britain heightened his sense of nationalism.

THE 'NEW CAMPAIGN'

Suffering bouts of depression and lethargy, Larkin sometimes neglected Liberty Hall for days on end, leaving union business to general president Tom Foran, Michael McKeown, and the no 1 branch committee, whose meetings were dominated by efforts to retrench on spending, and members' appeals for the price of a one-way ticket for the cross-channel ferry. Unusually, he also wanted to avoid facing distressed members or claims on his generosity. He diverted himself with the 'New Campaign', which involved himself, two ITGWU men described as 'Brothers Lennon and Donegan', Jack Carney as tour manager, and Delia's 'Irish Players' Dramatic Troupe'. The aims were twofold: to explain the position in Dublin to the British left – they spoke or performed to Clarion Clubs, ILP and British Socialist Party branches, and *Daily Herald* Leagues – and to raise funds for co-operatives to employ victimised workers. Jim claimed that his 'first visit to England last year' raised £1,900 and announced in October 1914 that a co-operative shop would be opened in Sligo followed by an underclothing shop in Dublin's Thomas Street under the auspices of the IWWU.[4] Delia's 'score of young men and maidens' included pipers and dancers, songs and plays, with a strong national accent. 'Irish songs and dances will be given,' *Liverpool Forward* announced, 'The national costume will be worn. From start to finish the plays will be acted by sons and daughters of toil.' The venues included Merseyside, Manchester, Huddersfield, Oxford, and London.[5] After speaking at the Corn Exchange in Oxford on 28 February 1914, Jim was taken to watch a debate on social reform at the university's Union Society, where he was amused by the sedate atmosphere and the mock parliamentary pomp. He was then accompanied to his lodgings with a giddy escort singing the 'Red Flag', and indulged the undergraduate juvenilia by calling for three cheers for the social revolution.[6]

When in London, Larkin operated out of the *Daily Herald* office, and the *Herald* influence was reflected in his deeper interest in the co-operative commonwealth and the guild socialism of A. R. Orage, S. G. Hobson, and *New Age*.[7] A *Daily Herald* League had been formed in Dublin during the 'Fiery Cross' campaign when the *Irish Worker* started to advertise the *Herald*, and, at Russell's prompting, W. P. Ryan had tried to develop a programme for Labour in *The Labour Revolt and Larkinism: The Later Irish Pioneers and the Co-operative Commonwealth*. The pamphlet envisaged Larkinism, the agricultural co-operative movement of Horace Plunkett and Russell, and politico-cultural forces like Sinn Féin and Conradh na Gaeilge, together remaking the primitive Gaelic communism romanticised by James Connolly in *Labour in Irish History*.[8] As late as 30 March, Larkin's mind was still on old quarrels in Britain, and he proposed to stand against the Prime Minister, H. H. Asquith, in his parliamentary constituency of East Fife in the next general election. Connolly suspected the hand of George Lansbury, editor of the *Daily Herald*, behind the idea and cabled Dublin: 'Myself and friends implore you not to oppose Asquith. If you do you will ruin your career. Leave that to fools like Lansbury.' Larkin went to Scotland anyway in early April before thinking the better of it.[9]

Larkin's interest in guild socialism came as a pleasant surprise to Arnold Wright, an admirer of the medieval guilds. For all their material success, the employers suspected that they had lost the propaganda war, and their Federation took the extraordinary step of paying Wright £500 to compile a history of the 'Larkinite movement in Dublin', the better to show that, in the concluding words of Wright's 'impartial' narrative, it was 'the crudest and cruellest emanation of Labour belligerency that modern history takes count of'.[10] In April, Wright's research took him to Croydon Park, where the man himself was in his shirtsleeves, pipe in mouth, directing the construction of a platform for a meeting.

> I found him at first unwilling to discuss the question, in view of the fact that Mr Connolly, his chief lieutenant, was bringing out a book on the subject of the strike, but eventually he opened his mind and we had a most interesting talk on the varied phases of the problem . . . A tall, loose-limbed man, with a slight stoop in the shoulders, he gave at the moment little impression of the popular idol; but we had not been speaking long before I discovered that the man was no ordinary type of agitator. His brain was full of ideas, crude and impracticable for the most part, but suggesting originality of thought and a wider outlook than that commonly attributed to him.[11]

Their subsequent discussion ranged over Larkin's views on guild socialism and *New Age*: 'recommended'; the Dublin employers: 'merciless' and less compromising than 'their English prototypes'; Irish industry: crippled by the reluctance of the banks to lend at less than 'impossible' rates; priests and politicians: 'the curses of Ireland'; the Hibernians: 'Catholic Orangemen . . . worse than Protestant Orangemen'; the slums: 'the fault of a corrupt Corporation'; corruption: 'rooted in jobbery and the registration system'; and Home Rule: 'the one thing . . . which would save Ireland.'[12]

If Wright was charmed, the ITGWU's no 1 branch committee disliked what they saw as self-indulgent distractions from immediate difficulties. The problem was compounded by the fact that while Larkin genuinely believed in the need for unions to undertake commercial projects, for financial as well as politically demonstrative reasons, he lacked the application to realise them. Delia enjoyed a minor success in establishing a small shirt factory under the aegis of the Women Workers' Co-operative Society in Liberty Hall. A Workers' Co-operative Stores, selling men's, women's, and children's wear was opened later at 31 Eden Quay.[13] Jim's expenditure – 'large expenditure' according to Foran – on Croydon Park, buying a cow, swinging boats, and tents, was portrayed as insensitive when thousands of union members were destitute. In reality, the situation was more complicated.

As the lockout progressed, the ITGWU's real income dwindled, but donations received through the Central Lockout Committee came to be 'considerably in excess of expenditure on strike pay' and a surplus was put aside each week in the safe in Liberty Hall. By Christmas, the safe contained about £7,500. What happened when Larkin returned to Dublin before Christmas says a lot about how the union was changing. Foran refused to tell him the size of the nest egg for fear he would squander it. The general secretary replied: 'I don't want to know the actual position; I only want to know is the Union safe.' Foran said it was.[14] When the Central Lockout Committee refused an appeal for a grant for Christmas bonuses, Larkin proceeded regardless. About £1,800 to £2,000 was disbursed in special payments, and three marquees were raised in Croydon Park to provide treats for 5,000 children. The no 1 branch committee wanted to spend £3,500 on paying off the mortgage on Liberty Hall, fearing the union might be evicted, and hold the remainder to cover anticipated post-lockout expenses. It was especially concerned about legal fees and particularly annoyed by Larkin's pursuit of appeals against a judgement in favour of stevedore Matthew Long. Larkin's last instruction to Connolly was to fight the case all the way to the House of Lords. Connolly obeyed, swallowing his conviction that it was 'money thrown away'.[15] Understandably, the committee was anxious about the day when the donations dried up. Excluding the special fund, its cash in hand on 6 January 1914 was a mere £144. In March 1914 the committee compelled Larkin to authorise the purchase of Liberty Hall before any further expenditure was approved. As Larkin saw it, the committee was deliberately frustrating the application of his social vision for the union. The dispute was not just about money, and the implications were serious. Due to his lengthy absences in Britain, and concentration on oratory rather than administration, Larkin had lost control of union management. Senior officers had come to resent Croydon Park as a personal hobby-horse of his, synonymous with his neglect of the union. Within days of his departure to the US, the no 1 branch committee discussed the upkeep of Croydon Park. Connolly initiated a review in March 1915 and in June the committee decided to surrender the lease.[16]

THE PARLIAMENTARY COMMITTEE, DUBLIN TRADES COUNCIL, AND PARTITION

Larkin's second term as chairman of the Parliamentary Committee did at least go smoother than the first. The Committee was now evolving into something like a permanent executive for the ITUC, taking a more pro-active role and providing a greater continuity of leadership. While it is difficult to be definitive, the evidence suggests that this owed more to William O'Brien, vice-chairman in 1912–13, and Tom Johnson, vice-chairman in 1913–14, than Larkin. Larkin frequently missed meetings of the Parliamentary Committee, and was absent from two of its major initiatives, a conferences with the British Labour Party in September 1913 and a deputation to Westminster in May 1914. Neither had he mobilised the Parliamentary Committee in the lockout. The Committee's annual report claimed it had been 'busily engaged during the year in connection with the dispute in Dublin'. Individual members had been, and the ITUC had observer status at some meetings during the lockout, but the Committee per se did not record any activity between September 1913 and March 1914.[17] Larkin headed to Glasgow for May Day 1914, to speak at rallies convened by the *Daily Herald* League, the Industrial Workers of Great Britain, and the Socialist Labour Party.[18] He left the Parliamentary Committee to press its concerns with the British Labour Party, on social legislation and relations with the party as well as partition, and send a delegation to Westminster on 12 May. Talks with John Redmond and Joe Devlin followed on 13th, and on 14th, through the IPP leaders, the delegation secured a long sought after audience with Augustine Birrell, Chief Secretary for Ireland, something British Labour had declined to deliver.[19]

Being out of the country so often, Larkin was unavoidably absent from most sessions of Dublin trades council in 1914. The council was still important to him, and he attended when possible, speaking at seven of its 19 meetings between January and September, and getting himself elected to its six member conciliation board in April. In June he had the council condemn a priest in Kingstown who was trying to form a non-militant 'yellow' trade union, and the council agreed, on his recommendation, to lobby the Archbishop of Dublin.[20]

One issue on which Larkin took a keen interest was partition. In March Asquith suggested that counties might be allowed to opt out of the Government of Ireland Act for up to six years. As the idea had been gaining ground in Unionist circles since 1912, and the Conservatives were likely to be back in power within six years, it was obvious that permanent partition was now a real prospect. The threat was reinforced by the 'Curragh mutiny' on 20 March, when General Sir Hubert Gough and 57 out of 70 army officers at the Curragh declared that they would resign their commissions rather than enforce Home Rule in Ulster. Larkin was furious at the consequences for his 'native' province. Not all colleagues shared his republicanism, but virtually all were convinced that partition would be disastrous for workers. Johnson put the conventional wisdom most cogently, and echoed Larkin's fears for Labour's chances in the Home Rule parliament:

> All their hopes of uniting the workers of the North and South would be destroyed. Organisation on sectarian lines would be extended and 'tightened up'. Employers would continue to use sectarianism and political issues to keep workers apart. Under any exclusion of Ulster scheme – even temporary – the effect on proposals for industrial legislation of a remedial character would be fatal for both North and South – the included and the excluded area. The included area would be predominantly rural and agricultural – its representatives in the Irish Parliament would hesitate to pass any measures of a beneficial character for the industrial worker for fear of repelling the Ulster farmer and capitalist. The cue of the Irish parliament would be to be conservative in legislation and administration with a view to inducing the Ulster party to come in. On the other hand the Ulster worker would be left outside the pale of either Irish or British parliament. Remedial measures brought before the parliament at Westminster would be left to apply only to Britain – Ulster being in a state of suspension – a good excuse would be available for restricting these measures to Britain and making them not applicable to Ulster.[21]

The Parliamentary Committee protested to Asquith, Birrell, and the party leaders at Westminster. British Labour replied that party officers were of a like mind with the ITUC on Ulster, adding, ambiguously, that 'anything the Party may ultimately agree to by way of amendment to the present Home Rule Bill will be agreed to in order to make any measure of Home Rule possible and with a view to creating circumstances that will eventually lead to complete

Home Rule'. It was not deemed a satisfactory position, and the Parliamentary Committee again complained that British Labour was taking its cue on Ireland from counsels other than Irish Labour.[22] On 27 March the Parliamentary Committee issued a 'Manifesto to the workers of Ireland'. Written by Larkin, its sentiments were more nationalist than Labourist:

> Fellow workers,
>
> Arouse! Awake! Arise! We are in the midst of a national crisis. The workers of Ireland have been kept asunder and divided in regard to political action during the past 30 years. They have been utilised and humbugged by the various political parties. And after that long period of waiting we find that the workers are the only class in the community whose interests are not consulted . . .
>
> To us of the Irish working class the division of Ireland into two parts is unthinkable. To us as Irish men the cutting off of that province or any part thereof which gave to our country such men as Shane O'Neill, Hugh Roe O'Donnell, Aodh Rua O'Neill, McCracken, Orr, Francis Davis, 'The Belfast Man', and the host of northern men who battled for freedom, and which from a labour as well as a national point of view is of such importance, is an act of pure suicide and should not be persisted in. We claim Ulster in its entirety, her sons are our brothers, and we are opposed to any attempt to divide us.
>
> As Irish workers we are not concerned with the officers of the British army taking the line they have, nor are we concerned, because of the effect their action may have on Britain's army, but we claim that what the officer may do in pursuance of his political and sectarian convictions, so too may the private in pursuance of his; and if today British generals and other staff officers refuse to fight against the privileged class to which they belong, so, too, must the private soldier be allowed to exercise his convictions against shooting down his brothers and sisters of the working class when they are fighting for their rights.
>
> If it is lawful for Carson to arm, it is lawful for us . . .
>
> THE WILL OF THE PEOPLE MUST PREVAIL. GOD SAVE THE PEOPLE![23]

Congress convened a mass indignation meeting in Dublin on 5 April, at which a resolution again displaced Labourist with nationalist arguments, and included a veiled allusion to the Citizen Army.

> That this mass meeting of Irish workers places on record its emphatic protest against the suggested exclusion of any portion of Ireland, whether temporary or permanent, from the provisions of the Home Rule bill, as we consider such exclusion would be a national disgrace, and, in addition, we feel that the separation of the democracy of Ulster from those of the other provinces would be a dire calamity. That in strongly and emphatically protesting against the recent attempt

of certain military officers to utilise the armed forces in the country for the purpose of furthering the interests of their class, we desire to impress upon the workers the necessity for learning aright and fully digesting the full significance of this action, and to in future apply it in a similar manner in the interests of their own class.[24]

REBUILDING THE CITIZEN ARMY

In March, Larkin had presided over the re-organisation of the Citizen Army. He had fallen out dramatically with Jack White in O'Connell Street on 11 January at a meeting in protest against a commission of enquiry into police behaviour during the lockout. Labour held the commission's terms of reference to be inadequate. White arrived from another platform to loud cheers. Distracted in full flow, Larkin rounded on him as 'the son of Sir George White, who defended the British flag at Ladysmith, the dirty flag under which more disease and degradation has been experienced than anything else I know of'. White stormed off the platform, upset at the reference to his recently deceased father rather than the flag. Larkin eventually apologised over ten years later. Meanwhile, White returned to drilling at Croydon Park, but relations between the two remained tense.[25]

White never managed to hold together the core of his force, and matters worsened with the end of the lockout, when the army lost its original sense of purpose and dwindled to company strength. A serious humiliation occurred on 13 March after White called on a meeting of unemployed workers at Liberty Hall to form a hunger-march to the Mansion House. A police baton charge dispersed the crowd on Butt Bridge, the Citizen Army escorts melted away and the press ridiculed them as 'the runaway army'.[26] White himself swung his shillelagh at the DMP before yielding to a severe clubbing and a nasty head-wound. He made the most of his days in court, enjoying the chance to beard the establishment. Larkin was not amused to see another playing that game, and actually complained of the magistrate's leniency.

> The law, moryah! must take its course. We say because Captain White is Captain White he is allowed to go free . . . Captain White and his counsel [were allowed] to turn the court into a theatre and enact a farce. But what a change when a poor, hard-working man who honestly admitted he had committed a common assault on a scab . . .[27]

It was Seán O'Casey who proposed the re-organisation of the Citizen Army in an interview with White. Both met with Connolly, Constance Markievicz, W. P. Partridge, and P. T. Daly, and all agreed to ask Larkin to preside over a public meeting in Liberty Hall on 22 March. With, according to O'Casey, 'the enthusiasm of young boy for a new toy', Larkin told the gathering that the army would have a uniform, a constitution, and an army council.[28] The uniform would be dark green with the Cronje hat popularised by the Boers. Arrangements were made later to acquire belts, haversacks, bayonets, and about a dozen rifles. The five article constitution, drafted by O'Casey, was intended to clarify the values and aims of the army and distinguish it from the Irish Volunteers. It affirmed the army as Labour and republican. Larkin insisted on the fifth article, requiring every member, if eligible, to be a trade unionist.[29] The army council included Larkin, as one of five vice-chairmen, O'Casey as secretary, Richard Brannigan and Markievicz as treasurers, and White as chairman; the Belfast-based Connolly was not a member. As Richard Braithwaite, Brannigan had been secretary of the Belfast Protestant Association and the man who put the infamous sectarian questionnaire to William Walker in 1905.[30] The Starry Plough appeared in April. Who designed the flag is unknown. Plausibly, given his love of literature and theatre, O'Casey believed it to be based on an idea of Larkin's, in turn inspired by Ryan's 1910 novel *The Plough and the Cross*, 'of which he sometimes spoke'.

> Jim Larkin had often complained about the common, dull, and gaudy banners carried by Labour Unions, all vulgar oilpainted things, and without much imagination. He mentioned that the Irish Citizen Army should show an example of what a flag could be like; and I, for one, assign the suggestion of the design to him.[31]

On 6 April Markievicz made a personal appeal to Dublin trades council for an army of 5,000 men.[32] Larkin spoke of each union contributing a unit, but the army was never embedded in the unions in this way, though endorsed by Dublin trades council. Recruitment drives consisted of White taking senior officers – including Larkin on occasion – to various points around Dublin in his motor car, and holding an open-air meeting. Enrolment remained sluggish.

Larkin took over as chairman of the army council in May. A self-confessed 'dictator', White was as averse as Larkin to conciliar governance, and suspected that the real function of the army council was to clip his wings. It was only a matter of time before something triggered his resignation.[33] It came when O'Casey opposed collaboration with the Irish Volunteers. A former IRB man himself, the cantankerous O'Casey was vehemently opposed to the Volunteers, and could not disguise his personal dislike of bourgeois elements like White and Markievicz. White decamped to command the Volunteer battalions in Derry. Wary of IPP influence, Larkin shared a suspicion of the Volunteers, but not O'Casey's hostility to republicans. In June the Volunteers accepted Redmond's demands for the appointment of 25 IPP nominees on their executive. Larkin's disgust was offset by the IRB's denunciation of the IPP take-over, and he paraded two companies of the Citizen Army with the Volunteers at the annual Wolfe Tone commemoration in Bodenstown on 21 June.[34] The commemoration had been initiated by Tom Clarke, treasurer and *de facto* 'head centre' of the IRB, in 1911 and was associated explicitly with the separatists.

Bodenstown marked a turning point in relations between the Citizen Army and the IRB. O'Casey claimed that in 1912 the IRB's Freedom Club had sought a pact with Larkin providing for mutual aid in elections and publicity, and that he and Seán MacDermott had formed a deputation to Liberty Hall.[35] If so, nothing much came of it until Larkin arrived at Bodenstown, where he was greeted warmly by Clarke.[36] The Citizen Army again marched with the Volunteers at the funerals of those killed at Bachelor's Walk on 26 July. 'Birrell's bloody bullies', as the *Irish Worker* put it, had been rushed to Howth earlier that day in 'William Murder Murphy's tramcars', to intercept the landing of 1,500 rifles from the *Asgard*.[37] They failed, and some of the rifles were dumped in Croydon Park, and a few purloined by the Citizen Army. Troops returning from Howth fired on a jeering crowd in the centre of Dublin, killing four and wounding 37. One of the few motion pictures of Larkin shows him in his black broad-brimmer walking tall at the head of the Citizen Army in the cortège. Evidently he had more success than White in building the nucleus of an army.

'ON THE THRESHOLD OF A NEWER MOVEMENT'

Writing to O'Brien on 8 June, Connolly hoped that the ITUC annual congress 'might act as a tonic on Jim and get him to act with vigour again'.[38] He did rally somewhat for the occasion, held on 1–3 June in the council chamber of Dublin's City Hall. This time he delivered the presidential address, the first to be given *ex tempore*. He sloughed off the lockout summarily as a failed attempt 'to starve them into submission', and then faced the future. It was what the delegates wanted. There was a sense among them that they had weathered the worst, and Larkin's affirmation, 'We are now on the threshold of a newer movement with a newer hope and new inspiration' was received with cheers. He emphasised the need for industrial unionism, a Labour party, and opposition to partition. The British Co-operative Wholesale Society, concurrently holding its annual conference in Dublin, was singled out for commendation. Having visited the Co-operative Exhibition in the Rotunda, he urged that co-ops, 'the safest line of advance', be taken as seriously in the south as they were in the north and Britain. Noting the irony of the venue, he referred to his expulsion from the Corporation and hopes of re-election, and concluded with an exhortation to live and die 'to win back, in the words of Erin's greatest living poet [Yeats?], for Cathlin ni Houlihan her four beautiful fields (loud and prolonged cheering)'. Those who expected an eloquent and historic oration were not disappointed, and Larkin's appeal for co-ops was more than rhetorical.[39] Weeks later he would tell an audience in Sheffield:

> Get in the cooperative movement. Make it a real cooperative movement. Build up round your Trade Union, as we do in Dublin, every social movement, every part of your material side of life. Make your centre of Trade Unionism a centre of all your life and activities.[40]

Connolly made his own historic contribution to the Congress by presenting each delegate with a copy of *Labour in Irish History*.

It was the most political Congress to date, with much of the business taken up with a new constitution, which changed the title of the ITUC to ITUC and Labour Party and of the Parliamentary Committee to the National Executive. Congress also discussed the composition of the party and its relations with its British counterpart, partition, which was condemned overwhelmingly, and the provisions of the Home Rule bill. Congress's demands for the schedules of the bill were reiterated, with some controversy over the choice of electoral system. In 1913 it was resolved unanimously that the government's decision to adopt proportional representation with the single transferable vote in constituencies returning more than two members should be applied to all constituencies. When Dublin trades council drafted a similar motion for Congress in 1914, Larkin had the electoral system changed to the alternative vote. At Congress, D. R. Campbell moved an amendment to reinstate the single transferable vote. O'Brien supported Campbell, and techy exchanges with the chairman suggest that his antipathy to Larkin was well advanced. Larkin, he ventured, with a studied barb, had been persuaded against proportional representation by Ramsay MacDonald's 'honeyed words' at the British Labour Party conference in Glasgow. Connolly secured an adjournment before the bickering escalated. After the resumption, Campbell's amendment was passed by 41–6 votes.[41] Larkin made a difficult chairman, interrupting speakers, making free with comment, and taking offence easily. Moving the vote of thanks, Thomas Cassidy, Typographical Society, Derry, congratulated him on 'a fine natural oration', adding: 'The only objection raised to his proceedings was that he arrogated too much of the time. But all would confess that Mr Larkin was an impartial Chairman. He had no respect for what delegate he sat upon.' Others were a trifle more circumspect. Larkin took it all with equanimity. 'He was a strong man,' he said, 'with any amount of confidence. He would love his enemies and beat his friends into doing things.'[42]

Soon after the Congress a dispute arose between Delia and the ITGWU's no 1 branch committee. There was widespread resentment in the union at Delia's arrogance and influence over Jim. Her brother found her a sinecure in the ITGWU's insurance section on its establishment, subsidising her real work as *Irish Worker* correspondent and accountant, and IWWU secretary. Suspicions of creeping nepotism would not have been eased by Pete's arrival in Ireland in 1913 and work as an ITGWU organiser in Dublin and Cork. He returned to England during the lockout, but two studio portraits of Pete as a public speaker, by commercial photographers A. H. Poole of Waterford, suggest he had given serious thought to a career as a full-time union official.[43] Delia had refused to provide accounts for the IWWU or her Dramatic Troupe's fund-raising tour of England after the lockout. The committee demanded the IWWU vacate the largest room in Liberty Hall, which it occupied rent-free.[44]

Jim submitted his resignation. No effort was spared to get the decision reversed. On Sunday 21 June, three bands and a great procession met him at Kingsbridge as he returned from the Wolfe Tone commemoration at Bodenstown. The throng declared that unless he stayed on, they would camp overnight at Croydon Park. The next day a special general meeting of the ITGWU packed into the Antient Concert Rooms, where Jim set out his position with a mixture of candour and dishonesty. He began by saying he had intended to leave for the good of the union. Recalling the ordeal of the lockout, he explained that he had been affected by 'strong emotion and physical disabilities', and was 'fighting depression and physical difficulties'. 'No one under God's sun knows what I have been through,' he said. He also referred to disappointing results in the recent Poor Law Guardians elections, and complained of lack of support from the no 1 branch committee. He wanted to set up a medical clinic, and a dental surgery in Liberty Hall, employ a family nurse, and start an open air school at Croydon Park for mentally disabled children. But the greatest obstacle was the 'penny-wise' committee, which was overly concerned with finance, forgetting that social schemes were 'an essential part of their work'. In addition, Countess Markievicz and Delia had been insulted. Throughout the oration the audience responded to his every entreaty for reassurance and the union officials were happy to soak up the censures, and lavish praise in return.[45] Whether Jim wanted to resign there and then is doubtful. The resignation ploy was a tactic to put manners on the no 1 branch committee. What he didn't say was that he was planning to leave, but would do so in his own time and on his own terms. He made another reference to his health in Trafalgar Square on 5 July, saying he was speaking 'against doctor's orders'.[46]

Larkin was in London, with Connolly, to attend the amalgamation conference of two major British trade union alliances, the NTWF and the General Labourers' National Council, in Caxton Hall on 8 July. Their presence was curious on several grounds. The ITGWU was not affiliated to either alliance, having been kept out of the NTWF by James Sexton, and with memories of the lockout all too fresh, neither Irishman was very welcome in Caxton Hall. Both were sceptical of this 'greater unionism', as it was called. A policy of amalgamation was the BTUC's response to the great unrest – and the most important legacy of the unrest for trade unionism. In 1912, 47 unions, with some 400,000 members, sought to rationalise themselves into five amalgamations. In 1913, three of the four railway unions formed the National Union of Railwaymen.[47] Connolly had argued, in articles in *Forward* and *New Age* in April and May, that 'greater unionism' would not only destroy the spontaneity and 'sporadic' action that were the weapons of victory in 1911, but was designed to do just that, and amounted to pouring the old wine of craft unionism into new bottles of industrial unionism.[48] Larkin too was critical of 'greater unionism' and its 'stagecoach' leaders. It was also likely that participation in the amalgamation would subordinate the ITGWU to a new UK federation, and ultimately assimilate it into a UK trade union. The explanation, perhaps, is that Connolly could not reject the logic of the OBU idea, and Larkin was concerned about the implications of developments in British trade unionism for his own union. He continued to monitor events in Britain, and had contributed to the recent debate in the NTWF on the employment of cheap Asian labour in Britain and British shipping, dismissing various racist solutions and saying the problem could be resolved 'in one hour' by organising 'the Lascars', as the Indian seafarers were called.[49] Both Irish delegates wanted the ITGWU to be affiliated on an international basis. James O'Connor Kessack told them to stop 'ranting about nationalism' and the conference thought they should be satisfied with provision for district machinery. Despite this setback, Larkin was among those urging amalgamation without delay. Frustrated with calls for caution, he shouted sarcastically at the chairman, 'I move that it be in twelve years' time.' It was agreed to amalgamate 'as soon as possible', but the timetable was overtaken by events in Europe.[50] Larkin pronounced the conference 'a qualified success'.[51]

After Caxton Hall, Larkin spoke at Sheffield, and then moved further north to speak at a Northumberland miners' picnic at Morpeth, and the miners' gala at Durham.[52]

THE WORLD WAR

On 22 March the *Irish Worker* deplored Dublin Corporation's motion of
sympathy to the Greek royal family on the assassination of King George I. If
anyone deserved sympathy, Larkin argued, it was the families of the '300,000
workers' murdered by the kings, czars, and sultans of the Balkans in their
recent wars. He quoted James Russell Lowell's American dialect poem: 'He
that takes a sword and draws it, and goes stick a fellow thro', Government 'aint
got to answer for it, God will send the bill to you.' His attitude to the world
war was the same, with the one big difference that England's difficulty was
Ireland's opportunity. The *Irish Worker* said little on the gathering storm in
Europe until Britain declared war on Germany on 4 August. Subsequently,
the war would preoccupy the paper. On 8th Larkin savaged 'the half-imbecile
beasts, who call themselves kings, emperors, kaisers, and czars, [and] launch
millions of men, built in the image of God, to destruction'. 'Remember,' he
continued, 'by taking Britain's side in this unholy war you are giving up your
claim that Ireland is a Nation . . . Stop at home. Keep your guns for your real
enemies'. A powerful editorial the following week pleaded with workers not
to let themselves be 'offered up as a sacrifice on the altar of the god of war . . .
to shoot and kill . . . men [with whom] they have no quarrel' for the same class
that starved them 12 months ago. In a now typical flourish, the class critique
concluded with an appeal to manliness and Irishness.

> It is for you to remember the great Queen who has drank the waters of bitterness
> for eight hundred years! Surely you will not disgrace the fathers that bore you?
> They suffered and died that she, "Our Dark Rosaleen", might enter into her
> inheritance.[53]

His antipathy to 'Judas' Redmond reached new heights. Redmond had pledged
Ireland's support for Britain should she declare war, and even before his
speech at Woodenbridge on 20 September, urging the Irish Volunteers to join
the war, he was depicted in the *Irish Worker* as a British recruiting sergeant.
Equally, Larkin made it plain that he was not pro-German, saluting the
Belgian resistance to the German invaders:

> We are with them heart and soul, because by their side and in their company, we
> are defending at the same time two great causes – the independence of small States
> and the sanctity of international obligations.[54]

On Sunday 16 August Larkin reviewed the Citizen Army at Croydon Park
and inspected one of their rifles, a German weapon of Franco-Prussian war

vintage. It was worth 5s 6d he said to general laughter, adding that if they wanted to win Ireland for Kathleen Ní Houlihan, they should get serviceable rifles 'immediately'. Fred Bower recalled that 'sometime' before his departure to the US, Larkin arranged for him to smuggle six guns from Liverpool to Dublin, packed in a crate marked 'Tombstone, With Care'. Bower reckoned the Irish respect for the dead would see it undisturbed.[55] A 'fully armed' Citizen Army marched up O'Connell Street on 30 August to mark the first anniversary of 'Bloody Sunday' and commemorate the 'Lockout martyrs'. Larkin concluded his speech with an affirmation that 'England's difficulty was Ireland's opportunity'. He said much the same at a rally in Cork a week later.[56] The war increased his interest in the Citizen Army, and he promised to assume 'active command'. In October a new army council was appointed, under 'Jim Larkin, CO'.[57]

From the defensive tone of his speeches, it is clear that Larkin felt he was swimming against a tide of war-fever, underpinned by what Labour would come to call 'economic conscription'. A Dublin mob had attacked German pork-butcher shops on the outbreak of the war, and the *Irish Worker* regularly deplored the loss of ITGWU men to the colours. Yet he need not have been so pessimistic. Labour activists at least refused to go with the flow. The ITGWU gave Larkin unquestioned backing. Dublin trades council protested against Redmond 'acting as a recruiting sergeant for the British Army', and affirmed its belief that 'Ireland should remain neutral as between England and Germany'.[58] And the ITUC executive, of which Larkin was vice-chairman, issued an anti-war manifesto on 10 August.[59]

'IS LARKIN GOING OUT, OR NOT?'

Larkin's departure was a messy affair which left his colleagues confused and increasingly doubtful about him. Coincidentally, in January 1914, nine Labour agitators were deported from South Africa to England. The subversion of free labour on the Witwatersrand by the importation of indentured Chinese 'coolies' had generated a furore in Britain in the run-up to the 1906 general election, Larkin himself had made a big issue of it as Sexton's political agent in West Toxteth, and this latest attempt to shackle South African trade unionists caused outrage. The rebels promptly mobilised to push Ramsay MacDonald into action, and the *Daily Herald* returned fire on Pretoria by despatching Tom Mann to South Africa. Larkin deplored British Labour's passivity on South Africa at Birmingham on 27 January, and spoke with Mann on 18 February at a rally for the deportees in London's East End. Dublin trades council lobbied the BTUC Parliamentary Committee to be included in a series of indignation meetings at which the South Africans would speak.[60] In March one of the deportees, Archie Crawford, delayed at Huddersfield to tell Larkin how much he was admired in South Africa. Crawford's partner and future wife, 'Pickhandle Mary' Fitzgerald, a doughty agitator in her own right, was Irish. Larkin said he hoped to visit the Rand at an early date. A lecture of Larkin's in Llanelli on 27 March was oddly entitled 'Dublin, South Africa, and socialism', though it dealt mainly with strikes in Britain.[61] Larkin was now taken with the idea of going 'right round', and tried to set up a tour of the US, South Africa, Australia, and New Zealand. On 28 April he wrote to Patrick Hickey, Wobbly and general secretary of the United Labour Federation of New Zealand, proposing to visit New Zealand in September to raise funds for co-ops in Dublin. On 30th he wrote to another Wobbly, Joe Pick of Cape Town, saying he might be in South Africa in a few months. Some letters revealed his demoralisation: 10 June, to the editor of *Forward*: '[I] have been out of humour both with myself and the world generally . . .'; 11 June, to Will Lawther, Durham miners' leader: 'I am dead tired . . .'; on 1 July he declined a speaking invitation from Lawther, and on 16 July replied to another request saying his going to America ruled out all engagements 'for some time'; also on 16 July, he wrote to Leon Reeves: 'as you are no doubt aware I am trying to get out of the country for a time.'[62]

But where to and to what end? In June Larkin told Connolly he was in contact with Haywood and gave the impression he was minded on a short, American tour. With an eye, as ever, on developing electoral politics, Connolly suggested he might fund-raise for the Labour Party in the US; a proposal Larkin later twisted to allege that Connolly beguiled him into travelling to America to be rid of his more popular chief.[63] For all their personal differences, and his frustration with despatching endless pleas to Liberty Hall for money for the Belfast office, Connolly appreciated the value of Larkin at the ballot-box and hoped he would stay in Ireland if his condition improved, but accepted O'Brien's view that it probably wouldn't and that a tour would be beneficial.[64] The dithering and deception continued. On 1 July Larkin wrote to Con O'Lyhane, New York, about crossing 'the big stream' in August 'to represent the new Irish Labour Party and our own Union'. O'Lyhane would become his primary contact in the US. Three years younger than Larkin and a trained chemist, he had worked with Connolly's Irish Socialist Republican Party in Cork, moved to London, led the Socialist Party of Great Britain, played a part in the Fiery Cross, and emigrated to the US in May 1914 to become a roving agitator and speaker, where he was known as Lehane or O'Lehane 'the man from Cork'. Larkin attended his farewell banquet. Also on 1 July, a letter went to 'Madam' [Markievicz?] saying

We are going through a very rough period over here but things must improve . . . I have one or two invitations from South Africa which I may accept and I would be glad of any advice from you or if you could put me in touch with anyone in the movement out there.[65]

Later that month Larkin spoke alongside Crawford at a rally for the South Africans in Croydon Park, and declared he 'would never leave Ireland so long as he had the confidence and support of the working class (cheers)'.[66] At the same time Connolly told O'Brien that Larkin intended to leave in September on a world tour, and suggested that Councillor Richard O'Carrroll and P. T. Daly travel as ITUC delegates and all be home by December for the elections.[67] On 10 August, the ITUC executive proposed a two-man US tour to raise funds for the Labour Party. To O'Brien's surprise, Larkin said he would rather go alone, and 'freelance'.[68] Writing on 18 August to Patrick Quinlan, a former colleague of Connolly's in New York, he explained candidly:

> I have not had a holiday for years, and I am not in love at present with the work here, and maybe the change would do good all round. I have had invitations from Canada, New Zealand, and Australia, and I was proposing taking a run right round with a view to collecting monies in advancement of the movement here at home . . .[69]

Another enquiry was despatched to the Workingmen's Union in Butte, Montana, where large numbers of men from Cork and Waterford had settled in the late nineteenth century to mine the 'copper mountain'. The Butte correspondent offered detailed advice and encouragement, with the warning that trade was 'dull' and he might be better off trying the colonies first.[70] On 22 August Connolly wrote to O'Brien: 'I am in a fog . . . Is Larkin going out, or not?'[71]

Relations within Liberty Hall were turning sour. In late August, the no 1 branch committee demanded that Delia pay for the use of a piano which she had appropriated for the IWWU's cultural activities. She refused and Jim declined to intervene. On 5 September, the committee requested Delia to take the IWWU elsewhere. When Jim threatened to call a general meeting to 'deal with the committee', the committee resolved to resign *en bloc*. Jim postponed the meeting. Connolly had told O'Brien on 5 September that Larkin would be gone in three weeks, and the *Irish Worker* of 12th noted he would soon be leaving. On 4 October, before the dispute with the committee came to a head, Jim announced his departure for the US. On the following day he asked Connolly to move to Dublin to take over the *Irish Worker* and the ITGWU insurance section. Daly was to take over the union. Connolly immediately urged O'Brien to canvass Foran and the no 1 branch committee for the acting general secretary's job, and penned a direct appeal to his boss on 9th.[72] Jim relented. Daly got the troublesome and thankless insurance work.

Larkin delivered a valediction at a carnival at Croydon Park on 18 October. Perhaps in homage to his destination, the Citizen Army mounted a spectacular display 'illustrating an Indian attack on an Irish Emigrant Train crossing the Western Plains, and its rescue by the United States Army'. The 'young Indian girls' were 'the centre of many admiring eyes'. John Simmons, the veteran secretary of Dublin trades council, then read an address. It was remarkably direct about 'the severe strain' of the lockout 'impairing your splendid constitution . . . hence the necessity for rest and recuperation', and hoped that 'with a restoration to your normal conditions of life, you will resume your propaganda in the cause of labour'.[73]

Larkin's last speech in Ireland was made at an anti-war rally in Cork City Hall on 22 October. Partridge had gone on ahead to handle the publicity. Larkin arrived late on the 8.35 pm train, and went direct to the City Hall. In fine form, he scorned the 'canards' about German and Austrian atrocities: 'What was the question at issue? It was the old never-ending struggle that has lasted in this country for seven hundred years . . . The question is the question of the Celt against Saxon despotism and brutality (applause)'.[74] The proceedings terminated with the singing of 'Who Fears to Speak of '98'. The day after, shadowed by two detectives, Larkin boarded the Liverpool boat at Kingstown with two suitcases and a black trunk.[75] He left astern a movement which still believed in him, and in his leadership of the lockout. The *Irish Worker* of 24 October appeared under Connolly's editorship, bearing the front-page strapline 'We serve neither king nor kaiser'.

Various theories were held on why Larkin went to America. Little credence was given to the remarks in his farewell statement in the *Irish Worker* of 24 October. The statement began by saying the visit was in response to US interest in aims and methods of the union. After a blistering denunciation of the world war, and the British Labour 'traitors' preaching 'racial hatred' in defence of it, it went on to invite ITGWU members to subscribe to his expenses at 6d or 1s per week. 'You pay all expenses and take all results . . . All monies accruing from my tour goes [*sic*] to re-build Liberty Hall and start productive works.' It was a strange, throwaway offer, reflective of the lack of preparation for the trip, and of difficulties between Larkin and the no 1 branch committee. The committee had granted him £10 on 13 October 1914 – which would just about cover his fare – and later agreed to ask members to defray his expenses.[76] Some, including friends like O'Casey, thought he wished to evade impending trouble over insurance money misspent on the 1913 struggle. One of Larkin's final acts in Ireland was to persuade O'Casey to attend the tuberculosis clinic in Charles Street. Certainly, the insurance section was a shambles, and nearly dissolved by the National Health Insurance Commissioners in 1914.[77] A more common speculation, expressed in Dublin trades council's eulogy, was that he needed to recuperate and would be back before too long.[78]

Back in an independent Ireland in 1923, and having sent very little money from the US, he denied that his mission was to raise funds for Liberty Hall, insisting that he had left on the appeal of Connolly, Clarke, and Patrick Pearse to get arms and ammunition. This was refuted by Mrs Connolly, Mrs Clarke, and John Devoy of Clan na Gael, the American counterpart of the IRB, but there may have been something in it.[79] The DMP believed that he was already receiving money from the Germans through Clan na Gael and that his 'real object' in the US was to 'advance German interests'.[80] Ten years on he swore an affidavit to a US judge that his purpose was 'to interest the workers of the United States in the condition of the Irish labour movement and with a view of getting material and political assistance for the revolutionary movement in Ireland'.[81] Whatever his immediate objective, there was a more fundamental motive. He had wanted to move on since December 1913. He had little to do with Belfast after 1907, or Cork after 1909. To say he was worn out is half true. He was tired of failure and running a crippled union. He needed action and success. Both Haywood and Carney believed the US to be the start of a world tour. Mercury was taking flight 'on spec'.

NOTES

1 UUMC, ITUC, *Annual Report* (1914), p. 38.

2 *New York Times*, 25–26, 29 December 1913. Speculation about a visit to the US and the possibility of being denied entry was also carried in Chicago. See *Day Book*, 7 January 1914.

3 Births Deaths Marriages Ltd, certificate, issued 2 August 2011, registration number 1182036.

4 *Irish Worker*, 21 October 1914.

5 *Liverpool Forward*, 13 February 1914; *Irish Worker*, 28 February–21 March 1914; Christopher Murray, *Seán O'Casey: Writer at Work, a Biography* (Dublin, 2004), p. 94.

6 *Irish Worker*, 7 March 1914.

7 Arnold Wright, *Disturbed Dublin: The Story of the Great Strike of 1913–14, with a Description of the Industries of the Irish Capital* (London, 1914), p. 260. Guild socialism was inspired by the ideas of John Ruskin and William Morris, and, more immediately, by Arthur J. Penty, *The Restoration of the Gild System* (London, 1906). *New Age* appeared in 1907.

8 *Irish Worker*, 29 November 1913.

9 C. Desmond Greaves, *The Irish Transport and General Workers' Union: The Formative Years, 1909–1923* (Dublin, 1982), pp. 128–9; Donal Nevin (ed.), *Between Comrades: James Connolly, Letters and Correspondence 1889–1916* (Dublin, 2007), p. 512.

10 Wright, *Disturbed Dublin*, p. 265; James Connolly, *Collected Works, Volume Two* (Dublin, 1988), p. 352.

11 Wright, *Disturbed Dublin*, p. 259.

12 Ibid., pp. 260–3.

13   Emmet O'Connor, *A Labour History of Ireland, 1824–2000* (Dublin, 2011), p. 95; *Workers' Republic*, 20 November 1915.

14   ITGWU, *The Attempt to Smash the Irish Transport and General Workers' Union* (Dublin, 1924), p. 77.

15   Long had won £200 compensation for an attempt by Larkin and others to compel him to join the Stevedores' Association. Larkin first appealed against the judgment in April 1913. In 1915 the House of Lords found against the ITGWU. See *Irish Independent*, 3 December 1912, 24–25 April 1913; ITGWU, *The Attempt to Smash*, pp. xvii, 130–1.

16   NLI, William O'Brien papers, 15676(2), parts 1–2; Francis Devine, *Organising History: A Centenary of SIPTU, 1909–2009* (Dublin, 2009), p. 57; on the Christmas treats for children see Emmet Larkin, 'James Larkin, Labour leader', in Donal Nevin (ed.), *James Larkin: Lion of the Fold* (Dublin, 1998), p. 5; ITGWU, *The Attempt to Smash*, pp. 77–8, 126–7.

17   UUMC, ITUC, *Annual Report* (1914), pp. 1–26.

18   *Irish Worker*, 9 May 1914.

19   UUMC, ITUC, *Annual Report* (1914), pp. 10–16.

20   UUMC, Dublin trades council minutes, 6 April, 29 June 1914.

21   UUMC, ITUC, *Annual Report* (1914), p. 12.

22   Ibid., p. 18.

23   *Irish Worker*, 28 March 1914.

24   J. Anthony Gaughan, *Thomas Johnson, 1872–1963: First Leader of the Labour Party in Dáil Éireann* (Dublin, 1980), p. 37.

25   Pádraig Yeates, *Lockout: Dublin 1913* (Dublin, 2000), p. 520; Jack White, *Misfit* (London, 1930), pp. 266–74.

26   Frank Robbins, *Under the Starry Plough: Recollections of the Irish Citizen Army* (Dublin, 1977), pp. 35–6.

27   White, *Misfit*, pp. 302–3.

28   Seán O'Casey, *The Story of the Irish Citizen Army* (London, 1980), p. 17.

29   *Irish Worker*, 22 August 1914.

30   John Gray, *City in Revolt: James Larkin and the Belfast Dock Strike of 1907* (Belfast, 1985), pp. 213–4.

31   Letters to Jack Carney and Gerald O'Reilly, David Krause (ed.), *The Letters of Seán O'Casey, Volume II, 1942–1954* (New York, 1980), pp. 144–5, 234.

32   UUMC, Dublin trades council minutes, 6 April 1914.

33   White, *Misfit*, p. 306.

34   Adrian Pimley, 'A history of the Irish Citizen Army from 1913 to 1916' (MSocSc, University of Birmingham, 1982).

35   Letter from Seán Ó Cathasaigh, *Evening Telegraph*, 7 March 1918.

36   Donal Nevin, 'The Irish Citizen Army, 1913–1916', in Nevin (ed.), *James Larkin*, pp. 259–60; *Irish Worker*, 16 May 1914.

37   *Irish Worker*, 1 August 1914.

38   Nevin (ed.), *Between Comrades*, p. 515.

39   UUMC, ITUC, *Annual Report* (1914), pp. 32–8.

40   *Daily Herald*, 16 July 1914.

41   UUMC, Dublin trades council minutes, 20 April 1914; UUMC, ITUC, *Annual Report* (1913), pp. 64–9; UUMC, ITUC, *Annual Report* (1914), pp. 63–4.

42 UUMC, ITUC, *Annual Report* (1914), p. 104.

43 Donal Nevin, 'Peter Larkin', in Nevin (ed.), *James Larkin*, p. 440; NLI, Poole collection, Peter Larkin, 2777, P_WP_2498; 2779, P_WP_2499. James O'Connor Kessack attacked Larkin for nepotism during the lockout. *Derry Journal*, 26 November 1913.

44 Theresa Moriarty, 'Delia Larkin: relative obscurity', in Nevin (ed.), *James Larkin*, p. 434.

45 *Irish Worker*, 27 June 1914.

46 Greaves, *The Irish Transport and General Workers' Union*, p. 132.

47 Elie Halevy, *A History of the English People in the Nineteenth Century, VI: The Rule of Democracy, 1905–1914 (Book II)* (London, 1952), p. 483.

48 See James Connolly, *The Axe to the Root and Old Wine in New Bottles* (Dublin, 1934).

49 Ken Coates and Tony Topham, *The History of the Transport and General Workers' Union: Vol. I, Part II, 1912–1922: From Federation to Amalgamation* (Oxford, 1991), pp. 544–5.

50 Ibid., pp. 523, 536–40; on the Larkin-O'Connor Kessack dispute see NLI, William O'Brien papers, 15679(9).

51 Eric Taplin, *The Dockers' Union: A Study of the National Union of Dock Labourers, 1889–1922* (Leicester, 1986), pp. 122–3; *Irish Worker*, 11 July 1914.

52 *Daily Herald*, 16 July 1914; NLI, William O'Brien papers, Henry Bolton to Larkin, 19 July 1914, 15679(1); *Durham Chronicle*, 31 July 1914.

53 *Irish Worker*, 8–15 August 1914.

54 Ibid., 29 August 1914.

55 Fred Bower, *Rolling Stonemason: An Autobiography* (London, 1936), p. 218.

56 *Irish Worker*, 5–12 September 1914.

57 Ibid., 29 August, 10 October 1914.

58 UUMC, Dublin trades council minutes, 21 September 1914.

59 *Irish Worker*, 22 August 1914.

60 *Derry Journal*, 28 January 1914; see Jonathon Hyslop, *The Notorious Syndicalist: J. T. Bain; a Scottish Rebel in Colonial Africa* (Johannesburg, 2004), pp. 1–2, 247; *Irish Worker*, 28 February 1914; UUMC, Dublin trades council minutes, 9–23 February 1914.

61 *Irish Worker*, 28 March, 4 April 1914.

62 NLI, William O'Brien and Thomas Kennedy papers, 33718/H(223); 33718/A (1–23).

63 Donal Nevin, 'Larkin and Connolly', in Nevin (ed.), *James Larkin*, pp. 404–5; Bertram D. Wolfe, *Strange Communists I Have Known* (New York, 1982), p. 64; Benjamin Gitlow, *The Whole of Their Lives: Communism in America – A Personal History and Intimate Portrayal of Its Leaders* (London, 1948), p. 38.

64 Nevin (ed.), *Between Comrades*, p. 515.

65 ITGWU, *The Attempt to Smash*, p. 165; NLI, William O'Brien papers, 15679(1); Nevin (ed.), *Between Comrades*, pp. 638–9.

66 *Irish Worker*, 25 July 1914.

67 Nevin (ed.), *Between Comrades*, pp. 515–7.

68 ITGWU, *The Attempt to Smash*, p. 166.

69 Ibid.

70 Letter to Larkin, 1 September 1914, NLI, William O'Brien papers, 15679(1).

71 Nevin (ed.), *Between Comrades*, p. 519.

72 Ibid., pp. 520–4.

73 *Irish Worker*, 24 October 1914.

74 Ibid., 31 October 1914; NAUK, CO 904/206/4, file 233B, James Larkin, 1914–15. The police put the attendance at 300.

75 NAUK, CO 904/206/4, file 233B, James Larkin, 1914–15.

76 ITGWU, *The Attempt to Smash*, p. 127.

77 C. Desmond Greaves, *Seán O'Casey: Politics and Art* (London, 1979), p. 148; Christopher Murray, *Seán O'Casey: Writer at Work, a Biography* (Dublin, 2004), p. 92; ITGWU, *The Attempt to Smash*, p. xiii, 165.

78 *Irish Worker*, 24 October 1914.

79 Gaughan, *Thomas Johnson*, pp. 265–6; ITGWU, *The Attempt to Smash*, p. 147; *Irish Independent*, 16 May, 12 June 1923; *Gaelic American*, 7 July 1923.

80 NAUK, CO 904/206/4, file 233B, James Larkin, 1914–15.

81 'Affidavit of James Larkin', made at the request of the US government on 21 January 1934, to assist the US in claiming compensation from Germany for acts of sabotage by its agents in the US during the First World War, reproduced in 'The Larkin affidavit', in Nevin (ed.), *James Larkin*, p. 298.

NINE

KAISER JIM, 1914–17

*America proved Jim Larkin's undoing. Like Antaeus his strength was great as long as he
was in touch with his mother earth. In America, he was out of his element.*
Bert Wolfe[1]

———

James Larkin's early career in the US is almost as enigmatic as his reasons for
going to America. On arrival, he associated with Clan na Gael. From January
1915 he moved closer to the Socialist Party and Labour unions. From November
1915 to October 1917 he worked with agents of imperial Germany. After that,
he joined the far left. Bert Wolfe's analogy with Antaeus reflected a widespread view on the American left, and one accepted by Larkin's biographers,
who have portrayed him as one who went to the US as a socialist agitator,
failed to find a role with his new comrades, and got sidetracked into working
for Clan na Gael and the Germans. The perception of Larkin as a good Labour
man fallen among republicans underestimates the centrality of nationalism to
his politics after 1908. The DMP's belief that his primary purpose in going to
the US was to work with the Clan and the Germans was a caricature, but it
should not be dismissed entirely. The DMP was sufficiently worried to arrange
to have him shadowed in the US, and considered employing a Pinkerton
detective if the American police would not oblige. Scotland Yard also believed
him to be in contact with Germans willing to supply arms.[2] Nothing was simple
where Larkin's personal motives were concerned. He was an anti-war socialist,
and a separatist who favoured an Irish alliance with Germany. He lived frugally
and could not be bought. Equally, he was constantly drawn to easy money,
which he spent as quickly and as mysteriously as he acquired it. He could be
mendacious and foolish, but was not malleable and always had a sharp sense of
his own interests. It beggars belief that he did not appreciate the consequences
of getting so close to Clan na Gael and the Germans. The most plausible explanation is that Larkin was willing to work with Labour, socialist, and republican
groups, and gravitated towards the last for financial reasons. There is no doubt
that he lost credibility on the left as a result.

The DMP's narrow view of Larkin's American intentions is contradicted
by his contacts with various socialists and the fact that he had a simple, open
plan: to make a living from public speaking, to travel, and, if and when the

mood took him, to move on to Australia and South Africa. He was open too on what he would say, and to whom. He told Con O'Lyhane that he was not going to speak 'for any Section', but was 'prepared to speak to any Section'. His topics would be: the new industrial movement, Labour in Ireland, what the worker wants, 'and other subjects'.[3] But in other respects, he was so casual as to imply that he was being taken care of financially by somebody, and that somebody could only be Clan na Gael. Nothing in his extant letters of enquiry to the US entailed any consideration of the logistics, costs, fees, or other expenses. After months of mulling over the possibility, he landed in New York with none of the things that speakers usually had prepared – advance publicity, an arranged lecture tour, a reception committee in each venue, advertising handbills, and pamphlets for sale at meetings. How much money he had with him is unknown.

Larkin didn't delay in Liverpool. He stayed over with Fred Bower and sailed for New York, second class on the *St Louis*, on 24 October, arriving on 2 November after a rough and extended passage.[4] Initially, the prospects looked good. Fame had preceded him, and newspapermen were immediately on hand seeking soundbites. The lockout had been well reported in the US, and the Clan organ *Gaelic American* had praised his attacks on John Redmond's war policy. Dismayed by Redmond, Irish Americans were swinging away from the United Irish League of America to Clan na Gael. While the Clan was as dominated by businessmen and politicians as the League, it was revolutionary. One of its top three personalities, John Devoy, was a typical die-hard Fenian willing to work with almost anyone – from the French Foreign Legion to the International Working Men's Association – to advance Irish independence. He was particularly sympathetic to a Labour-republican alliance. Larkin was hardly off the boat when the socialist paper, *New York Call*, published an interview, and he strained to make a good impression with plenty of American quotations.[5] Most socialists wanted to hear his message of opposition to the world war. Cut off from Germany by the naval blockade, war-related industries were mobilising behind the Allies and many Americans feared being dragged into a European war to fatten the coffers of corporate America. Yet within weeks it was all going wrong for Larkin. At least that was the perception of people like Wolfe, who saw a powerful force failing to realise his obvious potential. Whether Larkin was so unhappy as a maverick is less certain. But he did want more recognition, more influence, and more money. The lecture circuit could be lucrative. Hanna Sheehy Skeffington charged $250 for a talk in Butte, Montana in 1917, and ticket sales raised $584.50c.[6] Despite his renown and oratorical skill, and an ability to raise substantial donations from inspired audiences, Larkin never managed to get himself sufficiently organised to command big fees. By nature, he was an agitator rather than a public lecturer.

Usually, he spoke for nominal sums. He eventually found a generous sponsor, at the price of compromising his reputation.

After presenting his credentials to the Socialist Party of America, Larkin called to the offices of the *Gaelic American* with a note from Tom Clarke asking Devoy to 'do what he could for him'. [7] Larkin's services were promptly availed of. On 8 November, he spoke to 15,000 people in Madison Square Garden at a rally to celebrate the election of Meyer London as Socialist Congressman for New York's 12th district. He then set up the Four Winds Fellowship, a fraternity open to all trade unionists and socialists born in the British empire and opposed to the world war. In theory, the Fellowship was to be used to infiltrate anti-war militants into the unions and key war-related employments. To that end Larkin made contact with various Labour organisations, including the Western Federation of Miners, the Amalgamated Steel Workers' Union, and waterfront unions.[8] In practice, it was a personal soap-box and set the pattern for Larkin's preferred *modus operandi* over the next 20 years.

Clan na Gael was quicker to offer Larkin the chance of earning a living. The *Gaelic American* lionised him as Ireland's greatest workers' champion, and Devoy invited him to address a Manchester Martyrs memorial in Turn Hall, New York, on 15 November, to raise funds for the Irish Volunteers.[9] Larkin delivered a *tour de force*, combining romantic invocations of Kathleen Ní Houlihan with assertions that the working class never betrayed her. In reality, the class message was usually overshadowed at these meetings by the aspiration for Britain's defeat in the world war and calls for an Irish alliance with Germany, themes that Larkin endorsed fully. Devoy arranged for him to address a mixed German-Irish audience in the Academy of Music, Philadelphia on 24 November. The occasion had a theatrical finale. As Larkin, 'bitter, acrid, quivering with emotion', completed his denunciation of the common enemy, 'the curtains rolled back and the audience leaped to its feet with cheers at the spectacle. A company of Irish Volunteers, with guns at present arms faced a company of German Uhlans with drawn swords.'[10] At a banquet after the meeting he was introduced to the German and Austro-Hungarian consuls. Back in New York, he was approached by Captain Karl Boy-Ed, the German naval attaché, and offered $200 per week for propaganda and sabotage. Larkin replied that he was already engaged in organising strikes that would disrupt war-related industries through his Four Winds Fellowship. The Fellowship, he said, had 'created a number of stoppages at New York, Philadelphia, Newport (Mons) and New Orleans'. When Boy-Ed persisted, he explained that he did not want a German victory, favouring a military 'deadlock' leading to workers' revolts in the belligerent countries, and would not take money from the Germans or collude in sabotage on humanitarian grounds.[11] Larkin addressed at least two other Clan rallies in New York in December.[12] As early as January 1915, he had come to the attention of the French ambassador, Jules Jusserand, who reported to Paris that Kuno Meyer, the famous German Celticist, was making 'every effort to stir up German sympathies in Irish circles', and had 'publicly fraternised with the semi-anarchist politician Jim Larkin who is well known here . . .'[13]

The socialists too were hostile to the German connection. Compounding the problem, the press took every opportunity to sensationalise Larkin's meetings, giving prominence to his denunciation of Britain and support for Germany, highlighting heckling and disruption, claiming that he had called for bomb throwing, and referring to him an 'IWW agitator'.[14] One charge he rebutted was that he had called Old Glory a 'rag', pleading that it was the Union Jack to which he was referring.[15] His reputation as a syndicalist, and association with the Wobblies, alienated the right wing of the Socialist Party. In fact, he long declined to join any left-wing group in the US to avoid cramping his style. It was simply that his initial contacts were mainly with old friends of James Connolly, and he was known to have had the assistance of Big Bill Haywood during his Fiery Cross campaign. His religious views, which acquired a defensively Catholic character in exile, bewildered the mainly secular American left. Upton Sinclair had already created some prejudice in this regard in a letter to the *New York Times* of 31 December 1913, alleging that Larkin had refused to share a platform with Ernest Marklew, President of the British Socialist Party, on the grounds that he was divorced, and warning those in breach of church teaching on marriage 'to avoid the vicinity of Mr Larkin's cross'. Larkin made no public comment, but told Jack Carney that his objection was not to the divorce but to Marklew's treatment of his wife.[16] A legendary incident followed in New York's New Star Casino on 17 January, where the Socialist Party arranged a formal introduction for its Irish guest. The small attendance put him in defiant mood. 'Beginning with the Triple Entente and ending with Upton Sinclair [he] attacked everything outside Germany and his own movement.'[17] By contrast he praised the Kaiser as 'the one-armed saint of Germany'. Nonetheless, speaking for almost three hours, he held the audience spellbound until he unbuttoned his shirt to reveal a cross, and told his largely atheist audience: 'There is no antagonism between the Cross and socialism . . . I stand by the Cross and I stand by Karl Marx.' A few hecklers roared their disapproval.[18] Nor did he acclimatise to secularism over time. To many an American leftist, he was a 'Catholic Communist'.[19]

On landing in New York, Larkin had cabled Connolly promising 'a full report next mail'. He may have written also to Tom Foran.[20] In December 1914 he was dispirited to meet Nora Connolly off the boat, assuming that the 'Connolly' about to land was her father, James. Bob Briscoe, subsequently Michael Collins's chief gun-runner, unwittingly carried Nora's despatches past the immigration officials. He learned later that they were for the German ambassador, von Bernstorff.[21] On her father's instructions, Nora told Larkin nothing of what brought her to the US. Back in Dublin, she was debriefed by James:

> What do you think of Jim over there?
> Well – I got the impression that he was disappointed, and that people were disappointed in him.
> How?
> Oh, I don't know – as if he were too Labour for the Nationalist crowd and too National for the Labour crowd. You know.
> M'm. I do.[22]

While the Dublin press carried occasional reports of Jim's speeches, the union was totally unclear about his intentions. To draw the badger, William O'Brien despatched a four-page letter in February 1915, giving details of the Dublin municipal elections, which had gone badly for Labour.[23] He received a curmudgeonly, self-centred reply, peppered with pidgin Irish. Larkin was particularly annoyed that a lecture tour in Chicago for the Socialist Party, already announced in *New York Call*, had not been organised.[24]

> My dear Bill,
> Yours to hand safely. First news of real importance since I landed except what P. [Pete] brought. I received news from C. [Connolly] by Brennan, also note from C. insurance Office, and letter from R. Inchicore. I had already received returns of Election before C. letter arrived. [After commenting on the Dublin municipal elections, he went on:] I am doing well, moryah! Great bhoys the rebels of the Clan here, moryah! Thigen thu. Seddon and Bellamy were here before me, saw groupers and some of the heads of the SP [Socialist Party], Stitt Wilson etc. All of the leaders here AF of L [American Federation of Labor] and SP great friends of Ireland, Anti-British, moryah, thigen thu. My arrangements with SP Chicago, the tour under their auspices like the rising of '67, thigin thu [Con] Lehane had done nothing, was out on speaking tour when I arrived. Had never mentioned my intended arrival to anyone. Our attitude to war, especially from Irish standpoint admired by all the movement moryah! I am in good form and intend to make

good, but must have regular news. Send anything in connection with our movement, also copies of C's new Conquest [*The Reconquest of Ireland*]. Trade desperate
here. Estimated 5,000,000 (five million) unemployed. Some of them ships should
have been kept there. Will write soon.

Your Fiery X

Send me framed copy of Address signed.[25]

The address was presumably the illuminated valediction presented to him
by Dublin trades council. O'Brien sent an unanswered reply in May.[26] Adding
to Liberty Hall's frustration with the Larkins, Pete had arrived in New York
in late December 1914, interrupting Jim as he spoke to an IWW meeting
on the waterfront with 'Fellow worker speaker'.[27] The Wobblies made a point
of addressing comrades as 'fellow worker'. Pete was soon arrested, having
entered the US through working his passage from England under a false name
on the *Lusitania*. Following an appeal to the ITGWU, the no 1 branch
committee agreed unanimously to award his wife 30s a week while her
husband was in prison.[28]

February saw Larkin still in New York, living in a room at 4 Milligan
Place, a small alley in the West Village, then emerging as Gotham City's
'Little bohemia'. Here he held court, drinking endless cups of tea 'so strong
that it tasted like medicine', made from a kettle 'ever simmering on the
hearth'. More tea was taken in the Bronx with the Flynns, to whom Connolly
had recommended him. Mrs Flynn presented him with the green banner of
Connolly's Irish Socialist Federation, and he often spoke beneath it on the
waterfront. To his surprise, Mrs Flynn's daughters smoked cigarettes. He
advised her against such 'free ways'. Elizabeth Flynn, celebrated by the IWW's
official song-writer Joe Hill as 'the Rebel Girl', remembered him as 'gaunt . . .
with a rough-hewn face and a shock of graying hair' and 'very poor'.[29] The
apparent poverty may have been deceptive. Larkin liked to live abstemiously.
His one great personal indulgence was travel, and, from somewhere, he had
acquired the money to do it. In 1934 he recalled setting out on 'his own
itinerary', wandering 'for a number of months' about the US and crossing into
Mexico before returning to New York in April.[30] If this was wishful thinking,
he clocked up a fair mileage just the same. In February the *Gaelic American*
announced that he would spend a week in Pittsburgh and be available to any
Irish society 'at a nominal cost'.[31] On 27 February, he spoke in Boston, under
the auspices of the Boston School of Social Sciences. Police reports to Dublin
in March indicate that the lecture tour for the Socialist Party had gotten
underway and would last until 25 April. The tour took Larkin to Chicago and
to Providence, and other cities of the east.[32]

Superficially, Larkin was drifting away from Clan na Gael, so obviously so that the rift came to the attention of the Dublin press. Devoy said the New York socialists had turned him against the Clan, and that Clan activists were alienated by Larkin's attacks on them.[33] It may be too that the Germans wanted a more clandestine relationship. The British claimed to have intercepted a message from the Foreign Office in Berlin to their Washington embassy on 28 January advising Devoy: 'Support of Larkin entails loss of sympathy in many quarters of Ireland.'[34] A minute from the Irish Chief Secretary's Office to the DMP on 3 March noted: 'Larkin has dropped his German Uhlan and Irish Volunteer shaking hands & is at present an ineffectual socialist speaker.' There was no objection to a proposal from the Commissioner of Dominion Police in Canada to discontinue reporting on Larkin's speeches. The DMP's main concern was to secure evidence of treason – which it now had in plenty – and to have advance warning should Larkin try to return to Ireland. A request to Elizabeth to join him, in April, suggests her husband was settled on an indefinite stay in the US.[35] The DMP maintained its own informants in New York for some months, but its interest in Larkin faded until renewed alarm in 1917.[36] In reality, after the completion of his tour for the Socialist Party, Larkin developed deeper and more secret contacts with the Germans and certain people in Clan na Gael.[37] When in New York he continued his almost daily visits to Devoy in the offices of the *Gaelic American*.[38] Regular visits to Chicago and points further west indicate he was thinking of moving on from New York, where he had made too many enemies. An accident with a faulty stove in his room, which left him badly gassed, may have delayed his plans. A cable from 'Donnelly' to the ITGWU in June asked for $200 to meet his medical bills. Donnelly was probably J. E. C. Donnelly, a native of Donegal who had managed the American edition of the *Harp*, and was likely to have Connolly's confidence. The money was sent.[39]

OUT WEST

In July, O'Brien heard that Larkin had sent his children postcards from Utah.[40] Larkin was indeed in the west, and began a lecture tour of the Pacific states in San Francisco in mid July. Concentrating on three themes: the war, industrial unionism, and Ireland, he brought them together in a way that was open to misinterpretation.

In this war the workingmen are being used by both sides as tools. I believe the Allies are absolutely in the wrong, and personally I object to the British government at all times. England has been the bully of the world, and her outcry

against the German campaign in Belgium is humbug. England has always inter-
fered with the development of small nationalities. For every crime the Germans
have committed in Belgium, England has committed one hundred in Ireland.[41]

But he insisted 'We are not pro-German, as has been often said. We are pro-
human – for all mankind instead of for a limited nationalism that must always
breed wars'.[42] The talks drew good reviews, large attendances, and generated
enough press coverage to enable Connolly's *Workers' Republic* to pick up some
lengthy reports of speeches in San Francisco, San Pedro, and Fresno. The
Irish Worker had been closed by the censor in December 1914, and Connolly's
rather dry and monochrome replacement lacked the range of social and industrial copy that Larkin had been able to generate. The press in Ireland was
exploiting Larkin's absence to traduce him all the more, according to Connolly,
who was bothered by having nothing to offer in reply.[43] Aside from that, Larkin's
speeches brought a welcome touch of *Irish Worker* colour to the dreary *Workers'
Republic*. Unfortunately, he was prone to flights of fancy on what he had
achieved in his gallant and flawed efforts to create a working-class counter
culture in Dublin.

> Our whole life functions around our union . . . We are also shareholders in the
> Industrial Co-operative Distributing Society, from which we buy practically all
> our foodstuffs. Our women run a co-operative restaurant . . . we have our own park
> of sixteen acres, whereon we hold sports and gatherings every week-end. We have
> a co-operative hotel or guest house, where our members or friends can rent for
> nominal charge for week-ends . . . We have swing boats, hobby horses and sand
> gardens. We have hammocks swung from the trees so that the tired mother slave
> may hand over her baby to the volunteer girl nurses, who will look after baby while
> mother can go and trip the 'light fantastic' with her husband.[44]

The idyllic description was not calculated to raise funds for the impoverished
and retrenching ITGWU, and all the more poignant as the union was surrendering the lease on Croydon Park. And whatever about American audiences,
it is unlikely that breezy claims of how he had raised $3,500 for the ITGWU
in England after the lockout, had 'won the Dublin strike', been imprisoned
'thirty times', and worked in Ireland from the age of 12, did much for his
reputation in Liberty Hall. A critic of the hyperbole inspired Connolly to pen
a hilarious parody of the style, cleverly inverting it to satirise the Allied armies
and William Martin Murphy with comments like: 'We sadly missed Murphy's
trams in our recent brilliant advance backwards from Warsaw.'[45] One could
read Connolly as saying 'never mind, it's all eye-wash'.

Larkin's indifference to contact with the ITGWU is all the more curious as he kept himself informed of developments in Ireland. The Dublin Labour Party did reasonably well in a Westminster bye-election – its first such contest – in May 1915. When a vacancy arose in the Harbour constituency in August, Larkin cabled O'Brien from Hampton 354, 18th Avenue, San Francisco: 'Boys here think I should fight Harbour Division – money forwarded . . .' The no 1 branch committee wired Larkin that he would be nominated if the money arrived and Dublin trades council was open to the possibility of endorsing him.[46] The money never arrived, and Connolly advised Labour against entering the lists, pleading that it would be a distraction.[47] In all likelihood, he didn't want to cross his general secretary by fielding another candidate, and neither did he want his volatile boss back in Dublin as he pressed republicans for insurrection.

The public lectures did not solve Larkin's financial problems. The tour had drawn him closer to the IWW, and led to contacts with the Western Federation of Miners. The Federation had helped to inaugurate the IWW, though it disaffiliated in 1907. In September 1915 Larkin reverted to his old trade, and became an organiser for the Federation. For him, this was a regression. If the dream of a world tour had crumbled, he wanted to agitate, not organise. After some preliminary work in Phoenix and Tucson, Arizona, he was posted to one of the toughest stations, Butte, Montana. Shortly before his arrival, the *Montana Socialist* printed one of his speeches under the heading 'Germany: the friend of small nationalities'. It expressed the hope that 'all Ireland will not have to pay an awful price for the lying attacks of the conservatives upon the noble German Nation'.[48] The copper mining town of Butte was peculiarly amenable to this message. One quarter of its 30,000 residents were Irish-born or second generation Irish. The city boasted several fraternities echoing the spectrum of Irish politics, including the Robert Emmet Literary Association and the Ancient Order of Hibernians. As early as 1900, during the Boer War, the former had been courting an anti-British alliance with the city's 'German element'. As in Ireland, the separatists of the Literary Association were more sympathetic to the left than the Hibernians. Socialists won control of Butte City Council in 1913, and their enemies had since been waging a violent campaign to remove them from all positions of influence. In 1914, the largely Irish-run Butte Miners' Union, one of the founders of the Western Federation of Miners in 1893, had collapsed in a – literally – explosive dispute between members and officials in 1914, and it was Larkin's job to get the miners to rejoin the Federation. On 25 September 1915 he spoke in the Butte auditorium, saying it was a capitalist lie that socialists were against religion, that socialism was in keeping with Irish traditions, and that conservative Irish nationalists were 'frauds' who would leave a capitalist Ireland exploited by capitalist Britain. The next day he heard of the death of Keir Hardie, who had visited Butte in 1895, and proposed to hold a commemoration. His admiration for Hardie had been strengthened by Hardie's opposition to the wold war. The acting mayor, Michael Daniel O'Connell, barred him from the auditorium as he would be 'bad for harmony', and the sheriff had the Carpenters' Union deny him their hall. Larkin finally found a venue in the Finnish Workers' Club's Finlander Hall.[49] He turned the censorship into a free speech fight which attracted considerable interest in the press, and was noted in the *Workers' Republic*.[50] His efforts to unionise the miners were less successful, and he abandoned the project after some three weeks when the Germans offered him more lucrative work.

WORKING WITH THE GERMANS

The Germans had continued to cultivate Larkin. He and Devoy were chez Judge Daniel F. Cohalan the night Kuno Meyer brought Roger Casement's first message from Germany.[51] Casement had helped to establish the Irish Volunteers in November 1913, and Clan na Gael had financed his secret journey from New York to Germany via Norway in October 1914. On returning to New York in April 1915, Larkin was informed of 'antagonisms' between the German authorities and Casement which were hampering Casement's efforts to raise a liberation army from Irish prisoners of war. Thinking that one from a working-class background might do better, the Germans proposed that Larkin go to Germany via Spain, but 'for various reasons', the enterprise failed. Larkin suggested that Robert Monteith go in his stead. Monteith had served in the British army and was employed for many years as a foreman in the Ordnance Depot at Island Bridge barracks, Dublin. He joined the SPI in 1911 and was dismissed from his job on security grounds in November 1914. He then worked as a drill instructor with the Irish Volunteers in Limerick, and went to the US in August 1915. He was duly seconded by Clarke and arrived in Berlin in October.[52]

In the early summer, probably because of his financial difficulties, Larkin initiated a deeper collusion, and requested Devoy to act as a conduit for proposals to the Germans and the receipt of money from them. In the autumn, he was invited from Montana to Washington DC to meet the German diplomat, Count Georg Muenster zu Derneberg. Again, he was pressed to supervise sabotage on the waterfront, and again, he insisted subsequently, he refused. As an example of the kind of work he was willing to do, he cited the disruption of arms production through strikes in the Remington Arms companies in Bridgeport, Connecticut.[53] A strike for shorter hours had hit the Remington companies in July and led Remington and three other munitions companies to concede the eight-hour day. It is possible that Larkin or his Four Winds Fellowship were involved. He was based in New York at the time, and the press attributed the unrest to German agents.[54] Devoy claimed that an arrangement was made for the Germans to bankroll agitation of that kind. For political or legal reasons – he must have suspected he was under surveillance and in danger of being arrested as a saboteur – Larkin demanded that the monies be transmitted through Devoy, who agreed with reluctance, feeling he was being used. The total amount received is unknown. Devoy recalled a request for the substantial figure of $10–12,000 being readily accepted, but not the period involved.[55] It is likely that Larkin's departure from Butte coincided with the receipt of the first payment.

Thanks to the Germans, Larkin spent two years doing what he liked best: speaking, writing, editing, publishing, and travelling, ranging from coast to coast, and south of the border. In November he and Haywood were invited to Chicago to deliver the English-language eulogies at the cremation of Joe Hill.[56] Hill had been executed for an alleged murder in Salt Lake City, and his funeral was a huge occasion for the American far left. Larkin was deeply affected, and wrote the article 'Murder most foul' for the *International Socialist Review* on the first anniversary of his death. Jim made Chicago his base and a home for Elizabeth and the children.[57] Elizabeth had been living in Croydon Park. Jim had arranged that his, reduced, wages be paid to her and she received a weekly stipend of 50s up to January 1916.[58] When he asked her to join him in April 1915, and she appealed to Liberty Hall for expenses. Although the union donated £40, she lingered in Dublin until a further request to come over, and £100, followed in October and November.[59] After moving into other union accommodation when the ITGWU surrendered the lease on Croydon Park, Elizabeth sailed for New York with the two youngest boys in December. O'Brien took care to get a written testimony beforehand.

> To anybody, who may doubt my reason for leaving Croydon Park, I am going solely because Jim has cabled times without number requesting me to go to him. All concerned with the Transport Union without exception have done their very best to make my stay in Croydon Park happy and succeeded. I leave with great regret. L. Larkin.[60]

Jim's dislike of having to explain himself left Dublin in the dark about the significance of Elizabeth's departure.[61] In October, he sent the ITGWU £100 without any accompanying explanation. O'Brien wrote to O'Lyhane in November asking if he could shed any light on the mystery, and saying 'The Transport Union people are very uneasy about it all, but don't care to ask him bluntly for an explanation'. O'Lyhane and Larkin had been 'doing a lot of lecturing and agitating jointly and severally', but O'Lyhane, not shy himself about gilding the lily or self-promotion, offered no clarification, telling O'Brien that Larkin was planning a big fund-raiser for the union, was making arrangements to publish a weekly paper, and would 'no doubt' be in touch. The ITGWU reckoned that he was not coming back.[62] At least one fund-raiser was organised on 12 March 1916 under the auspices of the Chicago Federation of Labor. With Athlone-born John Fitzpatrick in the chair, Larkin spoke on 'Ireland, where she stands', with O'Lyhane in support. Admission was 25c, reserved seats 50c, and the posters declared that 'Total proceeds go to Irish trade and labor organisations'.[63] Larkin sent no more money to any Irish Labour body.

Connolly's intentions worried Larkin, who had formed a ridiculously egocentric view of what the Citizen Army would and should do. Larkin called repeatedly for action in Ireland. In early September, Kuno Meyer found him reassuring on preparations for the rising.[64] But he did not want Connolly grabbing the glory. Both his brother Pete and Francis Sheehy Skeffington carried home messages for Connolly to 'pull out of it', and in late 1915 or early 1916, Larkin cabled him 'not to move'.[65] The Easter Rising came as a bombshell. At once, Larkin grasped that he had been upstaged on a grand scale. The lockout, the biggest event in recent Irish history as far as the American press was concerned, had been overtaken. Adding salt to the wound, the American papers invariably connected him with events in Dublin, explaining the Rising as another revolt by the 1913 militants, and introducing Connolly and Constance Markievicz – the exotic Polish countess – as his former lieutenants. Some papers had him on the barricades in Dublin, others would note he was safely remote from the shooting.[66] For several days he remained incommunicado. When the press finally managed to reach him at home on the telephone on 29 April, the day Pearse and Connolly surrendered, his only comment was 'I have nothing to say on the Irish question'. Efforts to pursue the point were 'unavailing'.[67] Carney later defended the silence on the grounds that speaking out would have landed others in jail.[68] But Larkin's failure to offer an explanation spoke volumes. The Rising and Connolly's posthumous stature never ceased to rankle him. In private he frequently traduced his old underling, saying Connolly had destroyed the revolutionary force created in 1913 and that he should never have gotten mixed up with 'the poets'.[69]

It was a different matter in public. Once the worst of the shock had passed, Larkin offered public lectures on the Easter Rising and its personalities, and organised a commemoration in Cohan's Grand Opera House, Chicago, on 21 May. His nerves were badly unsettled. When Dr K. A. Zurawski of the Polish Federation condemned the English for murder in 'true Russian style', 'a dapper young man' in the fifth row, Matthew Thomas Newman, protested: 'I have lived in Ireland and my mother came from a long line of Ireland's best. But such ballyrot makes me ill. I say why do you try to put over such ridiculous drivel?'

> Larkin, who was sitting far back on the stage, arose, and, in a frenzy of anger, ran to the footlights. He jumped, clearing the orchestra pit and a high brass railing with apparant ease. A woman in the back of the theatre shrieked. When she started down the aisle she was recognised as Mrs Larkin. 'Be careful what you do to him!', she shouted to her infuriated husband. 'Jim, Jim! Think!
>
> Larkin seized Newman by the throat and choked him until he gasped for breath. Then he jerked him out of his seat and shook him until the offending one was speechless. After Larkin had torn Newman's collar away, he dragged him to the entrance of the theatre and tossed him out into the lobby. Then the meeting resumed.[70]

During his address, Larkin grabbed one of three rifles stacked on the stage and brandished it aloft.

In July Larkin was back in Butte to hail 'a working-class rising to keep Irish boys out of the British army'. The mask slipped a little as he went on to lambast patriots who 'knew nothing about Ireland . . . did nothing but talk a lot of sob stuff about Ireland in order to keep you Irish workingmen divided among yourselves . . . You lose your class . . . while listening to these mercenary phrase mongers talk . . . about Irish freedom'. When the editor of the *Butte Independent*, unofficial organ of the Butte Irish associations, rose to protest, Larkin rounded on him savagely.[71] That same month, in an obsequious, self-serving article in the *Masses*, he presented himself and Connolly as partners in building the ITGWU and the Citizen Army, and jointly drafting the 'declaration' of the insurgents. To impress readers of the leading monthly of the American revolutionary left, he claimed that the aim of the 'declaration' was 'a co-operative commonwealth . . . based on industrial democracy'. Justifying his absence from the action, he suggested that the Rising was premature and forced on the rebels by the threat of conscription. 'Though fate,' he added, 'has denied some of us the opportunity of striking a blow for human freedom, we live in hopes that we, too, will be given the opportunity.' An infuriated O'Brien read the article in the Glasgow *Forward*.[72] It was not that Larkin was bragging; in fact, he had been far more influential than Connolly before he left Ireland. It was his sheer mendacity that was so disturbing.

In June Larkin had been joined by Carney, who stayed with himself and Elizabeth at 1046 North Franklin Street, Chicago. Carney was like a pocket version of Big Jim: impassioned, eloquent, egotistical, cavalier with facts, fractious, and ferociously loyal to his role model. He claimed to have served the ITGWU in Dublin during the 1913 Lockout, and, more doubtfully, to have worked on the *Titanic* and fought in the Easter Rising. In the same month as the Rising he landed in New York on the *Snowden* from Glasgow, and in May he married the 24-year-old Mina Schoeneman, in Chicago, her native city. A talented artist and bohemian, Mina shared his lifestyle and politics and would express her own admiration of Larkin in sculpture. Carney's arrival allowed Larkin to realise his ambition to publish a paper, and together they produced the *Irish Worker* at North Franklin Street.[73]

> As soon as I arrived he decided to bring out an American edition of the IRISH WORKER. It was 16 pages in small 8 point type. The first page was a cartoon drawn by one L. S. Chumley, who was then drawing for Solidarity, the official organ of the IWW. I combed the British and Irish newspapers for news of Ireland, while Jim would dictate the main story. I would sit at the typewriter and he would dictate until all hours of the morning. We had 4,000 readers, mostly subscribers. We had to type the wrappers for the subscribers in addition to the preparation of the material for the paper and also arrange its make-up. As soon as we had carried the bags of mail to the post office we would be starting the next issue. Jim wrote as if he were in Dublin and offended many Irish-Americans. He singled out the late John McCormack, the singer, for attack for attending an Allied bazaar in Chicago and other pro-Ally Irish and Irish-Americans.[74]

The mast-head claimed to incorporate the *Harp* and the *Workers' Republic*, and the paper advertised its association with Easter Week.[75] The subscription rate was a hefty $2 a year. In February 1917 the San Francisco anarchist paper, the *Blast*, welcomed a third issue:

> In it the Irish radical movement finds a worthy champion and a reflection of the gallant spirits who last Easter week 'had not the strength to wait, but only the strength to die' ... *The Irish Worker* is a well-printed illustrated weekly of twenty-four pages ... The Blasters congratulate comrade Larkin on his enterprise and assure him of their loyal support. Faugh-a-Ballagh![76]

Both Larkin and Carney worked with the Congressional campaign of Socialist Party candidate Eugene Debs, which saw Debs well beaten by his Republican opponent, and Larkin travelled extensively as a speaker for the party.[77] He made a third visit to Butte in January 1917. O'Lyhane had spoken there in December, offering more or less the same message, and coevally a Pearse-Connolly Irish Independence Club was launched.[78]

Meanwhile, Larkin was living dangerously. In February 1916 the German military attaché in New York, Wolf von Igel, who had succeeded Boy-Ed, brought him to a sabotage plant at Hoboken, New Jersey, for a demonstration of how chemical explosives were manufactured. On 18 April von Igel was arrested at the German consulate as he awaited Larkin's arrival.[79] Larkin promptly left for Chicago, and began a campaign of agitation among miners in the western states. After speaking in the Dreamland Rink, San Francisco on 27 June he received an anonymous note warning him of a conspiracy to entrap the Irish-American labour agitator Tom Mooney.[80] In July, his presence coincided with two of the most notorious acts of German sabotage. The Bureau of Investigation (a federal secret service known from 1935 as the Federal Bureau of Investigation) knew he was in San Francisco – to meet the German consul – before the Preparedness Day Parade bomb on 16 July, in which several people were killed, and was visited daily by Mooney, who was sentenced to death for his part in the plot.[81] Larkin then travelled to New York to see Devoy, and was walking on Broadway at 2 am on 30 July when he heard a massive explosion on Black Tom Island in New York harbour. Over two million pounds of explosives, awaiting shipment to the Allies, had been detonated. Three men and a child were killed.[82] Larkin quickly returned to Chicago. In mid September he had another *rendezvous* with German agents, this time in Mexico City. On this occasion the Germans invited him to participate in bacteriological warfare, injecting 'disease cultures' into pack horses and mules.[83] His revulsion can be believed. Various sources attest to his love of animals.

HOME THOUGHTS

Elizabeth and the children returned to Dublin in August 1916, their fare paid by Clan na Gael.[84] Jim wrote to her in November 1916. His only extant letter to his wife provides a good illustration of his mentality and priorities:

My Dear Girl,

Two of your letters undated received this morning from Madison street office. How am I to convince you that I have written every week since you left and sent three extra letters in addition. I do not know whether this will reach you or not but surely you must that [*sic*] I worried uno death at the nonreceipt both of your letters and my reply,s [*sic*] I have had three letters from you and one cable there has been an enquiry from Dublin addressed to Nockels Sec. Fed. of trades Re. monies Forwarded I have written TF [Tom Foran] twice since you left informing him as to the amounts I had sent on they should have received £275 or 1375 dollars not much I know but you can explain how difficult it was to raise that out of my tours considering I was engaged on more important work for friends. £100 was forwarded to TF for Union. Then £5 to Daly And JC [James Connolly] for Trades Congress a further £5 to ec [executive committee] Union then draft on Munster Bank credit Daly and JC and £25 last remittances JC. A draft credited to school Master was returned here from Bank of Ireland for £25. Nockels has written officially. I cannot understand TF and the Boys do they think I was laying down on the job. If my advice had been followed there would have been another result advantage was taken of My position and difficulties of this were more anon Tell TF I am doing My utmost to compel friends to act square he should have received £375 from bricklayer. Now I want You to taken Fintan to good Doctor and get him examined he might be tubercular and he should be looked at once glad to hear the other Bouchals are well I sent three different set of toys gyroscopes etc. to them I have asked you in each of my previous letters to send me their Photos individually and together. What became of My picture and books etc. How is your folks especially Ralph I am trying to arrange about schooling expenses take care of Yourselves mind my lads see Jim learns his lessons and tell them to write to me each day it would only be writing exercise for them and I think You might write oftener and let me know who is living also send papers Good Night My Girl, I am sorry I let you return I did not think TF and the rest of the boys would forget so easy what we achieved together well there is a good time coming.

thine

Suemas[85]

Elizabeth passed the letter to Foran. The ITGWU resumed payment to her of her husband's salary of 50s per week in January, increasing it incrementally in these inflationary times to £8 per week by 1921. In October 1922 it paid £745 for 54 Upper Beechwood Avenue, a comfortable terraced house in Ranelagh, letting it to herself and the children at the 'less than normal rent' of £1 a week.[86]

Foran wrote to Jim in December 1916 asking for particulars of the monies allegedly sent to Dublin, and complaining of the lack of contact with the union. Neither the ITGWU nor Congress, he emphasised, had received money other than a £100 bank draft and '£350 from a friend, who did not say who it was from, last August'.[87] Jim replied on 22 January with some cryptic details on the monies. He then demanded an explanation of Connolly's action in Easter Week. 'I want you to see O'Brien, and get from him an authentic statement as to whether Skeffy [Sheehy Skeffington] delivered my message to Jim, and to give me reasons why they moved, when told not to move.' Following a request for fresh credentials – he had given his old ones to Samuel Gompers – and peremptory instructions on union officials, he said it was useless asking him to come home. 'Surely they know that if facilities offered – of any sort – I would be with them long ere this.' He ended with a promise of a fund-raising campaign to rebuild Liberty Hall, which had been shelled during Easter Week.[88] Meeting on 26 May 1917, the ITUC executive agreed to send him the following credentials:

The bearer, Mr JIM LARKIN, is the General Secretary of the Irish Transport and General Workers' Union, Liberty Hall, Dublin, which body he organised and led from one victory to another. He is past President of our National Executive and was Vice President on leaving here for America. Any assistance that can be given him will be esteemed as a great favour to his brothers in the Irish Labour Movement (Signed) P. Daly Secretary.[89]

Whether Larkin really wanted to go home at this point is open to question. Dublin Castle had adopted an order on 24 December 1914 under the Defence of the Realm Regulations prohibiting him from returning to Ireland. It was decided not to inform him for fear of the publicity he might make of it.[90] But he knew he had been barred from the British dominions, possibly from being denied entry to Canada, and had referred to himself as having been exiled by the British government.[91] At the same time, he didn't make an issue of it until 1919, and colleagues in Ireland would not have been aware of his circumstances. In September 1917 he applied to the British consul general in San Francisco for a passport for Shanghai. On being refused, he sought a passport for Ireland without pursuing the application.[92] There was also the option of travelling *incognito*, which, with his excellent waterfront contacts, would have been relatively easy. It never seemed to appeal to him.

IN AMERICA AT WAR

With America's entry into the war in April 1917, Larkin's situation became steadily more uncomfortable. In early 1917 the British embassy told the US State Department that he was active in a Chicago-based conspiracy to 'obstruct the manufacture of war materials'.[93] Coincidentally or not, the Bureau of Investigation began to track him from February 1917. Its initial efforts were concerned with his links with the Germans, and fairly episodic and amateurish. An agent in Chicago called to 10 North Franklin Street to find that the occupants 'knew nobody by the name of Larkin'. It cannot have been a secret that the *Irish Worker* was produced in 1046 North Franklin Street. However, other agencies were not so sluggish. The *Irish Worker* was suppressed and when Larkin continued to denounce the war he was arrested repeatedly. His new circumstances pushed him increasingly into conspiracy with Clan na Gael and the Germans. Carney's enigmatic recollection of the cloak and dagger goings on implies some collusion with Chicago policemen sympathetic to the Clan.

Jim went travelling being six and seven weeks at a time away from Chicago. On his return he would call meetings of the Clan na Gael. I was the messenger. I would meet a certain person, at this time one of the heads of the Chicago police, and hand him a note with instructions. I saw the men arrive for the meetings and checked on their numbers. Larkin knew how many would attend. So he must have been in close touch with the Clan.[94]

In June, the Espionage Act extended repression to all forms of anti-war activity. Now living at 211 East Eighteen St, Manhattan, Larkin was arrested on 22nd for speaking at the Queen's Labor Lyceum against the draft. He had singled out one of the several detective stenographers as 'an Irish stool pigeon, seated in the rear of this hall'. The same man detained him. Released on $500 bail, Larkin was tried, and acquitted.[95] He toyed increasingly with leaving the US. Following the February revolution, he spoke of going to Russia. Controversially, he received $2,000 from Clan na Gael to attend the socialist peace conference in Stockholm that summer, but again failed to get away. On 17 June he sent a cryptic telegram to Daly at the Trades Hall in Capel St, Dublin: 'Insist Partridge nominated don't homologate conference forward me credentials from party and movement address Huysmans proceeding east James Lawson.'[96] The DMP feared he was about to return and secured an order prohibiting himself, Monteith, and Liam Mellows from entering Ireland. Both Monteith and Mellows had been involved with the Easter Rising and subsequently escaped to America.[97] In August, rumours of Jim's impending immigration led the Prime Minister of Australia to confirm he would be prevented from landing.[98] Pete had arrived in Sydney in the autumn of 1915 and was soon arrested. In 1916 he was one of 12 Wobblies tried for arson and treason, and was sentenced to 15 years hard labour.[99] Other speculation had Jim leading anti-war protests by the Pearse-Connolly Club and the IWW in Butte.[100] In fact, Jim was embarked on an odyssey to Mexico as a courier for his German handlers at the behest of Clan na Gael. En route, in San Francisco, he helped a German contact recruit 'several men' for propaganda and sabotage in Vladivostok. He arrived in Mexico City on 17 September 'after many difficulties'. Here his secret career culminated in mid-October. Tired of his refusals to become a saboteur, the Germans broke with him, and had him robbed and left penniless.[101] His story is corroborated by two cables sent by him from Mexico to friends in the US – probably Clan na Gael men – pleading for money.[102] According to the Bureau of Investigation, he then worked with the IWW in San Francisco in December, before moving permanently to New York.

What did Larkin think he was doing getting so close to the agents of imperial Germany? As he would have it, he was, reluctantly, obliging Clan na Gael, advancing the cause of Irish freedom, disrupting munitions production, and promoting the anti-war policy of the American left. An affidavit on contacts with the Germans, written in 1934 for US law officers chasing damages from Germany for wartime sabotage, said repeatedly that he had refused to take money from the Germans, other than for travel expenses, and disdained to engage in acts of violence. He was also anxious to exonerate 'the revolutionary Irish organisation in America' from any 'act, hand, or part' in anti-American activity. The affidavit did not tell the full story. It never mentioned, for example, the lucrative deal he had done with the Germans through Devoy. He admitted to supplying the Germans with intelligence and contacts for sabotage work, and if he was so otherwise unco-operative, why did they give him first-hand knowledge of their sabotage operations, admit him to discussions of their plans, including the destruction of Black Tom, and chase him so persistently to turn saboteur?[103] Frank Robbins, an ITGWU emissary and later a bitter opponent, remembered him producing two sticks of gelignite from a suitcase in December 1916 with the words 'This is the kind of work we are doing here'.[104] There is no evidence of direct engagement in sabotage on Larkin's part. Even so, he came to be seen as a German agent, and there was an obvious self-indulgence about his wandering, freelance *modus operandi*. The break with the Germans compelled him to modify his lone star style, and return to the embrace of the American left.

NOTES

1   Bertram D. Wolfe, *Strange Communists I Have Known* (New York, 1982), p. 64.

2   NAUK, CO 904/206/4, file 233B, James Larkin, 1914–15; FO383/144, Metropolitan Police report on Baron von Horst, 7 September 1914. I am obliged to James Curry for this report.

3   ITGWU, *The Attempt to Smash the Irish Transport and General Workers' Union* (Dublin, 1924), p. 165.

4   Jim Larkin, *In the Footsteps of Big Jim: A Family Biography* (Dublin, 1995), p. 79; NAUK, CO 904/206/4, file 233B, James Larkin, 1914–15; *Chicago Daily Tribune*, 2 November 1914; *Indianapolis Star*, 3 November 1914.

5   Emmet Larkin, *James Larkin: Irish Labour Leader, 1876–1947* (London, 1965), p. 188.

6   David M. Emmons, *The Butte Irish: Class and Ethnicity in an American Mining Town, 1875–1925* (Chicago, 1990), pp. 390–1.

7   *Gaelic American*, 7 July 1923.

8   *Chicago Daily Tribune*, 9 November 1914; 'The Larkin affidavit', in Donal Nevin (ed.), *James Larkin: Lion of the Fold* (Dublin, 1998), pp. 298–312.

9   *New York Tribune*, 16 November 1914.

10   *Gaelic American*, 5 December 1914, quoted in Larkin, *James Larkin*, p. 192.

11   'The Larkin affidavit', pp. 298–312.

12   *New York American*, 7 December 1914; *Brooklyn Times*, 7 December 1914; *Gaelic American*, 26 December 1914.

13   Quoted in Jerome aan de Wiel, *The Irish Factor, 1988–1919: Ireland's Strategic and Diplomatic Importance for Foreign Powers* (Dublin, 2009), p. 255.

14 See for example, *Belvidere Daily Republican*, 28 November 1914; *New York American*, 7 December 1914; *Brooklyn Times*, 7 December 1914; and *New York Sun*, 18 December 1914.

15 *New York Tribune*, 4 December 1914. His letter was also published in *Wexford People*. I am obliged to Ida Milne for this reference.

16 *New York Times*, 29 December 1913; Larkin, *James Larkin*, pp. 192–5; Donal Nevin, 'Solidarity for ever', in Nevin (ed.), *James Larkin*, pp. 274–5.

17 *New York Tribune*, 18 January 1915.

18 Wolfe, *Strange Communists I Have Known*, p. 55; for a similar account see Benjamin Gitlow, *The Whole of Their Lives: Communism in America – A Personal History and Intimate Portrayal of Its Leaders* (London, 1948), pp. 38–9; NAUK, CO 904/206/4, file 233B, James Larkin, 1914–15.

19 Wolfe's description.

20 ITGWU, *The Attempt to Smash*, p. 134. Foran gave no details of this letter and may have been referring to the cable to Connolly, published in the *Irish Worker*, 14 November 1914.

21 Robert Briscoe, with Alden Hatch, *For the Life of Me* (London, 1959), p. 36.

22 Nora Connolly O'Brien, *Portrait of a Rebel Father* (Dublin, 1935), pp. 214–15.

23 William O'Brien, *Forth the Banners Go: The Reminiscences of William O'Brien as Told to Edward MacLysaght, D.Litt* (Dublin, 1969), p. 70.

24 NLI, William O'Brien papers, 15679(2).

25 Ibid.

26 Ibid., 15704(2).

27 Donal Nevin, 'Peter Larkin', in Nevin (ed.), *James Larkin*, p. 440.

28 ITGWU, *The Attempt to Smash*, p. 128; NLI, William O'Brien papers, 15672(2), part 2.

29 Elizabeth Gurley Flynn, *The Rebel Girl, an Autobiography: My First Life (1906–1926)* (New York, 1986), pp. 185–6; Larkin, *James Larkin*, p. 197.

30 'The Larkin affidavit', p. 301.

31 *Gaelic American*, 6 February 1915.

32 NAUK, CO 904/206/4, file 233B, James Larkin, 1914–15.

33 Larkin, *James Larkin*, p. 199.

34 NAUK, Cabinet papers, 'Intrigues between Sinn Féin leaders and the German government', CAB/24/117.

35 ITGWU, *The Attempt to Smash*, p. xix.

36 NAUK, CO 904/206/4, file 233B, James Larkin, 1914–15.

37 'The Larkin affidavit', pp. 301–2.

38 Larkin, *James Larkin*, p. 201.

39 Ibid., pp. 200–1; ITGWU, *The Attempt to Smash*, p. xix, 128; *Workers' Republic*, 29 May 1915.

40 NLI, William O'Brien papers, 15704(9).

41 *Northwest Worker*, 12 August 1915.

42 *Santa Cruz Evening News*, 17 July 1915.

43 *Workers' Republic*, 29 May 1915.

44 Ibid., 14 August 1915, reprinted from the monthly *International Socialist Review*, Chicago.

45 *Workers' Republic*, 14 August, 4–11, 25 September 1915.

46 ITGWU, *The Attempt to Smash*, pp. 70–1, 132–3; NLI, William O'Brien papers, 15679(2).

47 O'Brien, *Forth the Banners Go*, p. 71.

48 The speech may have been entitled 'Friends of small nationalities', it compared Germany, Britain, and Russia on their treatment of subject nations, but was headlined in the *Montana Socialist*

as 'Germany: the friend of small nationalities', which was indeed its thrust. *Montana Socialist*, 18 September 1915. Compare Emmons, *The Butte Irish*, p. 353, and Larkin, *James Larkin*, p. 204.

49 Emmons, *The Butte Irish*, pp. 340–55.

50 *Workers' Republic*, 13–20 November, 1915.

51 Larkin, *James Larkin*, p. 193.

52 'The Larkin affidavit', pp. 298–312; NLI, William O'Brien papers, 15674(1) part 1; aan de Wiel, *The Irish Factor, 1988–1919*, p. 184, 186; NAUK, CO 904/206/4, file 233A, James Larkin, 1915–19.

53 'The Larkin affidavit', pp. 298–312.

54 *Workers' Republic*, 7 August 1915.

55 Larkin, *James Larkin*, pp. 206–7.

56 *Bismarck Tribune*, 26 November 1915; *Workers' Republic*, 11 December 1915.

57 Larkin, *James Larkin*, p. 209.

58 NLI, William O'Brien papers, 15676(2), part 1.

59 For ITGWU payments to the Larkins see ITGWU, *The Attempt to Smash*, pp. xix–xx, 133–5.

60 NLI, William O'Brien and Thomas Kennedy papers, 33718/A(8).

61 Ibid.; William O'Brien papers, 15678(2).

62 ITGWU, *The Attempt to Smash*, p. xix, 133; Donal Nevin (ed.), *Between Comrades: James Connolly, Letters and Correspondence 1889–1916* (Dublin, 2007), p. 639; for O'Lyhane's oratorical view of Ireland and self-representation, see the *Eau Clair Leader*, 30 July 1915; *Washington Post*, 22 February 1916.

63 Larkin, *In the Footsteps of Big Jim*, p. 80.

64 Larkin, *James Larkin*, pp. 210–11.

65 ITGWU, *The Attempt to Smash*, pp. xxx–xxi; Larkin, *James Larkin*, p. 211.

66 See *Washington Post*, 29 April 1916; *Harrisburg Telegraph*, 29 April 1916; *Boston Post*, 30 April 1916; *Winnipeg Tribune*, 22 May 1916; *Brooklyn Daily Eagle*, 23 June 1917.

67 *New York Times*, 30 April 1916; *Atlanta Constitution*, 30 April 1916.

68 *Irish Worker*, 21 November 1931.

69 See for example RGASPI, minutes of the Anglo-American secretariat, 20 February 1928, 495/72/34–1/28; Wolfe, *Strange Communists I Have Known*, pp. 64–5; Frank Robbins, *Under the Starry Plough: Recollections of the Irish Citizen Army* (Dublin, 1977), p. 164; and Harry Wicks, *Keeping My Head: The Memoirs of a British Bolshevik* (London, 1992), p. 122.

70 *Belvidere Daily Republican*, 22 May 1916; *Greensboro Daily News*, 22 May 1916; Larkin, *James Larkin*, pp. 211–13; Nevin, 'Solidarity for ever', p. 275.

71 Cited in Emmons, *The Butte Irish*, pp. 358–9.

72 NLI, William O'Brien papers, 15679(15).

73 Richard Hudelson, 'Jack Carney and the *Truth* in Duluth', *Saothar* 19 (1994), pp. 129–39.

74 Jack Carney memoir on Larkin, written for Emmet Larkin and kindly passed on to the author.

75 NLI, William O'Brien papers, 15679(2).

76 *Blast*, San Francisco, 15 February 1917.

77 Manus O'Riordan, 'Larkin in America: the road to Sing Sing', in Nevin (ed.), *James Larkin*, p. 66; Bernard Brommel, *Eugene V. Debs: Spokesman for Labor and Socialism* (Chicago, 1978), p. 148.

78 Emmons, *The Butte Irish*, pp. 358–9.

79 Terry Golway, *Irish Rebel: John Devoy and America's Fight for Ireland's Freedom* (New York, 1999), p. 223.

80 *Blast*, San Francisco, 15 February 1917.

81 References to the Bureau of Investigation are from the Federal Bureau of Investigation file, James Larkin, 62–312, section 1. The file is not paginated; Larkin, *James Larkin*, p. 214.

82 Captain Henry Landau, *The Enemy within: The inside Story of German Sabotage in America* (New York, 1937), pp. 77–80.

83 'The Larkin affidavit', pp. 298–312.

84 John Devoy in the *Gaelic American*, 7 July 1923.

85 NLI, William O'Brien papers, 15679(2).

86 ITGWU, *The Attempt to Smash*, pp. xix–xx; *Irish Times*, 9 May 1925.

87 NLI, William O'Brien papers, 15679(2); letter from Foran 11 December 1916. The letter may have been sent by courier. Foran said he had 'already written through post'.

88 NLI, William O'Brien papers, 15676(2), part 1.

89 Irish Labour History Society Archives, ITUC national executive, minute, 26 May 1917.

90 NAUK, CO 904/206/4, file 233B, James Larkin, 1914–15.

91 See article in the *Workers' Republic*, 14 August 1915, reprinted from the monthly *International Socialist Review*, Chicago.

92 NAUK, CO 904/206/4, file 233B, James Larkin, 1914–15; file 233A, James Larkin, 1915–19.

93 Larkin, *James Larkin*, p. 216.

94 Jack Carney memoir. Chicago's police chief in 1917 was Herman F. Schuettler, a man regarded as strict but honest, with a record of repression of anarchists.

95 'The Larkin affidavit', p. 307; C. Desmond Greaves, *Liam Mellows and the Irish Revolution* (London, 1971), p. 128; *Brooklyn Daily Eagle*, 23 June 1917; *Daily Free Press*, 25 June 1917.

96 ILHA, ITUC minute book. W. P. Partridge was a Citizen Army veteran, imprisoned after Easter Week. Camille Huysmans was associated with the Second International.

97 NAUK, CO 904/206/4, file 233A, James Larkin, 1915–19.

98 Larkin, *In the Footsteps of Big Jim*, pp. 88–9; *Reading Times*, 31 August 1917.

99 Nevin, 'Peter Larkin', pp. 439–40; *Northwest Worker*, 15 February 1917.

100 *Oshkosh Daily Northwestern*, 20 August 1917.

101 Larkin, *James Larkin*, pp. 215–18; 'The Larkin affidavit', pp. 307–12.

102 Landau, *The Enemy within*, pp. 277–8; *Irish Worker*, 8 September 1923.

103 Landau, *The Enemy within*, pp. 276–7.

104 Robbins, *Under the Starry Plough*, p. 165.

TEN

RED JIM, 1918–23

The Soviet government of Russia is an ideal one and I am ready to live for it, work for it, and if need be die for it. Get ready, marshal your hearts, and get a disciplined army.
James Larkin, New York, 12 April 1919[1]

We'll go to Greenwich,
Where modern men itch
To be free
'Manhattan', Rodgers and Hart

——

Prior to the Mexico debacle, James Larkin had joined the Socialist Party of America, and in New York he became active in the party. As in 1914–15, he settled in the West Village, in MacDougal Alley off 6th Avenue. With a new wave of Irish agitators – the 'Easter Week exiles' – making their way to the US, and burgeoning support among Irish-Americans for republicanism after Easter Week, conditions were propitious for the politics he had been promoting since his arrival. The Irish cause became a mass movement. Friends of Irish Freedom, founded in 1916, had nearly 300,000 members in 1919. The American Association for the Recognition of the Irish Republic claimed 700,000 members in 1921. As in Europe, the war was pushing public opinion to the left, and Irish-America produced its own far left, the Irish Progressive League, launched in New York in 1917. The League sought to link the Irish cause with American social radicalism and international issues like recognition of Soviet Russia and peace in Europe. Though relatively small, with a core of about 150 activists in New York, it organised high-profile campaigns. Its membership included socialists with no Irish ties as well as comrades like Patrick Quinlan, Nora Connolly, and Frank Robbins.[2]

All of this was not entirely welcome to Larkin. The sudden elevation of once obscure acquaintances with their own version of revolution in the home country – a version that exalted James Connolly and 1916 rather than Big Jim and 1913 – wounded his pride. Privately, he contrasted their ability to manage the lecture circuit with his own disappointments in 1914–15.[3] Before Easter Week he had urged socialists not to forget the national – or at least – the Irish question. After Easter Week he barbed these appeals with criticism of nationalists. Now he complained of socialism being subordinated to nationalism. His abuse of republicans was so obviously driven by petulance that he lost credibility with the mainstream Irish-American left. Undaunted, he found a bailiwick of his own in the New York James Connolly Socialist Club, and then made the club premises the centre of a project to turn the Socialist Party into a communist party. Admiration for the Bolsheviks would shape his life over the next 15 years. It brought him renewed international renown as a revolutionary, and helped to erase some of the suspicion he had acquired from his collaboration with imperial Germany. It also led to his arrest and imprisonment in 1919–20, and deportation from the US in 1923.

BACON, EGGS, AND REVOLUTION

In February 1918 Hanna Sheehy Skeffington spoke to the Harlem branch   of the Socialist Party on 'The economic basis of the Irish revolution'. From the floor, Larkin demanded that the party put more of an emphasis on promoting socialism among the Irish.[4] Larkin had similar problems with remarks elsewhere by Nora Connolly, and believed that she was making derogatory statements about him and his relations with her late father.[5] Days later, the *Call* published an appeal from Con O'Lyhane for the formation of Connolly clubs.[6] Larkin requisitioned a premises for the New York James Connolly Socialist Club by breaking the lock on his Socialist Party branch rooms at 43 West 29th Street and moving in with the only possessions he needed: a mimeograph, a cooker, and a frying pan.[7] Billed as 'the first Commander-in-Chief' of the Citizen Army and 'in company with James Connolly . . . responsible for the radical movement which culminated in the Revolution of Easter week 1916', he was the main speaker at a preliminary meeting of the club on 15 March. The club was established formally at a rally in the Bryant Hall on St Patrick's Day.[8] Emmet O'Reilly served as president, Belfast-born Éadhmonn MacAlpine as vice-president, and Joseph McDonough as secretary.[9]

One of the Connolly Club's aims was to see Ireland 'develop along the lines of the forward peoples of the World', a veiled reference to Russia. In March or April, Larkin claimed to be in contact with Petrograd.[10] When Jack Reed addressed the club in May, Larkin was captivated. Recently back from Russia, the author of *Ten Days That Shook the World* was revitalising interest in the Bolsheviks. A fresh cause, free of *parvenu* Irish revolutionaries, was just the tonic for Larkin. With Jack Carney and MacAlpine he plunged his energies over the next 18 months into transforming the Socialist Party into a communist party. The Connolly Club became the national hub of the project, housing the editorial offices of his Socialist Party faction's *Revolutionary Age* and Reed's *Voice of Labor*. It was too a social centre after Larkin's heart, where comrades gathered 'to get information, to play pool, to eat ham and eggs made the way Jim Larkin wanted them made . . .'[11] Bert Wolfe recalled the presence of 'workingmen of all nationalities, Jewish cloakmakers, Scotsmen and Englishmen, Germans, Bulgarians, Yugo-Slavs, Russians, Greenwich Villagers. Wide-eyed they listened to the poetry of Larkin's speech, his intemperate polemics, his crotchets, his mixture of creeds'.[12] In a 'dark ugly' ground-floor flat in a 'dilapidated red brick tenement' in MacDougal Alley, directly behind Patchin Place, where Reed lived, Larkin had a second headquarters. Fusion of work and leisure was his preferred *modus operandi*. He lived, according to Benjamin Gitlow, the manager of *Revolutionary Age*, and otherwise an admirer, 'in utter disregard of cleanliness':

> Papers, pamphlets, books, rubbish, left-over food bits and dirty tea cups cluttered the place. Here sprawled over a large stuffed chair, the towering man held court. On the small gas stove tea was usually brewing, a dark concoction which Larkin drank by the bucketful. Here came emissaries from the four corners of the British Empire to report to the founder and commander of the Irish Citizens [*sic*] Army. His was an informal court. The haughty Larkin did not insist on ceremony but he did insist upon dominating the scene. He did not lack the human touch for he was a rough, congenial, witty gentleman who laughed loud and boisterously.[13]

To Gitlow, a former Bronx assemblyman and 17 years younger, he was

> an unusual organiser. He never gave one the impression that he was doing things. One never saw Larkin sitting at a desk, talking to a secretary, dictating letters or concerning himself with office details. More likely you would see him bent over a stove, frying eggs and bacon in a greasy pan. Yet he made the contacts he needed . . .[14]

In February 1919, the New York Socialist Party divided over the party's support for the erection of a Victory Arch to commemorate the world war. Radicals were outraged, the more so as the US army was one of the intervention forces in Soviet Russia. Larkin helped to organise a left section of the party with Reed, Rose Pastor Stokes, and Max Cohen.[15] His priorities led him to decline the leadership of the St Lawrence, Massachusetts mill strike in March. A glimpse of his activities in April is found in a Bureau of Investigation resume:

> Some of Larkins most prominent speeches together with their subjects are as follows: 'Greetings to the Russian Soviet Government' held at 66 East 4th Street, New York City.

April 3rd, 1919 'Propaganda Mass Meeting' held at 725–6th Avenue, New York City (Larkin, chairman)

April 4th, 1919 'The workers Council and the AF of L held at 66 East 4th Street, NYC.

April 11th, 1919 'Greetings to [redacted] 219 Sackman Street, Brooklyn, NY

April 13th, 1919 'Demand immediate release of all class war prisoners, and to protest against deportation'.

April 28th, 1919 Reception to [redacted] at Bryant Hall, 6th Avenue & 42nd Street. (Hall hired by James Connolly Club [redacted] Speakers [redacted] John Reed, Louise Bryant [redacted] James Larkin. Message from Debs read.

April 29th, 1919 Lecture and Concert on Lawrence Strikers at Burland Casino, Bronx, NY.

Larkin is a Socialist, Bolshevik, IWW agitator and propagandist. He is a very dangerous man of the 'roughneck type'. Spreads propaganda through labor unions.

He certainly had a flair for courting danger. A visit to C. E. Ruthenberg in Cleveland, en route from Chicago to New York, coincided with the Cleveland May Day riots, in which two workers were killed. Subsequently, the city mayor's house was bombed. Ruthenberg was charged with fomenting the unrest and Larkin was detained for questioning on 4 May.[16] On 21 June Larkin topped the poll in elections to a nine-man National Council of the Socialist Party left at a conference in the Manhattan Lyceum. MacAlpine was also elected. Larkin, Reed, and Gitlow were 'the big three' behind the majority view that the left should try to win control of the party at its national convention in August; a minority faction, dominated by the party's Russian language federation and Slavic bloc favoured the immediate formation of a communist party and walked out in protest.[17] The expulsion of the left from Socialist Party's national convention led to the creation of two parties in September; the Communist Party of America, with some 50,000 members, and the Communist Labor Party, which had about 10,000 members, but more anglophones. Critical of the former's penchant for European style Marxist jargon, and convinced of the need for the party to be 'American', Larkin joined the latter, where he still found himself at odds with the 'intellectuals'.[18] Carney was one of the party's five-man national executive committee.

The communist project earned Larkin the renewed attention of the Bureau of Investigation from early 1919. After very intermittent reportage on him in 1917–18, the Bureau had agents compile detailed accounts of speeches he gave in New York, Boston, Philadelphia, and Providence, Rhode Island. Frankly, he urged the formation of soviets and red guards in the US, his passionate admiration for events in Russia piqued by disappointment with America. One agent observed: 'Larkin mounted a table and began a fiery speech, which moved the audience to an extent that is seldom witnessed anywhere even at Socialist gatherings.' Informed that he could not be arrested under the Espionage Act, the 'special agent in charge' recommended, in March, that the immigration authorities be asked to consider deportation, adding 'We are extremely interested in the case'. In May, Bureau offices in Boston, Cincinnati, Pittsburgh, Detroit, San Francisco, New York, Cleveland, Philadelphia, St Paul, and Seattle were briefed on Larkin, a 'trouble breeder' engaged in 'Irish and IWW activities at various cities', and instructed to collect 'evidence of breaches of the US criminal code'.[19]

TROUBLE IN DUBLIN

Larkin's correspondence with the ITGWU became more frequent in 1918. Four ingratiating letters were sent to Tom Foran. His knowledge of events in Ireland was somewhat sketchy, but from English Labour papers he knew that the ITGWU was enjoying rapid recovery, and he was concerned about James Connolly's posthumous reputation and stories of friction between himself and Connolly. Astutely, he advised Foran not to let Labour be overshadowed by Sinn Féin and to be more assertive within the national movement. Again, he assured Foran that he would rather be in Ireland.

> My Purgatory continues. To bid good luck continually to exiles returning and yet to be denied that inestimable pleasure, hurts more than you can appreciate. May the curse of thousand years [sic] rest on those who prompted me to this undertaking.[20]

In October, Foran cabled, offering him a union nomination for Dublin's Harbour Division as a Labour candidate 'pledged to abstain from Westminster until Special Labour Congress decides otherwise'. There was an enthusiastic response on 14 October: 'Larkin accepts; run labour candidate; only insists no compromise; no political trading; will promulgate Irish Labour party's decision in all matters – Jim Larkin.'[21]

Of course, Labour ultimately decided not to contest the 1918 general election. It was probably after V. I. Lenin's call for a communist International in January 1919 that Larkin informed Foran: 'Our advice to you and those to be relied on is no conciliation with the Huysmans gang. We have opened up negotiations with Moscow officially.' On this, as on much else during his stay in America, Larkin's instructions to Dublin were ignored. Labour and the ITGWU-dominated Socialist Party of Ireland sent delegates to the Berne conference of Camille Huysmans' social democratic International Socialist

Bureau in February and never affiliated to the Communist International, or Comintern. The letter concluded with some concern about the union slipping away from him, and promised further couriers:

> some of our friends should be reminded that I will return maybe sooner that some would welcome. I have depended on you all these years hew to the line we laid down in 1908. Don't let a superficial success run away with you. Our fight in Ireland has not arrived yet make no mistake as to this. See to my wife and kids. See Jim and the other three kids are look[ed] after. I will not forget. Other men will arrive. Thine to the last.[22]

In reality, the ITGWU was slipping away from him. By December 1918, membership had soared from 3,500 in 1915–16, to 68,000. For the first time, it had become a nationwide structure, with a network of 210 branches. Larkin made an invaluable indirect contribution to the expansion by the example of his pre-war tactics, the sympathetic strike in particular.[23] His direct contribution, however, was zero, and the absence of a general secretary created managerial problems. Larkin's hopes that he could retain an influence through Foran were misplaced. Foran did not wish to continue the acting general secretary's role he had assumed after Easter Week. Instead he employed Séamus Hughes as financial and correspondence secretary, and became increasingly dependent on William O'Brien.[24] In December 1918, new union rules diversified power from the general secretary to a triumvirate of the general president, general secretary, and general treasurer. In effect, this meant Foran, Hughes, who was formally appointed assistant general secretary in May 1919, and O'Brien. Of the three, O'Brien emerged as the most powerful. Efficient, diligent, and persuasive at close quarters, he was also ambitious, arrogant, and ruthless enough to squeeze out those who bucked his managerial style. Some of Larkin's old loyalists were the initial casualties.

The most public confrontation was with P. T. Daly, whom O'Brien had long regarded as venal and incompetent, and Delia. Delia had resigned from the IWWU in July 1915 to work as a nurse in England. Daly brought her back to work in the ITGWU's insurance section in July 1918. Tensions surfaced immediately. O'Brien and Foran saw Daly as jealously appropriating the Larkin brand, and Delia was unpopular in her own right. When she was refused re-admittance to the IWWU, now under the management of Louie Bennett, there were allegations that it was all part of O'Brien and Foran's anti-Larkin agenda. Foran pleaded to Dublin trades council: 'I was "Jim Larkin" when he was away. I am satisfied that I did my duty by Jim Larkin . . .', and resolved to push Daly out of the union. In June 1919, he defeated Daly in the annual elections for the post of secretary of the ITGWU insurance section; a post that Jim had appointed him to. The day following, three clerks at Liberty Hall – Delia, Mícheál Ó Maoláin, and George Norgrove – struck against 'the usurpation of Jim Larkin's authority and the consequent victimisation of P. T. Daly'. Twelve others stayed at work. Daly, Delia, and Ó Maoláin mounted a protest campaign in Dublin and the provinces, backed by a weekly 'Larkinite' paper, *Red Hand*, edited by Delia. Daly trumped O'Brien on Dublin trades council, his old stomping ground, but failed to gain purchase within the ITGWU.[25] By the time Jim responded to appeals from the Daly faction, the storm had passed.

Jim regarded the dispute as a headache. There was no percentage for him in splitting the union or challenging the leadership, but he could hardly ignore people like Delia and his old friend Ó Maoláin. He sent Dublin two messages in August. The first, for publication in the ITGWU's *Voice of Labour*, read: 'To the Old Guard of the ITWU: Stand fast. I am returning. Take no side in this fratricidal strife going on in the Union. You and I will settle the matter, as we solved more serious problems in the past. This quarrel is but the growing pains of a lusty young giant.'[26] Privately, a sharp letter was carried home personally by MacAlpine. Introducing himself as 'Larkin's ambassador', MacAlpine handed it to Foran on 15 September. After berating Foran like an angry parent for allowing 'this fire to smoulder', Larkin ordered the closure of *Red Hand*, told both sides to patch up the squabble, and directed that Daly and others be reinstated. Underneath the furious tone, he affirmed confidence in Foran and dictated that the dissidents must 'submit to the Executive'. He signed off with another reference to 'the Old Guard': 'let us work together until the matters at issue are submitted to those who have a right to decide the fate of the Union – The Old Guard.' The notion that he and others of the pre-1914 vintage would control the union took no cognisance of changing circumstances. On 9 November the executive protested 'against the tone of the letter' and, in a reference to Daly's position, denied 'the right of any official of the Union to reverse a decision arrived at by the duly elected representatives of the members'.[27] It would also have been illegal under the laws governing approved insurance societies to have Daly reinstated without an election.

With Daly and his dissidents marginalised, O'Brien belittled Hughes at every opportunity, instigating his resignation from the union in July 1921. O'Brien did not even offer him a perfunctory note of thanks for his services, and tried to write him out of union history. Now *de facto* general secretary, O'Brien wished to be remembered as the architect of the glorious post-1916 expansion. None of this would have been possible without Foran's backing, and there is nothing to support the impression that Foran was at heart a decent old Larkinite being manipulated by O'Brien. O'Brien and Foran were a duo. Foran had the common touch O'Brien lacked. O'Brien did the managerial work for which Foran had little stomach. Coincidentally, what would become a familiar dichotomy in representations of O'Brien and Larkin – the dull, meticulous bureaucrat versus the flawed hero – was echoed in the second play to feature Larkin as a central character, Daniel Corkery's *The Labour Leader*, which opened in a Lennox Robinson production in the Abbey Theatre on 30 September 1919. Corkery drew on Larkinite conflict in Cork in 1908–9 to create Cork versions of Larkin and O'Brien in the strike leader Davna and the apparatchik Dempsey. Davna, violent and poetic, is depicted as a necessary product of brutal class oppression and the embodiment of a vision of how workers might be lifted out of it to a world of beauty. His alter ego, the rational, clerkly Dempsey, worries that he's a dangerous militant. The first act has a coalporter question the idea of giving Davna a secretary:

> And if ye give him a secretary his job will be to cut Davna off when he's giving us the history of Ireland in the tenth century, or giving us Shelley . . . And what would we know about him only for Davna? Or about the Red Flag? Or about anything at all.[28]

The Labour Leader drew packed houses, and the opening night compelled an intoxicated Pádraic Ó Conaire to wander onstage and sit at the feet of the cast. When the American Trotskyist and author of the *Studs Lonigan* trilogy, James T. Farrell, visited Larkin in 1938, his host rummaged through piles of books to find Farrell a copy of the play.[29] Surprisingly, O'Brien thought it a 'good study of Larkin'.[30]

Why Corkery's hero did not return is moot. References to going home in his correspondence became more forceful in 1918 and 1919. He was clearly tired of America by 1919, and was wont to let his audiences know it. In March, he called for a Soviet government in the US, saying he hoped he would be deported for the speech. His supporters claimed that he had been denied a passport 11 times by the British consulate in New York.[31] Yet, he did not raise a public protest about it until after July 1919, when he asked Foran to get Neil Maclean, Labour MP for Glasgow Govan, to table a parliamentary question. Maclean was informed that on 24 December 1914 Dublin Castle had barred Larkin from re-entering Ireland.[32] Even then, there was no bar on him entering Britain, and the man who helped smuggle Reed to Russia and Reed's papers on Russia into New York knew that there were other ways to travel.[33] The DMP warned of his 'probable return to Dublin' in July 1919, expecting he would just 'turn up' at Liberty Hall.[34] Foran moved a motion at the annual ITUC in August, condemning 'the British and United States governments in refusing passports'.[35] MacAlpine addressed Dublin trades council in October on the problem and the council considered a one-day protest strike. The British-based National Union of Railwaymen and the Railway Clerks' Association promptly dissented: Larkin's wartime association with the Germans had dented his popularity in Britain and Unionist Ireland. The trades council agreed to send its president, Desmond Logue, with MacAlpine, and Daly to lobby the Foreign Office in London with the strike threat in their pocket. At the request of the Labour Party whip, they were received by the Chief Secretary in the House of Commons on 11 November. By this stage, Larkin had been arrested, and all the Chief Secretary would do was assure the delegation that the Irish government had nothing to do with the arrest, promise to enquire as to the US government's charges, and review the case in the light of the arraignment.[36] On 15 November, Dublin trades council executive read a cable from Larkin, calling off the strike.[37]

DRAGNETS IN GOTHAM

Between 1917 and 1923, with America gripped by major strikes and a 'red scare', over half the states enacted 'criminal syndicalism' or similar statutes. Most of the others already had anti-sedition laws in place. New York had passed a Criminal Anarchy Law in 1902, after the assassination of President McKinley, but it had never been applied until 1919, when the New York Senate's Lusk committee was given powers which shocked liberal opinion. On 7 November, Lusk agents made a series of raids on what the press usually termed 'anarchists', 'communists', or 'reds'. The next day, a 'journalist' got access to MacDougal Alley, told Larkin the Lusk committee would like to see him, and took him to join 2,000 other suspects held in an auditorium. Savouring the joke, Larkin hailed the comrades with a laugh, and jovially made fun of the police.[38] Among his personal effects was a false passport. Two days later he was one of 20 selected for test case accusations of 'criminal anarchy', a charge many thought unconstitutional. The 'crime' was of advocating the violent overthrow of the government. Larkin and Gitlow, the biggest fish in the net, were arraigned for their part in publishing the Socialist Party's 'Left-wing manifesto' in *Revolutionary Age* on 5 July 1919. Waiting for their case to be processed at the Old Police Headquarters in Manhattan, they chatted calmly, Larkin smoking his pipe and leaning his 'rangy, angular body' against a doorpost, before a large crowd of supporters. In the throng was Dr Pat McCartan, Dáil Éireann's envoy to the US. Asked to explain his presence, he replied sceptically, 'I have merely come to watch the interesting process by which American courts make anarchists.'[39] The litigation commenced on 13

November with Larkin's counsel pleading in the Municipal Court that the 'criminal anarchy' statute violated the constitution. When the plea was dismissed, Clan na Gael produced the $15,000 bail, John Devoy providing $5,000 from the estate of his late brother, Michael.[40]

Released on 20 November, Larkin resumed political activity with a jaunty insouciance about what lay ahead. At a Communist Labor Party rally in the Manhattan Lyceum, he described the Lusk committee as 'microbes', 'men with the mind of an amoeba', and 'a body with the vile odor of the skunk'. Teasing the police stenographers, he called for a 'Soviet army', before adding 'Of course, I mean we have got to meet together in a drilled manner, come early, stay throughout the meeting, and then be dismissed by the Chairman'.[41] The left generally tried to subvert the scare with ridicule, joking about '10 days that will shake the United States (with laughter)'.[42] Off the record, Larkin knew his situation was serious. His appeal failed, Chief Magistrate William McAdoo, who hailed from Ramelton, handed him over to the Supreme Court, and the entire New York bomb squad was assigned to serve the warrant.[43] He now came before Justice Bartow S. Weeks, who made plain his prejudices against the left. As Weeks quibbled about granting bail, Larkin could be heard whispering to his counsel, 'Tell the judge that some of the money came from Irish sympathisers.' On 4 December, Larkin cabled Foran saying he expected 'five to ten', and asking to see Young Jim 'to give him instructions for the future'.[44]

Others were not so sure about the future. The Bureau of Investigation was informed of an alleged conspiracy by four New York Irish republicans to poison Larkin with cyanide lest he jump bail, stowaway for Ireland, and 'arouse the Irish Socialist vote against the Sinn Féin'. In the most bizarre aspect of the plot, a stoker bearing a 'striking resemblance' to Larkin would go to Ireland in his place, to urge Labour support for Sinn Féin. Often alarmist and comically uninformed on Larkin's background, the Bureau noted soberly that he was under close watch and 'there are little chances that he will make any attempt to escape trial as he considers himself a Martyr to the cause'.[45]

An equally mysterious, but more corroborated, intercession came from the British. In February Scotland Yard enquired of Alexander Rorke, Assistant District Attorney and state prosecutor in the trial, if the charges against Larkin might be dropped to allow him to travel to South Africa for six months. The British consul in New York made repeated enquiries as to the case and the feasibility of leniency or an appeal. Rorke exploited the requests to blacken Larkin's name with Irish nationalists. Bumping into Devoy on 29 July 1920, he took him to his office and showed him the incriminating evidence. Devoy issued a damning statement on what he'd seen.[46] In October, Archie Crawford, president of the South African Federation of Labour, tried to undo the damage with an explanatory cable to T. J. O'Flaherty, secretary of the Larkin Defense

Committee in New York. According to Crawford, he had a conversation in England in March with a 'high authority, not LG [Lloyd George] but one with all the necessary power' in the British government, who cleared the way for Larkin to get a passport for South Africa. Crawford and Larkin had met in England in March 1914, when the former was one of the South African deportees. He had since returned to South Africa, abandoned revolutionism, and led the South African Federation of Labour to support the world war.[47] His Irish-born wife, 'Pickhandle Mary', would soon be delegated by the South African government to the International Labour Organization in Geneva. One could understand the British wanting to oblige Crawford, and Crawford wanting to help Larkin. Why the British would help Larkin or want him in a colony on the verge of major industrial conflict is less obvious. Rorke detected the hand of the Lusk Committee, which had a reputation for using agents-provocateurs, behind it all; and possibly the British thought that Larkin would make ideal material for their propaganda associating the Irish struggle with Bolshevism, or be of service as a critic of Sinn Féin.[48] Crawford's cable did Larkin some service. The *Call* sprang to his defence as 'an Irish proletarian . . . internationalist and revolutionist', insisting that Rorke had deliberately distorted the facts.[49]

More predictable intervention came from J. Edgar Hoover. Hoover had an obsession with communists, and, formerly head of the Justice Department's Enemy Aliens Registration Section, he regarded deportation as the best way to deal with them. In January 1920, as head of the General Intelligence Division of the Bureau of Investigation, he ordered that a brief be prepared on Larkin's activities with a view to deportation. In February, the Bureau requested an unabridged transcript of the trial on completion, and Hoover sent Rorke a copy of W. P. Ryan's book *The Irish Labour Movement from the 'Twenties to Our Own Day* with the suggestion he read the pages on Larkin. Hoover could not have been reassured by Ryan's mythologisation of the great man as 'trans-human, colossal, legendary', and asked Rorke to note that Larkin was 'born in Ireland and taken to New York in his infancy', perhaps the only time that New York has been confused with Newry.[50] He requested the return of the book 'as soon as it has served your purpose', and when Rorke said he hadn't received it, posted another copy. At Rorke's request, Hoover supplied documentation from Britain on Larkin's birth and criminal record, and on his own initiative provided Rorke with a file of Larkin's speeches.

By the opening of the trial on 7 April, Larkin's apprehension was being confirmed. He had been indicted with Isaac E. Ferguson, Ruthenberg, and Gitlow – all members of the National Council of the left – and Gitlow had already received a sentence of five to 10 years.[51] Larkin conducted his own defence as usual, though he was advised privately by Jeremiah O'Leary, a lawyer and president of the American Truth Society, founded in 1912 'to combat the influences which are now enslaving American finance'. O'Leary had also established the wartime paper *Bull*, to combat the anti-neutrality bias of what he termed 'the anglo-press'.[52] Like an obstreperous barrackroom lawyer, Larkin deployed delaying tactics, challenging 'bourgeois' talesmen in pursuit of a 'proletarian' jury, and earning repeated rebukes from Justice Weeks for enquiring after their investments and social beliefs. He in turn criticised the beak as 'heterogeneous, conglomerate, and illogical'.[53] The self-defence created some embarrassment for the bench when Weeks decided he'd suffered enough aspersions on his impartiality and proposed to commit Larkin to the city prison, the Tombs, for contempt. He then realised that the case couldn't continue without the defendant. But a threat to revoke his bail and lodge him in the Tombs when not in court drew an apology from Larkin and a plea that he was suffering from a cold and from stress.[54]

Weeks finally revoked his bail on 26 April and had him detained in the Tombs, to criminalise him in the eyes of the jury, in Larkin's opinion. Larkin was also allowed to take the witness stand and ask and answer his own questions. The cross-examination came from Rorke. He did not belabour the fact that his beliefs, not his deeds, were on trial, and his defence consisted mainly of an elaboration of those beliefs and the ethics of revolutionary struggle. Despite his newfound Bolshevism, his philosophy remained an eclectic stew of Christianity, socialism, syndicalism, communism, and Irish national-ism, all after his own fashion. The one change which Bolshevism appears to have induced in his values was a slight shift from nationalism to internation-alism. He called himself a 'nationist' rather than a 'nationalist', meaning that he cherished distinctive national cultures while regarding political nationalism as narrow and 'foolish'. Devoy was not pleased. Most observers thought he had gained enough sympathy to divide the jury. Instead, on 28 April, it found him guilty in less than an hour. On 3 May he was sentenced to five to ten years' imprisonment. Only one party comrade, Gertrude Nafe, dared defy the judge's warnings against protest in court, standing silently while the sentence was being read. The prisoner was then fingerprinted and measured at the Criminal Identification Bureau at police headquarters, and placed by Sheriff Knott with convicts bound for Sing Sing prison, Ossining, New York.[55]

Hoover's worries were not allayed. He continued to furnish Rorke with snippets of information, and complained that Larkin 'seems to be engaging again from behind prison walls in his usual propaganda'. Both feared that friends would smuggle him papers, and to discourage visitors he was transferred on 15 June to Clinton prison, Dannemora, near the New York–Canadian border. The authorities pleaded that the Sing Sing could not handle the volume of mail arriving for Larkin.[56] Sing Sing was old and grim, with 'small, narrow stone chambers crowded with four to six inmates sleeping in each cell', but it had enjoyed an enlightened governor who introduced a model regime.[57] Clinton prison was harsher. In July, a journalist with the *Call* wangled an interview, and reported a marked deterioration in his appearance. Rumours that he had contracted consumption led to renewed international protests and questions in the House of Commons from Britain's first communist MP, Colonel L'Estrange Malone. Clinton had an ironic association with tuber-culosis as tubercular prisoners were sometimes transferred there for the crisp, curative air of the Adirondacks. The protests had an effect. Larkin was given an outdoor job, supervising a convict gang, and November saw him back in Sing Sing, where he could liberally receive visitors, who kept him supplied with money and books.[58]

Politics was important in protecting Larkin from the routine violence of prison life. He recalled:

> the ordinary criminal entering an American prison must join a gang or he don't get very far. We who were political prisoners, though not recognised by the Law as politicals, were recognised by the government within the prison. We were looked up to, consulted about home, legal matters, in fact all inside and outside activities affecting the lives of our unfortunate brothers. We would be engaged for hours every night writing to sweethearts wives, mothers, lawyers, and most of our leisure time was occupied drafting and writing petitions for clemency . . .

He still described himself and his fellows as 'buried alive'.[59] His most famous visitor, Charlie Chaplin, went to see him at the invitation of Galway-born libertarian socialist, adventurer, and celebrity author, Frank Harris.

> Larkin was in the shoe factory, and here he greeted us, a tall handsome man, about six foot four, with piercing blue eyes but a gentle smile. Although happy to see Frank, he was nervous and disturbed and was anxious to get back to his bench. Even the warder's assurance would not allay his uneasiness. 'It's bad morally for the other prisoners if I'm privileged to see visitors during working hours,' said Larkin. He said he was treated reasonably well, but he was worried about his wife and family in Ireland, whom he had not heard from since his confinement. Frank promised to help him.

Chaplin sent presents to Elizabeth and the children.[60] Carney recalled being invited to Hollywood with Pete Larkin to speak on Big Jim to Chaplin, Charles Ray, and Milton Sills, among others, when his chance to meet the stars was cut short by Jim's release.[61] Jim's relations with Elizabeth were strained. She had joined him briefly in 1919, but at Easter 1922, R. M. Fox found her reluctant to campaign for his release, and 'plainly uneasy' about her husband's return to Ireland, which was now rumoured to be a possibility if Al Smith won the New York gubernatorial election in November. A leftish Democrat and Irish-American, Smith was expected to be sympathetic. Neglected by him so often, Elizabeth had reason to fear that Jim would return to destroy the measure of peace she enjoyed in Dublin.[62]

Larkin was later moved to Great Meadow, Comstock, a relatively comfortable, open prison, where he was put to work in the laundry and spent 'several hours daily tying up sheets, pillow cases etc for the prison departments'.[63] He was managing to keep an eye on Irish affairs, and had despatched a long, thunderous denunciation of the six 'traitors', 'helots', and 'Judases' who signed the 'foul and destructive' Anglo-Irish Treaty, four days after the Treaty was signed. His suggestion that they hang themselves from London Bridge was excessive. On 13 December the statement reached O'Reilly in New York, and on 28th it was received by the *Voice of Labour*. The *Voice*'s editor, Cathal O'Shannon, published it along with a note dissociating the paper from the violent language used against the signatories, despite being 'absolutely and completely opposed' to the 'political and social opinions' of most of the 'Ratificationists'. This reference to social differences was missing from Larkin's ultra-republican rant, which was grounded in a ferocious hatred of the 'blood-soaked, tyrannical Empire'.[64] Months later, Larkin impressed Countess Markievicz as appreciative of the conditions in Comstock, and 'well up in everything that is going on at home, except about the late Commandant [Connolly]'. But his frustration showed in complaints against both the British and Free State governments for blocking his release, and Devoy and fellow Clan leader Judge Daniel F. Cohalan for not getting him out. Beneath the outward assurances, Markievicz sensed his fretfulness.

> The real tragedy for a man like Jim is the confinement, and the isolation. There he is, a man of great brain and tireless energy, shut up with a crowd of Blacks, Chinese, and criminals of every race, located at the back of beyond, and hearing daily of the dire stress of the country to which he belongs.[65]

Larkin shared this race consciousness. It was typical of the times and inevitable that any Labour activist in New York would acquire it. One memoir of his prison days detailed the various races and his fascination with their different characteristics. At the same time, he did not hold any race to be inherently inferior. Of the African Americans, he wrote:

> Then we had over one hundred negroes, 'bad niggers' as the average citizen would say. I have lived in close and intimate relationship with these bad niggers. They

were much of a muchness with the average man. One thing I found out. The negro is no longer a Slave, mentally, physically, or politically, and America is going to wake up some morning and find out. Some of the most earnest students in the prison school were these same bad niggers, and some of the whitest [ie. most honest] men we ever met in this world had black skins just as some of the blackest hearted scoundrels we ever met had white skins. Outwardly the nigger was a wilful, saucy, singing no-give-a-damn sort of cuss. My analysis – close and sympathetic – a man obsessed with sorrow and acquainted with grief and yet realising his position determined to alter it and for the betterment of society [*sic*]. They were a never ending source of study and delight.[66]

As editor of the *Irish Worker* he would tell socialists who faulted 'native' labour for its lack of militancy that the fault lay in colonial oppression. 'The White man when he goes abroad in other people's countries is always accustomed to giving himself a very grand certificate for this own virtues . . . Can any Socialist fundamentally believe that one nation is entitled, because of its nationality, to go and dominate over another nation . . .'[67]

From the moment of his incarceration, Larkin had been exploring legal avenues to freedom. On 30 December 1920, his application for a certificate of reasonable doubt had been rejected in the New York Supreme Court by Justice Cohalan.[68] In March 1922, as the red scare subsided, there were rumours that he would be pardoned by Governor Miller to mark Ireland's first St Patrick's Day as a free country. Leo Healy, one of his several lawyers, promised he would go home to unite Collins and de Valera. The Republican state chairman agreed that England had pardoned 'worse'. And Tom Johnson made a special appeal from Irish Labour for the liberty of 'Irish political prisoners' in a St Patrick's Day message to the 'workers of America'.[69] The optimism was unfounded. On 6 May, he was freed by the appeal court on a writ of reasonable doubt, only to be re-arrested at Comstock on a second criminal anarchy indictment, taken to the Tombs, charged with violating immigration laws, and served with deportation warrants. He finally walked into a contingent freedom two days later, after Mrs Charles Brooks of the Bronx paid the $15,000 bail. According to James J. Barry, another of his attorneys, friends of Larkin were ready to raise up to $300,000 in bail.[70] There were friends too in Moscow. Grigori Zinoviev, president of the Comintern, cabled the International's 'warmest greetings to the undaunted fighter released from the "democratic" prisons'.[71] The Soviets had followed his case with interest. On 13 August 1920 foreign commissar G. V. Chicherin suggested to the Politburo of the VKP(b) (All-Union Communist Party (Bolsheviks)) that Mrs Zinaida Mackenzie Kennedy, a British spy who had been handled by MI6 agent Paul Dukes, be exchanged for Larkin, or, 'as a last resort', the first big American spy in Soviet custody,

Xenophon Dmitrievich de Blumenthal Kalamatiano. The Politburo approved, subject to Chicherin reaching an 'understanding' with the Cheka. The Americans declined the offer. When the US later asked for the return of Captain Kirkpatrick of the American interventionist force in Russia, the Soviets agreed on condition that Larkin be freed.[72] In February 1922, Larkin had been elected to the Moscow Soviet to represent the Moscow International Communist Tailoring Factory by a union of tailors, most of them returnees from the US. A number of other class war prisoners in America were similarly honoured, but the Soviets forewent efforts for the release of Gitlow and Ruthenberg to make a special plea that Larkin be allowed to take his seat.[73]

A less exotic chalice was proffered by the Labour Party as it mobilised for its first general election; a nomination for North Dublin. Larkin evidently understood that Labour's participation would make the party a prop of the pro-Treaty constitution and replied on 5 June 1922:

> Decline emphatically. Charge you and all comrades to remember the purpose of the Union – an injury to one, etc. What of Ulster? Damn politics, and politicians, especially carellists [careerists?]. Let them clean up the mess. Ulstermen's Defence Alliance formed here. We want ship. Remember 1913. Send us 20,000 dollars to furnish ship: ours. Volunteer crew of loaders ready. We will get food cargo here. Red hand. Raise fiery cross. Be true to the principle of the dead and living nation. For the sake of the children of Ulster, fail <u>not</u>. Publish. – Jim.[74]

The Ulster Defense Alliance and the food ship became a frenetic crusade, driven by an obvious personal stress. On 6 August, looking older than his years, his face puffy, his brow a 'pronounced frown', he delivered a three-hour oration, entirely on Ireland and the terror in Ulster, at a picnic of the 'Kevin Barry-Nora Connolly Clubs' at Windsor, Connecticut. Irish Labour leaders, he assured his audience, would follow his orders. He spoke too of forthcoming fund-raising rallies in Cleveland, Butte, and San Francisco. The project drew him back towards Irish republicans, who were all the more eager to embrace allies as national unity collapsed at home. New York communists took a sceptical view of his latest 'pet organisation', and concluded he would never make a permanent home in the radical movement. For the authorities, he was still dangerous. Ruthenberg and Ferguson had been granted re-trials in July, but Larkin and Gitlow had their appeals rejected.[75] On 29 August his Defense Committee threw a party, where he received gifts of clothes and other comforts for his renewed confinement in Sing Sing. On 31st, he was back in custody.[76] Gubernatorial clemency now was his only hope.

KATHLEEN LOOKS FOR HER MAN IN THE WEST

From the time of his arrest, socialists from New York to New Zealand formed groups to campaign for Larkin's release and raise funds for his legal expenses. A few prominent New York Irish-Americans and the American Civil Liberties Union at the behest of the Larkin Defense Committee did the crucial work. The committee had been formed originally in Chicago by John Fitzpatrick of the Chicago Federation of Labor, and worked with the Irish Progressive League and Irish-American Labor League, which was more or less the New York Connolly Club.[77] Its publications had a strong socialist republican slant, and linked Larkin with Fintan Lalor and James Connolly. 'Kathleen ní Houlihan,' wrote Carney, 'though she lies bleeding and broken looks for her man in the west.'[78] Éamon de Valera, of whom Larkin would normally speak with respect, did nothing to help during his visit to the US as President of the Republic, and may have been hostile, but Harry Boland and the Republic's consul in New York made every effort through legal channels.[79] When the American Liberty Club telegrammed Michael Collins, asking the Provisional Government to petition the US government, the cabinet requested a report from its US envoy. On seeing Rorke's evidence on the British intercessions for Larkin, Collins took no further action. Ironically, Rorke himself now favoured clemency and had appealed to New York's Governor Miller, pointing out that all belligerents in the recent war had freed their political prisoners except the US. Senators, congressmen, judges, and sheriffs added their voices.[80]

Various Irish bodies joined the international chorus. In a letter to the Glasgow-based Socialist Labour Party, Delia reported protests by Richard Corish, mayor of Wexford, the corporations of Dublin, Kilkenny, Sligo, and Drogheda, Kildare and Westmeath county councils, Athlone, Bray, Navan, Killarney, Mallow, Carlow, New Ross, and Kells Urban District Councils, and Bandon Town Commission.[81] Killarney's objection to the sentence 'inflicted on Mr Jim Larkin for his stand against Capitalism on behalf of the Toilers of the World' was filed by the Bureau of Investigation. A patently peeved US consul told Fermoy Urban Council that its protest would not be forwarded to Washington.[82] Unionist Ulster was more understanding of the American position. Moira District Council assured the US government that the conviction was 'just and righteous'.[83]

Dublin trades council formed a defence committee, of which Delia became secretary. Identified with the Larkinite wing of the city's fractious trade union movement, the committee complained of ITGWU inaction.[84] In truth, Foran did what he could, and was genuinely sympathetic, though it was no secret that ITGWU leaders expected trouble should Larkin return. On 20 November 1919, Foran assured the New York Connolly Club of ITGWU support, and offered to pay Larkin's legal costs. In June 1920, the ITUC urged the annual congress of the American Federation of Labor to use its power to free Larkin. The cable was received in silence. On 21 July there was a less than half-hearted 24 hour 'general' strike, called by Dublin trades council and discountenanced by Congress and Liberty Hall. About 1,500 workers, mainly dockers, responded, and Delia led a march on the American consulate. Later that year, after a delay caused by the denial of travel permits by the US consul, Foran escorted Young Jim to see his father, without the permits.[85] In 1922 Pete accepted his suggestion of a 'daring act' to free his brother, and travelled to New York with an escape plan in mind, which Jim rejected. Foran also maintained a friendly correspondence with the New York Larkin Defense Committee, whose secretary, O'Flaherty, endorsed the ITGWU's hostility to 'the freak release committee of Dublin' and confirmed his committee's 'thorough agreement with the policy of the Union in regard to Larkin'.[86] O'Brien did the minimum consistent with giving his titular boss no excuse for fault-finding. In November 1921 he ignored Seán O'Casey's requests, as secretary of the Jim Larkin Correspondence Committee, for an interview. O'Casey's committee aimed to encouraged people to write to Larkin and had postcards printed to make the job easier. He and Larkin corresponded about his plays, *The Crimson in the Tricolour* and *The Seamless Coat of Kathleen*. Larkin repaid the debt by seeing the Broadway production of *The Hairy Ape*, a play about a brutish ship's stoker seeking meaning in a world determined by the money men. Returning to Dublin 'full of it', he sparked O'Casey's passion for the work of Eugene O'Neill.[87]

O'Flaherty later broke with the New York committee. He and Larkin became bitter enemies over the latter's policies on his return to Ireland, and over the handling of subscriptions to the committee. Thousands of dollars donated to the release campaign were never accounted for. Some accused Larkin or his supporters of spending the money on other causes.[88] Larkin subsequently alleged in Moscow that O'Flaherty and the American Communist Party had stolen $50,000 raised for his defence.[89] Following O'Flaherty's resignation, Carney's wife, Mina, shouldered the brunt of the work. Mina enlisted the help of prominent Irish-Americans, including the chaplain of the 'Fighting 69th' regiment, and Archbishop Patrick Hayes of New York. Other champions of the cause included Norman Thomas, associate editor of the *Nation*, Presbyterian pastor, and Christian socialist.[90] With the election of Smith as governor, a window opened. Smith's victory in itself confirmed that the 'red scare' had abated, and he granted a hearing for a pardon on 9 January. Larkin was due for release in January 1924 in any case, with allowances for good behaviour. Pleaders attended from a formidable team of 'respectable' US and Irish nationalist bodies, such as: the American Association for the Recognition of the Irish Republic, the Daughters of the American Revolution, and the Speakers' Bureau for American Independence, as well as the Irish Progressive League. Governor Smith concluded that here was 'a political case where a man has been punished for the statement of his beliefs . . . during the period of unusual political excitement following the close of the war . . .' Senator Clayton R. Lusk was disgusted.[91] A special messenger brought the news from Albany to Ossining, and Warden Lewis Lawes immediately went to Larkin. 'I am awfully thankful', he told Lawes, 'I never deserved to be sent here in the first place.' At 5 pm on 17 January, convict no 50945 left Sing Sing with a free pardon.[92]

TO DUBLIN OR MOSCOW?

Larkin's last weeks in the US involved a bizarre cocktail of conspiracies, contradictions, and confusion as to his politics and eventual destination. He first went to New York's West Village, operating out of 53 Jane Street, the office of his Defense Committee, before taking up residence at West 33rd Street.[93] Churlishly, he informed the American Civil Liberties Union that he would not have accepted the pardon had he known that others convicted with him of the same crime were to stay in jail.[94]

Soon after his release, Jim cabled Elizabeth to say he would be back in Dublin shortly.[95] Hoping to return in a blaze of glory, he then reactivated the food ship project. In Chicago's Ashland Auditorium, speaking with Carney and Sheehy Skeffington, he claimed that there was an assassination plot afoot to stop him going to Ireland, and implied that it involved a conspiracy of Irish-Americans and US authorities. Nonetheless, he was going home, he said, to fight for a republic, and would work with de Valera, adding 'I condemn certain political activities of the Irish bishops, but I am and will remain a Roman Catholic'. Fifteen hundred dollars was raised with the help of the local Connolly Club, and Larkin toured New England for the Ulster Defense Alliance. He and Carney inspected boats on Long Island, New York, and Larkin interviewed the sales manager of the US Shipping Board in Washington DC.[96] The Defense Alliance also applied, unsuccessfully, for a loan from the Garland Fund, a philanthropic foundation which aided a variety of left-wing projects. As the Fund was run by a 'who's who' of the far left, it was an embarrassing snub. The Alliance executive denounced them as 'anti-Irish'.[97] In late February, British police searched the quartermaster of the SS *Carmania* and found a note from Jim to Delia saying he hoped to be in Dublin by Easter Sunday with a relief ship. The information was passed on to the Vice-Regal Lodge.[98]

The note to Delia did not prevent all of the intelligence people monitoring Larkin from forming the impression that he was tacking away from Irish republicans and the idea of returning to Ireland. The explanation may be that Larkin's troubled mind was never going to let him work in harness with any organisation, and as the prospect of collaborating with the anti-Treatyites in Ireland loomed larger, his contrary individuality reasserted itself. Fifty-three Jane Street had become the centre of liaison between communists and Irish republicans. It was a worrying development for the Free State representative in Washington DC, Professor T. A. Smiddy, who knew that the 'irregulars' were soliciting communist aid, and the Soviets were courting Larkin.[99] Larkin was well placed to close the circle and enlist his waterside contacts for gun-running. Smiddy had hired the private detective agency run by the sons of William J. Burns, Director of the Bureau of Investigation, to track Robert Briscoe, the IRA's gun-runner in chief, and collect evidence against Larkin. In February the Free State army's Director of Intelligence informed his London counterpart, Lt-Colonel J. F. C. Carter of Special Branch, of a suspected smuggling operation between New York and London involving Larkin and Briscoe.[100] Yet within weeks Smiddy was gleefully telling Dublin that Larkin had split his supporters by denouncing the 'Republican bourgeois' and demand-ing that de Valera adopt a Labour programme. Smiddy reckoned he was now 'very reluctant to return to Ireland', and more interested in communism than republicanism.[101] From London, the Communist Party of Great Britain advised the Comintern that the IRA had despatched 'someone' – probably Dan Breen in the opinion of the Comintern's Anglo-Saxon referent – to America to secure Larkin's support.[102]

The Comintern had written to Larkin on 3 February acclaiming his release 'with great joy', and extending an invitation to visit Soviet Russia 'at your earliest opportunity . . . to discuss a number of burning questions affecting the inter-national revolutionary movement'.[103] Here was an opportunity to do commercial as well as political business with the Soviet government, and return to some-thing more attractive than the drudgery of union work. Foran cabled on 6 February, conveying the ITGWU's laconic 'satisfaction' with Larkin's release, and seeking the date of his return.[104] But divers antagonists continued to dog the food ship project. Police prevented Larkin from speaking at Providence, Rhode Island, and Hibernians managed to silence him at Worcester, Massachussetts. On trying to reach Quebec in March, where Sheehy Skeffington and Pete had earlier organised with Montreal Communists, he was told that he had been barred from Canada since 1915, detained in Montreal for four hours, and deported back to the US.[105]

On 23 March, he replied belatedly to Foran, and asked for £5,000 to buy a steamer. When Foran sought details, a wire on 28 March enquired of the

Portrait of a youthful Jim Larkin. Reproduced courtesy of Getty Images Ireland.

Elizabeth Brown, probably on her wedding day in 1903.

Pete Larkin, posing for a professional photographer, Poole of Waterford, in 1913. Pete was hoping to become an ITGWU organiser at this time. Reproduced courtesy of the National Library of Ireland.

Mr. W. M. Murphy, J.P.

William Martin Murphy. Larkin's nemesis in 1913, but Murphy lost the propaganda war. Reproduced courtesy of the National Library of Ireland.

Larkin during the Belfast dock strike in 1907. Labourite and loyalist, Alex Boyd, in the straw hat, would turn against Larkin when he founded an Irish union. Reproduced courtesy of Dr Frank Boyd.

Home is the hero. Larkin on return from the United States, 1923. Reproduced courtesy of the RTÉ Stills Library.

Larkin family: Jim, Elizabeth, Young Jim, Denis, and Fintan during the lockout.

The world famous photo of Larkin, taken on his return to Dublin in 1923. Reproduced courtesy of the RTÉ Stills Library.

Larkin, probably taken when he visited Moscow in 1924. Reproduced courtesy of RGASPI.

Jack Carney in Moscow, probably 1925. Reproduced courtesy of RGASPI.

The WUI Band. The social side of trade unionism was always important to Larkin and a big part of his appeal. Reproduced courtesy of Irish Labour History Society.

Lying in state with a guard of WUI and Citizen Army veterans. Note his clasped hands, the crucifix, and the Starry Plough. Reproduced courtesy of the RTÉ Stills Library.

WUI banner. Larkin as the public history would remember him. Reproduced courtesy of the RTÉ Stills Library.

International Brigaders at the Larkin statue in Dublin's O'Connell Street, now a symbol of the city, Labour, and solidarity. Reproduced courtesy of the Irish Labour History Society.

Liberty Hall, marking the centenary of the lockout. Reproduced courtesy of SIPTU, Liberty Hall.

money salted away from the 1913 Lockout subscriptions, and already spent on expenses arising from the lockout and the purchase of Liberty Hall; the same cache that had caused friction between Larkin and the no 1 branch committee in 1913–14.[106] The cable also claimed, in a transparent reference to Russia: 'have monopoly contract certain Eastern Government, after relief work done', implying that the ship would be a long-term investment. Of course, Larkin's characteristic secretiveness meant that his business plans were not clear to anyone else, and the very thought of the ITGWU – currently being pounded by a wage-cutting offensive in an economic slump – purchasing a golden chariot for Larkin to restore his imperious command, showed how out of touch the general secretary was. It is significant too, that since 1917 his correspondence was with Foran, rather than the more powerful O'Brien. In fact, in his cable of 28 March, Larkin addressed Foran as 'Acting Secretary' and asked 'Who are your executive?' O'Brien, in particular, resented the self-seeking demands on the union's purse. The ITGWU had paid Elizabeth over £2,000 in her husband's absence, covered his medical expenses in 1915, and subvented Young Jim's visit to him in prison. Despite his capacity for fund-raising – in 1937 he declared to the Irish High Court that he possessed $2,000 on re-entering Ireland, on which he lived following his suspension as ITGWU general secretary in June 1923 – Larkin's total remittances to his union from the US amounted to a paltry £450. Nor had he done any work for the union. Foran wired a definitive 'no' to the financial requests on 9 April.[107]

Foran's refusal led to a change of plan. Larkin decided he would go to Moscow before Dublin. Implicitly, he was prioritising aid from the Soviets for a life of freelance agitation over working with the ITGWU. Privately, he sounded out the British consul in New York about a passport for Germany, Austria, and Russia before returning to Ireland. The consul informed Archbishop Hayes in one of his regular briefs to His Lordship.[108]

DEPORTATION, AND FABRICATION?

Carney claimed that he and Larkin hastened to Washington DC, forcefully lobbied the Secretary of Labor for a deportation order, and got Larkin onto Ellis Island within 24 hours.[109] In fact, a deportation was impossible without judicial evidence, and the Department of Labor as well as the Bureau of Investigation had been chasing the evidence since 1920. Their lack of success implies it couldn't be found. Despite the violence of his speeches, his advocacy of a soviet government and red guards, and even his legal conviction in 1920, the necessary proof that he had actually demanded the violent overthrow of the US government remained in doubt, and it has been argued that the

Bureau of Investigation stretched the evidence.[110] On Larkin's release from Sing Sing, Burns, as Director of the Bureau, collated reports from field offices and found that 'certain statements are quoted and attributed to Larkin but copies of the reports in which the statements appear cannot be located'. On 23 January 1923 he wrote to his New York 'Special Agent in Charge' asking if quotes attributed to Larkin at a meeting in the Odd Fellows Hall, New York in 1919, could be proven. Despite a negative reply, Hoover offered to prepare a deportation case for the Department of Labor, and obtained a copy of the Department's file on Larkin. When the file turned out to be similar to the Bureau's own, Burns wrote to the Department on 5 March, supplying one additional piece of evidence:

> concerning the meeting at Odd Fellows Hall, New York City, on February 16, 1919 at which Larkin commanded his audience to rise and swear allegiance to the Red flag. At this meeting, according to our records, Larkin made an appeal for money, using such slogans as 'Every Dollar Kills the Capitalist', and 'Give now or the Boss will Take it Away Later'.

This was hardly the required smoking gun, but Burns went on:

> After very careful examination of all the information in our files, it is very evident that James Larkin is a person who fully comes within the provisions of the immigration law providing for deportation of an alien who advocates the overthrow of the Government of the United States by force or violence. It would be very desirable to effect his deportation at an early date for, as you no doubt have noted, he has been upon a speaking tour throughout the country in the interests of radicalism.

A deportation warrant was issued on 18 April. Believing their quarry intended to evade the warrant by absconding to Philadelphia, the Bureau had detectives of the New York Police Department's bombs squad arrest him at 3.50 pm on 19th. Charged with being an alien anarchist, he was turned over to the immigration authorities, and taken to Ellis Island. His personal possessions were simply abandoned.[111] Larkin told the bombs squad he had no wish to go to Ireland and would prefer to settle in Palestine. Palestine may have been a throwaway jest. The *New York Times* reported him laughing and chatting with his guards.[112] The comment on Ireland might have reflected real apprehensions. That evening Maurice Leon, a well-known New York lawyer, appealed to the British consul to give Larkin a passport. The next day, the consul declined the request for a passport for Germany, Austria, and Russia, and offered one for the UK only.[113] Smiddy had warned Dublin that Larkin's return would present 'a grave problem for the Government', but when the British enquired in February if the Free State would object to the issue of a passport, the cabinet raised no objection; the Free State's Criminal Investigation Department counselled that a passport was preferable to deportation, which would prevent him from returning to the US.[114] With the passport issue finally resolved, he was deported! On 21st, in good spirits, under the eyes of two Bureau agents, he boarded the *Majestic* for Southampton. Carney shadowed him, below decks, as a stoker.[115] That same day, news of the deportation was carried in Moscow's *Pravda*.[116]

After a chequered start, Larkin ended up making an impact in the US, as an anti-war agitator, a founder of American communism, and a famous political prisoner. There was nonetheless an air of unfulfilled promise to his stateside sojourn. To his comrades on the far left, he seemed a strange, lonely, implacable rebel wasting his energies on the fringe when he might have been leading his people at home. Even Carney, urging him to dictate a memoir in 1946, suggested it be in three volumes, covering 1907 to 1910, 1911 to 1914, and 1923 onwards, leaving out the American decade entirely.[117] Imprisonment created a tragic image of Larkin as the gaunt idealist 'that life is crushing'.[118] It also won him renewed and more far flung international renown as a revolutionary political agitator. And that was the path he intended to pursue. The Communist Labor Party had liberal access to the coffers of the Soviet mission to the US – Larkin had shared a platform with head of mission Ludwig Martens, the man who pawned Russian jewels for $20,000 worth of valuta from Dáil Éireann – and if he could milk the Soviets as he had the Germans, a pleasant life of oratory, writing, and travel lay ahead.[119] But his self-indulgent lifestyle in the US had stripped away the last constraints on his egotism and discipline. He had shown in 1918 how destructive his jealousy could be, gratuitously offending many Irish and Irish-American sympathisers. And he was not willing to understand how Ireland and the ITGWU had changed since 1914.

NOTES

1   FBI file, James Larkin, 62–312 Section 1.

2   David Brundage, 'American Labour and the Irish question, 1916–23', *Saothar* 24 (1999), pp. 59–66.

3   See his comments in letters to Foran in 1918, ITGWU, *The Attempt to Smash the Irish Transport and General Workers' Union* (Dublin, 1924), pp. 166–8.

4   C. Desmond Greaves, *Liam Mellows and the Irish Revolution* (London, 1971), p. 154.

5   David M. Emmons, *The Butte Irish: Class and Ethnicity in an American Mining Town, 1875–1925* (Chicago, 1990), p. 357; ITGWU, *The Attempt to Smash*, pp. 167–8.

6   O'Lyhane was planning to publish his own paper *World Republic*, but within a year he had died of influenza while jailed in Hartford, Connecticut. *Co-operative News*, 18 April 1918; FBI file, James Larkin, 62–312 Section 1.

7   Greaves, *Liam Mellows*, p. 154; Bertram D. Wolfe, *Strange Communists I Have Known* (New York, 1982), pp. 54–5.

8   NLI, William O'Brien papers, 15679(4).

9   Ibid., 15679(2).

10   ITGWU, *The Attempt to Smash*, p. 167.

11   Benjamin Gitlow, *The Whole of Their Lives: Communism in America – A Personal History and Intimate Portrayal of Its Leaders* (London, 1948), p. 21.

12   Wolfe, *Strange Communists I Have Known*, pp. 54–5.

13   Gitlow, *The Whole of Their Lives*, p. 39.

14   Ibid., p. 42.

15   Jacob A. Zumoff, *The Communist International and US Communism, 1919–1929* (Leiden, 2015), p. 36.

16   *Chronicle-Telegram*, 4 June 1919.

17   Gitlow, *The Whole of Their Lives*, p. 42.

18   Emmet Larkin, *James Larkin: Irish Labour Leader, 1876–1947* (London, 1965), pp. 219–34; Manus O'Riordan, 'Larkin in America: the road to Sing Sing', in Donal Nevin (ed.), *James Larkin: Lion of the Fold* (Dublin, 1998), pp. 67–9.

19   FBI file, James Larkin, 62–312 Section 1.

20   Undated letter to Foran, received in Dublin, April 1918, ITGWU, *The Attempt to Smash*, p. 167.

21   Ibid., p. 71.

22   An excerpt is in ibid., p. 168; the full letter in NLI, William O'Brien papers, 15679(2).

23   Emmet O'Connor, *Syndicalism in Ireland, 1917–23* (Cork, 1988), chapters 1–2.

24   See Thomas J. Morrissey, SJ, *A Man Called Hughes: The Life and Times of Seamus Hughes, 1881–1943* (Dublin, 1991), pp. 86–143. For the ITGWU see C. Desmond Greaves, *The Irish Transport and General Workers' Union: The Formative Years, 1909–1923* (Dublin, 1982), pp. 194–250.

25   Thomas J. Morrissey, SJ, *William O'Brien, 1881–1968: Socialist, Republican, Dáil Deputy, Editor and Trade Union Leader* (Dublin, 2007), pp. 145, 170–5.

26   *Voice of Labour*, 20 September 1919; *Evening Telegraph*, 19 September 1919.

27   ITGWU, *The Attempt to Smash*, pp. 135–6.

28   Daniel Corkery, *The Labour Leader: A Play in Three Acts* (Dublin, 1920), p. 26. See also Padraig G. Lane, 'Daniel Corkery and the Cork working class', *Saothar* 28 (2013), pp. 43–9.

29   Micheál MacLiammóir, *All for Hecuba: An Irish Theatrical Autobiography* (London, 1946), p. 88–9; Quoted in 'Larkin in literature and art', in Nevin (ed.), *James Larkin*, p. 406.

30   Morrissey, *William O'Brien*, p. 182.

31   FBI file, James Larkin, 62–312 Section 1.

32   William O'Brien, *Forth the Banners Go: The Reminiscences of William O'Brien as Told to Edward MacLysaght, D.Litt* (Dublin, 1969), p. 74; *Parliamentary Debates House of Commons*, 18 August 1919, vol. 119, col. 1977–8; 19 November 1919, vol. 121, col. 942.

33   Gitlow, *The Whole of Their Lives*, pp. 20, 28.

34   NAUK, CO 904/206/4, file 233A, James Larkin, 1915–19.

35   UUMC, ILPTUC, *Annual Report* (1919), p. 134.

36 Séamus Cody, John O'Dowd, and Peter Rigney, *The Parliament of Labour: 100 Years of Dublin Council of Trade Unions* (Dublin, 1986), p. 131; *Irish Independent*, 30 October 1919; NAUK, CO 904/206/4, file 233A, James Larkin, 1915–19.

37 NLI, William O'Brien papers, 15704(6).

38 Gitlow, *The Whole of Their Lives*, p. 42; NLI, William O'Brien papers, 15679(15); *Lincoln Evening Journal*, 13 November 1919; *New York Times*, 29 November 1919.

39 *Lincoln Evening Journal*, 12 November 1919; *Washington Post*, 27 November 1919; *Harrisburg Telegraph*, 10 November 1919; *Brooklyn Daily Eagle*, 10, 16 November 1919.

40 *The Times*, 14 November 1919; Terry Golway, *Irish Rebel: John Devoy and America's Fight for Ireland's Freedom* (New York, 1999), p. 264; *New York Times*, 19 May 1921.

41 *New York Times*, 29 November 1919.

42 Maximilien Cohen, 'Long live the Communist Party! 2,500 seized in raids', *Communist World*, 15 November 1919.

43 *Evening World*, 26 November 1919.

44 *Brooklyn Daily Eagle*, 1 December 1919; NLI, William O'Brien papers, 15678(1).

45 The plot must be regarded as doubtful, the more so as the informant alleged that one of the four assassins was Pat Quinlan, an IWW organiser and friend of Larkin, but not the Patrick Quinlan who had been a member of Connolly's Irish Socialist Federation.

46 NLI, William O'Brien papers, 15679(13).

47 · Jonathon Hyslop, *The Notorious Syndicalist: J. T. Bain; a Scottish Rebel in Colonial Africa* (Johannesburg, 2004), pp. 269–70.

48 NA, DT files, S2009.

49 *Call*, 30 October 1920; FBI file, James Larkin, 62–312 Section 1.

50 Ryan wrote that Larkin was 'born in the neighbourhood of Newry' and 'taken to England in his infancy', but a confusion of Newry and New York is the only explanation for Hoover's statement. W. P. Ryan, *The Irish Labour Movement from the 'Twenties to Our Own Day* (Dublin, 1919), pp. 170–2.

51 *Ogden Standard-Examiner*, 2 April 1922; On the trial see Donal Nevin, 'Solidarity for ever', in Nevin (ed.), *James Larkin*, p. 277; O'Riordan, 'Larkin in America: the road to Sing Sing', pp. 69–71; Larkin, *James Larkin*, pp. 239–43; and R. M. Fox, *Jim Larkin: The Rise of the Underman* (London, 1957), pp. 136–48. British and Irish Communist Organisation, *The American Trial of Big Jim Larkin, 1920* (Belfast, 1976) provides a transcript.

52 Jerome aan de Wiel, *The Irish Factor, 1988–1919: Ireland's Strategic and Diplomatic Importance for Foreign Powers* (Dublin, 2009), p. 269, 278.

53 *Harrisburg Telegraph*, 6 April 1920; *Muskogee Times-Democrat*, 8 April 1920; *Huntingdon Press*, 9 April 1920.

54 *New York Times*, 23 April 1923.

55 Ibid., 4 May 1920.

56 *Brooklyn Daily Eagle*, 20 June 1920.

57 Charles Chaplin, *My Autobiography* (London, 1964), p. 306.

58 NLI, William O'Brien papers, 15678(1); Larkin, *James Larkin*, p. 244; *Boston Post*, 22 October 1920.

59 *Irish Worker*, 22 December 1923.

60 O'Riordan, 'Larkin in America: the road to Sing Sing', p. 72; Donal Nevin, 'On Larkin: a miscellany', in Nevin (ed.), *James Larkin*, p. 473.

61   *Irish Worker*, 21 November 1931.

62   Nevin, 'On Larkin: a miscellany', p. 486; Fox, *Jim Larkin*, p. 152.

63   NLI, William O'Brien papers, 15678(1).

64   *Voice of Labour*, 7 January 1922.

65   Jim Larkin, *In the Footsteps of Big Jim: A Family Biography* (Dublin, 1995), pp. 81–3.

66   *Irish Worker*, 22 December 1923.

67   Ibid., 15 March 1924.

68   *Brooklyn Daily Eagle*, 17 December 1920; *San Francisco Chronicle*, 31 December 1920.

69   *New York Times*, 15 March 1922; *Times-Herald*, 16 March 1922; *Washington Post*, 16 March 1922; *Daily Messenger*, 17 March 1922.

70   *Winnipeg Tribune*, 8 May 1922; *New York Times*, 7 May 1922.

71   Larkin, *James Larkin*, pp. 245–6.

72   RGASPI, 17/3/102–2. I am obliged to Svetlana Lokhova for this information. On Kirkpatrick, see NA, Department of Foreign Affairs, ES Box 28, file 185.

73   FBI file, James Larkin, 62–312 Section 1; UCDA, Desmond Fitzgerald papers, P80/385(11).

74   ITGWU, *The Attempt to Smash*, p. 72; Larkin, *James Larkin*, p. 256.

75   *Oneonta Star*, 13 July 1922; *Brooklyn Daily Eagle*, 13 July 1922.

76   FBI file, James Larkin, 62–312 Section 1.

77   Larkin, *James Larkin*, p. 245; Greaves, *The Irish Transport and General Workers' Union*, p. 284. In October 1920 the Larkin Defense Committee comprised Peter Nunan, Grocery Employees' Association, chairman, T. J. O'Flaherty, secretary, Emmet O'Reilly, Actors' Equity, treasurer, Richard Bryan and Patrick Rowley, International Steam Engineers, Thomas McDermott, Motion Picture Operatives, and Will McGreevy, Gertrude Kelly, and Ann Gourley. NLI, William O'Brien papers, 15679(15); FBI file, James Larkin, 62–312 Section 1. In November 1921 the members were: Mrs Dudley Digges, chairwoman; O'Reilly, secretary-treasurer; Wayne Arey; Egan Clancy; Ryan; Rowley; Kelly; John Taaffe; McDermott; and McGreevy. NLI, Seán O'Casey papers, 37993.

78   Cork Workers' Club, *Convict No. 50945: Jim Larkin, Irish Labour Leader*, Historical Reprints no 12 (Cork, *n.d.*).

79   NLI, William O'Brien papers, 15678(1); Nevin, 'Solidarity for ever', pp. 294–5.

80   NA, DT files, S2009; NLI, Joseph McGarrity papers, 33364(2/8).

81   *Socialist* (Glasgow), 1 July 1920.

82   *Londonderry Sentinel*, 10 July 1920.

83   *Charlotte News*, 16 July 1920.

84   The others on the committee were Barney Conway, chairman, Michael Connolly, treasurer, Seamus McGowan, Henry Dale, Stephen Hastings, and Mícheál Ó Maoláin. See Larkin, *In the Footsteps of Big Jim*, p. 87.

85   *Altoona Tribune*, 16 June 1920; *Arkansas City Daily Traveler*, 21 July 1920; *Lawrence Daily Journal-World*, 21 July 1920; *Ogden Standard-Examiner*, 21 July 1920; *New York Times*, 22 July 1920; NLI, William O'Brien papers, 15678(1), 15676(2); ITGWU, *The Attempt to Smash*, pp. 137–8.

86   Greaves, *The Irish Transport and General Workers' Union*, p. 316; NLI, William O'Brien papers, 15678(1).

87   David Krause (ed.), *The Letters of Seán O'Casey, Volume I, 1910–1941* (London, 1975), pp. 97–100, 842; David Krause (ed.), *The Letters of Seán O'Casey, 1955–58, Volume III* (Washington, DC, 1989), p. 376.

88 Ronan Fanning, Michael Kennedy, Dermot Keogh, and Eunan O'Halpin (eds), *Documents on Irish Foreign Policy, Volume II, 1923–1926* (Dublin, 2000), p. 82.

89 RGASPI, Arthur MacManus to the Anglo-American secretariat, reporting Larkin's statement to the Profintern executive, 495/72/91. I am obliged to John E. Haynes and Jim Monaghan for this reference.

90 NA, letter from Gloster Armstrong, British Consulate General, New York, 12 January 1923, 2011/25/958.

91 Larkin, *James Larkin*, pp. 245–8; *Ogden Standard-Examiner*, 18 January 1923; *Brooklyn Daily Eagle*, 18 January 1923.

92 O'Riordan, 'Larkin in America: the road to Sing Sing', p. 65; NA, report from Gloster Armstrong, British Consulate General, New York, 2011/25/958.

93 UCDA, Desmond Fitzgerald papers, P80/385(71/3).

94 Nevin, 'Solidarity for ever', p. 278.

95 *Freeman's Journal*, 27 January 1923.

96 FBI file, James Larkin, 62–312 Section 1; *Irish Worker*, 5 January 1924; *Irish People* (Chicago), February 1924; NA, DT files, S2009; Jack Carney memoir on Larkin, written for Emmet Larkin and kindly passed on to the author.

97 *Fitchburg Sentinel*, 18 April 1923.

98 UCDA, Desmond Fitzgerald papers, P80/385(31).

99 Fanning et al (eds), *Documents on Irish Foreign Policy, Volume II*, pp. 31–4, 80–2.

100 UCDA, Desmond Fitzgerald papers, P80/385(15).

101 Fanning et al (eds), *Documents on Irish Foreign Policy, Volume II*, p. 82; UCDA, Desmond Fitzgerald papers, P80/385(69/6).

102 RGASPI, Anglo-Sachischer Referent An das Sekretariat, 23 April 1923, 495/89/20–3.

103 RGASPI, Comintern to Larkin, 3 February 1923, 495/89/12–1.

104 For the cables between Foran and Larkin, February–April 1923, see ITGWU, *The Attempt to Smash*, pp. 141–2.

105 FBI file, James Larkin, 62–312 Section 1; Fanning et al (eds), *Documents on Irish Foreign Policy, Volume II*, p. 32; *Irish Worker*, 5 January 1924.

106 Larkin, *James Larkin*, pp. 248–9, 264.

107 ITGWU, *The Attempt to Smash*, pp. xix–xx; NLI, William O'Brien papers, 15679(6).

108 UCDA, Desmond Fitzgerald papers, P80/385(71/3).

109 Larkin, *James Larkin*, pp. 248–9; Jack Carney memoir.

110 See Claire A. Culleton, 'James Larkin and J. Edgar Hoover: Irish politics and an American conspiracy', *Éire-Ireland* 35 (fall/winter 2000–1), pp. iii, iv, 248–50.

111 UCDA, Desmond Fitzgerald papers, P80/385(69/7); 'The Larkin affidavit', in Nevin (ed.), *James Larkin*, p. 312.

112 *New York Times*, 20 April 1923.

113 FBI file, James Larkin, 62–312 Section 1; *Irish Worker*, 5 January 1924; NA, DT files, S2009; UCDA, Desmond Fitzgerald papers, P80/385(72).

114 Fanning et al (eds), *Documents on Irish Foreign Policy, Volume II*, p. 33; NA, DT files, S2009.

115 Larkin, *James Larkin*, pp. 248–9.

116 RGASPI, Anglo-Sachischer Referent An das Sekretariat, 23 April 1923, 495/89/20–3.

117 Alan J. M. Noonan, '"Real Irish patriots would scorn to recognise the likes of you": Larkin and Irish-America', in David Convery (ed.), *Locked Out: A Century of Irish Working-Class Life* (Dublin, 2013), p. 72.

118 Lola Ridge, 'To Larkin', in Theo Dorgan, 'Larkin through the eyes of writers', in Nevin (ed.), *James Larkin*, pp. 107–8.

119 Gitlow, *The Whole of Their Lives*, p. 57; *Brooklyn Daily Eagle*, 16 November 1919; Theodore Draper, *American Communism and Soviet Russia* (New York, 2003), pp. 202–3.

ELEVEN

THE MORALS OF A EUROPEAN
FOREIGN MINISTER, 1923–4

Had Jim Larkin had the vision to play ball at that time, he could have had the Irish
Transport Union practically delivered to him on a platter.
Gilbert Lynch[1]

—

Shortly after returning to Dublin, James Larkin addressed a meeting at which a photographer captured the famous iconic pose subsequently portrayed on banners and in the monument on O'Connell Street (see plates p. x). In the photo, none of those around him seem animated by the voice, the upraised arms, or the open palms bidding the world to arise. It is as if they feel that Big Jim is playing Big Jim. Beneath Larkin's soaring frame sits a worried Tom Foran, his shoulders hunched with tension, looking like he wishes he – or Larkin – were somewhere else. The photo speaks volumes about the difference between 1913 and 1923, and Larkin's inability to see this. Foran had every reason to be worried. Within weeks Larkin would split the ITGWU, and the event would overshadow his second career in Ireland.

Everyone expected trouble on Larkin's return. In particular, William O'Brien anticipated a challenge to his command of the ITGWU and prepared his ground. Historians have rationalised the divide in terms of the personal, industrial, or political differences between Larkin and O'Brien, incredulous that the hero of 1913 could instigate something so disastrous to gratify his vanity. Incredibly, the schism was entirely of Larkin's making, and driven by the most contradictory and self-defeating motives. Larkin wanted to continue the kind of freelance agitation he had pursued in America with financial help from Soviet Russia. As he didn't want union work, and the ITGWU was anxious to retain his goodwill at a time of acute industrial conflict, a mutual accommodation seemed possible initially. But Larkin soon found he couldn't bear the thought of others running 'his' union. Nor could he confine his attack to O'Brien or marshal a reasoned critique of the ITGWU leadership. Throwing caution to the wind, he made enemies on all sides. This was not rational behaviour. It flowed from the needs or prohibitions of an unbalanced personality, in which egotism had given way to egomania, problems probably aggravated by the loss of Elizabeth.

The split could not have come at a worse time for Labour. Since the onset of a slump in 1920, employers had been pressing for pay cuts and Labour was losing the fight. General workers were among the last sectors to avoid the knife, and bracing themselves for the bosses' 'big push'. In these circumstances, the ITGWU executive reckoned, Larkin's antics looked all the more irresponsible and workers would close ranks against him. This indeed proved to be the case in the provinces, where Larkin had few contacts. In Dublin on the other hand, he had a personal relationship with the workers, in contrast with the more bureaucratic style of the executive leaders, and was synonymous with militancy at a time when members were beginning to doubt the union's resolve. Certainly, he had the potential to rally the majority of ITGWU members in Dublin to his side. And yet, he preferred to put his case in the court of law rather than the court of public opinion. 'Mr Larkin has had a somewhat rackety career,' commented the *Manchester Guardian*, 'but not one that would quite have made us expect to see him sink from the moral level of an average carter or goods guard to that of an average European Foreign Minister.'[2]

'LIKE A LION IN THE ZOO'[3]

On disembarking at Southampton, Larkin was welcomed by P. T. Daly with a deputation from Dublin trades council, who briefed him on their disputes with O'Brien. The O'Brien-Daly antagonism had caused the ITGWU to lead the formation of a rival Dublin Workers Council in 1921, leaving the smaller trades council dominated by communist sympathisers and Larkinites. On the quayside too was Willie Gallacher of the Communist Party of Great Britain (CPGB) who took Larkin to London for the weekend to meet other leading comrades, Arthur MacManus and Bob Stewart. The three Scots advised him to get a handle on changes in Ireland before proceeding to Moscow. A complicating factor was the existence of the Communist Party of Ireland (CPI), founded by Roddy Connolly in September 1921. The Comintern had charged the CPGB with a fostering role over the fledgling CPI, much to the resentment of the Irish. The British had a poor opinion of the party, its policies, leadership, and the size and quality of its membership, and hoped it could be overhauled with Larkin's help. Larkin had other ideas, but under Comintern protocol, if he wanted to deal with the Soviets, he couldn't act independently of the CPI.[4]

On Monday 30 April, Big Jim caught the Irish mail at Euston, and landed at Dún Laoghaire just after 5.25 pm. Delia, Patrick Colgan, whom she had married on 8 February 1921, and some 40 supporters were waiting to greet him. Hands deep in his pockets, he looked dour, ignoring shouts of 'Welcome home, Jim, we want you back'. But walking down the gangway with Young Jim he cut a familiar figure in a black overcoat and black broad-brimmer, hooked-stem pipe between his teeth, and on the pier he declined the photographers' requests to pose, obliging them to take group shots. Three hours later he steamed into Westland Row, to be met by Elizabeth and the younger boys. Firemen at the nearby Tara Street Station hung out a banner saying 'Welcome back Jim'. A crowd of 4,000 followed a brake and a band to Liberty Hall, where he spoke from an upper window. Opening with a homage to James Connolly, 'the greatest Irishman of his generation', he spoke of how Connolly, Tom Clarke, and Patrick Pearse had gone down to the quayside with him as he took the ship for America, how he had given them 'his promise in life', and how the British had prevented him from returning to Ireland.

Justifying his departure in 1914 and absence during the independence struggle would have a huge importance for him. There was much to criticise about the ITGWU's record, he said, but now was the time for forbearance and unity. He deplored the assault on nationalists in Belfast, before moving on to what would become a major theme of the homecoming speeches: peace and the need for an immediate, unconditional end to the Civil War.[5] The ITGWU executive learned of his return from a newspaper ad. Foran was there to receive him. O'Brien thought he should not be indulged and snubbed the occasion. The two had a frosty re-acquaintance on Wednesday. 'Hello Bill. You've got grey,' said Larkin. O'Brien replied: 'Yes Jim, and you've got white.'[6]

O'Brien and Foran had already got the union onside at a special conference of the executive and 75 branch delegates on 24–25 April. Convened to adopt new rules designed to centralise control in the union, the conference was also availed of to limit the power of the general secretary. Foran read the cables exchanged between himself and Larkin between 6 February and 9 April, detailing his refusal to send money to the US. A proposal from James Fearon, once more with the Newry branch and with the CPI, that 'consideration of the matter be deferred until Larkin's return' was withdrawn in favour of unanimous agreement that the executive's action be endorsed, and the matter be discussed further when Larkin came back. The conference then approved amendments to the rules which extended the triumvirate format of 1918 into a five-man collective leadership. The general president and vice-president were to have a broad competence over policy, including industrial relations. The general secretary's duties were confined to recruitment, organisation, education, propaganda, and general administration. There was also to be a financial secretary and a political secretary. All major decisions were to be taken jointly, and could be referred to the national executive by the general president and one other executive officer, or any three executive officers. Reservations expressed related only to procedural points and the wisdom of having a political secretary. No one seemed bothered that Larkin was to be locked into a collective leadership. The conference agreed unanimously to refer the rules to the branches for approval and adjourn to await Larkin's arrival.[7]

On 4 May, Larkin attended a meeting convened to reacquaint him with the ITGWU executive. He seemed unsure of what direction to take. After expressing disappointment over the refusal to send him £5,000 to purchase a ship and its lack of trust in him, he announced he was going to Russia immediately, 'where he had important work to do', and that he would resign as general secretary the following day and be an ordinary member, if the executive permitted. Taken aback, Foran proposed he embark on a tour of the branches to get a better understanding of the situation. To O'Brien's surprise, he agreed and asked that no public statement be made on differences between himself and the executive. He also paid his union dues – £11.10s in arrears – in two payments that month.[8] On 8 May organiser Charlie Ridgway optimistically informed Bill McMullan, secretary of the ITGWU's Belfast branch, that Larkin would be in Belfast in June to deal with the 'Dockers question' and would 'do good work with the English Unions there'. The letter was intercepted and discussed by the Belfast government, which had expected that Larkin would be expelled from the Free State and flee to Northern Ireland, creating 'a serious situation'. The Northern Home Affairs minister assured his colleagues that if Larkin entered 'Ulster' he would be interned forthwith.[9] Over the next two weeks, Larkin was the soul of moderation, and addressed his oratory primarily to calls for peace. Éamon de Valera had ordered an IRA ceasefire from 30 April, but the Civil War had not yet been terminated formally. Larkin actually prepared his speech for a Connolly commemoration on 13 May, and pleaded with republicans to disarm: 'Give up your arms . . . [do not mind] words about allegiance, and giving up guns [so long as you keep] the principles of Ireland a nation, one and indivisible.'[10] He also made the fateful claim that he had gone to America to procure munitions at the behest of Connolly, Tom Clarke, and Pearse.[11]

The day after at the reconvened ITGWU rules conference, Larkin made a long statement on his mission to America, denying that he had gone to raise funds for Liberty Hall and repeating his claim that he went for Connolly, Clarke, and Pearse, 'to rebuild a Nation', not Liberty Hall. Adding to the air of conspiracy, he requested that most of the address be kept off the record. He offered little resistance to the new union rules, objecting only to the creation of the post of political secretary. Again he complained about the executive's refusal to fund the 'food ship', but appeared more concerned with Russia, saying that 'He had arranged a monopoly of trade between Ireland and Russia, and he would be going to Russia shortly with the permission of the Union, but would not be very long away'. At the same time, he assured the conference that he had no time for the CPI's criticisms: 'why take notice of these little wasps?' One delegate expressed his relief: 'of all the meetings he had ever attended he had never been better pleased than here today. The people who had been prophesying about what Larkin would do on his return would evidently be disappointed . . .'[12]

Larkin was not so easy on Labour Party leader Tom Johnson. Complaints that Labour TDs 'were not properly representing the workers in the Dáil' led to Johnson being summoned to the afternoon session. Rather foolishly, Johnson dismissed Larkin's request to defend the party's record, saying he had attended only to answer questions. The questions came, the sharpest of them from Larkin, who concluded with a comment often taken as self-deprecation but probably directed at Johnson:

> Don't submit your minds to any one man. Think these problems out for your-selves. A leader who can lead you out of the wilderness can lead you back again. If there is a thinking, intelligent movement, no leader can mislead you.[13]

Johnson replied that he was not a leader, just a spokesman, appointed by accident.[14]

What was to be a two-month tour of the branches began on Sunday 20 May.[15] Accompanied by Jack Carney, Larkin spoke at Wexford, New Ross, Waterford, Dungarvan, Clonmel, Mallow, and Cork. Everywhere, he was received as a celebrity, and the *Voice of Labour* provided enthusiastic coverage. Repeatedly he called for peace and voluntary IRA disarmament. Then, at the end of May, he made an unscheduled visit to Limerick, where he had arranged for Carney to cable him to return to Dublin.[16] The gloves were coming off. We can only speculate on Larkin's timing. Certainly, he had seen enough to know much had changed, and was not the man to sit patiently and perfect a campaign to take back 'his' union. On 30 May, he summoned O'Brien to his office. O'Brien in turn called for Foran, rejecting his pleas to go to a race meeting, and the two found Larkin 'pacing up and down like a lion in the zoo'. Foran quickly excused himself, leaving the 'lion' to growl about all the mistakes made in his absence. The argy-bargy drifted to the American mission. Once again, Larkin said he had been sent by Connolly, Pearse, and Clarke. Unfortunately, in the climate of the time it seemed not just bumptious but irreverant to be calling on three dead heroes of Easter Week as apologists for his absence from the national revolution. Kathleen Clarke had written to the press asking for evidence, and she was backed in the controversy by Lillie Connolly, and John Devoy. In July Devoy published a front-page attack in the *Gaelic American*, reprinting letters from Mrs Clarke, Mrs Connolly, and O'Brien all refuting Larkin's claims.[17] Larkin made no reply. It was not his style to explain, and the full story would probably have revealed a few less noble reasons for leaving. But the fact that he had some connection with Tom Clarke and Clan na Gael – a guiding one in the eyes of the DMP in 1914 – and that he had reiterated the claim again and again over the coming weeks, suggests that there was an element of truth in it, even if his version embellished some facts and ignored others. O'Brien says he bit his lip for the sake of the union, but he hated dishonesty and was seething with anger about it. He told Larkin he knew it to be untrue, and suggested they put the case to a jury appointed by the Irish Labour Party and Trade Union Congress (ILPTUC). It may have been the tipping point. The next day, Larkin called a meeting of the no 1 branch in the La Scala theatre.[18]

'THERE IS THE DEVIL'S WORK IN DUBLIN ...'[19]

On Sunday 3 June, some 2,500 out of 11,000 members of the no 1 branch took their seats in the La Scala for an operatic tragedy. Foran chaired. O'Brien was in Sligo dealing with branch affairs. Since Larkin's return, he had deliberately stuck to a 'business as usual' regime to keep his composure. Foran opened with a conciliatory prelude. They had been called, he said, to allow the branch to meet the general secretary, and 'He was sure they were all delighted to have him back again'. Larkin began with a review of how he had built the union, and why he had gone to America. He soon got bogged down in petty, *ad hominem* details about who did what. Most of his complaints related to finances and the withholding of money from him. The nub of his grievance was that the ITGWU was no longer as he knew it. The pre-1914 achievements were forgotten and he had been badly treated. Connolly's status really nettled him: 'He agreed that it was the sacrifices of James Connolly that built up the Union, but who sowed the seed? The employers were massing for an attack on them now, and how were they going to fight it with this spirit of antagonism in the Union.' Oblivious to the bitter irony, Larkin rambled over an incoherent series of allegations of misappropriation of funds in 1913–14, and subsequent maladministration, and argued that the recent rules conferences were illegal, and that some members of the executive held their posts illegally. Time and again, he came back to O'Brien. Foran was his friend, but he could not work with O'Brien, the Machiavelli of it all. The argy-bargy ended with exchanges between Foran and Larkin over whether O'Brien was doing his job properly. Larkin said he would call a meeting of the executive immediately.[20]

The meeting took place on 5 June. At the outset, Larkin demanded O'Brien's resignation from the executive on the ground that he was a salaried TD. He further protested that the new rules were invalid, on the ground that they were submitted to the Registry of Friendly Societies without the authority of the executive, that the delegate conference which approved them was not convened in accordance with the 1918 rules, and that no meetings of the no 1, no 3, no 5, and Limerick and Newbridge branches had been held to ratify them. In Waterford too, the branch secretary had failed to convene a meeting on the rules because of the big farm strike. Foran pleaded that the absence of meetings was the fault of branch officials, not the executive, that 97 branches had approved the rules to date, with only seven voting against, and that Larkin had broadly accepted the rules at the conference on 14 May, which Larkin denied. Technically, Larkin had a point, and Foran implicitly conceded as much in proposing the rules be put to a ballot of the members. Implicitly too, Foran was distancing himself a little from the approach taken by O'Brien, who tabled an amendment that the rules be ratified by a delegate conference. Larkin spurned the gesture. After an adjournment and resumption at 7.30 pm, he asked Foran if he was going to allow O'Brien's amendment to be put to a vote. When Foran said he was Larkin handed him a prepared statement announcing his withdrawal from the meeting. O'Brien's amendment was then put and defeated: only he and Tommy Ryan, Waterford, supported it. Foran's motion was adopted, and it was agreed to submit the questions raised by Larkin to a vote of the entire membership.[21] One can understand the appeal of challenging the rules. If declared invalid, the union leadership was completely undermined. But it was an extraordinarily litigious way to carry on in the middle of a class war, and it alienated the entire executive, which was confident of membership backing.

What is striking about the sheaf of letters and telegrams from provincial branches on the dispute is the common opinion that the trouble was driven by Larkin's ego rather than policy issues and that it amounted to an attack on themselves as much as the executive. Larkin's tour of the branches in May had exposed his arrogance.

> The attitude he adopted at Cork was that of a Czar – he was the be all and the end all of the Union – the great I am, Who Am, and Who will be. With the expansion of the Union, however, the days of Czardom are over. When we, who are the rank and file, elect our Executive we do so for a set purpose, and that is to manage the affairs of the Union to our satisfaction. I have yet to learn that we gave a mandate to Larkin or to any other person to carry the Union pedlar-wise on his back.[22]

Typical was the following resolution: 'That this Committee of the Waterford Branch IT&GWU pledges its support to the Executive (that has been elected by the votes of the rank and file of the Union) in any action taken to preserve democratic rule & prevent dictation from any quarter.'[23] While the correspondence was from officials, these were officers who had an impressive record of leading militancy since 1917, and knew their troops.

But Larkin had more shots in his locker. On 10 June, he addressed the no 1 and no 3 branches, and introduced two new lines of attack, exploiting the rank and file suspicion of officialdom which tended to be more endemic in the bigger Dublin branches, and offering to take care of members denied mortality benefit by the ITGWU in his absence. Before the no 3 branch in the Olympia theatre, he read a list of documents purporting to show misuse of funds by executive member Thomas Kennedy, a close friend of O'Brien who deputised for him as general treasurer on occasion. Larkin denied Kennedy a hearing, and turned the assembly into a kangaroo court. Almost every one of the 1,200 present voted for his suspension from the union, pending an investigation. Foran and O'Brien watched helplessly: no match for the demagogue in full flight. They too were 'suspended'.[24] That was the end of any semblance of democracy in Larkin's campaign within the union. Henceforth he would resort to the putsch, the law, and the political stroke in search of a quick and easy victory.

Next morning, Larkin led a march of about 100 workers through the streets to seize Liberty Hall and the ITGWU head office at 35 Parnell Square, and refuse admittance to the suspended officers. When O'Brien and Foran arrived at Parnell Square and were stopped at the front door, they called out the clerical staff, most of whom responded, and departed quietly. An emergency meeting of the executive suspended Larkin as general secretary, and secured an interim injunction to prevent him or his agents interfering with their duties. Larkin quickly handed over the keys of Liberty Hall. Perhaps he thought he could retain Parnell Square, and carve a bailiwick out of the ITGWU as simply as he had annexed a base in 1918 from the Socialist Party in New York. But the executive persisted, obtaining a mandatory injunction on 18 June. On the following day, the Parnell Square premises was surrendered without resistance.[25]

The revival of the *Irish Worker* on 15 June extended Larkin's offensive to the 'God save the King Labour Party' and its 'English, anti-Irishman' leader, who was born not far from himself in Liverpool. Of course Johnson was a different kind of Scouser. His correct English voice, polite style, and air of 'constant appraisal', seemed proof positive that the contrast between Labour's rhetorical radicalism and *de facto* moderation amounted to deliberate duplicity. In January he had infuriated republicans by canvassing privately for the Treaty, in breach of Labour's notional neutrality. Even by his own fearsome standards,

Larkin developed an extraordinary hatred of Johnson, and could not pass him in the street without offering abuse.[26] The *Irish Worker* made the cause no clearer. A few Larkinites tried to rally the rank and file and get branches to pay subscriptions to an office at 45 Luke Street on the south quays, but the man himself failed to generate a campaign.[27] By mid July the public still knew little of the reasons for the ITGWU's internal trouble, and Larkin appeared to be working 'apart and in obscurity'. He had already ruled out contesting the forthcoming general election, expressing disdain for Dáil Éireann, and his most prominent political act that month was to speak at a reception in the Mansion House for Mrs Terence MacSwiney; who was just back from the US, where she had worked hard for his release from prison. To a large audience, he delivered a panegyric on the life of her late husband beneath a banner inscribed 'One leader only, and that James Larkin'.[28]

THE AUTUMN CRISES

Deepening the split, the industrial storm broke on 16 July. Since April, the ITGWU had been negotiating with the Shipping Federation on pay cuts for seamen, and hoped that a settlement would also prevent a threatened confrontation on the docks. When a section of Dublin seamen refused to compromise, the ITGWU detected Larkin's influence. The breakdown of talks with the Shipping Federation encouraged the feared national dock dispute. On 16 July, 3,000 dockers struck against a pay cut of 2s per day. The dispute triggered a wave of similar employer demands, marking the final phase of the wage-cutting offensive. It was a disastrous development for Labour, which left the pillars of the movement – the Labour Party, the ITGWU, and the ILPTUC – looking pathetically weak. Since May, Larkin had grasped a blatant weakness in Labour Party strategy; its stolid refusal to exploit the political instability to force the government to restrain the employers. The cabinet took seriously his threat to disrupt the forthcoming general election failing a settlement of strikes. On 1 August it agreed to request employers to postpone wage cuts for three months, during which conferences would be convened under government auspices. The dock employers rejected the appeal, but it was heeded in some quarters. The ITGWU backed the dock strike as it seriously engaged the no 1 branch, and as it supplied the strike pay, Larkin took unofficial command of the Dublin dockers and excoriated the union executive: 'three in one – one in three – Employers' Federation – Labour Leaders – Government Officials – the organised Strike Breakers!'[29]

Hamstrung by the split, the ILPTUC Annual Congress on 6 August scarcely addressed the crisis. Larkinites and republicans aggressively picketed the opening of the Congress in Dublin's Mansion House. Larkin had promised there would be no Congress, and tried to invoke the law to stop it. He himself was listed as an ITGWU delegate, with an address at Elizabeth's house, 54 Upper Beechwood Avenue, but Larkinites in the ITGWU's no 1 branch claimed that their branch delegates were not properly elected. After his supporters had jostled and jeered the Congress delegates, Larkin obstinately contested for the chair of the national executive against Luke J. Duffy, and was trounced by 147–27 votes.[30] It was as if he was defying his erstwhile admirers to make his 'calvary', as he put it in the *Irish Worker*, which republished, without any explanation or response, grave accusations against him from Mrs Connolly, Devoy, and others.

The general election on 27 August was another disaster for Labour. Larkin endorsed four candidates nominated by Dublin trades council, and a fifth in Tipperary. He ignored the CPI's marginal input, which amounted to publishing a programme, calling for votes for Labour and Sinn Féin, and endorsing two candidates.[31] The Larkinites' electoral target was Labour, more than anything else. O'Brien's campaign was harassed, and Johnson had his meetings heckled by Larkin in person. The election was a big disappointment for Labour. Expecting to build on an excellent showing in 1922, the party saw its share of the vote fall from 21.3 per cent to 10.6 per cent.[32] O'Brien's vote collapsed and he lost his seat. Larkin was blamed of course, but the party was paying the price of its irrelevance to the industrial struggle. On aggregate, the Larkinites did no better, winning 4,500 votes, but Daly's good showing in Dublin North restored some political credibility to Dublin trades council.[33] In September, Larkin proceeded to form his own political machine, the Irish Worker League (IWL); the name suggested it was to be analogous to the *Daily Herald* League, with which he had worked in Britain during the lockout.

Over the summer and autumn, ITGWU branch officials tried to heal the rift, and deputations met Jim on a number of occasions in Delia's flat in 17 Gardiner's Place, where he lodged with the Colgans, Pete, and Carney. Pete had been released from jail in August 1920, following a 'free the Sydney 12' campaign, backed by the Australian labour movement. The New South Wales government acknowledged implicitly that the evidence against him was doubtful. After resuming political activity in Australia, he left for England in May 1922, toured the US, and finally settled in Dublin in 1923.[34] With Patrick Colgan, an ex-Citizen Army man and a future officer of the Workers' Union of Ireland, the Gardiner's Place household offered a congenial atmosphere for a man married to the movement, and an open door to a procession of suppliants, militants, and political literati like Liam O'Flaherty, Peadar O'Donnell, and Seán O'Casey.[35] Stewart joined them in January 1925 and described the large living room as:

a clearing house for all problems political and economic or even purely domestic. As people came and went there were no introductions so that you had not the faintest idea whom you were speaking to . . . In all this welter of coming and going, discussion and argument, Big Jim would sit in his easy chair talking to everyone, butting in the conversation and lighting match after match trying to get his pipe going, so that after a while he was entirely surrounded by burnt matches.[36]

According to O'Casey, it was Jim's decision not to live with Elizabeth, and O'Casey thought it unwise and unjust. Then again, R. M. Fox formed the impression in 1922 that she didn't want him back, and there were rumours of a liaison between herself and Foran.[37] Jim clammed up where anything so private was concerned, and not even his closest friends would broach the subject with him. The parting was not amicable, and the couple usually liaised through Delia or Carney. Money proved to be a chronic problem, as it always was with Jim. Elizabeth was unable, or Jim was unwilling, to pay the rent on her house in Upper Beechwood Avenue following his suspension as general secretary, and in May 1925 the ITGWU took a court action for repossession. Elizabeth offered to pay the outstanding amount, £63.5s owed up to October 1924, but the court gave judgement for possession, with costs.[38]

Following the ILPTUC congress, a steering committee was appointed to convene an 'Unofficial Rank and File Delegate Conference' to seek a resolution. Larkin attended a meeting of the no 1 branch on 26 August, convened to elect delegates to the conference. He declared statements of the steering committee to be incorrect, spoke for an hour on matters unrelated to the purpose of the meeting, and withdrew. The no 1 branch decided not to boycott the conference.[39] On 31 August, the conference elected an investigation committee and asked both sides to abide by its findings. The executive agreed, providing that Larkin would too. Larkin declined. Gilbert Lynch, then an official of the Dublin no 3 branch, recalled:

there was no doubt about it but that the sympathy of the majority of delegates attending that conference was with Larkin . . . But Jim was not content with being the centre of the shop window – he wanted no one in the shop window with him. His full authority as general secretary would have been restored, but that wouldn't satisfy him. The price of reconciliation for Jim was that he must not only be restored as general secretary, his suspension removed, but he must be restored to the position he had in the union before he left in 1914 – he must be again complete dictator. They reasoned with him, they argued with him, they tried to cajole him, but they couldn't move him from this – Foran, O'Brien, Kennedy and the rest must go![40]

On 27 September, the investigation committee reported that it would be pointless to call another conference.[41]

O'Brien now opened a propaganda war, publishing the investigation committee's report as a leaflet entitled 'Larkin ignores members' authority'. Another leaflet was headed 'Is it jealousy?' 'Why is Larkin attacking the Transport Union Executive? Because he ran away in 1914 and returned in 1923 to find the Union a powerful and nation-wide organisation . . . Larkin cannot bear to think that the Union survived his absence.' And another leaflet asked 'Is it the Employers who pay Larkin and Daly to attack the Transport Union?'[42]

Once the election was over, there was less pressure on the government to restrain the employers. Larkin called a meeting in the Mansion House to establish a 'Workers' Co-operative Shipping Company', but it was another of his many good ideas for which he lacked the discipline to bring to fruition.[43] On 26 October, the unions in the dock strike accepted a cabinet proposal that the dockers accept a 1s per day cut, pending an enquiry into wage rates. On Larkin's advice, Dublin dockers voted 687–433 to fight on. The ITGWU executive dismissed the ballot and withdrew strike pay. On 29 October, Larkin and Daly issued a call for a general strike for the release of 8,000 or so republican prisoners, hundreds of whom had been on hunger strike since 14 October. Writing on ITGWU stationery and signing himself 'General Secretary', Larkin made a separate and desperate offer to President W. T. Cosgrave, promising to end all strikes – save the intractable Waterford farm strike – on government terms in return for the release of the prisoners. Cosgrave sent him a curt rejection by return of post.[44] Dublin dockers then accepted the pay cut, and allied occupations suffered related reductions.[45] Larkin's next fight would be against the ITGWU in Dublin Castle, where the Askwith enquiry had convened in 1913.

EXPULSION

The hearing for legal cases against the ITGWU and its counter cases against Larkin opened before the Master of the Rolls, Mr Justice Charles O'Connor, in the High Court's Chancery Division on 12 February 1924. In *Foran and Others v. Larkin*, the ITGWU sought injunctions against Larkin entering union premises or obstructing union officials. In *Larkin v. the Irish Transport and General Workers' Union, Thomas Foran, William O'Brien, Daniel Clancy, Michael Duffy, Michael Hill, Thomas Kennedy, Michael McCarthy, and Thomas Ryan* – the union executive – the plaintiff argued that the union had used funds for political purposes, without having a legal political fund, contrary to the provisions of the Trade Union Act (1913). This contention was based ultimately

on the infamously anti-trade union Osborne Judgment of 1909, in which the
Law Lords ruled that it was illegal for unions to use funds for political purposes.
The 1913 Act modified the judgement to allow a union to make political contributions if its members had voted to create a political fund. Unions regarded the
Act as too restrictive, and Larkin's invocation of it embarrassed the communists.
Larkin further contended that union rules adopted on 20 December 1918 had
not been properly endorsed by the branches – the two biggest branches, no 1
and no 3 had not voted on them – and therefore the executive and their subsequent actions and rules were illegal; and that Foran and O'Brien had broken
the rules in withdrawing £7,500 from union funds without the knowledge of
the general secretary.

Why fight a case you can't win? Why would a proven agitator turn his back
on mass mobilisation to invoke anti-union legislation? The ITGWU executive
suspected he was trying to 'hold up the machinery of the union' or embarrass
it financially.[46] The more likely explanation is that Larkin was senselessly
litigious and headstrong. He could not resist the temptation to act as his own
legal counsel, or reproduce verbatim reports in the *Irish Worker*. As counsel, he
was more than usually disorganised, vituperative, petty, and unfair to witnesses,
notably Foran, whom he said had 'from the hour he left . . . injured his family'.[47]
The accusation was another of the personal thrusts that made the split so
venomous. While the ITGWU rebutted it openly, rumours that Foran had
come between Jim and Elizabeth persisted.

The court found against Larkin on 20 February, leaving him with legal
costs of £1,300.[48] The judge's summing up was damning, and deplored his
wasting the union's time and money, and his 'entire want of business capacity
[and] entire absence of a sense of duty'. On 3 March, O'Brien wrote one last
time to his general secretary on behalf of the executive, inviting him to say why
he should not be suspended or expelled from the ITGWU. On 13th, Larkin
said he would be appealing the court ruling, and no action should be taken in
the meantime. Dublin trades council had already called a mass meeting to
open a 'Larkin sustentation fund'. The next day the executive voted unanimously to expel him from the union.[49]

THE SPLIT CEMENTED

There the matter might have lain. The *Irish Worker* reported a number of
branches deploring the executive's decision and passing votes of confidence in
Larkin. Advertisements of branch meetings continued to appear in the paper.
But Big Jim did not appeal against the court ruling, and his response to the
expulsion was to busy himself with the IWL, an indication that he had shifted

his priorities to Moscow. In January he had applied for passports for himself and Young Jim to travel to Berlin on transport-related business. What that business was, the Larkins would not say, and the applications, made through the Department of External Affairs, were refused by the British government. In fact, arrangements had been made to take them from Berlin to Moscow. The next invitation to Moscow was to attend the fifth world congress of the Comintern in June. Big Jim was keen to discuss his own financial relations with the Soviets, and decided it could not be postponed. The want of a passport was not a serious obstacle. All he had to do was slip on board a ship in England, and that was made easier on 27 May when the Soviets opened a regular freight-passenger line between London and Leningrad. He left Dublin on 2 June. Whether the liner service influenced his timing is not known, but it's curious that he never liked to travel rough in adult life. The Irish government would later query how he managed to travel without a passport.[50]

Larkin was scarcely out of the country when the crisis in the ITGWU came to a head. In May a dispute had broken out in Alliance and Dublin Gas. On 20th, the gas workers voted 407–44 to invite Larkin to a meeting in the Mansion House.[51] Strike action was approved by the no 1 branch, but O'Brien refused strike pay because of Larkin's involvement. Larkin then asked all ITGWU members to pay their subscriptions to the gas workers' dispute committee. Barney Conway led 45 Larkinites to occupy Liberty Hall until arrested by the army.[52] On the same day, Larkin spoke from a window in Liberty Hall for the last time, and called a dock strike which secured the release of the men. They were soon back in custody for refusing to 'give bail for future behaviour'. The campaign for their release provided a rallying point over the next five weeks and left the ITGWU looking like it was in cahoots with an anti-union government and an army with a record of strike-breaking. Meanwhile, the gas company reached a satisfactory settlement with the workers, not the ITGWU. It was a huge blow to O'Brien. He regained possession of Liberty Hall on 28 May, but did not re-open it for union business until 1927. A 'new Larkin union' was rumoured to be on the cards.[53]

On departing for Moscow, Jim instructed Pete 'under no circumstances' to break with the ITGWU.[54] For the moment he was financially buoyant with the balance of the money he had taken home from the US, and had no need of a union, and he claimed later that he hoped to win back the masses through the IWL.[55] He was naïve to think the momentum for a split could be put on hold while he got on with his Soviet agenda, though it would be entirely in keeping with his subjectivity. He was equally naïve to ignore his brother and son's ambition for union jobs and a slice of the action. In fairness, Pete and Young Jim had a political agenda. They did not share Big Jim's egocentric view of events, and were encouraged by the objective basis for a split.

If Jim's war on the ITGWU executive was personal, the membership divide echoed the earlier divisions of the European left into communists and social democrats. Congress had been transformed during the economic boom from 1917 to 1920, with affiliated membership burgeoning from under 100,000 to 225,000. Growth, against a backdrop of revolution at home and abroad, had stimulated a revival of syndicalist ideas introduced by Connolly and Larkin, and by 1919 Congress was theoretically committed to revolutionary objectives. When boom yielded to slump, an inexperienced leadership, intoxicated by four triumphal years, pledged to 'hold the harvest', and resist all wage cuts on a united basis. Instead, Congress soon discarded its syndicalist pretensions, and from 1921 to 1923 trade unions suffered successive defeats in conventional, sectionalist strikes.[56] For Labour to have promised so much and delivered so little generated extensive rank and file disillusionment. And while the ITGWU executive could boast an impressive record of resistance to wage cuts up to the summer of 1923, that claim was in tatters by 1924. In a letter to the CPGB in June 1924, Young Jim affirmed that the WUI would be a communist union, and implied that he had favoured a split for some time and had been awaiting an opportunity.[57]

On 30 May, Pete had notified ITGWU members that a Port, Gas, and General Workers' Provisional committee would receive all union dues until further notice, and on 15 June Pete and Young Jim launched the Workers' Union of Ireland (WUI). John Lawlor, one of Big Jim's 'old guard', an athlete and a much travelled man, became general president. A head office was established initially at Luke Street, and later at 31 Marlborough Street, which was christened – of all things – 'Unity Hall'. While few of the officials defected, 16,000 workers, two-thirds of ITGWU's Dublin membership, joined the WUI; as did 20 out of 300 provincial branches.[58] The WUI immediately appealed for financial aid to the CPGB. In a letter to Gallacher, Young Jim implied that the union would be an integral part of the communist movement and that he had favoured a split for some time.

> We are at last moving forward and everything depends upon our good work. One small omission and everything could be ruined again. This explains our fears in the last week . . . Our newspaper is beginning to establish itself and it is of the utmost importance that there are no interruptions in its publication. The fact that we have called the new union the 'Workers' Union' occurred because of our political line. We now have a 'Workers' Union' just as we will in the future have a 'Workers' Party'.[59]

The British declined to help, citing the policy of the Profintern, the trade union equivalent of the Comintern, opposing the creation of parallel unions.[60]

Not for the last time, they underestimated the length to which Moscow was prepared to go to accommodate its prize recruit.

It is difficult to gauge how seriously Big Jim regarded the loss of the ITGWU in the summer of 1924. Clearly it was a source of deep personal frustration. Whether he saw it as an irretrievable blow to his status, as he would do by the 1930s, is another question. There is no mystery as to why he threw away the unchallenged position he held as ITGWU leader. He was not interested in taking over the organisation as it was in 1923. It was not that he wanted his old power back: he wanted his old union back. Some evidence suggests that he would have been content to wrest the heart of the union in Dublin from the executive, and leave them the remainder. Either way, he wanted to sweep away the existing structures, and surround himself with a loyal band. If Foran and O'Brien had laid the ITGWU at his feet, he would have turned it into what the WUI became; a small, Dublin-based union, centred on himself. But he had no plan. He was not acting rationally. Moreover, he was not in love with trade union work, and impatient to acquire some greater status without bothering to build a support structure among the rank and file. His contacts with republicans in the US in 1922–3 had encouraged him to believe that a statesman's role in peace making awaited him. When that illusion crumbled, he still had the Russian card to play.

NOTES

1 Aindrias Ó Cathasaigh (ed.), *The Life and Times of Gilbert Lynch* (Dublin, 2011), p. 50.

2 *Manchester Guardian*, 13 June 1923.

3 From William O'Brien's description of Larkin, *Forth the Banners Go: The Reminiscences of William O'Brien as Told to Edward MacLysaght, D.Litt* (Dublin, 1969), p. 78.

4 Bob Stewart, *Breaking the Fetters: The Memoirs of Bob Stewart* (London, 1967), p. 148; C. Desmond Greaves, *The Irish Transport and General Workers' Union: The Formative Years, 1909–1923* (Dublin, 1982), p. 317; Emmet O'Connor, 'Jim Larkin and the Communist Internationals, 1923–9', *Irish Historical Studies* 31:123 (May 1999), pp. 358–61.

5 *Workers' Republic*, 5 May 1923; NLI, William O'Brien papers, 15679(23).

6 Donal Nevin, 'Titan at bay', in Donal Nevin (ed.), *James Larkin: Lion of the Fold* (Dublin, 1998), p. 77.

7 ITGWU, *The Attempt to Smash the Irish Transport and General Workers' Union* (Dublin, 1924), pp. 145–6; Irish Labour History Society Archives, Dublin, ITGWU, *Draft Rules of ITGWU*, 1923.

8 ITGWU, *The Attempt to Smash*, pp. 142–3; Francis Devine, *Organising History: A Centenary of SIPTU, 1909–2009* (Dublin, 2009), p. 132; O'Brien, *Forth the Banners Go*, p. 77.

9 Public Record Office of Northern Ireland, Belfast, Cabinet papers, CAB/4/71/19; CAB8G/15. I am obliged to Seán Byers for this reference.

10   Emmet Larkin, *James Larkin: Irish Labour Leader, 1876–1947* (London, 1965), p. 259.

11   J. Anthony Gaughan, *Thomas Johnson, 1872–1963: First Leader of the Labour Party in Dáil Éireann* (Dublin, 1980), p. 265.

12   ITGWU, *The Attempt to Smash*, pp. 147–8.

13   Ibid., p. 148.

14   Gaughan, *Thomas Johnson*, pp. 264–5.

15   Ibid., p. 260.

16   Greaves, *The Irish Transport and General Workers' Union*, p. 318.

17   O'Brien, *Forth the Banners Go*, pp. 77–81; ITGWU, *The Attempt to Smash*, p. 147; *Irish Independent*, 16 May, 12 June 1923; *Gaelic American*, 7 July 1923.

18   O'Brien, *Forth the Banners Go*, pp. 77–81; NLI, William O'Brien papers, 15679(23).

19   NLI, ITGWU papers, 27062, correspondence with branches, June–July 1923, J. P Hayes, Lehenagh branch, Summerstown Quarry, Cork, to head office, 21 June 1923.

20   ITGWU, *The Attempt to Smash*, pp. 146–59.

21   Ibid., pp. 157–9.

22   NLI, ITGWU papers, 27062, correspondence with branches, June–July 1923, J. P Hayes, Lehenagh branch, Summerstown Quarry, Cork, to head office, 21 June 1923.

23   NLI, ITGWU papers, 27062, correspondence with branches, June–July 1923, Waterford branch to head office, 14 June 1923.

24   ITGWU, *The Attempt to Smash*, pp. 159–60; Devine, *Organising History*, p. 151.

25   *Manchester Guardian*, 13–22 June 1923; Devine, *Organising History*, pp. 151–2.

26   Gaughan, *Thomas Johnson*, p. 378; *Cincinnati Enquirer*, 14 March 1922.

27   Devine, *Organising History*, p. 152.

28   *Manchester Guardian*, 2, 16, 28 July 1923.

29   Devine, *Organising History*, pp. 136–8.

30   UUMC, ILPTUC, *Annual Report* (1923), p. 43, 87; *Manchester Guardian*, 7 August 1923.

31   Emmet O'Connor, *Reds and the Green: Ireland, Russia and the Communist International, 1919–43* (Dublin, 2004), p. 88.

32   For general election results see Michael Gallagher, *Political Parties in the Republic of Ireland* (Manchester, 1985), pp. 158–9.

33   Arthur Mitchell, *Labour in Irish Politics, 1890–1930: The Irish Labour Movement in an Age of Revolution* (Dublin, 1974), p. 189.

34   Donal Nevin, 'Peter Larkin', in Nevin (ed.), *James Larkin*, pp. 439–43.

35   Theresa Moriarty, 'Delia Larkin: relative obscurity', in Nevin (ed.), *James Larkin*, p. 437.

36   Stewart, *Breaking the Fetters*, p. 149.

37   Donal Nevin, 'On Larkin: a miscellany', in Nevin (ed.), James Larkin, p. 487; R. M. Fox, *Jim Larkin: The Rise of the Underman* (London, 1957), p. 152.

38   C. Desmond Greaves, *Seán O'Casey: Politics and Art* (London, 1979), p. 123; Nevin, 'On Larkin: a miscellany', p. 486; *Irish Times*, 9 May 1925.

39   Devine, *Organising History*, pp. 135.

40   Ó Cathasaigh (ed.), *The Life and Times of Gilbert Lynch*, p. 50.

41   ITGWU, *The Attempt to Smash*, pp. 160–1; Gaughan, *Thomas Johnson*, pp. 266–7.

42   Thomas J. Morrissey, SJ, *William O'Brien, 1881–1968: Socialist, Republican, Dáil Deputy, Editor and Trade Union Leader* (Dublin, 2007), pp. 220–1.

43 Devine, *Organising History*, p. 139.

44 NA, DT files, Larkin to Cosgrave and reply, 29 October 1923, S2009; Devine, *Organising History*, p. 138.

45 Emmet O'Connor, *A Labour History of Ireland, 1824–2000* (Dublin, 2011), pp. 123–7; Larkin, *James Larkin*, p. 270.

46 Devine, *Organising History*, p. 155.

47 ITGWU, *The Attempt to Smash*, xii, p. 95.

48 RGASPI, Harry Pollitt, report on the situation in Ireland, 17 April 1924, 495/100/168–1/3.

49 Morrissey, *William O'Brien, 1881–1968*, pp. 224–5; *Irish Worker*, 1 March 1924.

50 NA, DJ, Larkin file, JUS 8/676; RGASPI, ECCI to Larkin, 2 June 1924, 495/89/27–5; *Irish Worker*, 27 September 1924.

51 Larkin, *James Larkin*, pp. 280–1.

52 Ibid., pp. 279–80; Nevin, 'Titan at bay', p. 80.

53 Morrissey, *William O'Brien*, pp. 225–6; Devine, *Organising History*, pp. 156–7.

54 Devine, *Organising History*, p. 158.

55 RGASPI, Larkin to Zinoviev, undated [1925], 495/89/32–13/26.

56 For unrest between 1917 and 1923 see Emmet O'Connor, *Syndicalism in Ireland, 1917–23* (Cork, 1988), pp. 96–167.

57 RGASPI, Larkin Jr to Willie Gallacher, 16 June 1924, 495/84/27–6/7.

58 Larkin, *James Larkin*, pp. 280–2; Donal Nevin, 'Larkin and the Workers' Union of Ireland', in Nevin (ed.), *James Larkin*, pp. 342–3.

59 RGASPI, Larkin Jr to Willie Gallacher, 16 June 1924, 495/84/27–6/7 [translated from a copy in German].

60 RGASPI, Larkin Jr to Gallacher, 16 June 1924, and reply, 18 June 1924, 495/89/27–6/9; report on Ireland, 495/89/104–98.

TWELVE

MY WAY AND NO WAY, 1924–6

Jim Larkin and his most immediate associates can think of nothing else but Jim Larkin. It is difficult to argue or venture any opinion that does not coincide with his own, and yet the man is undoubtedly a leader.

Harry Pollitt, 17 April 1924[1]

—

James Larkin's engagement with communism in Ireland is usually seen as a quixotic sidelight to his union work. In reality, he had intended Soviet Russia to be the rock on which he would base the rest of his life. On returning to Ireland, he had planned to go to Moscow, only to be diverted by his fight with the ITGWU executive. While that fight was his priority until expelled from the union, he had continued to intrigue with the CPGB, pressing the British to get the CPI liquidated and have the Comintern deal directly and exclusively with himself. The CPGB and the Comintern were happy to comply up to a point. The CPI was small and ineffective. Its leader, Roddy Connolly, was regarded as insubordinate, arrogant, headstrong, and not very effective. By contrast, Larkin was a powerful agitator, with some outstanding achievements to his credit. Furthermore, whereas the CPGB's interest in Ireland was British and Irish centred, the Comintern took a wider view, and was more concerned with Ireland's global potential to involve the Irish diaspora in communism and embarrass British imperialism. Here too, as an internationally known personality, Larkin appeared to be an exceptional asset. The communists knew he would be difficult to work with. They did not realise he would be impossible, and assumed that in a worst case scenario he could be used as a figurehead with a party built around him.

Larkin's relations with Moscow were the most tortuous page in the most tragic chapter of his career. His aim was to secure funding. He did not expect the Soviets to bankroll him as freely as the Germans had done between 1915 and 1917, and proposed they open commercial ventures with Ireland. But the communists wanted Larkin to create a party first and foremost, with the lure of aid and trade to follow. With his pathological aversion to any form of supervision or accountability, a party was just what Larkin could not create. And his problems were compounded when he found himself saddled with the leadership of the WUI. As he stood on the poop deck of the *Tobolsk* en route to

Leningrad, a first-class cabin at his disposal and a flattering reception in Moscow ahead, he had no idea of what Pete and Young Jim were doing behind his back in Dublin, and little did he know that he was about to enter the most miserable period of his life.

SHAFTING THE CPI

The *Workers' Republic* had denounced the changes proposed at the ITGWU conference in April 1923 and was vituperative about 'Judas' Foran for betraying Larkin's confidence and colluding with 'Bouncer' O'Brien to hogtie Big Jim.[2] Larkin met the CPI's central committee in early May and made 'vague references' to his relations with the Comintern, leaving the committee to ask Moscow what those relations were 'as this is absolutely necessary to enable us to define our position towards him'. Subsequently he treated the party with silent contempt.[3] A British special branch report observed that his attitude to the CPI was 'very doubtful', noting: 'A friend who has been in close touch with him since he returned from America says he is not the man he was, there is something missing mentally, but is still a force to be considered. His name alone means much to the Dublin docker.'[4] The CPI's inner thoughts were much the same. '[Q]uestions are being constantly asked . . . as to our attitude towards Larkin,' it admitted in June. Yet following his split with the ITGWU executive, the CPI offered him 'all support'.[5] Communists needed no reminding of their own disputes with William O'Brien. While dismayed by the imbroglio, the Comintern's pursuit of Larkin continued. The Executive Committee of the Communist International (ECCI), the controlling body of all communist parties, wrote to him on 6 August saying it had hoped to see him earlier and offering a flight to Moscow from Germany.[6] Arthur MacManus, first chairman of the CPGB, and now colonial secretary of the Comintern and a member of its presidium, despaired of Larkin taking an extended break from his war with O'Brien and urged the ECCI to have a representative meet him in Holland, France, or Germany. 'The task of the reorganisation of the entire Irish movement,' he advised, 'should be undertaken almost immediately.'[7]

MacManus got his chance to push for re-organisation when disputes within the CPI in the wake of the general election led the ECCI to ask the CPGB to investigate. Though born in Belfast and a former seminarian, he had little sympathy with the peculiarities of Irish radicalism. Already convinced that the CPI was too republican and scarcely Leninist, he compiled a damning report. The second part of the report dealt with Larkin. Unprompted, Larkin had 'emphatically' encouraged MacManus to have the CPI dissolved. While the IWL had yet to indicate anything specific of its politics, MacManus believed it intended to recruit 'more or less militant workers not only in Ireland but in Great Britain and America as well', and promised that the CPGB would discuss developments with Larkin at the earliest opportunity. The report recommended the liquidation of the CPI; the politburo of the CPGB endorsed it unanimously.[8] In January 1924, the ECCI dissolved the CPI, instructing members to join the IWL.[9]

Larkin visited London in January and got the CPGB to circularise comrades urging the formation of IWL branches in Britain. A London branch was founded in March by Éadhmonn MacAlpine and held public meetings near the Elephant and Castle.[10] In February MacManus informed the Comintern of what would be a consistent theme in CPGB policy on Ireland: that instead of trying to build 'an absolutely ineffective and valueless Party such as existed recently', it would be better to establish a broad-based workers' party. Larkin demurred as he wanted a direct line to the ECCI and no adulteration of his standing in Moscow, but after several meetings, he agreed that the IWL would push for a workers' party.[11] MacManus was not the last man to think he had the measure of Big Jim:

> You must not imagine that we, on this side, do not fully understand Larkin and all the difficulties of his strong personality and hasty thinking. We appreciate this to the full, but we considered that his capacity for attracting the masses around him and for stimulating them into action was just the essential thing that was required in Ireland at the moment. We also felt that if, side by side with his activities in this direction a strong, co-ordinated group . . . could be built up around him that by this means an organised revolutionary movement might become a possibility. To effectively establish this, however, takes time, as both the process of following and working closely with Larkin on the one hand and at the same time training and developing the Communist group around him on the other, is a very delicate job.[12]

For his part, Larkin could not yet feel secure from critics and rivals. He had envisaged the IWL as a loose campaign force rather than a party, and had spoken airily of developing an international network to mobilise the diaspora behind struggles in Ireland. To date, only Dublin and London branches had emerged, and the former did little more than occasional fund-raising for striking gas workers and republican prisoners' dependents. Meetings were often cancelled simply because Larkin could not be present. CPI veterans were drifting out in disgust, and they were encouraged by the *Irish People*, organ of the Irish American Labor League and edited by T. J. O'Flaherty in Chicago. O'Flaherty denounced Larkin for his 'aversion to advice or criticism':

Those who would think for themselves and offer him wise counsel he spurns, while the lap dogs who profess to worship him, he takes to his bosom. This and his overweening vanity are responsible for the series of blunders he has committed since his arrival in America in 1914 and since his return to Ireland.[13]

In April the *Irish People* reported that the CPI's 'best elements' were attempting to build the nucleus of a new party in workers' republican clubs and Connolly education clubs.[14] Ever anxious to acquire intelligence on Ireland, the ECCI invited CPI veterans in the 'Irish Republican Workers' Party' to send a delegate to the Comintern's fifth world congress.[15] However, no more was heard of the party.

It seemed that the CPI veterans could create structures, but not members, and Larkin was averse to structures, but did have supporters. The IWL had enrolled 500 members on its inauguration. On 27 January 1924 Larkin spoke to 6,000 people in College Green at an IWL and Dublin trades council commemoration to mourn the death of Lenin, 'master mind of the twentieth century.'[16] On his first visit to Ireland on 12–13 April, Harry Pollitt despaired over the depth of the divisions caused by the Civil War and the ITGWU split. With the CPI despatched, Jim had no further use for the British, and resisted any CPGB involvement with Irish affairs. Pollitt found him unforthcoming as to his plans – 'Nothing that we may say or do will influence him', he told London – but he was impressed with Larkin's popularity.[17] A pocket of Larkinism developed in north Tipperary, due to dissatisfaction with the ITGWU in its Nenagh and Roscrea branches, fanned by their own internal disputes. In Roscrea, locked out roadmen arranged a fund-raising hurling tournament between Laois and Offaly for Palm Sunday and appealed to Larkin to attend. Promised an audience of thousands, he turned the occasion into an IWL and trades council excursion, complete with two bands and a commissariat.[18] Pollitt found:

a mass of streamers welcoming Larkin to [Roscrea]. Over 500 workers paid 7s. each to travel by excursion with Larkin . . . last Sunday he called a meeting in Dublin to demand that all the [political] prisoners be set free. I am assured that it was one of the largest meetings ever seen in the city.[19]

After Larkin threw in the sliothar in the hurling match – refereed by the secretary of the Tipperary county board and won by Offaly – the proceedings in Roscrea closed with a big demonstration for the release of political prisoners, addressed *inter alia* by Pollitt. Pollitt reckoned the IWL had a 'tremendous chance' if Larkin would take it seriously. The CPGB concluded that Pollitt's report fully justified its policy on Ireland. The Roscrea ITGWU was inspired to set up a co-operative shop and milk supply for the town – a venture close to Larkin's heart – and Dublin trades council and the IWL decided to hold regular excursions, organising one for Wexford in May, featuring a Gaelic football match between a Dublin and Wexford selection.[20]

In May, Larkin made his first visit to the Durham coalfields since 1914, speaking on 5 May at the annual Labour Day rally in Spen, and then at Anfield Plain, before walking three miles through the woods to overnight with an old comrade. The next day he addressed two meetings in Newcastle on Tyne. At each venue he called on the Labour government to release Irish political prisoners. He then journeyed to London to advise comrades of the IWL and hear 'the pregnant words of wisdom' of Shapurji Saklatvala, originally a Parsi from Bombay, and known as the CPGB's 'red Indian'.[21] Like Larkin, 'Sak' was a former ILP'er turned Bolshevik by the October revolution. The London IWL was suspiciously more animated than its mother ship in Dublin, and the *Irish Worker* was not embarrassed to advertise the fact. The Dublin IWL was doing little other than organising public meetings and excursions and operating a cheap food outlet from 17 Gardiner's Place, where workers could buy sardines at 3d a tin and Scotch oatmeal for 3d a lb.[22] Fitful progress occurred in the wake of Pollitt's visit. At a conference in the Mansion House on Easter Sunday, a draft constitution was adopted and a formal membership scheme introduced. The IWL's objective was a workers' republic, and its methods were to be education and organisation, industrial, economic, and political. Dermot Stewart and P. T. Daly, and CPI veteran Bob Murray were nominated for chairman. John Nolan, Stewart, Michael Sutton, Barney Conway, J. McMahon, Daly, James Mitchell, Murray, Mrs Farrelly, William Vickers, Hilary Williams, Michael Connolly, Vincent Atkinson, and John Farrelly were nominated for the executive. The proposed officers were mainly Dublin trades council activists. Murray, soon dropped out in protest at the IWL's inactivity.[23] For no obvious reason, elections for an executive were deferred to 4 May, and then postponed, ostensibly for want of a venue. It was hardly coincidental that Larkin was bound for Durham that day. The *Irish Worker* then announced the elections would be on 19 May and then on 26th, and then on 2 June, by which time Larkin was off to Moscow.[24] Another former CPI man, George Pollock, warned the ECCI that Larkin would never develop a party and was best confined to trade unionism. Known in Ireland as George McLay, Pollock had moved from Scotland on the outbreak of the world war and worked in Dublin as an insurance agent, so often the last resort of the unemployed white-collar revolutionary.[25] He was a shrewd critic of Larkin. Regardless, Larkin was invited to the fifth world congress of the Comintern 'as a representative of the Irish working class'.[26]

IN MOSCOW'S VAULTS

On 4 June Larkin made his way to Hay's Wharf, on the south bank of the
Thames, where he boarded the ARCOS (All-Russian Co-operative Society)
ship *Tobolsk*. A special cabin had been reserved for him on the poop deck. To
the bemusement of the captain, an Irishman, his only luggage was 'a handbag
containing a change of under-clothing and a few books'.[27] Just one other
passenger was a delegate to the Moscow conferences: Dora Montefiore, who
had famously organised the ill-fated 'Save the Kiddies' scheme during the 1913
Lockout and was travelling as a representative of the Communist Party of
Australia. She thought highly of Jim, and had helped Delia's campaign to get
him released from jail in the US. On 12 June they arrived in Leningrad, where
they were met by a young Russian lady who could communicate with Dora
through German, and driven to a hotel before taking the night train to Moscow.
Dora was impressed with their accommodation in a new international sleeping
carriage. Jim was taken aback. Despite her protestations that it was normal in
Russia, he, 'with true Irish chivalry', declined to share their compartment,
where he had been assigned the upper berth. After much searching, he slumped
into a seat in a third-class carriage after 1 am. At 9.30 am, they steamed into
Moscow, and were taken to the Comintern's hotel, the Lux, for tea with
Scottish friends, and then to their hotel on Red Square. Conditions in Russia
were still difficult, and no food or milk was to be had at the hotel.[28]

The fifth Comintern congress opened on 17 June. Dora described the occasion:

> The opening ceremony of the Congress took place in the great [Bolshoi] Theatre
> where tier upon tier of gilded boxes and balconies were filled to overflowing with
> cheering workers. Greetings in every western and eastern language were hung on
> the sides of the theatre, and the young pioneers (the boy scouts of the Soviet
> Republic) ran back and forth with messages from platform to audience, and saluted
> the *International*, as it thundered from floor to roof. The following day the first
> session of the Congress was held in one of the two great front halls of the Kremlin
> Palace ... On this occasion, and in honour of the dead leader [Lenin], the huge gilt
> chandeliers and the front of the platform were draped in a very fine black crepe. The
> second great hall was used by the typists and stenographers, whilst in a large dining
> room two or three hundred delegates dined every day at three o'clock ... On the
> afternoon of this first session the delegates filed out of the Congress hall, and
> walked in silence, four or five deep along the terrace, through the narrow Kremlin
> gate on to the Red Square, our goal being a visit to Lenin's tomb.[29]

There were 406 delegates from 41 countries, and Larkin did not find them
congenial. 'I do not belong to those kinds of people who make a living by

attending congresses,' he later told Comintern chairman Grigori Zinoviev, 'I detest such people.'[30] Even continental socialists were non-plussed by the Russian penchant for long, scholastic debates, factional polemics, and theoretical formulation. Refinement of theory was all the same to Larkin, for whom communism was just the old class struggle in new clothes, and the Comintern a crock of gold. He seldom spoke publicly in Russia, preferring to confine himself to short comments on familiar topics, and made his parochial interests very plain during the debate on the national and colonial questions.

> I mount this tribune with some deference, and only at the request of Comrade Zinoviev, who said the congress was interested in Ireland. I have failed to notice it. The congress seems interested only with those parties which have the biggest membership . . . I appeal to you comrades to turn your eyes to the Irish proletariat. We are not confined to Ireland. We have millions in England, Scotland, the United States, Australia and South Africa. It is the duty of the Communist International to get this great mass, mostly proletarians, interested in the great Communist movement.[31]

His one other speech during the congress's 30 or so sessions endorsed the CPGB's support for 'united front' tactics with the British Labour Party, and disputed the ECCI's view that the British working class was moving left.[32] At the end of the congress, he was elected to the ECCI, which was all the more remarkable as he was not even a member of a communist party.

As the Comintern congress closed on 8 July, the third world congress of the Profintern opened the same day. To a considerable degree, the delegates and the agenda were the same. Again, Larkin's presence was anomalous, as the WUI – or should one say the ITGWU? – was not yet an affiliate. Deeming himself, quite rightly, to be an expert on industrial conflict, Larkin played a livelier part in the debates. In the process he revealed his ideological and temperamental differences with Bolshevism, and uninterest in, or naivety about, the politics of the Moscow congresses. The Profintern had by now abandoned hope of communist control of western Labour. The overarching aim of its third congress was to harden the position of communists against social democrats and their International Federation of Trade Unions at Amsterdam, and intensify pressure for a new trade union International that would include the communists. Regardless, Larkin emphasised the importance of co-operatives to the trade union movement, recalling a big lockout in Dublin 'some years ago' and how food ships from the British co-operative society had 'procured the victory of the struggle'.[33] The muddle as to the outcome of the 1913 Lockout was less than honest. Behind the scenes, he was lobbying for a Soviet backed co-operative in Dublin.[34]

Larkin was more in tune with the Profintern's British policy, which was to promote a united front and 'boring from within' by creating fractions within existing unions. The fractions would come together in August as the National Minority Movement, and operate as the British section of the Profintern. At the same time, Larkin thought it 'amazing that we should accuse the Amsterdam people of unreality while we ourselves have been nursing all the illusions that have been spread in the course of this single session [about Britain being on the verge of revolution].'[35] Later he took a paper by Aleksandr Lozovsky, the Profintern's general secretary, on 'The strategy of strikes' at face value, and ridiculed the idea that industrial conflict could be ordered along military lines.[36] The pair remained on bad terms. It was foolish to have offended a key man in what would be the WUI's International, but Lozovsky was just the sort of man Larkin hated, and the want of tact was not entirely on Larkin's side. An intellectual and tireless pamphleteer, with no experience of manual labour, a poor opinion of trade union leaders who collaborated with capitalism, and an abrasive style, Lozovsky was an odd choice to lead the Profintern. In fact he was so unpopular that the Soviets had replaced him with the genial Mikhail Tomsky, head of the All-Russian TUC, on a delegation to Britain in April 1924. One British communist satirised Tomsky as a dove 'flitting around Eccleston Square [TUC headquarters] cooing "I'm not Lozovsky, I'm Tomsky".'[37]

After the Profintern congress closed on 20 July, Larkin went sightseeing. He later claimed to have been made a chief of battalion in the Red Army – an honour conferred on a few westerners – and travelled 11,000 miles around Soviet Russia, visiting Nizhny Novgorod, the Caucasus, and Georgia. Back in Dublin on 25 August, he was obviously chuffed to have been treated as a priv- ileged guest. Following a parade to the Mansion House, headed by a banner inscribed in Russian: 'Greetings to the Revolutionary Transport Workers of Dublin from the Moscow Transport Workers', he boasted of his election to the ECCI as 'one of the 25 Commissioners to rule and govern the earth'.[38] O'Brien wondered why the Comintern needed the other 24. He was not alone. Some Larkinites thought he had made himself a 'laughing stock'.[39] In fact, he had been elected as one of 26 candidate members of the ECCI, which contained a further 44 members.[40] No one grasped the real source of his elation. Buried in the speech was a reference to his having secured 'an agreement and pledges for the establishment of direct commercial relations with Russia'. The *Irish Worker* promised a detailed and truthful account of Soviet Russia, 'let who will be offended.' Alas, the series never got beyond 'From Dublin to Leningrad'.[41]

LEADING THE WUI

In some respects Larkin's position in the autumn of 1924 was stronger than it had been 12 months earlier, now that the leaders of the Labour Party, Congress, and the ITGWU were discredited by the slump, and Moscow had corroborated its supreme confidence in him. If denunciations of Soviet Russia were not uncommon in the provinces, communism had yet to acquire the odium with which it was invested by the resurgence of Catholic social power in the 1930s, and Labour divisions produced a sizeable constituency for communism in Dublin. In addition to the IWL's 500 supporters, the WUI claimed a membership of 15,754 in December 1924; with 22 branches in Dublin city and county, and one each in Abbeyfeale, Bray, Dundalk, Nenagh, and Roscrea. A further 5,000 workers were affiliated to Dublin trades council.[42] The Civil War created another propitious field as the IRA cast about for a road back. With help from Russia, British communists, and republicans, Larkin had the opportunity to construct his own movement, and become something bigger than a union leader. Instead, he was to face disappointment and humiliation, betrayed by a personality that left him endemically quarrelsome, violently averse to criticism or accountability, and plagued with a persecution complex. The frustration with the WUI was not confined to the ITGWU. An ILPTUC manifesto against Larkin in September 1924 referred pointedly to 'personal jealousies, sectional envy, partisan hatreds'.[43]

Big Jim had little choice but to accept the loss of the ITGWU as a *fait accompli* and assume the post of general secretary in the WUI. He inherited a baptism of fire. From June onwards, inter-union disputes broke out in the construction of the fishmarkets, the docks, and the cinemas, as the WUI struck against the employment of ITGWU members. Big Jim was saddled with subventing 3,000 members involved in six major strikes. Reeling from lost strikes and falling membership, the ITGWU spent double its income in 1923–4, and the WUI was sure it could finish it off with one big push.[44] On 9 August, the *Irish Worker* declared:

> The Transport Union card is nothing but a pass to a scab. There is only going to be one labourers' union in Ireland and that will be the Workers' Union, which has earned its place by right of conquest.[45]

This was Pete's policy, but Big Jim allowed it to continue. Worsening his mood, he was coming under financial pressure and would be declared a bankrupt in the High Court on 21 November for failing to pay costs arising from his litigation against the ITGWU.[46] Privately, he disowned the WUI's first flush of militancy, blaming the 'terrible inability' of incompetent functionaries, including Pete, 'super-revolutionaries', and 'careerists' for taking the union to the brink of insolvency. He also claimed that the circulation of the *Irish Worker* had fallen by 50 per cent in his absence.[47] Of course he had the prestige to rein in the militants, but that would have compromised his image.

The ITGWU riposte was uncompromising; for the rest of his life O'Brien nursed an obsession with Jim, filing all sorts of petty details about him in his personal effects. By August, the *Voice of Labour* was carrying stories of assaults by the 'OBU Defence League' on WUI agents trying to carry the union to the provinces.[48] Though confident the Larkins would bankrupt their union, O'Brien was happy to help the police and employers accelerate the process. On 29 November a police detective reported that he was having informants enrolled in 'Larkin's mob' 'through the medium of the ITGWU'. That same day the *Voice* proclaimed that in future ITGWU members would take the place of WUI strikers unless they were engaged in a genuine trade dispute. The inter-union war had a serious propaganda dimension too. Both sides distributed abusive handbills, and Larkin sometimes devoted half the *Irish Worker* to the ITGWU.[49] O'Brien probably compiled *The Attempt to Smash the Irish Transport and General Workers' Union*, a selection of documents on Larkin and the split, and the *Voice* printed what was later published as *Some Pages from Union History: The Facts Concerning Larkin's Departure to America*. After his members had prevented Larkin from speaking in Sligo in December 1924, the local ITGWU branch secretary cabled O'Brien: 'Send ten dozen copies of *The Attempt to Smash* immediately.'[50]

There was one dispute that Big Jim disowned immediately on his return, at the meeting in Mansion House on 25 August, and which would have terrible personal consequences for him. Two strikes had broken out at the Great Southern and Western Railway works at Inchicore on 12 August, one involving a wage demand by millwrights' helpers and running shed workers, which was settled quickly, and the other a demarcation dispute between vicemen in the WUI and fitters in the Irish General Railway and Engineering Union. The craftsmen at Inchicore had a reputation for militancy and zealous defence of demarcation. The General Railway and Engineering Union had emerged out of the Irish Engineering Industrial Union – itself a breakaway from the Amalgamated Society of Engineers – after the Engineering Industrial Union accepted a cut in settlement of the long-running dispute in 1921–2 known as 'the railway crisis'.[51] Jim's animus was probably stirred by Seán McLoughlin. McLoughlin was famous as 'the boy commandant' of Easter Week, promoted to the rank by James Connolly himself as the General Post Office garrison made its last stand. He was subsequently active on the far left in Ireland and Britain. Described by the special branch as 'undoubtedly the strong man of the movement', he was one of the few CPI comrades to join the inner circle of Larkinites and welcome the foundation of the WUI.[52] He was unanimously elected secretary of the WUI's no 2 branch. McLoughlin's fame would not have commended him to Jim, and during the strike he ran foul of Pete and Delia. According to his memoir 'How Inchicore was lost', he had argued against strike action, on financial grounds, only to have Pete dismiss his caution. Pete, he wrote, 'did everything in his power to make our position impossible', adding that the strike committee complained constantly about his dictatorial methods. McLoughlin also claimed that a lorry of the Rapid Transit Company, owned by Delia and her husband, had driven through a picket line at Kingsbridge. Jim said he knew nothing of the Rapid Transit Company, though it operated out of 17 Gardiner's Place. Privately, according to Jack Carney, Jim was devastated. In 1948, when his animosity towards Delia was at its height, he told Seán O'Casey:

> She did more harm to the Big Fellow than any of the employers. In 1926 [*sic*] she and Pat Colgan, during a carters' strike, organised the Rapid Transport [*sic*] Company. They made lots of money because all the other carters were out. From that day to the hour of his death, Jim never spoke to Delia. They lived in the same house and sat at the same table but no word passed between them.[53]

The story is corroborated by Bob Stewart, who was seconded to Dublin by the Comintern in January 1925.

> All the time I was in Dublin I lived with Larkin and his sister Delia and his brother Peter . . . Jim did not speak to Delia and Delia did not speak to Jim, so they had to talk to each other through Peter. When Peter was missing I was used as the go-between. It was a dreadful position for grown-up people to create, particularly when to make any political headway friendship and comradely tolerance were an absolute necessity.[54]

McLoughlin believed that from the outset Big Jim was intent on ending the dispute 'at any cost', and excluding him from its leadership. By September, the WUI was concerned simply with getting the men their jobs back. On 12 September the Great Southern and Western Railway offered to take all the men back other than 100 or so whose places had been filled by strike-breakers. McLoughlin wanted to hold out for no victimisation, but Jim accepted the Great Southern's offer and blamed the debacle on McLoughlin. Recriminations between the two men led to a showdown at the Inchicore Picture House on 4 October. Before 200 union members and the WUI executive, the friction descended to new depths. McLoughlin won a victory of sorts as the atmosphere turned against the executive and Jim walked out. But it had obviously become impossible for McLoughlin to stay in 'Larkin's union', and he moved to

England. The vilification did not end. Jim accused him of absconding with branch funds and sent his version of events to the CPGB.[55] McLoughlin wrote his own account, which found its way into O'Brien's private papers.

By March 1925, Larkin was getting a grip, and made the first of ever greater retrenchments of WUI ambitions, offering to recognise ITGWU cards in divided employments.[56] His troubles intensified. Two libels actions, by Tom Johnson, and Denis Cullen, Bakers' Union, saddled the WUI with a bill of £1,600 for legal expenses in 1925. Johnson, who suffered routine vilification in the *Irish Worker*, was persuaded by his colleagues to sue Larkin and the Gaelic Press for an article published on 24 May 1924. A statement of his saying it might be necessary 'to organise a civilian army to do productive work', was twisted to imply that he was calling on the government to deploy the army against the unemployed. Big Jim said the offending item had been written by Young Jim, though he took responsibility and told the court he would have been more vituperative himself. The judge awarded Johnson £500 damages against Big Jim and £500 against the Gaelic Press. Cullen was the victim of a leaflet claiming he had voted for wage cuts in Grangegorman, and won another £1,000 in damages. Big Jim refused to pay and was declared a bankrupt.[57] The *Irish Worker*, a flabby caricature of its pre-war self, ceased production after 9 May. It was also in May that the ITGWU won its court case against Elizabeth for possession of 54 Upper Beechwood Avenue.

Worse followed in July, when the Coal Merchants' Association locked out ITGWU and WUI workers 'until a satisfactory guarantee is obtained that the men employed in the coal yards will work amicably together'. Many employers had long been urging similar action, and in August the Dublin Employers' Federation pledged support to the coal merchants, in a determined attack on Larkin's methods. On 12 August, ITGWU members resumed work 'to end the tyranny of the Larkin family organisation in the coal trade', enabling colliers to be unloaded under police protection.[58] The WUI men replied desperately, launching a mass assault on ITGWU dockers at the North Wall on 2 September. In separate incidents, a bomb was thrown into a dock shed housing ITGWU members, and groups of men visited homes of ITGWU workers and intimidated their families.[59] When the ITGWU supplied coal delivery drivers to break the WUI resistance, Larkin threatened sympathetic action wherever deliveries were made, but only the gas workers struck in sympathy, and they were compelled to return the next day. Larkin also tried to sustain the struggle by importing a substantial quantity of 'unity coal', which was sold directly to WUI members and to the needy. By mid-September, the merchants were on the point of victory, and the WUI eventually ordered its men back to work.[60] Having inherited a surplus of £472 from the turbulent second half of 1924, the WUI ended 1925 with a deficit of almost £4,800.

Fortuitously, employers did not press on to smash the union, content to have checked its militancy.

By most criteria, Larkin was proving to be a disastrous union leader, and the financial anxieties and the burden of administration had a depressing effect on him. There were to be regular complaints from the Registry of Friendly Societies about delays in filing annual returns, and anomalies in the accounts supplied. Larkin's legendary disregard for money was in truth selective, and he showed a hard-headedness where his vital interests were concerned. Strike pay plummeted from £9,344 in 1925, to £45 in 1926, and £131 in 1927, rising to an annual average of £1,100 for 1928–30. Working expenses, on the other hand, consumed an increasing proportion of revenue up to 1928, when they amounted to 99 per cent of income; by the mid 1930s the proportion was still high at around 60 per cent. Another outgoing was personal loans. Each week, Larkin would hear hard luck cases and offer assistance. Loans to members rose from 2 per cent income in 1924 to 20 per cent in 1930, and at least half the money was never recovered and written off.[61] Larkin had always regarded membership figures as a strategic weapon rather than a fact, and the WUI was not alone in supplying exaggerated statistics to the Registry of Friendly Societies. From 1924 to 1940, the WUI registered annual official membership figures of between 14,500 and 17,000. The very stability of these figures makes them unreal. Between 1924 and 1930, union membership in the Free State declined from 126,000 to 70,000. And the drop was steepest in transport, where density fell by 60 per cent.[62] The ITGWU shrank from 51,000 members in 1925 to 15,000 in 1929.[63] While the WUI enrolled a few thousand 'non-benefit' members, its true strength can be gauged from annual subscriptions – each member being worth about £1 per annum – which fell from £9,212 for the second half of 1924, to £9,026 for 1925, and £5,830 for 1926, a figure not consistently exceeded until 1931. Big Jim also insisted that the WUI had numerous branches outside Dublin, whereas Young Jim told Moscow in 1930 that all of the provincial branches had collapsed.[64]

Dissent within the WUI compounded the disillusionment. Larkin liked to operate on a personal and verbal basis, and never kept records. His coat pocket served as his filing cabinet. When necessary he would sift through the contents, and throw away anything no longer active. That had always been his way, but it suited his purpose. In the absence of documentation and procedure, it was harder for dissidents to challenge the general secretary, or for outsiders to gather hostile evidence. Moscow's agents knew little of the union's internal state, and were chary of penetrating what was understood as Larkin's fief. In reality, the WUI was more akin to a medieval kingdom. Branches could function autonomously provided they didn't thwart the king. He made the big decisions, controlled the major resources, and simply withheld his support from anything he didn't approve of. He expected obedience, and was given to attribute failure to disloyalty or conspiracy. Carney reported the detection of ITGWU agents in the union after the 1925 coal strike.[65] O'Brien probably had spies in the camp, and certainly had a highly placed informant in 1929 who noted rumblings on the executive about Larkin's dictatorial style and junkets to Russia. Larkin had his own spy in Parnell Square. Tom Bell, a Comintern agent, claimed the WUI to be 'continually in a state of turmoil by the quarrels between Larkin and the [branch] secretaries' over finance.[66]

By 1929, the dirt was getting into the public domain. Jack Dempsey publicly accused Larkin of dishonesty while in Moscow for the Profintern congress in 1928.[67] A docker, and hardened hit-man, proud of sharing a moniker with the US boxing champion, Dempsey had been convicted of two assaults on ITGWU members. In one, at the fishmarkets in 1924, the victim stood little chance against villains named Jack Dempsey and James Bond. Dempsey received two-months hard labour. Undeterred, he and Barney Conway waylaid a senior ITGWU man, Frank Robbins, in 1925.[68] In April 1929, Dempsey published accusations of misappropriation of WUI funds by the Larkins.[69] Big Jim had had his suspicions of Dempsey. When Dempsey visited Moscow for the Profintern congress in 1928, Larkin warned the other WUI delegates to be careful of what they said to him. Sure enough, Dempsey accused Larkin of dishonesty. In Moscow, Larkin could blame it all on Lozovsky's intrigues.[70] He did not have to worry about the Soviet police. But after Dempsey repeated the charge in Dublin, the Department of Justice enquired of the Garda commissioner if legal action could be taken. The Gardaí agreed that the allegations were 'substantially correct', but added that Larkin had squandered 'thousands of pounds from Moscow within the past few years', and hinted that action might be counterproductive:

> The international communist press have howled out time and time again about the strategical importance of Ireland – not from the military standpoint, but because it is universally known that Ireland contains within herself a potentially revolutionary people at England's front door, and the CI demands that Ireland should be the 'Afghanistan' in the enemy's own camp (England), and because Larkin has failed to create such a situation there are fairly powerful influences at work to oust him.[71]

Within months, Larkin was in open dispute with officers of his no 3 branch, and prosecuting the secretary, John Bohan, for possession of the branch premises and financial records. Bohan filed countercharges against Larkin for not having held an audit of the WUI's books for three years.[72] In October, 'as a result of internal trouble in the WUI', a laundry section opted to transfer to the ITGWU.[73] Declining in stature, more vulnerable to criticism, and commensurately more anxious to stifle dissent, Larkin met the challenge with cunning inactivity. Bohan claimed that no executive elections had been held since 1926, and in 1932 Joe Troy of the Revolutionary Workers' Groups told Moscow that the WUI had convened no annual conference for four years, or branch elections for six to eight years, and that the only meetings held involved Larkin speaking for hours on some political issue unrelated to trade unionism.[74] In 1928, a proposed housing scheme for union members, 'Unity Park' in Drumcondra, foundered in a way suggestive of poor communication between the general secretary and his executive.[75]

Larkin's hopes of bringing culture to the workers suffered from the same want of completion. O'Casey had been thinking of basing a play on him since October 1922, but his ardour was dampened by the splits of 1923–4, and he told Lady Gregory he was avoiding his hero: 'because I love the man and am afraid he would bring me into the movement. And I do not think it will succeed on his present lines, but through art and culture and the people of culture.'[76] There was deception, or self-deception, here. People of culture were just what Larkin wanted. Perhaps O'Casey feared being saddled with union work that would take time from his writing. He had nothing to do with Delia's players once established with the Abbey Theatre. Or perhaps he needed distance to preserve his dramatic vision of Larkin. No man is a hero to his valet. O'Casey was both inspired by Larkin's visit to Russia in 1924 and embarrassed by the Mansion House speech he made on his return. Larkin kept in touch, taking a serious interest in the plays. Carney urged O'Casey to send him a copy of *The Silver Tassie*, and reported back: 'He thinks it is great stuff but is somewhat sceptical of its being staged in London.'[77] In 1925 Larkin approached O'Casey to get permission from Lady Gregory to present *The Rising of the Moon* at the Queen's Theatre. When her Ladyship later asked O'Casey about rumours that Larkinites would disrupt a meeting about building a gallery to accommodate the Hugh Lane collection of modern art, he assured her that Larkin's criticism of the cost of the project was intended simply to highlight the lack of spending on workers' housing and that he was a great admirer of Lane, with whom he claimed to have had dinner in the US. Larkin also helped Mícheál Ó Maoláin organise An Cumann Cosanta na Gaeltachta in Dublin.[78]

THE FLY IN THE RED WEB, 1924–6

Larkin's industrial record had its redeeming features; his political project degenerated into an ignoble mess. He knew that the Soviets would not give him a blank cheque to be a free agent, and the price of a productive relationship with Moscow would be the regularisation of the status of the IWL and WUI as communist organs, the creation of other Comintern agencies in Ireland, and collaboration with Comintern officials. And still he could not deliver.

It took six months to resolve the role of the WUI and IWL. On 20 November 1924, at a meeting with Willie Gallacher, Tom Bell, Arthur MacManus, and a Comintern emissary from the Communist Party of Germany, Jim refused to engage in realistic discussion and rejected interference from Moscow as well as London. Predicting that Jim would eventually 'turn against us', the German referent recommended the cultivation of links with radical republicans.[79] Pete travelled to Moscow in December to join a commission comprising representatives of the Comintern, the Profintern, the CPGB, and the Minority Movement. His report to the commission complained of persistent obstruction from the CPGB, and condemned the ITGWU for collusion with the Free State government and the British unions in Ireland for regular scabbing. It also introduced another nagging problem for Moscow in its dealings with the Larkins: the difficulty of obtaining reliable, or even relevant, information. Pete put WUI membership at 30,650 and IWL membership at 6,000.[80] Yet Pete's statement compared favourably with later despatches from his brother, which told of the tremendous advances of communism in the Free State, despite:

> the most fearful combination of corrupt, politically ignorant, and blood-soaked tyrants that ever masqueraded as a government. Mussolini, Horthy, Primo de Rivero have much to learn from our democratic Premier, Cosgrave, who was formerly a bar tender in a low class public house (drinking den), and his Fidus Achates Kevin O'Higgins a lawyer.[81]

Pete presented too a memorandum proposing a mutual recognition treaty or a trade agreement between Soviet Russia and the Free State.[82] Three salient bones of contention emerged in discussions on the commission. First, the British favoured a reconciliation of the ITGWU and the WUI, with communists forming a revolutionary fraction in the merged union. Secondly, the Larkins wanted the CPGB to campaign for the withdrawal of British unions, 'outposts of British imperialism', from Ireland. The CPGB tendered no ideological objections but was apprehensive. The party was concerned to emphasise that the Minority Movement was 'not out to disrupt the unions, or to encourage any new unions'.[83] Thirdly, the CPGB wanted the IWL to be a broad workers' party, embracing a communist fraction. The British also wanted a group of young republicans invited to Russia for political and military training, an idea the Larkins suspected as an attempt to outflank them. Other differences related chiefly to the role of British communists in Ireland, and the IWL in Britain.[84]

An accord was endorsed by the presidium of the ECCI on 7 January 1925. The WUI was recognised as the Profintern's voice in Ireland, and was to convene a conference, by May at the latest, to formulate statutes, an economic programme, and proposals for united action with other unions and trade unionists. Communists in reformist unions were to build revolutionary fractions. The IWL was to be transformed into a political party after the WUI conference. Irish trade unionism was accepted as independent of Britain. Irish sections were to deal directly with Moscow (ie. not through Britain), and have a permanent representative there. The Profintern and Comintern were to have representatives in Ireland. Irish Worker League or WUI activities in Britain were to be co-ordinated with the CPGB or the Minority Movement, and vice versa; and communists in both countries were to fight for the withdrawal of British unions from Ireland. With Big Jim's approval, a group of young republicans was to be invited to Moscow. The *Irish Worker* was to be supported, and the *Daily Worker*, organ of the Workers' Party of America, was to cease its attacks on Big Jim.[85] The source of this annoyance was O'Flaherty, author of the famous 'As we see it' column, and a critic of Jim's policy towards the ITGWU. As the column was very popular and O'Flaherty was rarely sober, he defied party and Comintern strictures on what was an indefensible breach of communist protocol. Jim consistently complained about him.[86]

The ECCI resolution said nothing on aid or trade, which were, for Jim, the crucial part of the package. Subsequently he complained to Zinoviev that following his visit to Russia in 1924,

the promises made by you, by M., T., and L. [probably Dimitri Manuilsky, rapporteur on the national question at the fifth Comintern congress, Tomsky, and Lozovsky], apart from the miserable £100 which didn't even cover my costs, were the only comradely gestures received. Your suggestion of a personal link by [sending] a ship or goods or even the very presence of your emblem would have been of immense value.[87]

He also referred to promises 'concerning the founding of a co-operative and the means to do so'. The ECCI did allocate £1,000 to Ireland, but Jim wanted the money immediately, control over the Comintern's Irish budget, and a Soviet trade initiative with the Free State. Instead the balance of the money – £900 – was lodged with the CPGB for the establishment of a press in Ireland. Comintern officials put nothing in writing concerning trade relations, possibly for fear of compromising Narkomindel, the People's Commissariat of Foreign Affairs, as the Soviet Foreign Ministry was called.[88] It may well have been a wise precaution. Two letters pertaining to Larkin were among 'a mass of documents' seized by the British police in arrests of CPGB leaders in October

1925; both were passed on to the Irish authorities.[89] Over the next four years there were regular, if less specific, references to money allegedly promised for the WUI by Zinoviev and Lozovsky. The Soviets made no admissions, though they did send small amounts.[90]

'ALL HIDEOUS CHAOS'[91]

Bob Stewart arrived in January 1925 to help implement the plan of action. 'Larkin was the biggest problem,' Stewart recalled, 'because he always personalised his politics. He would denounce this scoundrel and that scoundrel, in fact almost everyone in Ireland was a scoundrel.'[92] But billeted in 17 Gardiner's Place, he could see Jim's lighter side and appreciate his personal problems. The pair got on well – their common horror of drink assisted – and Stewart did not exaggerate in saying 'I was one of the few men he really trusted politically'.[93] Already Larkin's impatience with Moscow was mounting as his financial troubles deepened. He made a second visit to Russia in February for the fifth enlarged plenum of the ECCI, only to discover it was postponed to March. On returning through London he was informed by A. J. Bennett that aid depended on progress, for which he blamed the CPGB.[94]

Stewart first set up sections of two Comintern fronts, International Class War Prisoners' Aid (ICWPA) and Workers' International Relief (WIR). Their inaugural mission would be to channel relief to victims of the near famine conditions along the western seaboard and to republican prisoners' dependents. In many parts of the west, dreadful weather in 1924 had led to the total failure of the potato crop and made the saving of turf impossible. The *Irish Worker* put the number in distress at 75,000, and, possibly due to a typographical error, the figure of 750,000 was cited by WIR internationally.[95] In the spring the Free State government started a scheme to supply seed oats and potatoes, but in September the Department of Agriculture estimated that 5,000 families were still unable to provide for themselves.[96] Larkin became president of the Irish section of WIR, Stewart was secretary, and they were joined on the executive by officers of Dublin trades council, the IWL, and radical republicans like Charlotte Despard, Maud Gonne, Hanna Sheehy Skeffington, and Peadar O'Donnell. The ILPTUC declined a request from international WIR to participate: Johnson humbugged with objections to 'souperism' and more honest protest against the leadership of 'a man whose life is spent destroying solidarity and disrupting the Irish Trade Union Movement'.[97]

The WIR central office in Berlin intended the 'Irish action' to be of international significance. Willi Münzenberg, the Comintern's propaganda 'wunderkind', demanded a big effort, with funds raised in Russia, the US, Canada, and Australia, and the famine blamed on both the Free State government and British imperialism.[98] The potential for enlisting the Irish abroad was obvious. There was also a diplomatic dimension. In 1924 elements in the British TUC had mooted unity talks between the International Federation of Trade Unions and the Profintern. A British TUC delegation had visited Russia and co-sponsored an Anglo-Russian joint advisory council on Labour unity. The fifth enlarged plenum of the ECCI attached 'immense importance' to the Anglo-Russian rapprochement, and WIR hoped its aid to their recent colony would impress the British on the value of international fraternity.[99] In May the British government notified Tim Healy, the Free State governor general, that 'considerable prominence is being given in the Soviet press to the situation in Ireland'. *Pravda* had published an article by Larkin, illustrated with photos of 'a fat and prosperous' priest and starving women and children, calling for the despatch of a 'Red Relief Ship' to Dublin.[100] Larkin and Mrs Despard addressed a WIR conference in London in April, chaired by George Lansbury, MP, at which prominence was given to victims of the recent earthquake in Japan, and famine in Germany and Ireland. Helen Crawfurd, international secretary, announced that £1,017 had been received for Ireland.[101] The WIR committee in Dublin concentrated its efforts on the worst affected areas, in south-west Donegal and Mayo. By 31 May foodstuffs to the value of £725 had been distributed through local committees to some 400 families in these areas.[102]

The Irish operation ran into terminal difficulties over the summer and autumn. Larkin lashed out on all sides, blaming intrigues against him in Ireland, the British for their imperialist attitudes, accusing O'Flaherty of embezzling funds in the US, and Berlin for doing nothing to stop it all.[103] Gallacher travelled to Dublin in July to rescue WIR from collapse. Larkin complained that every promise made to him in Moscow had been broken, and left Gallacher speechless when he said he had read CPGB correspondence on Ireland in the Comintern archives. A grant of £100 from the Profintern temporarily deflated the crisis. But a bigger pitfall lay ahead. Lansbury's visit to Dublin on 24 July to present WIR with £500 from the Russian Red Cross again inflamed Larkin's suspicion that the British were trying to belittle him. Though Lansbury had championed the Fiery Cross in 1913 as editor of the *Daily Herald*, Larkin had developed a strong antipathy to him. In fact the CPGB had wanted Larkin to present the cheque; Lansbury, a noted pacifist and humanitarian, was chosen on the insistence of the Russian Red Cross.[104] Neither was Berlin too pleased with events. The whole point of a front was to broaden support, and WIR's policy was to foster trade union unity and united front tactics. In Ireland, however, it was compelled to back the WUI in its quarrel with Congress and the ITGWU.

Larkin had cabled Berlin on 22 August 1925 for aid to open WIR food dispensaries for 'children of locked out Dublin dockers'. The Berlin executive approved unaware of the implications until Congress attacked WIR for backing Larkin's war against the Irish Labour movement. Trade unionists on the British WIR executive complained of being placed in an impossible situation. Lansbury threatened to withdraw, and Mrs Sheehy Skeffington and others resigned. When Münzenberg asked the Profintern for advice, Larkin submitted a long, unapologetic report. In a detailed rebuttal, WIR concluded that its Irish committee had 'the worst possible consequences' for the front internation-ally.[105] No more was heard of WIR in Ireland, but there were humiliating consequences after the arrest of leaders and the seizure of 'a mass of documents' at King Street, London, headquarters of the CPGB and the Minority Movement, in October. The British Home Secretary, Sir William Joynson-Hicks, selected one of Larkin's letters to illustrate the unscrupulousness of the communists to his parliamentary opponents.

> I am not blaming the members of the Communist party. I am blaming England for allowing itself to be duped and to be dependent on instructions from Moscow and on money from Moscow. Before I finish, the hon. Member for Bow and Bromley [Lansbury] challenged me to read a letter regarding himself, and he will forgive me if I read one to the secretary of the Communist party here, dated 19th September, 1925, dealing with the Irish question. I think the hon. Member must have received some money, but I am not suggesting improperly, of course. They write: 'When money has been sent to help the famine area, the British party, instead of using it for the Workers' Union in Ireland, distributed it through Lansbury, a hypocrite'. Forgive me.
> MR LANSBURY: That is all right.
> SIR W. JOYNSON-HICKS: It goes on to say: 'He presented it to the Soup Kitchen Brigade.' The hon. Member and I have fought here side by side, and I want to let him know that these men are not really friends of his. They are not friends of the Labour party. [hon. members: 'We know it!'] We want the Labour party to realise what is being done by the Moscow Brigade here. [HON. MEMBERS: 'We know it!'] In that case, if you know it, why are you complaining of our position to-day?[106]

In 1926 a British parliamentary paper publishing a selection of the seized papers actually stated that Larkin had purloined famine relief funds for the WUI.[107]

The Irish section of ICWPA had been founded in Dublin in March 1925, and the executive included representatives of the WUI, IWL, and republicans. By December ICWPA had 1,000 members in Dublin and Belfast, and several small groups elsewhere. The Dublin group sponsored a Lenin commemoration in Banba Hall in February 1926. 'Wonderful day,' noted Mrs Despard. Two months later the group's involvement with Roddy Connolly's Workers' Party of Ireland (WPI), an attempt to develop an alternative to the IWL, caused ructions between WUI members and others on its executive. 'The great Jim will tolerate nothing of which he is not the boss,' Mrs Despard confided to her diary. 'The great Jim' made a rare appearance at the next meeting to make the point in person and unchivalrously 'denounced certain of the members as antiques'.[108] 'Things are about as bad as they can be in Dublin,' reported an international ICWPA representative in October.

> What are we to do? Dissolve MOPR [ICWPA] and place it in control of another group? This is impossible. That would mean open war with Larkin and we could not as yet stand against him. Also the whole position would have to be in consultation with ECCI as big political issues would arise.[109]

SORTING OUT THE PARTY

A key aim of the communist fronts was to lay the ground for a party. As the CPGB wanted, it was to be called the Workers' Party of Ireland, and neither the manifesto nor the draft constitution mentioned communism. With weeks to go to the launch date of 24 May 1925, Stewart believed that good progress was being made, and the CPGB released £50 from its Irish fund for the preparations. But as the deadline approached, Larkin became increasingly contrary, and 'could not find room' in the *Irish Worker* to publish the manifesto. Then, after going about 'with the manifesto in his pocket for days', and telling Stewart not to worry, he refused to sign it, and declined to attend the launch. Hundreds did attend and 200 applied to join, but Stewart knew it was pointless to proceed.[110] Bennett despatched a gentle rebuke, followed by an assurance that £1,000 was available for a press, and that he was willing to negotiate for a Profintern office in Dublin. Larkin refused to receive the letters. Once again he was spiting himself. Local elections were due in June. A few candidates sought his endorsement, and Larkinites in Nenagh achieved some success.[111]

Stewart and Bennett remained sympathetic. At the time – the penny would drop eventually – Stewart rationalised that the root cause of the sabotage was finance. Swallowing a sense of personal betrayal, he advised E. H. Brown, British representative at the Comintern, that Larkin was holding out for three concessions: £1,000 for the WUI, control over Comintern funds for Ireland and direct communication with Moscow, and a Soviet initiative to open commercial relations with the Free State.[112] Brown endorsed the first two demands, significantly omitting any reference to trade, and added that the Comintern might send Larkin a personal letter deploring O'Flaherty's articles.

The alternative, he argued, could well be the collapse of the WUI and the basis for a mass party.[113] An ECCI commission recommended the release of the £900 held in London, with £250 to be used for the WUI and £650 for the party; the appointment of Bennett to negotiate with Larkin and control funding for Ireland with power to increase the Irish budget; and a letter on the gadfly O'Flaherty.[114] The ECCI agreed, with minor amendments, and Zinoviev wrote a personal letter to Larkin expressing sympathy with his 'severe difficulties'; Larkin resented the implication. The seed capital for the party was never sent, and the WUI was still looking for the £250 in 1928.[115]

Carney's arrival in Moscow in August 1925 as the Irish resident representative did nothing to improve Anglo-Soviet-Irish understanding. Carney had returned to America in 1924 to edit *Labor Unity* in San Francisco. He left California in April 1925 at the Comintern's request, but then found himself stranded in New York, awaiting instructions, when the ECCI encountered difficulties with Larkin. Ironically the CPGB urged his expedition to Moscow in the belief that he would be a settling influence on Larkin and 'very serviceable in pushing for a Workers' Party'.[116] Carney had acquired a solid reputation from his record in the US, but where Big Jim was concerned, a ferocious loyalty dissipated all reason. In September at an ECCI orgbureau inquest, he attributed the absence of a party to the financial burden on the WUI work, which had been receiving £400 a week in income and spending £1,900 a week in strike pay until brought to the verge of bankruptcy, CPGB sabotage, and the ECCI breaking its promises of big financial aid. It was agreed that a commission be appointed to 'examine how far promises to Larkin had been made and not kept' and prepare material for future ECCI plena.[117] In October, another inaugural conference of the party was abandoned. As in May, Stewart had made the arrangements, and Larkin did not turn up.[118] Aside from the business of the party, Stewart had angered Larkin by arranging for a visit to Russia by a republican delegation in June.

A bigger problem was bubbling over, more visceral as it affected Larkin's livelihood. The Minority Movement had been dismayed by the January 1925 agreement's provision for a campaign for the withdrawal of British unions from Ireland. As Minority Movement secretary, Pollitt told Moscow that it would multiply the disruption in Irish Labour and 'stir up more difficulties' with unions in Britain and nothing would be done pending talks with Larkin.[119] Larkin had attended a Minority Movement conference in London in January and gave it a rapturous report in the *Irish Worker*.[120] Outraged by Pollitt's determination to renege, he walked into the Movement's annual conference in London in August in a foul mood. Brushing aside a hearty reception, he showered abuse on those present, including the Dublin delegates, and declared that he would clear the British unions out of Ireland. Gilbert Lynch gives a flavour of the style in his memoirs.[121] To Larkin's fury, in September the British helped Dublin trades council start an Irish Minority Movement, with backing from 35 trade unions, union branches, and trades councils.[122] Both sides to the dispute submitted extensive reports to the Profintern. The Minority Movement, as usual, pleaded that any action against the amalgamateds would simply cause more division, and suggested the central schism, between the ITGWU and the WUI, be addressed through communist fractions in both unions.[123] Carney might have done better. Even the CPGB acknowledged the necessity of an independent Labour movement in Ireland. Instead Carney tendered a shoddy presentation, short on facts, long on Larkin's heroic record, and studded with sweeping assaults on his enemies.[124] Lozovsky, the most sceptical of the Soviets on Larkin, dismissed it sarcastically, complaining that it was impossible to get concrete information from the Irish and that 'Comrade Carney speaks as if Ireland had the very worst reactionaries and the very best revolutionaries'.[125]

The ECCI had passed the dispute to a prestigious commission, which included Pete Larkin. Accepting the British case, it proposed that a new autonomous all-Ireland Minority Movement be created, dealing independently with Moscow.[126] Carney's standing in Moscow never recovered. The British länder secretariat got the ECCI to suspend decisions on Irish affairs pending a discussion with Larkin. Carney lost his salary from the Comintern and he went to work for the Profintern, not a comfortable station given the enmity between himself and Lozovsky. The Profintern too sought to bypass him. When Larkin left his faithful friend twisting in the wind by refusing to communicate with Moscow, Lozovsky suggested he return to Dublin. 'During the two years that I have acted as Irish representative I have not received any friendship from the CI,' Carney wrote in 1927.[127]

Dublin trades council duly planned to re-launch the Irish Minority Movement on 14 February 1926, with Jim and Tom Mann, chairman of the British Minority Movement, as the star speakers. It made no sense for Larkin to oppose the trades council. It was his only ally in the Labour movement, and had granted a loan of £200 to the WUI, which was so short of funds that it had affiliated to the council for 1,000 members, with a promise to affiliate the remainder when finances allowed. Nonetheless Larkin pulled out of the meeting at the last minute, saying he had not been given adequate notice. The council then resolved to sever all ties with him.[128] With Stewart's return to England and Dublin trades council's breach with Larkin, Roddy Connolly and his associates despaired of the IWL. In March 1926 they decided to establish the WPI. Resolutions at the party's founding conference advertised its roots in ICWPA and hinted at collusion with the CPGB.[129]

The British general strike on 3 May in opposition to the miners' lockout brought a brief unity on the fractured left. Larkin rushed out a cheap, stencilled edition of the *Irish Worker* on 2 May, declaring: 'Workers of Ireland the fight in Britain is your fight.' Dublin trades council issued a daily stop press *Dublin Labour Bulletin* from 8th. After the collapse of the general strike on 12th the rival Irish communist groups gave discrete aid to the British miners, who fought on until December. The WUI blacked British coal imports for 11 weeks, until coal was discharged under guard. It also raised funds for the miners and hosted three Welsh choirs, five Scottish pipe bands, and 'what is called a jazz band'. Larkin would later complain bitterly of the CPGB's feeble support for his efforts.[130] He had never abandoned his suspicion of King Street. Soon after the foundation of the WPI, he hastened to London, most likely to register a protest with the CPGB about collusion with Connolly, and raised stormy opposition to the new party within ICWPA. When the WPI gave notice of a May Day rally, he employed his usual stratagem of announcing a demonstration of his own. Anxious to avoid a clash, the WPI yielded, and Connolly's son also surrendered 'Connolly day' – 12 May – to Larkin, who rarely uttered a good word about his old subaltern in private. Larkin staged an impressive commemoration, which the unemployed association band concluded with the 'Internationale'.[131]

As a prospective communist party, the WPI's future depended on the Comintern. McLay had written to the ECCI on 29 April, requesting affiliation.[132] Ominously, the ECCI informed Larkin that 'Our information points to the fact that this Party [the WPI] is to be considered a Communist Party ...', and demanded a 'detailed report on the conditions which hitherto prevented the carrying out of the decisions of the ECCI'.[133] On 12 July Carney sent a long report to the ECCI. This time he was careful to include figures, if not facts, and WUI membership was put at 18,000. The WPI was described as an 'eyesore' of ne'er do wells, greedy for 'Russian gold'. On Larkin's failure to develop a party, Carney conceded he had no explanation.[134]

The ECCI referred the dispute to its seventh enlarged plenum, which met between 22 November and 16 December. Hoping to gain intelligence on Ireland, the ECCI invited the WPI to send a delegate, together with 'an exhaustive report on the economic and political situation of Ireland' and 'detailed facts on the entire labour movement'.[135] The WPI was unable to afford representation at the plenum but Larkin was sufficiently stirred to attend, though recovering from illness, probably pneumonia: an ECCI transcript described it as 'serious Rumania'.[136] He brought with him two documents, a detailed application for a loan of £4,000 to revive the *Irish Worker*, and a political review. The review ended with a reminder of the importance of the Irish throughout the world and concluded, in the name of the 'Irish Communist Party', that 'they must be Bolshevised'.[137] The empty rhetoric no longer deceived anyone in Moscow. When Larkin blamed his difficulties on the CPGB's imperialist attitude, the British delegate calmly pointed out that for all its faults the CPGB existed and the Irish party did not.[138] At a Profintern commission on relations between Irish and British affiliates, he attacked the British at length for their performance during the miners' lockout, and demanded an end to Minority Movement activity in Ireland. Waving the polemic aside, Lozovsky asked for facts, and the British made it clear they thought it better to move on without Larkin.[139]

Despite this the dispute had a favourable outcome for Larkin. The ECCI refused to sanction the CPI's 're-establishment' in the shape of the WPI and told the CPGB to stop intriguing in Ireland. Larkin was promised that in future Irish revolutionary organs would deal independently with the Comintern.[140] Assuring Larkin of its co-operation, the CPGB urged Connolly to comply with the ECCI decision.[141] At an aggregate meeting on 27 March, Connolly moved that the party be dissolved in the interests of communist discipline. The motion was defeated heavily in favour of an appeal to the ECCI.[142] The appeal concluded with a despairing offer to work with Larkin despite his 'egocentric nature' and determination to destroy any attempt at building a workers' party. The Comintern never replied.[143]

Larkin was now, as the Garda put it, 'unpopular with all parties'. It was not a choice of my way or no way. As he could neither collaborate nor delegate, there was no way. He had alienated his friends. The WUI was in decline and impoverished. The IWL was moribund. The British were working behind his back in cultivating alternative allies in Ireland. There was no sign of Soviet commercial links with the Free State, and the Comintern was obviously unwilling to release substantial funding before the creation of a party. A man described by the Department of Justice as 'a dangerous revolutionist' in 1924, would generate 'no cause whatsoever for anxiety about his relations with Russia' during the British general strike of 1926.[144] But one consolation remained: Moscow still believed that if little could be done with Larkin, nothing could be done without him.

NOTES

1   RGASPI, report on the situation in Ireland, 17 April 1924, 495/100/168–1/3.

2   *Workers' Republic*, 5 May 1923.

3   ITGWU, *The Attempt to Smash the Irish Transport and General Workers' Union* (Dublin, 1924), p. 148.

4   NAUK, British special branch report no 206, 17 May 1923, CAB 24/160.

5   *Workers' Republic*, 9–16 June 1923.

6   RGASPI, Comintern presidium to Larkin, 6 August 1923, 495/89/20–5.

7   RGASPI, MacManus to the secretariat, ECCI, 5 September 1923, 495/89/22–65/66.

8   RGASPI, report by MacManus and the Politbureau of the CPGB, 11 October 1923, 495/38/7–236/241.

9   RGASPI, MacManus to Comintern secretariat, 11 October 1923, 495/18/210–52/55; MacManus to Kuusinen, 2 February 1924, 495/38/7–243/44; MacManus to the Workers' Party of America, 2 February 1924, 495/38/7–245/48; McLay to ECCI, 26 June 1924, 495/89/27–13.

10   NA, DJ, Larkin file, JUS 8/676; *Irish Worker*, 15 March 1924.

11   RGASPI, MacManus to Kuusinen, 2 February 1924, 495/38/7–243/244.

12   RGASPI, MacManus to the Workers' Party of America, 2 February 1924, 495/38/7–245/248.

13   *Irish People*, December 1923.

14   Ibid., April 1924.

15   RGASPI, ECCI to CPI, 8 April 1924, 495/89/27–3; ECCI to secretary Irish Republican Workers' Party, formerly Comparty, Ireland, 2 June [1924], 495/89/27–4.

16   Charlie McGuire, *Sean McLoughlin: Ireland's Forgotten Revolutionary* (Pontypool, 2011), p. 121; *Irish Worker*, 2 February 1924.

17   RGASPI, Harry Pollitt, report on the situation in Ireland, 17 April 1924, 495/100/168–1/3.

18   *Irish Worker*, 29 March, 5–19 April, 3–17 May 1924.

19   *Nenagh Guardian*, 19 April 1924; RGASPI, Harry Pollitt, report on the situation in Ireland, 17 April 1924, 495/100/168–1/3.

20   *Nenagh Guardian*, 5 April 1924; *Irish Worker*, 3, 17 May 1924.

21   *Irish Worker*, 10–19 May 1924.

22   Ibid., 10 May 1924.

23   Mike Milotte, *Communism in Modern Ireland: The Pursuit of the Workers' Republic since 1916* (Dublin, 1984), p. 74. Whether an executive was elected is unclear, as is the claim that it included US heavyweight boxing champion Jack Dempsey. There was a Dublin Larkinite of the same name, but Larkin had some contact with the boxer. According to the *Irish Worker*, 1 August 1931: 'In the Head Office of the Workers' Union of Ireland there hangs a large autographed picture of Jack Dempsey. The Unity Boxing Club, run by members of the Workers' Union of Ireland, have a promise from Jack that whenever he comes to Europe he will visit their headquarters – Unity Hall . . . When the Labour Movement along the Pacific Coast of the USA needed help they knew they could rely upon Jack'. The *Irish Worker* ran a series on Dempsey's life story over the coming weeks.

24   *Irish Worker*, 3–24 May 1924.

25   RGASPI, McLay to the ECCI, 26 June 1924, 495/89/27–10/14; NA, report on the CPI, S5074a; I am obliged for information on Pollock to his grandson, Tara Flynn, Pennsylvania.

26   RGASPI, ECCI to Larkin, 2 June 1924, 495/89/27–10/14.

27   *Irish Worker*, 27 September 1924.

28   Dora Montefiori, *From a Victorian to a Modern* (London, 1927), chapter 15.

29   Ibid.

30   RGASPI, Larkin to Zinoviev, 495/89/32–13/26.

31   Donal Nevin, 'Workers of the world', in Donal Nevin (ed.), *James Larkin: Lion of the Fold* (Dublin, 1998), p. 336; Milotte, *Communism in Modern Ireland*, pp. 75–6.

32   Milotte, *Communism in Modern Ireland*, p. 76.

33   RGASPI, third Profintern world congress, fourth session, undated [1924], 534/1/31–34/35.

34   RGASPI, Larkin to Zinoviev, undated [1925], 495/89/32–13/26.

35   Emmet Larkin, *James Larkin: Irish Labour Leader, 1876–1947* (London, 1965), pp. 277–8.

36 Ibid.

37 Daniel F. Calhoun, *The United Front: The TUC and the Russians, 1923–1928* (Cambridge, 1976), pp. 12–13; Kevin Morgan, *Bolshevism and the British Left, Part Three: Bolshevism, Syndicalism, and the General Strike: The Lost International World of A. A. Purcell* (London, 2013), pp. 127–8.

38 Larkin, *James Larkin*, p. 279; Nevin, 'Workers of the world', p. 337.

39 *Irish Times*, 30–31 March 1956; NLI, William O'Brien papers, Sean McLoughlin, 'How Inchicore was lost', 15670.

40 Jane Degras (ed.), *The Communist International, 1919–1943: Documents, Volume 2, 1923–1928* (London, 1971), p. 572.

41 *Irish Worker*, 20–27 September 1924.

42 Séamus Cody, John O'Dowd, and Peter Rigney, *The Parliament of Labour: 100 Years of the Dublin Council of Trade Unions* (Dublin, 1986), pp. 139–47; for WUI membership and finances see NA, WUI file, 369T A.

43 NLI, ILPTUC, *Annual Report* (1925), p. 35.

44 Francis Devine, *Organising History: A Centenary of SIPTU, 1909–2009* (Dublin, 2009), p. 158.

45 Donal Nevin, 'Titan at bay', in Nevin (ed.), *James Larkin*, p. 80; Larkin, *James Larkin*, p. 284.

46 NA, DT, election to Dáil Éireann and 'unseating' of James Larkin Sr, an undischarged bankrupt, 1927–8, S5562.

47 RGASPI, Larkin to Zinoviev, undated [1925], 495/89/32–13/26.

48 *Voice of Labour*, 30 August 1924.

49 NA, DJ, Larkin file, JUS 8/676; Larkin, *James Larkin*, pp. 283–4.

50 NLI, William O'Brien papers, 15679(5).

51 Pádraig Yeates, 'Craft workers during the Irish revolution, 1919–22', *Saothar* 33 (2008), p. 46.

52 NA, report on the CPI, S5074a.

53 NLI, Seán O'Casey papers, Carney to O'Casey, 27 July 1948, 37989.

54 Bob Stewart, *Breaking the Fetters: The Memoirs of Bob Stewart* (London, 1967), p. 149.

55 McGuire, *Sean McLoughlin*, pp. 127–9.

56 Larkin, *James Larkin*, p. 284.

57 *The Irish Reports* (1925), the Law Library, Dublin; Larkin, *James Larkin*, p. 284; J. Anthony Gaughan, *Thomas Johnson, 1872–1963: First Leader of the Labour Party in Dáil Éireann* (Dublin, 1980), pp. 272–6; Devine, *Organising History*, p. 216.

58 Larkin, *James Larkin*, p. 285; *Voice of Labour*, 22 August 1925.

59 Gaughan, *Thomas Johnson*, pp. 270–1.

60 Larkin, *James Larkin*, pp. 285–6.

61 Devine, *Organising History*, p. 223.

62 Kieran Allen, *Fianna Fáil and Irish Labour: 1926 to the Present* (London, 1997), p. 27.

63 C. Desmond Greaves, *The Irish Transport and General Workers' Union: The Formative Years, 1909–1923* (Dublin, 1982), p. 321.

64 RGASPI, joint report on WUI, S. Murray and J. Larkin Jr, 2 August 1930, 495/89/63–19/27.

65 RGASPI, report on Ireland, 495/89/104–40/41.

66 RGASPI, report to the Politsecretariat and Anglo-American secretariat, ECCI, 26 November 1929, 495/89/64–64.

67 UCDA, Seán MacEntee papers, 'Notes on communism in Saorstát Éireann', P67/523(5), p. 11.

68 NLI, ITGWU papers, 27041(1), 27041(3), 27044, 27048.

69 ILHA, Cathal O'Shannon papers, COS 93/12/152A(P); NLI, William O'Brien papers, 15679(9).

70 UCDA, Seán MacEntee papers, 'Notes on communism in Saorstát Éireann', P67/523(5), p. 11; RGASPI, statement from Larkin on WUI disaffiliation from the Profintern, undated [1929], 495/89/104–137; ILHA, Cathal O'Shannon papers, COS 93/12/122a(P).

71 NA, DJ, Larkin file, JUS 8/676.

72 RGASPI, report to the Politsecretariat and Anglo-American secretariat, ECCI, 26 November 1929, 495/89/64–64; NLI, William O'Brien papers, 15679(11).

73 NLI, William O'Brien papers, 15679(6), 15679(11); *Irish Independent*, 22 October 1929.

74 *Evening Herald*, 30 October 1929; RGASPI, Murray and Troy, report on the situation in Ireland, at the Anglo-American secretariat, 495/72/188–182.

75 NLI, William O'Brien papers, 15679(6).

76 Christopher Murray, *Seán O'Casey: Writer at Work, a Biography* (Dublin, 2004), p. 163.

77 Ibid., pp. 137–8, 205.

78 Éamon Ó Ciosáin, *An t-Éireannach, 1934–37: Páipéar Sóisialach Gaeltachta* (Dublin, 1993), p. 27; David Krause (ed.), *The Letters of Seán O'Casey, Volume I, 1910–4* (London, 1975), pp. 122–4, 255–6; Murray, *Seán O'Casey*, p. 205.

79 RGASPI, Betrifft Bewegung in Irland, 21 November 1924, 495/89/26–1/6.

80 RGASPI, reports to the German representation, Moscow, 21, 26 November 1924, 495/89/26–1/6; reports from Peter Larkin, 1924, 495/89/26–25/38, 495/89/104–88/101.

81 RGASPI, report from Larkin, 1926, 495/89/110–136/42.

82 RGASPI, memorandum on Ireland, undated [1924], 495/89/103–15.

83 Allen Hutt, *British Trade Unionism: A Short History* (London, 1975), p. 99.

84 RGASPI, John Pepper, 'Der Konflikt der Irish Workers League mit der Communist Party Gross-Britanniens', 27 December 1924, 495/89/26–22/24.

85 RGASPI, protokoll nr 18 der Sitzung des Präsidium des EKKI, 7 January 1925, 495/2/37; Resolution on the Irish question of the presidium of the ECCI, 7 January 1925, 495/89/28–22/24; 'The immediate tasks of the Profintern in Ireland', 1925, 534/6/77–20/22; minutes of the Executive Bureau, Profintern, 7 January 1925, 534/3/107–34. In 1920 the Communist Labor Party and a faction of the Communist Party of America had united as the Workers' Party of America, which also served as a legal front for the illegal Communist Party of America. The Workers' Party changed its name to the Workers' (Communist) Party of America in 1925 and to the Communist Party of the USA in 1929.

86 RGASPI, Pepper to ECCI secretariat, 14 September 1925, 495/89/30–6.

87 RGASPI, Larkin to Zinoviev, undated [1925], 495/89/32–13/26.

88 RGASPI, Brown to the secretariat, 20 June 1925, 495/89/30–5.

89 British Parliamentary Papers, *Communist Papers: Documents Selected From Those Obtained on the Arrest of the Communist Leaders on October 14, 21, 1925*, Cmd.2682 (1926), xxiii, 585; UCDA, Seán MacEntee papers, 'Notes on communism in Saorstát Éireann', P67/523(5), p. 22.

90 RGASPI, resume of comrade Stewart's letter, 9 June 1925, 495/89/30–9/10; Inkpin to Bennett, 10 July 1925, 495/100/242–3; Larkin to Zinoviev, 1926, 495/89/32–13/26.

91 'And in the labour world it's all hideous chaos', PRONI, Charlotte Despard papers, diary, 4, 7 February, 23, 29 April 1926, D/2479/1/9.

92 Stewart, *Breaking the Fetters*, p. 149.

93 Theresa Moriarty, 'Delia Larkin: relative obscurity', in Nevin (ed.), *James Larkin*, p. 437; Stewart, *Breaking the Fetters*, pp. 149–50.

94 RGASPI, Larkin to Zinoviev, undated [1925], 495/89/32–13/26. The fifth enlarged plenum met between 21 March and 6 April, its first meeting since July 1924. Bennett, alias D. A. Petrovski, was born in Russia as Max Goldfarb. Comintern representative to the CPGB, and director of the propaganda bureau of the ECCI, 1927–9, from 1929 he worked with the Soviet secret police.

95 *Irish Worker*, 14 March 1925; NA, DT, L. S. Amery to T. M. Healy, 18 May 1925, S4437.

96 NA, DT, secretary, Department of Agriculture to the President, 23 September 1925, S1693.

97 RGASPI, constitution d'un Comité Irlandais de secours, undated, 538/2/29–69; NLI, Hanna Sheehy Skeffington papers, notice of committee meeting, 8 April 1925, 24,117; ILPTUC, *31st Annual Report for 1924–25* (1925), p. 37; *Irish Worker*, 7 March 1925.

98 RGASPI, IAH, Antrage des Genossen Münzenberg in der Sitzung des Zentralkomitees, 21 February 1925, 538/26/26–31.

99 Jane Degras (ed.), *The Communist International, 1919–1943: Documents, Volume 2, 1923–1928* (London, 1971), p. 184; RGASPI, comité central du Secours Ouvrier International au Comité Anglo-Russe pour l'unité syndicale, 4 April [1924], 538/2/27–33/34.

100 NA, DT, L. S. Amery to T. M. Healy, 18 May 1925, S4437.

101 RGASPI, Secours Ouvrier International, 27 February 1925, 538/2/29–32; La famine en Irlande, 5 March 1925, 538/2/29–33; Conférence du Secours Ouvrier International a Londres, 19 April [1925], 538/2/29–40/42.

102 *Irish Worker*, 14 February, 7–14 March, 2 May 1925; RGASPI, constitution d'un Comité Irlandais de secours, undated, 538/2/29–69; Internationale Arbeiterhilfe, Bericht über Hilfstaetigkeit, 31 May 1925, 538/2/27–67/74.

103 RGASPI, Larkin to Zinoviev, undated [1925], 495/89/32–13/26; Larkin, Bericht über die Arbeit der IAH in Irland, 21 September 1925, 495/89/32–27/39.

104 Albert Inkpin, general secretary of the CPGB, described Lansbury as 'one of the worst and most subtle enemies of our party'. RGASPI, Inkpin to Bennett, 10 July 1925, 495/100/242–3.

105 RGASPI, Münzenberg to the Profintern, undated, 538/2/27–160; Larkin, Bericht über die Arbeit der IAH in Irland, 21 September 1925, 495/89/32–27/39; L. Gibarti, Bemarkungen zum Bericht des Genossen James Larkin über die irische Aktion der IAH, undated, 495/89/32–40/44.

106 British House of Commons debates, 1 December 1925, vol. 188, cols 2101–2.

107 British Parliamentary Papers, *Communist Papers: Documents Selected From Those Obtained on the Arrest of the Communist Leaders on October 14, 21, 1925*, Cmd.2682 (1926), xxiii, 585.

108 PRONI, Charlotte Despard papers, diary, 4, 7 February, 23, 29 April 1926, D/2479/1/9.

109 RGASPI, report on ICWPA, Irish section, for Anglo-American secretariat, 15 November 1926, 495/89/36–59/61. See also Carney's comments on ICWPA in RGASPI, report on Ireland, undated [1926], 495/89/104–18/45.

110 RGASPI, to the Irish working class [Workers' Party of Ireland manifesto, 1925], 495/89/106–34/36; see model statutes for a communist party, drafted by the ECCI orgbureau, Degras (ed.), *The Communist International, Volume 2*, pp. 172–9; Milotte, *Communism in Modern Ireland*, pp. 79–80; Stewart, *Breaking the Fetters*, p. 154.

111 RGASPI, E. H. Brown, Resumee des Briefes von Stewart, 9 June 1925, 495/89/30–9/10; Larkin to Zinoviev, undated [1925], 495/89/32–13/26; *Nenagh Guardian*, 7 November 1925.

112 RGASPI, E. H. Brown, Resumee des Briefes von Stewart, 9 June 1925, 495/89/30–9/10.

113 UCDA, Seán MacEntee papers, 'Notes on communism in Saorstát Éireann', P67/523(5), pp. 22–4; RGASPI, Brown to English section, Comintern, 9 June 1925, 495/89/30–11/13.

114 RGASPI, Brown to Comintern secretariat, 20 June 1925, 495/89/30–5. Of course, £50 from the fund in London had been spent on the intended launch of the Irish party.

115 RGASPI, Larkin to Zinoviev, undated [1925], 495/89/32–13/26; protokoll nr 70 der Sitzung des Büro des Sekretariats des EKKI, 22 June 1925, 495/20/948; IWL questionnaire, 2 February 1928, 495/89/49–1/3. Larkin also wrote separately to Lozovsky on 13 March 1928 asking him to settle 'this long outstanding financial irritation', 534/7/286–86.

116 RGASPI, Inkpin to Bennett, 10 July 1925, 495/100/242–3; Carney to the ECCI, 20 July 1927, 495/89/42–3.

117 UCDA, Seán MacEntee papers, 'Notes on communism in Saorstát Éireann', P67/523(5), pp. 24–6; RGASPI, L. Gibarti, Bemarkungen zum Bericht des Genossen James Larkin über die irische Aktion der IAH, undated, 495/89/32–40/44.

118 RGASPI, recommendations [to the Irish commission], undated [1926], 495/89/28–27/28.

119 RGASPI, Pollitt to the Profintern, 5 February 1925, 534/7/26–38/39.

120 *Irish Worker*, 31 January 1925.

121 RGASPI, Pollitt to Lozovsky, 2 September 1925, 534/7/26–154/156; Aindrias Ó Cathasaigh (ed.), *The Life and Times of Gilbert Lynch* (Dublin, 2011), pp. 50–2.

122 Cody, O'Dowd, and Rigney, *The Parliament of Labour*, pp. 139–47.

123 RGASPI, report, undated [1925], 495/89/104–153/161.

124 RGASPI, remarques du Cam. [J. T.] Murphy, undated [1925], 495/89/28–28; report on Ireland, undated [1925], 495/89/104–162/183.

125 RGASPI, minutes of the executive bureau, RILU, 28 January 1926, 534/3/150–255/265.

126 RGASPI, report to ECCI secretariat, 12 January [1926], 495/89/28–31; Irish resolution on trade union work, undated [1926], 495/89/33–2/3.

127 RGASPI, Carney to the secretariat, 17 March 1926, 495/89/36–1; Carney to Lozovsky, 17 March 1926, 495/89/36–2; minutes of the meeting of the executive bureau, RILU, 28 January 1928, 534/2/150; Carney to Comintern, 20 July 1927, 495/89/42–3.

128 Cody, O'Dowd, and Rigney, *The Parliament of Labour*, p. 142.

129 RGASPI, McLay to ECCI, 24 June 1926, 495/89/34–4; WPI report, undated [1926], 495/89/34–10. In October 1925 the British Labour Party annual conference refused to consider the affiliation of the CPGB. Communists then launched a 'national left wing movement' with the *Sunday Worker* as its organ.

130 RGASPI, Larkin at Profintern session, 21 December 1926, 534/3/173–119/130.

131 *Irish Hammer and Plough*, 22 May 1926; PRONI, Charlotte Despard papers, diary, 12, 18, 23, 29 April, 1, 4, 9 May 1926, D/2479/1/9; RGASPI, Larkin at Profintern session, 21 December 1926, 534/3/173–119/130.

132 RGASPI, McLay to Comintern, 24 June 1926, copy of letter forwarded 29 April, 495/89/34–4; McLay to secretary, CPGB, 20 April 1926, 495/89/34–1.

133 RGASPI, John Pepper to Larkin, 29 May 1926, 495/89/34–2.

134 RGASPI, report on Ireland, undated [1926], 495/89/104–18/45.

135 RGASPI, Pepper to McLay, 14 October 1926, 495/89/34–5.

136 RGASPI, minutes, executive bureau, RILU, 21 December 1926, 534/3/173–113.

137 RGASPI, letter from Larkin and statement, undated [1926], 495/89/110–136/47.

138 RGASPI, protokoll nr 83 der Sitzung des Präsidiums des EKKI, 20 December 1926, 495/2/64a–63/101.

139 RGASPI, session, 21 December 1926, 534/3/173–119/130.

140 RGASPI, protokoll nr 84 der Sitzung des Präsidiums, 7 January 1927, 495/2/70–7/8; Irish draft resolution, undated [1927], 495/3/3–15/17.

141 RGASPI, CPGB to Larkin, 9 February 1926, 495/89/42–1; CPGB to Connolly, 8 February 1927, 495/89/42–2.

142 RGASPI, statement by the executive, WPI, April 1927, 495/89/46–8; *Workers' Republic*, 2 April 1927.

143 RGASPI, WPI to the ECCI, 30 March 1927, 495/89/46–1; report on the IWL, 22 February 1928, 495/89/50–51/69.

144 NA, DJ, Larkin file, JUS 8/676.

THIRTEEN

RETREAT FROM MOSCOW, 1927–9

From the sublime to the ridiculous is but a short step.
Napoleon I, 1812

—

The late 1920s should have seen an enhancement of James Larkin's importance within the communist world. The quarrels and setbacks of 1925–6 did not diminish Moscow's interest in Ireland. Globally, the Comintern was becoming more interventionist and more concerned with realising its dream of one world communist party. Bolshevisation, adopted as a slogan at the fifth world congress in 1924, was refined at the fifth enlarged ECCI plenum in 1925 and at the sixth world congress in 1928. In addition, the Comintern was moving towards the political sectarianism against moderates for which Larkin had become notorious. Bitterly disappointed with the outcome of the general strike in Britain, Aleksandr Lozovsky penned a pamphlet, *British and Russian Workers* (December 1926), describing the TUC leaders, in language he might have borrowed from Larkin, as 'slippery eels'. The Anglo-Russian Joint Advisory Council was dissolved in 1927, and the Comintern ended its united front policy for Britain, and everywhere else, in 1928 with the adoption of the third period theses. The theses contended that the Bolshevik revolution occurred in a time of advance, and was followed by a phase of bourgeois recovery and stabilisation. Now the capitalist world was entering a third period, of heightening economic crisis and class conflict, in which employers would turn in desperation to fascism. As the future would be either fascist or communist, leftists who refused to work with the communists were ultimately 'social fascists', and Comintern affiliates should expose them for what they were.

Unfortunately for Larkin, his personality problems would not allow him to exploit the new dispensation, and everything seemed to change for the worst. Bolshevisation entailed the creation of regional secretariats within the Comintern apparatus to monitor affiliates. The IWL and WUI came under the Anglo-American secretariat, and the scrutiny of mainly British communists with more experience – and scepticism – of Larkin than the Russians. The spat over the WPI led the Comintern to decide that it should have permanent representatives in Ireland to work with Larkin. A shift in tone became evident in 1927 when Moscow demanded the activation of the IWL or else. The Comintern also concluded that it would have to work around Larkin rather than through him, and opportunities unfolded with the opening of the International Lenin School as the Comintern's 'cadre forge', and the development of links with republicans. By 1928, Larkin was also growing concerned about the growth of clerical anti-socialism. When the Soviets finally initiated commercial links with Ireland, and cut Larkin out of their commercial operations, he decided he had had enough.

THE COMMUNIST TD

Larkin took a limited interest in elections up to 1927. The dissolution of Dublin Corporation between 1924 and 1930 deprived him of an obvious political outlet. His one intervention in the June 1927 elections was to hold an eve of poll meeting in central Dublin and deliver a two-hour rant against all and sundry on the left; WPI officials were accused of misappropriating funds during their CPI days and the *Workers' Republic* compared him to 'an infuriated animal . . . stamping on the wreckage' he had made.[1] Changes in Moscow's supervisory procedures would soon challenge the self-indulgence. Jack Carney returned to Dublin and was replaced in Moscow with Iosef Fineberg, a former member of the British Socialist Party and now a Comintern functionary. The Comintern also tried to make progress in Ireland through two resident agents: Christian Hilt, a Norwegian, and Jack Leckie, a Glaswegian.[2] In mid-1927 it adopted a more efficient system wherein Hilt's reports from Dublin were reviewed by Fineberg over a period, making it possible to compile a moving picture of events instead of reacting to snapshots. Hilt's fairly optimistic despatches raised an eyebrow with Fineberg, who thought him 'impressed too much by the Irish comrades', adding 'but he appears to be finding them out'.[3]

The ECCI had approved another Irish offensive on 7 June, and some weeks later Hilt began his three-month residency in Dublin to push for a party.[4] A change of regime seemed at hand. Labour had won 22 seats in the general election, the still abstentionist Fianna Fáil won 44, and Cumann na nGaedheal clung precariously to power with 47 seats. Hilt employed the carrot at first, urging Moscow to consider Larkin's appeal for Soviet diplomatic relations with the Free State. The assassination of Kevin O'Higgins, Minister for Justice, on 10 July, prompted him to resort to the stick. The government responded to the crisis with a Public Safety bill, proposing additional powers for the army and Garda, and to declare vacant the seats of abstentionist TDs. Hilt presented Larkin with a formal ECCI demand for action on 26 July.[5] An IWL meeting on 29th agreed to establish a weekly paper and a bookshop, draft a political programme, and organise a labour unity meeting.[6] But it was to Fianna Fáil that Larkin turned. Days earlier a WUI contingent had marched in the funeral procession of Fianna Fáil TD Constance Markievicz and, to the indignation of Count Markievicz, Fianna Fáil let them carry the red banner presented to Larkin in Moscow.[7] On 3 August Larkin called on Éamon de Valera to convene a meeting of groups to oppose 'the tyrannical measures of the government'.[8] When de Valera obliged, only he and Larkin turned up for the conference, which lasted all of ten minutes. Larkin applauded Fianna Fáil's decision to sit in Leinster House on 12 August, and colluded with Fianna Fáil in the general election it precipitated.

The IWL fielded three candidates in the election: Big Jim in North Dublin, Young Jim in County Dublin, and John Lawlor in South Dublin. Aside from a demand for the release of political prisoners, their election address outlined a long list of specific, incremental demands.[9] Carney mounted a hectic campaign, organising five to ten meetings each night. The IWL's main target was the Labour Party. Labour had challenged Big Jim's nomination on the grounds that he was an undischarged bankrupt, and both sides swapped merciless abuse during the campaign.[10] Big Jim hounded Tom Johnson's meetings in person, and on one occasion was physically attacked by Johnson's son.[11] His united front tactics towards Fianna Fáil paid a dividend, and he was supported by Fianna Fáil candidates, as well as by Willie Gallacher and Shapurji Saklatvala, currently MP for Battersea North.[12] The outcome was a fleeting triumph. The League won 12,500 votes, and Big Jim romped home on the first count with 7,490 votes, the only communist ever elected to Dáil Éireann. Young Jim helped unseat Johnson. Labour took its revenge in instigating Big Jim's disqualification from Dáil Éireann as a bankrupt.[13] The Comintern offered to clear the debts, but as they arose out of the litigation involving the ITGWU and Johnson, Larkin refused. Instead, he staged an alternative 'tattoo' to the grand finale of Dublin Civic Week in September, leading a torchlight parade from Marlborough Street to Burgh Quay, opposite Liberty Hall, where he told a large crowd of what he would do if he could take his Dáil seat.[14] The ECCI sent a detailed policy statement, endorsing his anti-imperialist united front line, but advising him to turn his guns on Fianna Fáil rather than the Labour Party.[15]

The outcome of the election merely confirmed the ECCI in its view that conditions had long been favourable for a party, and that Larkin had been the principal obstacle. Fineberg thought his motivation in activating the IWL was purely to come 'into the limelight'. Larkin continued to fudge about developing a party without 'guarantees', and when Hilt assured him that aid would be forthcoming:

> Larkin replied that he had been given many promises before that were not carried out, with the result that he had got into heavy personal debt. Apparently this

interview bore an extremely heated character because the representative says that it brought him to the state that the seriously thought of leaving the country.[16]

Hilt was not the best man to handle Larkin. He suffered a nervous breakdown in 1929 and was given a quieter job as a translator for the VKP(b). Carney tried to put the IWL on some kind of footing, and a press appeal for members attracted 200 letters of enquiry.[17] But when Hilt left Ireland in October, Larkin's procrastination again predominated.

BY-PASSING LARKIN

Moscow had already begun to outflank Larkin. Fineberg observed in August that unless cadres could be found to counterbalance him, the proposed party would be 'at the constant mercy of [his] caprices'.[18] The outcome was the despatch of students to the Lenin School. Whereas none of its initial 75 places were allocated to Ireland when the ECCI discussed its establishment in March 1926, the school would eventually admit 20 Irish students, almost as many as it took from Switzerland, and Moscow wanted more.[19] Suspecting mischief afoot, Big Jim had been reluctant to delegate anyone other than Young Jim, but his favourite son was keen to repair relations between Dublin and Moscow. For the moment, the project worked to Big Jim's advantage. It removed a few hot-heads from Dublin and Young Jim persuaded the ECCI that the IWL executive would push for the formation of a party.[20] Big Jim hoped the scholar revolutionaries would give him some leverage in Moscow. He got a rude awakening when he wrote to Laszlo Rudas, the Lenin School's Hungarian pro-rector, requesting financial assistance for some students, and appraising others. Rudas, a strict old Bolshevik, rebuked him for political interference and told him to deal with students through the correct channels.[21]

A second key development was the cultivation of links with a transformed IRA. In November 1925 the IRA declared its independence from Sinn Féin, and acquired a younger, more radical leadership. The formation of Fianna Fáil dealt a body blow to Sinn Féin, bringing the IRA to the fore in the surviving republican movement. The army council appropriated Sinn Féin's *An Phoblacht* and appointed Peadar O'Donnell as editor. The socialist slant given the paper by O'Donnell complimented changes in the composition of the IRA. As membership dwindled, it assumed a more plebeian hue.[22] By October 1926 republicans were preparing anti-Poppy Day protests under the rubric of the League Against Imperialism, which would soon be a communist front.[23] Prior to the tenth anniversary of the Bolshevik revolution, an International Trade Union Relations Committee was formed in Dublin to send a delegation to

Moscow for the celebrations. The ten-man visiting party included three WUI members and Mick Fitzpatrick, a veteran of the CPI, assistant secretary of the Irish National Union of Vintners', Grocers', and Allied Trades' Assistants, and a member of ICWPA and the IRA army council. Fitzpatrick had had some contact with Hilt during the latter's Irish residency. He had further discussions with Comintern leaders in Moscow, and was appointed to the presidium of the newly established International Friends of Soviet Russia.[24] Larkin also travelled for the celebrations, embarking at Cobh on the *Bremen* for its home port on 24 October.[25]

The ECCI meanwhile grappled with the more embarrassing consequences of the election, which its critics on Britain's far left were quick to exploit. Larkin had called on workers to vote IWL and Fianna Fáil, the WPI had endorsed the Labour Party and Fianna Fáil, while the CPGB urged votes for the IWL, Labour, and Fianna Fáil, for which it was denounced by the WPI.[26] 'More communist trickery' scoffed the *Socialist Standard*, organ of the Socialist Party of Great Britain. Supplements on Ireland during the hustings in the *Sunday Worker* included interviews with Mrs Despard and Maud Gonne of the WPI, and Saklatvala made contacts with the WPI when in Dublin. The Anglo-American secretariat drafted a detailed brief on policy, endorsing the IWL's tactics in the general election, but advising a more critical line towards Fianna Fáil and less hostility to the Congress based labour movement. It also urged the IWL to become active in the provinces and the six counties, and sugared an appeal for co-operation with the CPGB with the suggestion that the withdrawal of British unions from Ireland might be raised in the 'near future'.[27]

THE NINTH PLENUM AND THE FOURTH WORLD CONGRESS

Larkin's infamous temper was already being provoked by Hilt's successor. Leckie's mission was to organise the IWL with a head office separate from the WUI, install Carney as secretary and editor of a weekly paper, liaise with the recent WUI delegation to Russia regarding publicity, scout for suitable candidates for the Lenin School, and meet with Fitzpatrick. The plan was have a party convention by Easter and confine Larkin to propaganda work. A subsidy of £2,000 was to be made available for the party paper. Leaving Moscow on Christmas day, Leckie spent some time at home in Scotland, and landed in Dublin in mid-January 1928. It was a fruitless journey. Larkin and Carney fobbed off his naïve requests to meet the IWL executive and see IWL records, which in all likelihood did not exist. Leckie's persistence drove Larkin into a towering rage, and he lodged a formal protest with Nikolai Bukharin, who had succeeded Zinoviev as head of the Comintern, about his interference and negotiations with 'terrorists and feudists'. Leckie had been in contact with George McLay and Fitzpatrick, and while the WPI was a beaten docket, Larkin scented a threat in Fitzpatrick and was already doing what he could to keep him offstage.[28] The WUI withheld the log books of their delegates to the October revolution celebrations in Moscow from the International Trade Union Relations Committee, preventing it from publishing a souvenir of the visit. The delegates did address several meetings in Dublin, and one in Roscrea, to publicise the trip, but Larkin was in no hurry to start a branch of Friends of Soviet Russia. Only when Fitzpatrick advertised his intention to proceed did he convene a meeting in the Tivoli Theatre on 22 January at which, following a lantern slide show, he and Mrs Despard founded Irish Friends of Soviet Russia.[29] Leckie left Ireland, sadder and wiser, on 1 February.

A week or so later, Larkin and Carney arrived in Moscow for the ninth ECCI plenum. Bukharin spent three hours discussing religion with Larkin, in an effort to elucidate his troublesome Irish enigma. Larkin's defence of the Catholic Church, while foregoing the opportunity to attend mass, left the Comintern chief no more enlightened.[30] Bukharin also invited him to speak in the closing stages of the great debate between Leon Trotsky and Josef Stalin on whether the revolution needed to be international or could survive in one country. Larkin, as usual, declined to comment on Russian affairs, and then offered to draft proposals to heal the rift between the two Soviet leaders. Almost alone among the plenum delegates, he saw the dispute as inter-personal. Nonetheless he inclined to Stalin's side of the argument. Anomalously, he always would favour Stalin and organisation over Trotsky and agitation. Delivering a lecture to 2,000 people at the Moscow Soviet on Ireland, trade unions, and the peasantry, he asked the audience to 'hold up the hands of Stalin'; perhaps the only analogy ever drawn between Stalin and the biblical Joshua.[31] He seemed keen to please his hosts. At the plenum he endorsed the third period tactic of hostility to social democratic parties, criticising the CPGB's reservations about the application of the line.[32]

The green monster resurfaced where Larkin's record and interests were at issue. Harry Wicks, from Battersea, who could marvel at the power of his oratory, recalled his pettiness before English students at the Lenin School:

> [he] opened by casting his eye round us and making some sneering remark about 'all you little Lenins!'. His main theme turned out to be the unlikelihood of a Communist Party ever taking off in Ireland. What stuck in my gullet most was that, for some reason or other, he was very critical of James Connolly. Emphasising the stranglehold of the Catholic church, he went out of his way to note that even Connolly had died in its arms. Now, that may well have been. But Larkin was loading the blame for his current difficulties onto Connolly.[33]

There is no record of Larkin saying anything similar to the Irish section, which organised 'a fine concert with some of the best singers in Moscow and Connolly's photo over the stage' to mark the thirteenth anniversary of his execution.[34] In the plenum's trade union commission Larkin indulged in personal attacks on the CPGB leaders, faulting their record during the miners' lockout, and complaining of the Minority Movement's refusal to campaign for the withdrawal of British unions from Ireland.[35] In the Irish commission he turned his wrath on republicans to discourage Soviet and CPGB contacts with the IRA, presenting a marathon and exceptionally personal diatribe, which *en passant* condemned Connolly's alliance with bourgeois nationalists in 1916, and descended to such exhaustive, petty criticism of the British that the normally meticulous Comintern secretaries abridged the minutes.[36] Despite this terrific subjectivity, Larkin largely got his way. The ECCI modified its directive on Ireland to emphasise that the IWL should operate independently with the proviso that it should seek to win over the best elements of Sinn Féin and the IRA, and recommend electoral transfers to Sinn Féin candidates.[37] Larkin's relations with Lozovsky were more brittle, and a seething antipathy between them worsened to the point that they nearly came to blows. He told Lozovsky that the WUI executive wanted to break with the Profintern unless promises of financial help were made good.[38]

On a lighter note Larkin described with unusually gentle sarcasm his difficulties in obtaining cultural propaganda from the leaden Soviet bureaucracy:

> After a long and wearisome lecture from Mme Kameneva [cultural relations department] who felt that she had a message to deliver, and a victim to appreciate it, I convinced her that there were some people in Ireland who are really one [*sic*] removed from the amoeba stage of life ... She gave me an album containing coloured reprints from many of the Russian painters. A very interesting compilation. I was going to take it with me because I have had such interesting experiences in the USSR regarding promises. But Mme Kameneva would insist that she would send it on along with other interesting matter, by mail. Up to this writing, neither greetings or album, nor other interesting matter has ever reached this land of primitive people.[39]

Before hurrying home to fight the bye-election for his Dáil seat, Larkin did receive copies of *The Battleship Potemkin* and another film, which were confiscated as 'inflammable' contraband by the authorities in England, but later returned.[40]

The wrangling continued at the fourth world congress of the Profintern. The WUI delegation presented a questionnaire to Bukharin implicitly critical of Leckie and Comintern contacts with the CPGB, the WPI, and the IRA, and enquiring whether the ECCI would pay the WUI £247 allegedly allocated to it by the Profintern in 1925. Larkin wrote separately to Lozovsky, urging him to settle 'this long outstanding financial irritation'.[41] Larkin also complained about Fineberg, and Carney carried a written request that Seán McAteer, alias David Twist, be appointed special representative of the IWL and WUI in Moscow, to prevent the Irish sections being 'directed, or misdirected' by the Anglo-American secretariat.[42] Originally from Edentober, near Dundalk, McAteer had travelled to the US in 1915 and joined the Wobblies. Larkin knew him from 1917 at least, when he recommended him to the German agent Carl Witzke for sabotage and propaganda work against Tsarist Russia in Vladivostok.[43] McAteer was active subsequently in the Citizen Army during the Civil War, and fled to Russia with CPGB collusion following a post office raid in Liverpool in 1923.[44] His lack of documentation being a problem, Pete and Big Jim intervened to get him admitted to the VKP(b) in 1925, which was essential to securing work with the Comintern and a major advantage to a career elsewhere. The ECCI declined to appoint him as IWL representative, and McAteer ended his days running the seamen's Interklub and later working for the port authority in Odessa. As a foreigner, he was vulnerable during the Terror, and was shot as a spy by the NKVD in 1937.[45] The congress itself brought more controversy. Aside from Jack Dempsey condemning Larkin as dishonest, Carney announced the WUI's disaffiliation because the Profintern would not compel the Minority Movement to apply its policy on British unions in Ireland. In a rambling speech, he referred too to the financial burden on the WUI.[46] The breach was healed with promises of solidarity. Six months later, the Profintern was complaining of having heard nothing from the WUI.[47]

Aside from everything else, Larkin had come to regard the Profintern link as a liability. As his confidence in revolutionary trade unionism drained away, he was rattled by stirrings of Catholic anti-communism. The first of what were intended to be annual 'Catholic social weeks' had been organised in April by the Federation of Catholic Young Men's Societies, and featured lectures by P. J. S. Serrarens, secretary of the International Federation of Christian Trade Unions. The secretary of the Dublin trade union unity conference, which was sponsoring merger talks between the rival trades and workers councils, attended and attacked communist trade unionism and the presence of Irish students in the Lenin School, and Serrarens received favourable coverage in the *Irishman*, organ of the Labour Party. Larkin made a mountain, to Moscow, out of the molehill, ignoring the fact that the lectures had generated little interest in Labour circles, and the *Irishman* was taken to task by Frank Robbins for seeming to encourage Catholic trade unionism.[48] Of genuine significance was the amalgamation in November of Dublin trades council and Dublin Workers Council. As Moscow feared, the 'all red' council's communist sympathies were not carried over into the new body, leaving the WUI further isolated.[49]

Larkin's illusions about an alliance with Fianna Fáil were dispelled when the party refused to give him a free run in the bye-election for his Dáil seat in April. He came third in the contest, with 8,232 votes. Hilt returned to Dublin on 27 April to oversee the transformation of the IWL into a party. An issue of the *Irish Worker* appeared on 12 May, with a print run of 5,000 copies. On 13th, about 30 people from Dublin, Belfast, Limerick, and Tipperary attended a conference of the IWL at which the ECCI position on Ireland was endorsed, and Carney elected provisional general secretary. Hilt and Larkin then set off to Berlin for a conference with the Western European Bureau, which handled Comintern liaison with the west. Carney despatched an ebullient report on IWL activities in August, adding a warning that Comintern collaboration with the IRA 'must be stopped'.[50] In reality, nothing had changed or would change.

ROTTEN OLD PETROL

The final break came after Russian Oil Products Ltd (ROP), a London-based division of Soviet Russia's Naptha Syndicate, opened a depot in Dublin in July 1928. A vestige of the company still trades in Ireland as TOP Oil. The Anglo-Russian trade agreement of 1921 made possible the establishment of ROP in August 1924. Importing oil from Batum and dumping it at very competitive prices, ROP soon captured 20 per cent of the British petroleum market, and the nickname 'rotten old petrol' became a familiar joke to British schoolboys. A surge in the price of gasoline on the world market in 1928 made ROP's ZIP motor spirit even more competitive. Russian Oil Products was just the sort of thing that Larkin had been seeking for Ireland and since 1924 he had made repeated claims of promises that the Soviets would become commercially active in Ireland. Hilt pressed his case from July 1927, and in November of that year Maxim Litvinov, assistant commissar of Narkomindel and a former resident of Belfast, and Anatoli Lunacharsky, commissar of education, held a promising discussion on a trade exchange with the Irish representative in Geneva.[51] Larkin pushed again for Soviet 'diplomatic and economic penetration' of Ireland in February 1928, emphasising that considerable potential existed for trade in grain, oil, and timber. The Soviets, he said, agreed to address the question 'without loss of time', though Iveagh House's enthusiasm for an exchange casts some doubt on Narkomindel's sense of urgency.[52] Subsequently the WUI's co-operative approached the Soviet timber trust in London, without results. Unfortunately for Larkin his reputation in business was no more reliable than that in politics. In 1927, as in 1925, he had imported 'unity coal', lost money on the venture, and failed to clear his debts with merchants in Liverpool.[53] Trade with Soviet Russia was another of Larkin's bright ideas frustrated. The Free State and Soviet governments were blowing hot and cold about links at this time. A major contract for the export of Ford tractors from Cork led to the drafting of a commercial treaty in July 1930, but when the Soviets began building their own tractors, the Irish side got cold feet over the political implications.[54]

Russian Oil Products developed into a sizeable operation in Dublin, employing 90 people, including some high-profile sceptics on Larkin, like Roddy Connolly.[55] When Larkin protested that the company was using non-union labour, Bukharin cabled Dublin to say that the work in question was sub-contracted, and that ROP hired union labour only.[56] Larkin then protested that while ROP had approached the Labour Party and was engaging members of the ITGWU and – almost as execrable in his eyes – the British-based Amalgamated Transport and General Workers' Union, it had made no contact with himself and had refused to hire some WUI members. In September he travelled to London to see the senior manager, Rouben Terakopoff, and warned he would end up 'on the Rock Pile in Siberia'.[57] Terakopoff laughed at him, and an outraged Larkin wrote again to Bukharin, and had Carney infringe protocol by beseeching Irish students at the Lenin School to register a formal objection.[58] Carney threatened to withdraw the students from Moscow, complained of Bukharin's failure to fulfil his promises, and announced that the Russian banners presented to the WUI would be returned. Doing his best to turn a crisis into a drama, Carney told Leckie:

> I would rather be a Trotskyite and be wrong than be right among those at the centre . . . Warn other representatives that they must not come here. Our head office is on the third floor, and the drop is none too small.[59]

On foot of a protest from the Irish students, the Anglo-American secretariat raised the matter with the ECCI secretariat, and assured Dublin that an ROP official from London would 'clear up the whole situation'. As for Bukharin's promises, the Anglo-American secretariat told the IWL that they were 'contingent' on receipt of intelligence from Larkin, and until then nothing could be done.[60]

The Comintern conceded that ROP had made mistakes, but the Soviets were not willing to deepen their dependency on a man who had lost their confidence. In addition, and despite the fact that it employed communists and spies and was watched by MI5 and the Garda, ROP was a genuine commercial enterprise to earn valuta.[61] Larkin made his last trip to Russia in January 1929 to ensure that his appeal reached the highest authorities.[62] In a weasel-worded letter he pleaded that unless the dispute was resolved in the WUI's favour, membership opinion would compel him to resign from the union executive, and his place might be taken by non-communists.[63] Stalin heard the case on 7 February at a meeting of the VKP(b) politburo. On the proposal of Lozovsky and Grigori Sokolnikov, soon to be Soviet ambassador to Britain, the politburo agreed that the Soviet trade representative in London should review the ROP apparat in Ireland in the light of Larkin's allegations, and that ROP be directed to employ trade union labour only; preference was to be given to the hiring of WUI members, but the union was not to be allowed organise a monopoly of ROP employees and no deals were done with Larkin on the sale of fuel.[64]

For all his earlier indignation, Carney did not see the ROP affair as a breaking point. On 19 February, before Larkin returned, he wrote fraternally to Lozovsky seeking Profintern help with propaganda work. It was probably soon after that that Larkin severed his official ties with Moscow.[65] In two undated documents, he announced his political retirement from 'active work', and asked the Comintern to keep faith with the Irish at the Lenin School, stressing that Young Jim was his own man and an earnest communist. Moscow respected this request. It was more cynical about the claim that the IWL remained a genuine affiliate under Carney's leadership. Larkin was less reticent in declaring the WUI's irrevocable disaffiliation from the Profintern, blaming the Profintern's lack of financial support for the union, and Lozovsky for intriguing against him with the WUI delegation to Moscow in March 1928. He also stated that the WUI was 'constantly under fire' for its Profintern membership.[66] It is true that attitudes were changing, as the Catholic Church began to awaken to its social power. It is true also that Larkin realised that Moscow was preparing to by-pass him through the IRA left – which he had tried to stop – and through the Irish at the Lenin School, which he could hardly oppose as this group included Young Jim. Yet the ROP business had enormous, and secret, significance for him. After all, the Soviets did agree to 'clear up' ROP and give preferential treatment to the WUI. It would be consistent with Larkin's character and aims in his relations with Moscow if the refusal to do a deal with him on the sale of oil was the real breaking point. It amounted to final proof that he was never going to obtain from Russia the money to be free of the burden of union work. Just how sore he felt over his treatment by ROP management would be revealed in 1930.

Surrendering his status as an international communist leader signified the end of grand ambition. Very quickly, Larkin lost international visibility, and his reputation suffered. For one who liked acclaim, travel, and sharing platforms with globally renowned revolutionaries, it could not have been an easy decision.

He was a proud man, and had suffered enough humiliation, but again, there was shrewd calculation in the decision. He knew he wasn't going to get anything more out of Moscow, so why put his union in the firing line for the ungrateful reds? The WUI was his bread and butter, and he was quite pragmatic about it. Though his communism had not amounted to anything of substance, the retreat from Moscow signalled his abandonment of revolutionism in trade unionism. In politics, the process would take a little longer. For the moment, he clung to the dream that had become so wrapped up with his image, and hoped to remain a communist of sorts. But if he was shaken by Catholic power in 1928, he would find much worse to come.

NOTES

1   *Workers' Republic*, 18 June, and first issue October 1927.

2   RGASPI, Carney to ECCI, 20 July 1927, 495/89/42–3; report on the IWL, 22 February 1928, 495/89/50–51/69.

3   RGASPI, digest of communications received from representative [in] Ireland, undated [August 1927], 495/89/104–184/189.

4   RGASPI, minutes of sub-committee to consider letter to IWL, 22 December 1927, 495/89/40–13.

5   RGASPI, digest of communications received from representative [in] Ireland, undated [August 1927], 495/89/104–184/189; to the executive committee, IWL, 26 July 1927, 495/89/42–4/7.

6   RGASPI, report of IWL meeting, 29 July 1927, 495/89/42–18/19.

7   *Wilmington News-Journal*, 18 July 1927.

8   J. Anthony Gaughan, *Thomas Johnson, 1872–1963: First Leader of the Labour Party in Dáil Éireann* (Dublin, 1980), p. 302.

9   RGASPI, IWL election address, September 1927, 495/89/47.

10 Séamus Collins, 'The situation in Ireland', *Communist International*, 1 February 1928, pp. 53–6.

11 Gaughan, *Thomas Johnson*, pp. 302, 309, 324–5; Donal Nevin, 'Workers of the world', in Donal Nevin (ed.), *James Larkin: Lion of the Fold* (Dublin, 1998), p. 339.

12 RGASPI, digest of communications from representative in Ireland, undated [September 1927], 495/89/45–40/44.

13 Collins, 'The situation in Ireland', pp. 53–6; NA, DT, election to Dáil Éireann and 'unseating' of James Larkin Sr as an undischarged bankrupt, 1927–8, S5562.

14 Christopher Murray, *Seán O'Casey: Writer at Work, a Biography* (Dublin, 2004), p. 196.

15 RGASPI, ECCI to IWL, 495/3/46–207/11.

16 RGASPI, digest of communications from representative in Ireland, undated [September 1927], 495/89/45–42.

17 Ibid.

18 RGASPI, digest of communications received from representative [in] Ireland, undated [August 1927] 495/89/104–189; digest of communications from representative in Ireland, 22 September 1927, 495/89/45–44.

19   RGASPI, sixth ECCI plenum, 8 March 1926, 495/164/500–50/82; letter to Irish students, 8 February 1930, 495/89/65–6; Barry McLoughlin, *Left to the Wolves: Irish Victims of Stalinist Terror* (Dublin, 2007), pp. 30–1; José Gotovitch and Mikhail Narinski et al (eds), *Komintern, L'Histoire et les Hommes: Dictionnaire Biographique de l'Internationale Communiste en France, en Belgique, au Luxembourg, en Suisse et a Moscou (1919–1943)* (Paris, 2001), pp. 595–8.

20   RGASPI, minutes of sub-committee on IWL, 22 December 1927, 495/89/40–13/14.

21   Barry McLoughlin, 'Proletarian academics or party functionaries? Irish Communists at the International Lenin School, Moscow, 1927–37', *Saothar* 22 (1997), pp. 63–79.

22   Dónal Ó Drisceoil, *Peadar O'Donnell* (Cork, 2001), pp. 40–4; Brian Hanley, *The IRA, 1926–1936* (Dublin, 2002), p. 11, 114.

23   PRONI, Charlotte Despard papers, diary, 8, 22 October 1926, D/2479/1/9.

24   NA, DT, memo, September 1931, S5864B; RGASPI, Irish Labour Defence League annual report, 7 July 1929, 539/3/644–2/5; report on the IWL, 22 February 1928, 495/89/50–51/69.

25   *Irish Independent*, 25 October 1927.

26   *Workers' Republic*, first issue October 1927.

27   RGASPI, ECCI to IWL, undated [December 1927], 495/3/46–207/211; Collins, 'The situation in Ireland', pp. 53–6.

28   RGASPI, IWL to ECCI, 2 February 1928, 495/89/49–1/10.

29   RGASPI, letter from Fitzpatrick, 31 March 1928, 495/89/52–24/25; report on the IWL, 22 February 1928, 495/89/50–51/69.

30   Letter from Carney in Donal Nevin, 'Larkin and Connolly', in Nevin (ed.), *James Larkin*, p. 400.

31   Jack Carney memoir on Larkin, written for Emmet Larkin and kindly passed on to the author. For further praise of Stalin see the *Irish Worker*, 18 July 1931.

32   Emmet Larkin, *James Larkin: Irish Labour Leader, 1876–1947* (London, 1965), pp. 291–2.

33   Harry Wicks, *Keeping My Head: The Memoirs of a British Bolshevik* (London, 1992), p. 122.

34   Cited in McLoughlin, *Left to the Wolves*, p. 30.

35   RGASPI, ninth ECCI plenum, fifth sitting, 13 February 1928, 495/167/75.

36   RGASPI, minutes of the Anglo-American secretariat, 20 February 1928, 495/72/34–1/28.

37   RGASPI, the immediate tasks of the IWL, 7 April 1928, 495/3/62–25/29.

38   Larkin, *James Larkin*, p. 297; RGASPI, statement from Larkin on WUI disaffiliation from the Profintern, undated [1929], 495/89/104–137.

39   RGASPI, report on films, cultural relations, economic and diplomatic penetration, undated [1928], 495/89/104–133/136.

40   Ibid.

41   RGASPI, IWL questionnaire, 2 February 1928, 495/89/49–1/3; Larkin to Lozovsky, 13 March 1928, 534/7/286–86.

42   RGASPI, Larkin to Piatnitsky, 13 March 1928, 495/298/19–6; Larkin to Comintern, 18 April 1928, 495/49/49–16.

43   Larkin, *James Larkin*, pp. 217–18.

44   I am obliged to D. R. O'Connor Lysaght and Barry McLoughlin for details on MacIntyre. See also McLoughlin, *Left to the Wolves*, pp. 219–83.

45   RGASPI, Larkin to Piatnitsky, 13 March 1928, 495/298/19–6; letter from Larkin, 18 April 1928, 495/89/49/–12/16.

46   RGASPI, Profintern congress, eighth session, 22 March 1928, 534/1/68–19/27.

47 RGASPI, Profintern to WUI, undated [1928], 534/6/79–33.

48 RGASPI, letter from Larkin, 18 April 1928, 495/89/49–12/16; *Irishman*, 21–28 April 1928.

49 Séamus Cody, John O'Dowd, and Peter Rigney, *The Parliament of Labour: 100 Years of the Dublin Council of Trade Unions* (Dublin, 1986), pp. 148–50; RGASPI, report to the ECCI from Christian Hilt, 6 June 1928, 495/89/50–39/42; Profintern to WUI, 6 July 1928, 534/6/79–28/31.

50 RGASPI, letter from Larkin, 18 April 1928, 495/89/49–12/16; report to the ECCI from Christian Hilt, 6 June 1928, 495/89/50–39/42; report from Carney, 8 August 1928, 495/89/50–43/50.

51 RGASPI, memorandum on the establishment of direct relations between the USSR and the Irish Free State, undated [1927 or 1928], 495/89/107–1/5; Ronan Fanning et al (eds), *Documents on Irish Foreign Policy, Vol. III, 1926–1932* (Dublin, 2002), M. MacWhite to Joseph P. Walshe, 30 November 1927, p. 162.

52 Fanning et al (eds), *Documents on Irish Foreign Policy, Vol. III*, memorandum by the Department of External Affairs to Diarmuid O'Hegarty (Dublin) on Irish Free State commercial relations with the USSR, 7 April 1930, pp. 522–4.

53 RGASPI, report on films, cultural relations, economic and diplomatic penetration, undated [1928], 495/89/104–133/136; Gaughan, *Thomas Johnson*, pp. 272–6; Donal Nevin, 'Titan at bay', in Nevin (ed.), *James Larkin*, p. 79.

54 Matt Treacy, *The Communist Party of Ireland, 1921–2011: Vol. I, 1921–1969* (Dublin, 2012), pp. 53–4.

55 Ibid., p. 26.

56 RGASPI, Bukharin to Larkin, 28 July [1928], 495/89/49–17; note, undated [1928], 495/89/52–5.

57 *Irish Worker*, 22 November 1930.

58 RGASPI, Profintern to Guser, Larkin's statement, 6 February 1929, 495/89/56–1/7; *Irish Worker*, 22 November 1931; Carney to Heimo, 17 September 1928, 495/89/52–6; Carney to Larkin Jr, 6 November 1928, 495/89/52–13/15.

59 RGASPI, Carney to Jack [Leckie], 16 October 1928, 539/3/643–1/6.

60 RGASPI, Anglo-American secretariat to Piatnitsky, 20 November 1928, 495/89/49–11; Anglo-American secretariat to IWL, 1 December 1928, 495/89/49–20.

61 NAUK, file on ROP, HO 144/17917; Krivitsky file, KV2/805.

62 Nevin (ed.), *James Larkin*, contains a photo of Larkin with Transcaucasus delegates to the seventh all-union conference of Mestrans, dated January 1929, but there is no other evidence of a visit.

63 RGASPI, Profintern to Guser, Larkin's statement, 6 February 1929, 495/89/56–1.

64 RGASPI, protocol no 63 of the politburo, 7 February 1929, 17/3/725–1/2. I am obliged to Barry McLoughlin for this reference. *Workers' Voice*, 31 May 1931.

65 RGASPI, Carney to the Party Convention of the Workers' (Communist) Party, 27 January 1929, 515/1/160–1/3; Carney to Lozovsky, 19 February 1929, 534/7/266–93/94.

66 RGASPI, letters from Larkin, undated [1929], 495/89/49–18, 495/89/104–137.

FOURTEEN

THE LARKINTERN, 1929–33

I'm the Committee now; I'm the Union!
Red Jim, in Seán O'Casey, *The Star Turns Red*, Act II

—

At 55 years of age, and believing himself to be younger, James Larkin was by no means ready for any form of retirement, and hoped to carry on as leader of a movement, reviving the *Irish Worker* in October 1930. The plan was to develop the WUI as a reformist union while continuing the IWL as before, allowing him to combine self-interested pragmatism with self-indulgent radicalism and be his own personal communist. The ambition was frustrated by Moscow and Rome.

Larkin's breach with Moscow was not known in Dublin for some months, and he continued to receive communist emissaries and, on occasion, upstage his rivals with counter-demonstrations.[1] George McLay first heard of the ECCI's new Irish policy in London in September 1929 and advised the Connolly Club, which was preparing to transform itself into a party 'adhering to the programme' of the Comintern.[2] The arrival of agents of the Comintern's Irish commission that September promised an end to the andrewmartins. The commission's aim was to build a party that would be Bolshevised, ie. grounded in Leninism, ready to operate under Comintern rules, and loyal to Moscow. Great care was taken to ensure that the party would not go the way of its predecessors. The communists first traded as the Revolutionary Workers' Party, then from November 1930 as the Revolutionary Workers' Groups (RWG), and only from June 1933 did they dignify themselves as a communist party and become the second CPI. It might have been worse for Larkin. The Comintern was currently in its 'third period' phase, guided by the slogan 'class against class'. Larkin's case illustrates how flexible the ECCI could be, even at the zenith of Bolshevisation. In Ireland, the third period line was not to be applied towards Larkin or the IRA until the party's future was secure. In the interim, Moscow sought to keep him on-side, at best as the figurehead of the proposed party, at worst as a benign neutral. Neither option commended itself to Larkin, who knew it was just a matter of time before he was marginalised.

Rome's intervention was more unexpected. Catholic policy on communism changed fundamentally in 1930. The Vatican had regarded the disestablishment of the Russian Orthodox Church after 1917 as an opportunity, and sought a concordat with the Soviet government permitting Roman clergy to prose-lytise in Russia. The Soviets admitted an apostolic delegate who ordained priests and bishops between 1925 and 1927, but following recognition from the British and American governments, they turned less co-operative.[3] By 1928, Pope Pius xi had concluded that open confrontation with communism was only a matter of time. Pius was already championing Catholic action as a social and political answer to the world's descent into crises, and the Irish faithful were starting to respond with the creation of Catholic social studies circles. The call to Catholic action was reinforced by one of the most influential papal encyclicals, *Quadragesimo Anno*, in 1931, marking the fortieth anniversary of the first papal encyclical on the labour question. In theory, Catholic action was an alternative to capitalism and communism, in practice its targets were modernism, liberalism, and socialism. When Pope Pius publicly condemned Soviet persecution of Catholics in February 1930, expiatory masses were said throughout the Catholic world. After saying nothing on the subject in the 1920s, when it had greatest cause for concern, the Irish hierarchy waged its most complete onslaught on communism between 1930 and 1933, and made communism a political taboo for the next 30 years.

Even the WUI became problematic. Its perennial financial difficulties were intensified by the profits squeeze that came with the Great Depression. Larkin's enthusiasm for militancy was found wanting, and together with in-creasing criticism of the lack of internal democracy, it eroded his confidence, and drained away the acclaim that fuelled his drive. Larkin's response was to retreat into a more obscure individualism. It was not the kind of answer he would have given before, and it showed that he was getting tired and demoral-ised. He neither opposed the communists, nor assisted them or allowed them any influence in the WUI. His response to clericalism was less enigmatic, and there is no doubt that he was intimidated by the sudden upsurge of Catholic anti-communism, which mobilised the most comprehensive anti-radicalism he had ever experienced. For the first time in his life he flinched from moving to the left of his rivals. In 1932 the IWL was discarded for an 'Independent Labour' ticket in politics, and the WUI became more of a personal, than a personality driven, union.

COLD SHOULDERING THE COMINTERN

A tense relationship with the communists continued to 1932, suffered by Moscow in the hope of winning Larkin over or fear of provoking his wrath. At the same time, the Comintern was determined to be free of dependence on its treacherous Irish ally. An opportunity had arisen when Josef Stalin initiated a

general chistka or purge of Bukharinites and other 'right-wing' elements opposed
to his forced collectivisation policies; Nikolai Bukharin himself was removed
from power in the Comintern, eventually arrested, given a show trial, and shot.
Purges had their various uses. When the chistka reached the Lenin School in
September 1929, it provided an excuse to cleanse the students of all suspect
sympathies. Harry Wicks described the process as gruelling, with the whole
school assembling in the auditorium day after day for weeks on end to watch
each teacher and student being grilled before the dignatories of the VKP(b)'s
chistka commission.[4] For the Irish, the virus was deemed to be Larkinism.
Suspected Larkinites were isolated from the revision of policy on Ireland, and
Tom Bell had Young Jim removed as the anglophone sector's 'partorg', or
party organiser; a prestigious post which entailed responsibility for the politics
and academic progress of students. Bell, a Scottish Canadian and not to be
confused with the Glaswegian of that name who wrote *Pioneering Days*, had
worked with the Irish commission in Moscow and would lead its three-man
team in Dublin.[5] He had little regard for the peculiarities of the Irish situation
and was impatient to apply the third period theses in Ireland. Objections from
Young Jim, Pat Breslin, Seán Murray, and Charlie Ashmore about their 'progressive and intentional exclusion . . . from discussions on Irish questions', led
to an official investigation. It found in favour of the Irish, but Young Jim was
not reinstated as partorg. Like other students, Young Jim was subjected to
Stalin's newly prescribed therapy of Bolshevik 'self-criticism', in which comrades
were encouraged to expose their weaknesses before the party. No doubt
Young Jim was not alone in hating the practice. 'It is correct,' he admitted

> that it was difficult to extricate myself from Larkin's influence, but the school has
> helped me in this. I hope that it will be always possible for me, as a party-member,
> to reach the correct point of view in all questions and that we will only have to take
> Larkin's influence into account in as much as he shares our views.[6]

Though strained, the confession can be corroborated. He freely acknowledged
his father's peculiarities in 1930 and Irish colleagues later recalled him as 'fairly
objective' on the subject.[7] Moscow meanwhile prevailed on him to advise his
father of moves ahead and ask him to keep silent. In time, the ECCI hoped,
he would entice the big man back into the fold. Inclined naturally to think the
better of his father, Young Jim shared this optimism, but found his role as
intermediary uncomfortable. Father and son shared a deep respect – Big Jim
scarcely refers to his other children in extant records – without being very commu-
nicative. Young Jim was reserved and shy, and it was Jack Carney, for example,
who wrote to allay his worries about a difference between his parents over
Elizabeth's financial allowance – Carney himself having interceded to resolve

the problem – and promise to see about a suit and a camera he had requested. Moreover, the suit and the camera were to come out of Carney's pocket.[8]

In September 1929 Bell and Bob Stewart arrived in Dublin with orders not to disturb 'the big noise'. A third member of the commission, Dan Buckley, was to work in his native Cork.[9] Moscow's courting of Larkin irritated the Dublin-based communists, who were thoroughly disillusioned with him. Having to pull punches was all the more tortuous while the Comintern's policy of 'class against class' urged implacable opposition to reformists and deviation-ists.[10] Big Jim's uncharacteristic silence about the web being spun about him kept the communists guessing. He had told Moscow that he wished to retire from politics; a claim echoed by Young Jim.[11] But Bell had no faith in Moscow's benign scenario and warned that Larkin had promised to 'settle their hash'.[12] On 26 October Bell sent the politsecretariat a dismissive report on the Dublin left. The WUI, he wrote, had become a reformist union, and Larkin's 'outra-geous conduct' made it impossible to use the IWL as a basis for a party. He was scarcely more positive about other radical groups.[13] On discovering in December 1929 that the Profintern had invited Larkin to its next plenum, he, Stewart, and Buckley promptly complained to the ECCI that 'when we started this work we understood that the policy of the Comintern was to work inde-pendently of Larkin', and demanded a clarification of Moscow's position.[14] The communist *Workers' Voice* tendered guarded criticism of WUI reformism, usually taking care to avoid attacks on the man himself.

In the summer of 1930 the ECCI resolved to advance the process of Bolshevisation by extending 'class against class'. Following reports from Bell and Stewart in March, a 2,700-word resolution arguing for the launch of a party was drafted for a meeting of the Anglo-American secretariat on 20 April. Acknowledging the challenges posed by the confusion of ideas and fear of clerical and reformist Labour hostility, the paper advised that these could best be tackled through doctrinal clarity, the application of 'class against class' to the IRA and Larkin.[15] In June and July the ECCI dictated several drafts of a 2,000-word letter to comrades in Ireland. The ECCI's most important revision was to demand continued diplomacy towards Larkin. The WUI remained, in ECCI parlance, 'the open revolt of the militant proletariat in Dublin against the treachery of the Labour Party and trade union leaders.' Whether Moscow really believed this, despite intelligence from Dublin to the contrary, is doubtful. The ECCI was anxious to get a WUI delegation to the forthcoming fifth Profintern congress and to plant the seeds of a communist fraction within the union. Young Jim carried the instructions home when he and Murray returned from the Lenin School in July 1930.[16] In the communists' first personal approach to Big Jim, they met him in July. During an 'extremely difficult' audience, they found him 'very embittered', especially that Stewart, with whom he had been close, had not been in touch. Russian Oil Products also remained a sore point. Tentatively, Murray and Young Jim concluded that an accord was possible if the big man was handled with sensitivity.[17] Sensitivity was hardly a forte of the ROP management. In September the company opened a new installation in Dublin port in the presence of Soviet diplomats. One of the guests at a banquet that evening in the Gresham Hotel was William O'Brien, who assured his hosts that Irish Labour had no objection to 'foreign capital'.[18] The *Worker's Voice* tactfully ignored the occasion. Big Jim soon had his revenge with the recall of Rouben Terakopoff, and ROP's financial director, Dr L. B. Rabinovitch, to Moscow for having become too influenced by capitalism. A vicious editorial in the *Irish Worker* – 'Delousing ROP' – gloated over the horrors of Stalinism.

> All things come to those that wait . . . We have waited Rabinovitch's brother and lady [*sic*]. They are on the Rock Pile in Siberia. Terakopoff laughed when we told him what awaited him. *Now for the others*. Big Fleas have little fleas upon their backs, and so ad infinitum. A cold blast from the East will kill off not only the Big Fleas, Rabinovitch, Terakopoff, but others will popoff.
> Soviet flea powder is slow to act, but very salutary and sanitary.[19]

Terakopoff and Rabinovitch sought asylum in Britain.[20] In Dublin, ROP would be plagued by inter-union disputes between the WUI and ITGWU.

The ECCI tried to appease Larkin by criticising the application of the line on Ireland, and its failure to differentiate between the WUI and unions 'where the bureaucracy is now completely social-fascist'. Bell was rebuked for 'political mistakes and [a] generally sectarian attitude', and recalled to Moscow. Young Jim, Murray, and Bill Denn, another graduate of the Lenin School, were to comprise the new leadership, assisted by Stewart. There was also to be an investigation of ROP.[21] Big Jim was not placated, and his son's position became ever more awkward.

Despite the tension, Big Jim continued to share the communist outlook on many issues. The *Irish Worker* lavished praise on Soviet Russia and the 'Shannon schemes' of the five-year plan, the Shannon hydro-electric scheme having been the mightiest engineering project of the Free State. Like the communists Jim was sceptical about Saor Éire, criticising its lack of intellectual ballast, he damned the Labour Party for its anti-republicanism, and endorsed the third period line, applying its logic to one of his pet hates in the Labour movement, the well-heeled leader of the Irish Women Workers' Union:

> The issue in Germany is: FASCISM versus COMMUNISM, with every party, apart from the Communist Party, supporting moves towards a Fascist dictatorship. It is

for this reason that the British Labour government supports the capitalists of Germany. As the crisis in Germany develops the Social Democrats are being more and more exposed, with the Communist Party increasing its support.

Miss Louie Bennett, the pacifist, becomes a supporter of Fascism.[22]

With her 'respectable middle-class' background, as she put it herself, her bungalow in salubrious Killiney, and her moderate and moderately confusing ideas, the gentle Miss Bennett was an easy target. The Larkins also remembered how Bennett had taken over the Women Workers' Union on Delia's departure to London in 1915, and how the union refused to re-admit Delia on her return to Dublin in 1918. Bennett could be firm when it suited her.[23]

THE INDUSTRIAL FRONT

The friction between Big Jim and the communists extended into industrial relations and to the British-based unions, 'the greatest bulwark of British imperialism in Ireland', according to Delia. 'IRISH WORKERS IN IRISH UNIONS' urged Jim,

> welded together into one fighting Irish Labour Movement is the only policy for Irish workers. Any other policy will be a waste of time and barren of results . . .
>
> In the broad field of international action you have not been behind when the call for international solidarity has gone forward. It is in no narrow national sense that you are now advised to organise into Irish unions . . .[24]

It did not help that for all three elements, Jim, the communists, and the British unions, transport was a key sector, and of all sectors in the still contracting trade union movement, transport was worst hit. Rationalisation in the five years after 1926 led to wage cuts and some 5,000 redundancies. The WUI countered with a recruitment campaign, and between 1928 and 1930 it enrolled 400 busmen and 700 labourers in the railway shops at Inchicore and Broadstone. Big Jim became chairman of an inter-union 'council of action' at the Inchicore railway works. The council's acceptance of job losses and ten per cent pay cuts following a strike in February 1929 generated a fresh resolve to challenge him.[25] He remained chairman and claimed credit for forcing the Great Southern Railway to withdraw 600 dismissal notices in 1931. Emboldened, Jim led a Mansion House conference of railwaymen to initiate a national campaign for the nationalisation of the railways.[26] While equally averse to Britain's 'labour imperialists', the communists were aghast at Larkin's appeal for national rather than revolutionary unions. Noting his continuing collaboration with the

National Union of Railwayman, they derided the policy as opportunist and camouflage for moderation. Larkin could claim some vindication in 1933 when the British Minority Movement secretariat conceded the poor fighting record of key cross-channel unions in Ireland, and belatedly concluded that Irish conditions required a native trade union movement.[27]

The biggest struggle of the period for communists was the Dublin building strike. With fractions in the WUI, the ITGWU, and the Irish National Union of Woodworkers, the RWG had some hope of influencing events. Ashmore and Denn were leading members of the Woodworkers and the union had concluded a solidarity pact with the Forest and Woodworkers' Union of the Soviet Union.[28] In December 1930 RWG militants created a rank-and-file group to encourage opposition to a proposed wage cut.[29] After 12 January, when 3,000 workers struck officially, the rank-and-file group pressed for an extension of the dispute. Three hundred workers attended a conference convened by the group on 18 February.[30] However when the strike ended in April, with acceptance of a modified pay cut, the RWG had lost as much as they had gained. Union leaders had refused to accept any communist influence over strike policy. The National Union of Woodworkers had severed its connection with the Soviet Forest and Woodworkers' Union on receiving no help from Russia other than literature.[31] Relations with Big Jim had worsened. In one instance he walked off a platform at College Green rather than speak with communists, and the *Workers' Voice* denounced his leadership as 'bankrupt'.[32]

In line with the turn to class, the *Workers' Voice* published weekly letters on conditions in various employments, especially linen mills. One exposé evoked a response in the Dublin mill of the Greenmount and Boyne Linen Company, at Harold's Cross. On 16 February the company posted notice of a ten per cent wage cut. The 230 employees promptly struck for a 20 per cent wage increase.[33] Without a trade union they faced a daunting challenge. The communist presence on the strike committee led to their isolation by the Labour movement and attempts to link the dispute with a similar strike in Lurgan were countered by union officials.[34] On 18 March employers tried to re-open the mill with the backing of 16 employees and police escorts. The Labour Defence League helped to mobilise mass pickets on a daily basis.[35] The RWG persuaded the workforce to join the WUI, for want of something better, and in late April Big Jim addressed several mass meetings. His brief rapprochement with the RWG extended to that year's May Day celebrations, when the WUI band led the communist parade in Dublin, and 400 people turned up to hear Young Jim and Bill Rust, CPGB.[36] The defeat of the Greenmount strike in mid-May was not unmitigated. The workers were promised their jobs back, and 200 remained members of the WUI.[37]

The autumn saw Murray emerge as the guiding figure of the RWG. Young Jim was retained in the higher echelons because of his name. It was Young Jim that International Labour Defense, the US wing of International Red Aid, contacted when trying to arrange rallies in Ireland for Mrs Ada Wright, a mother of the 'Scottsboro boys' – eight African Americans falsely convicted of rape in Alabama. Big Jim had publicised their case in the *Irish Worker*.[38] What the Larkins thought of de Valera's refusal to admit Mrs Wright to the Free State is not known. Internally, there were growing complaints of Young Jim failing to make best use of his corporation seat and allowing himself to be constrained by his father: 'unless he is rooted out of the Larkin family concern his effectiveness for the party is going to be very poor', noted one RWG report.[39] Family was the operative word, for Larkin was turning the WUI into an extended family. He had always believed that a union's remit should not end at the factory gate. 'Unity Hall,' he boasted, 'is more than the Head Office of the Workers' Union of Ireland; it is a social centre where the men, women and children of the Dublin working class can enjoy themselves.' There was no doubt about who was the patriarch. Inviting members to a boxing tournament in the hall, he asked them to show their 'appreciation': 'Of course, Jim Larkin will be there. Did you ever know him to miss anything where his own were concerned? It will be worth your money to watch him watching the fights.'[40] With such a personality cult, it was easy for him to exclude the communists and other dissident voices from the WUI. Carney had put the union's membership at 18,000, and if the ECCI knew him to be prone to exaggeration, it is unlikely that it realised that the actual muster was closer to 6,000 by 1929, the union's internal affairs being shrouded in an obfuscation which baffled observers in Dublin no less than Moscow.[41] In response to criticism of the RWG's failure to develop a united front with the WUI, Jim Troy told Moscow that infiltration of the union was impossible. It had held no annual conference for four years, or branch meetings for over six years, and the only meetings permitted were those dominated by Big Jim, who would ramble on for hours on whatever took his fancy.[42] An RWG review in 1932 identified four main obstacles: state repression, labour reformism, the Catholic Church, and the 'virtual' collapse of Larkinism.[43]

'A REPUBLICAN BY CONVICTION, A DOCTRINAIRE REPUBLICAN'[44]

The elections for the new Dublin Municipal Council exposed differences in the Revolutionary Workers' Party, the communists' current flag of convenience, on what to do about Big Jim. Bell wanted a harder line than his editorial board, but his stock was waning as comrades, 'Even the comrade from Coleraine', grumbled about his alcoholism.[45] Obviously, it would not have commended him to Big Jim. On 27 September 1930 the *Workers' Voice* urged readers to vote for the IWL candidates, who 'are standing on a platform of struggle against the renegade reformist Labourites'. The communists fielded two candidates and were given some grounds for optimism. Out of a total poll of almost 70,000, Esther MacGregor, a tenants' leader, received a disappointing 129 votes, but Young Jim was elected for the south city centre area with 967 first preferences, or half the quota.[46] Obviously, the name mattered. The IWL, still representing itself as communist, won 5,940 first preferences, though of its 12 candidates only Big Jim was returned. He had exceeded the quota on the first count with 2,637 votes and was returned for electoral area no 2, comprising Clontarf, Drumcondra, and Glasnevin.[47]

At noon on 14 October he walked back into the chamber from which he had been excluded in 1912. It was a sweet moment for him, and brought forth all his venom against 'the foul, vicious, political thuggery' of his fellow councillors, especially the populist Alfie Byrne, 'the shaking hand of Dublin'. Big Jim announced that while he would prefer to vote for 'a nominee of my own class', he would vote for Seán T. O'Kelly for Lord Mayor, because 'I am a Republican by conviction, a doctrinaire Republican'.[48] He was also an enthusiast for Fianna Fáil's tariff protection policy, an indignant critic of Trinity College – 'the Trinity of evils: privilege, bigotry, obstruction' – and a passionate opponent of poppy day.[49] 'The World War has not been forgotten', he warned in one of several philippics.

> Here in Ireland we have the British Legion to for ever remind us of it. Every November the soil of Ireland is degraded by the sellers of poppies. The blood of those who died is distilled into gold to further strengthen the bonds of slavery.[50]

Immediately after the election, Big Jim revived the *Irish Worker: An t-Oibridhe Gaodhlach* and prepared to make the IWL more active, with Carney as secretary. 'A number of Comrades have determined it shall live,' he explained:

> Who am I that I should refuse to carry out an order? I am always described as a Dictator, etc, etc. In fact I am an overworked subservient slave, but free because I know that I am a slave, and enjoy my slavery, knowing that without freedom for my class I must continue to be a slave.[51]

The 1930 numbers ran to four pages and cost 1d. The editor appealed to readers to form a limited company to finance the paper, and was able to double the size in 1931. Content usually featured items on working conditions, news of the WUI, snippets on sport, mainly soccer, boxing, and billiards, and longer opinion articles, written mainly by Larkin. The quality of editorial pieces varied from vituperative sniping at his opponents on the right and on the left, to incisive criticism of government policy, broadsides on industrial relations, timely alarms on European fascism and Japanese aggression in China, naïve encomiums of Soviet Russia, and a considerable number of items on America, its labour bosses, gangsters, banksters, and boxers. Some contributions, on women workers and domestic servants among others, were signed 'DLC', probably Delia Larkin Colgan. All in all, it offered a readable and unique perspective, hungry to thunder against exploitation, malpractice, corruption, and humbug on every side. The communists remained sceptical. On 4 October the *Workers' Voice* declared that the IWL 'had no programme other than that of its leader, Jim Larkin, senr, who posed as "The Friend of the Poor"'. The next issue contained an apology from the editorial board, explaining that the remark was not in conformity with the party's united front policy towards the IWL. But Bell could not restrain his antipathy. At an IWL 'open forum' on unemployment in the Mansion House on 23 November, Big Jim denounced the 'obscurantist campaign' to strangle the *Workers' Voice*, which was being hounded from printer to printer by Catholic pressure groups. Shortly afterwards, Big Jim's Camac Press, at 68 Old Kilmainham Road, which printed the *Irish Worker*, began producing the *Workers' Voice* also. Incredibly, the *Voice* lambasted a chunk of his Mansion House speech, calling for tariffs, as 'tripe'.[52] When the communists reconstituted the Revolutionary Workers' Party as the RWG in November 1930, Big Jim stayed aloof.

Over the following year it became obvious to the RWG that if he was not going to 'settle their hash', neither would he co-operate with them. Not even the proscription of various republican and pro-communist groups in the government induced 'red scare' of October 1931 induced Big Jim to reconsider his solo style. Curiously, the IWL was not on the proscribed list, though Garda Commissioner Eoin O'Duffy had considered including the WUI.[53] Big Jim denounced the repression, slammed the passivity of Fianna Fáil, and observed that the first sod for the altar for the Eucharistic Congress was turned on the day the government introduced the Public Safety bill. But he was just not a team player. On Sunday 18 October the WUI Brass and Reed band led a march to College Green, where thousands protested against the Public Safety bill. Young Jim and Carney spoke with Murray. Big Jim was conspicuous by his absence.[54]

THE WALK TO CANOSSA

On 21 November 1931 Carney assured readers of the *Irish Worker* 'Jim Larkin is OK', and denied accusations that he was drifting to the right. In truth, his hero was withdrawing into the quietest phase of his career. Pete's death in Baggot Street Hospital on 15 May 1931 was a heavy blow. Jim gave him a 'red funeral', without clergy, on a Sunday to boot. Despite the increasingly clerical atmosphere, there was an impressive turnout, and the WUI provided as much ceremony as it could muster for the procession from Unity Hall to Glasnevin. The chief mourners included 'Mrs J. Larkin'. Jim penned a biographical series 'The story of a man' in the *Irish Worker* over the following month.[55]

The 1932 general election was the last hurrah of red Larkinism. Moscow insisted the RWG contest the forthcoming general election in all possible constituencies under the slogan 'For an independent workers' and farmers' republic'; Young Jim Larkin was to be nominated in North Dublin and WUI branches drawn into a united front.[56] Big Jim had other ideas and fought North Dublin himself, as a communist on the old IWL platform of enmity towards the Labour Party and support for Fianna Fáil – compelling the RWG to switch Young Jim to the less propitious South Dublin and make a token effort for Troy in North Dublin. On polling day 'a vociferous army of young-sters, plentifully bedecked with red sashes and red jerseys and carrying red flags' paraded through the streets in Big Jim's support, and Shapurji Saklatvala accompanied him on a tour of the polling stations. The RWG mounted a big effort, producing a campaign paper, *Vanguard*, 60,000 election addresses, and thousands of leaflets for specific groups like the unemployed and republicans.[57] Young Jim polled 917 votes, and Troy 170.

After his own disappointing tally of 3,860 first preferences, Big Jim forsook revolutionism, retiring the IWL, and discontinuing the *Irish Worker* after 12 March.[58] The assault from the right was multi-layered, and prosecuted through the bishops and the Cumann na nGaedheal government, newspapers, journals, lay and clerical groups, middle-class study circles, more demotic fraternities like the Catholic Young Men's Association and parish sodalities, and a few dedicated counter-communist organisations like the Catholic Unemployed (Able-Bodied) Men's Association and St Patrick's Anti-Communism League.[59] Enjoying some protection from their name, the Larkins escaped the worst of the clerical repression visited on the communists and their publications, but pressure was brought to bear. Advertising in the *Irish Worker* dried to a trickle in 1931, and the paper complained of a boycott by 'every corrupt politician, every profiteering shopkeeper, every labour fakir, and the enmity of the Garda Síochána in such places as Bray and elsewhere'. Sixty shops stopped selling it, and newsboys and their families were threatened with loss of work. An appeal to readers in the last issue for a guaranteed 1s a week came too late.[60] For months back it was all too evident that the paper had become disconnected from objectivity. Issues were written entirely by Big Jim and Carney, peppered with eulogies of Jim, and padded with cartoons, photographs, and serialised book chapters. It was not quite the end of Big Jim's editorial career. A cheaply produced bulletin, *Truth That Is News*, appeared from October 1932 to January 1933 when the WUI ran a strike in the *Irish Press*. Proceeds from sales went to the newsboys, for whom Larkin was a champion. He had organised them in 1911, and they reminded him of the two glorious years that stretched between the summers of 1911 and 1913. '[T]he JIM LARKIN of '13 is still much to the fore', claimed the bulletin, and it did reveal some flashes of his old spirit, and even his lingering sympathy with Russia.[61] He admired the Soviet Union to the last, courageously defended it, and never renounced communism. From what he said about ROP management he admitted the existence of the Gulag, and was uncritical of it. Whether he knew of the mass terror and routine judicial murders is unclear. Undoubtedly he believed the Soviet propaganda about the five-year plan, and possibly thought the collective advance of workers outweighed the rights of a few bourgeois individuals. Privately, there were reservations about 'real existing socialism'. In 1935, a starry-eyed John de Courcy Ireland – down from Oxford and about to begin a life on the Irish left – was pained to hear him talk of authoritarianism, shoddy workmanship, and a corrosion of idealism in Russia.[62] As yet, it was not in his nature to explain or apologise; so the public policy was silence, underpinned by a determination to put his red reputation behind him. Moscow's demands for a united front with WUI militants, and repeated attempts by the RWG to organise a WUI fraction, were frustrated by 'the weakness of our leadership inside the union', and the absence of branch meetings; a remarkable indication of Big Jim's iron rule, as Carney, Young Jim, and Barney Conway, were prominent on CPI platforms after the party's foundation in 1933.[63]

For most Dubliners, participation in the Eucharistic Congress in June 1932 was a walk to Canossa and the symbolic end of red Jim. He was, of course, ambivalent on the church and always appreciative of Catholics who were doing good social work. Subsequently, the Legion of Mary, which had been obliged to vacate its house in the Liberties, was allowed to meet in a nearby WUI office and later in Unity Hall.[64] And his absence from what Dublin trades council called a 'magnificent event' would have intensified his quarantine.[65] His stock was falling in any case. When he fought North Dublin in the January 1933 general election as an 'Independent Labour' candidate, the designation he would adopt in all elections up to 1942, his vote dipped to 2,792. In June 1933, he unexpectedly lost his seat on Dublin Corporation. A reasonable showing on the first count was not sustained by transfers. Young Jim, standing for the CPI, finished bottom of the poll.[66]

The retreat from revolution did not spare the WUI from reaction in 1933. Fanned by lenten pastorals and lenten missions, anti-communism reached a crescendo in late March. It would be only the first of several attempts to crush communist organisations in Dublin over the next four years.[67] On Sunday 26 March communist meetings in central Dublin were broken up. Next evening several hundred demanded entry to the RWG's headquarters, Connolly House, and proceeded to smash windows until dispersed by the Garda. On Tuesday Connolly House was besieged again, and the mob went on to attack the Workers' College, the National Unemployed Movement's office, and Unity Hall. On Wednesday, thousands made a third assault on Connolly House, and stoned the Workers' College. Thursday, the final night of terror, saw another attack on the Workers' College. After being held back by Gardaí, the crowd moved on to sing hymns outside the offices of the National Unemployed Movement and Unity Hall.[68] When the storm abated, a few sympathisers from Connolly House called round to find that Denis Larkin had put his lifelong hobby to use by photographing the wreckage.[69]

Another kind of closure to the revolutionary years occurred after Christmas 1933 from an intervention by John J. McCloy and Casimir P. Palmer, who were representing the US government in its pursuit of $40 million compensation for German wartime sabotage in the US. McCloy spent ten days in Dublin breaking down Larkin's suspicion and reluctance to assist what he called 'money groups'. Big Jim drove McCloy about the city, regaled him with stories of America, and recommended a George Bernard Shaw play at the Abbey Theatre. As his sentiment shifted, he asked Young Jim why he shouldn't make a statement. There were a few reasons. He could be seen as turning informant on former confederates, providing justification for the US engagement in the world war, and embarrassing the campaign for the release of Tom Mooney, one of America's most famous political prisoners. Less than three years earlier the *Irish Worker* had published 'Tom Mooney's appeal to the world labour movement from San Quentin Prison, California' in 18 instalments.[70] Young Jim stayed silent. Eventually, Big Jim's anger at the German denials made up his mind, or so he said. Early on New Year's Day, McCloy was summoned to a deserted Unity Hall. With Carney typing away, Big Jim dictated his extraordinary affidavit entirely from memory in a 'trance-like state', oblivious to McCloy, finishing up at 12.30 am on 2 January. It was sworn in the presence of the US consul general in Dublin. The sensational detail was more than McCloy expected. It led US Supreme Court judge Owen J. Roberts to rule that Germany had to respond to the accusations, and saved the American case from collapse. Excerpts were leaked to the American press, which head-lined the implication in sabotage of Ernst Hanfstaengl, a Harvard-educated member of Chancellor Hitler's inner circle. Leaked too was the revelation that McCloy promised his informant £50 for legal expenses. On learning of the stiff fee, the Germans claimed McCloy had bought a confection of lies.[71]

The final phase of Larkin's life as a revolutionary, which began with his embrace of syndicalism in 1910, was over. That he had not abandoned revolutionism on breaking with Moscow is indicative of his deep and sincere anti-capitalism, and of the centrality of revolutionism to his public persona. The attempt to be a revolutionist on his own terms had been as messy and enigmatic as anything that had gone before. He gave it up, not for that reason, but because he had lost faith in the possibility of revolution, even if he still hoped the possibility would return. Less kindly, one could also say that the forces of reaction were too strong.

NOTES

1   RGASPI, Ben Ainley to the political bureau [CPGB], 25 August 1929, 495/89/59–1/3.

2   UCDA, Cowan family papers, Séamus McGowan papers, McLay to the secretary, James Connolly Workers' Club, September 1929, P34/D/34(24).

3   See Anthony Rhodes, *The Vatican in the Age of Dictators, 1922–45* (London, 1973), pp. 131–40.

4   Harry Wicks, *Keeping My Head: The Memoirs of a British Bolshevik* (London, 1992), p. 92.

5   RGASPI, A. J. Bennett to the political secretariat, ECCI, 24 July 1929, 495/3/151–96.

6   Barry McLoughlin, 'Proletarian academics or party functionaries? Irish Communists at the International Lenin School, Moscow, 1927–37', *Saothar* 22 (1997), pp. 68–70.

7   RGASPI, joint report on WUI, S. Murray and J. Larkin Jr, 2 August 1930, 495/89/63–19/27; information from Joe Deasy.

8   RGASPI, Jack to Jim, 8 November 1928, 495/89/52–13.

9   RGASPI, draft letter to the comrades in Ireland, 4 July 1930, 495/20/25–25/28.

10 RGASPI, report, from Bell[?], 27 October 1929, 495/89/54–34, *Workers' Voice*, 5 April 1930.

11 RGASPI, Arthur [?] to Frank [?], 17 November 1929, 495/89/54–53.

12 RGASPI, Tom Bell to Bell, 27 October 1929, 495/89/64–63.

13 RGASPI, preliminary report on the present situation and on our Irish policy, 26 October 1929, 495/89/54–19/25; Arthur [?] to Frank [?], 17 November 1929, 495/89/54–53/63a.

14 RGASPI, Bell, Buckley, and Stewart to the ECCI, 5 December 1929, 495/89/54–76.

15 RGASPI, draft resolution on Ireland for meeting of Anglo-American secretariat, 20 April 1930, 495/89/61–2/9.

16 UCDA, Seán MacEntee papers, 'Notes on communism in Saorstát Éireann', pp. 34–8, P67/523(5).

17 RGASPI, joint report on WUI, S. Murray and J. Larkin Jr, 2 August 1930, 495/89/63–19/27.

18 *Irish Times*, 26 September 1930.

19 *Irish Worker*, 22 November 1930.

20 House of Commons debates, 24 November 1930, vol. 245, cols 874–5; NAUK, nationality and naturalisation, HO 144/17914.

21 RGASPI, draft resolution on Ireland, 1 September 1930, 495/89/61–19/22.

22 *Irish Worker*, 8 August, 26 September, 3 October 1931.

23 Rosemary Cullen Owens, *Louie Bennett* (Cork, 2001), pp. 64, 124–5; Mary Jones, *These Obstreperous Lassies: A History of the Irish Women Workers' Union* (Dublin, 1988), pp. 29–30.

24 *Irish Worker*, 15 November 1930. The editorial was signed 'DLC'. *Irish Worker*, 27 June, 11 July, 8 August 1931.

25 RGASPI, Ben Ainley to the political bureau, 25 August 1929, 495/89/54–1.

26 *Irish Worker*, 5, 26 September 1931.

27 RGASPI, Troy, letter to RWG on RILU in Ireland, 29 June 1932, 495/89/73–1/12; National Minority Movement report, 534/7/53–42.

28 RGASPI, Dublin building trade dispute, RS [Bob Stewart] and SM [Seán Murray] to Robin [Page Arnot?], 17 March 1931, 495/89/69–2; an den Nationalen Holzareiterverband Irlands, 495/89/69–4/6.

29 *Workers' Voice*, 6, 20 December 1930, 10 January 1931.

30 Ibid., 21 February 1931.

31 RGASPI, Troy before the Anglo-American secretariat, 10 June 1932, 495/72/188–6.

32 RGASPI, report from Ireland, 22 March 1931, 495/89/67–54; CPI, *Communist Party of Ireland: Outline History* (Dublin, 1975), p. 30; *Workers' Voice*, 31 January 1931.

33 *Workers' Voice*, 21 February 1931.

34 RGASPI, material about Ireland (From the Irish brigade in the Lenin School), 21 May 1932, 495/89/80–15/18.

35 *Workers' Voice*, 28 March 1931.

36 NA, DJ, Workers' Revolutionary Party, JUS 8/691.

37 RGASPI, [RWG] secretariat, 22 March 1931, 495/89/65–40/42; *Workers' Voice*, 2 May–27 June 1931.

38 *Irish Worker*, 6 June 1931; James A. Miller, Susan D. Pennybacker, and Eve Rosenhaft, 'Mother Ada Wright and the international campaign to free the Scottsboro Boys, 1931–1934', *American Historical Review* 106:2 (April 2001), pp. 387–430. I am obliged to Andrew H. Lee for this reference.

39 RGASPI, report re. national meeting of RWG, 5–6 November 1932, 495/89/82–14/18; abridgement of report of Neptun, 26 January 1931, 495/89/64–2/3; report from secretariat, 31 January 1931, 495/89/65–1/4; to the secretariat, Ireland, 26 February 1931, 495/89/65–20.

40 *Irish Worker*, 23 January 1932.

41 Officially, the WUI claimed 15,095 members in 1928, and 16,159 in 1929, but it gave its income for these years as £4,337 and £6,335 respectively, and each member was worth about £1 per annum. NA, Registry of Friendly Societies files, WUI file, 369T.

42 RGASPI, Troy before the Anglo-American secretariat, 495/72/188–182.

43 NLI, Donal O'Reilly papers, resolution, uncatalogued, ACC.5891.

44 Larkin describing himself in the *Irish Worker*, 18 October 1930.

45 Emmet O'Connor, *Reds and the Green: Ireland, Russia and the Communist International, 1919–43* (Dublin, 2004), p. 159.

46 *Irish Times*, 29 September–2 October 1930; *Thom's Directory, 1931* (Dublin).

47 *Irish Times*, 29 September–2 October 1930; *Workers' Voice*, 27 September–11 October 1930.

48 *Irish Worker*, 11–18 October 1930.

49 Ibid., 7, 21 March 1931.

50 Ibid., 1 August 1931.

51 Ibid., 25 October 1930.

52 Ibid., 29 November 1930; *Workers' Voice*, 29 November 1930.

53 Mike Milotte, *Communism in Modern Ireland: The Pursuit of the Workers' Republic since 1916* (Dublin, 1984), pp. 108–11.

54 *Irish Worker*, 24 October 1931.

55 C. Desmond Greaves, *Seán O'Casey: Politics and Art* (London, 1979), p. 151; *Irish Worker*, 23 May–27 June 1931.

56 RGASPI, Anglo-American secretariat to Ireland re-elections, 7 January 1932, 495/89/75–1.

57 RGASPI, general election, February 1932, 495/4/205–12/14. The RWG's election fund provided £30; where the remainder came from is unclear.

58 RGASPI, results of the Irish Free State elections, undated [1932], 495/72/197–14/16.

59 Emmet O'Connor, 'Anti-communism in twentieth century Ireland', *Twentieth Century Communism: A Journal of International History* 6 (2014), pp. 59–81.

60 *Irish Worker*, 12 March 1932.

61 *Truth That Is News* 1:33, 37, undated [January 1933].

62 John de Courcy Ireland, 'As I remember Big Jim', in Donal Nevin (ed.), *James Larkin: Lion of the Fold* (Dublin, 2012) , p. 448.

63 RGASPI, S. Murray, Ireland, group organisation, 8 June 1932, 495/89/78–30/32.

64 Donal Nevin, 'On Larkin: a miscellany', in Donal Nevin (ed.), *James Larkin*, p. 476.

65 Matt Treacy, *The Communist Party of Ireland, 1921–2011: Vol. 1, 1921–1969* (Dublin, 2012), p. 53.

66 *Irish Times*, 28–29 June 1933.

67 Mary M. Banta, 'The red scare in the Irish Free State, 1939–37' (UCD, MA, 1982), p. 138; *Irish Workers' Voice*, 1 April 1933; NA, DJ, Garda reports, 8 April, 14 June 1933, JUS 8/711.

68 Banta, 'The red scare in the Irish Free State', p. 135, 263, fn. 54; Luke Gibbons, 'Labour and local history: the case of Jim Gralton, 1886–1945', *Saothar* 14 (1989), p. 91; Michael Farrell, 'Anti-communist frenzy', *Irish Times*, 28 March 1983.

69 *Irish Times*, 26 January, 29–31 March 1933; Eoghan Ó Duinnín, *La Nina Bonita agus an Róisín Dubh; Cuimhní Cinn ar Chogadh na Spáinne* (Dublin, 1986), p. 81.

70 This point is made in Manus O'Riordan, 'From Sing Sing to sing and sing: the 1934 Larkin affidavit', *Irish Political Review* (October, December 2011). See the *Irish Worker*, 18 October 1930, 21 March, 4 April–13 June 1931.

71 Captain Henry Landau, *The Enemy within: The inside Story of German Sabotage in America* (New York, 1937), p. 278; Chad Millman, *The Detonators: The Secret Plot to Destroy America and an Epic Hunt for Justice* (New York, 2006), pp. 238–44; *New York Sun*, 6 April 1934; Peter Conradi, *Hitler's Piano Player: The Rise and Fall of Ernst Hanfstaengle, Confidante of Hitler, Ally of FDR* (New York, 2004), pp. 119–21; *Dunkirk Evening News*, 14 June 1934; *Gettysburg Times*, 7 April 1934; *San Bernardino County Sun*, 22 April 1934.

FIFTEEN

ISHMAEL, 1934–40

'I am an Ishmael . . .'
Big Jim Larkin to the ITUC[1]

———

'I am Ishmael', James Larkin's ringing rebuke to the 1942 ITUC, was largely untrue of the 1940s, and said more about his frustration at being stigmatised for old transgressions and denied the acceptance he deemed his due. But it certainly had much truth about it in the 1930s. He had come a long way from being the prophet Isaiah in 1913. Jack Carney observed in January 1934: 'Jim is not so active at present. I think he made a mistake in 1923, but he has kept [faith with] the past.'[2] Keeping faith meant silence and isolation, nursing the WUI, and rebuilding his electoral base to regain his corporation seat and achieve more intermittent success in general elections. From 1935 he managed to claw his way back into the wider trade union movement in Dublin, gradually building trust and consolidating new friendships. It was a time when the world of Labour began to settle on an even keel, when revolutionism continued to ebb, trade union membership recovered, and support for an increasingly conservative Labour Party consolidated. Big Jim's personal life too acquired a settled character. Elizabeth's circumstances became more stable in 1932 when she moved into a house in St Agnes's Park, Crumlin, with her youngest son, Barney, and Bridie Goff, a Citizen Army veteran. Subsequently, she and Barney would move again, to a flat in 10 Warrington Place. In her final years she had the consolation of a quiet life, the love of her sons, the devotion of two pet dogs, and the opportunity to indulge her interest in gardening and portrait and landscape painting. Her granddaughter, Stella McConnon, remembered her as 'a very gentle person. Quite quiet'. Differences with Delia appear to have been resolved, and Big Jim had moved with the Colgans to the salubrious 41 Wellington Road, by 1928 at latest.[3] At home with the Colgans, he enjoyed a peaceful life and, whenever possible, would retire each night at 10 pm with an armful of reading matter, to a dusty book-lined room and lights out at 3 am.[4]

THE WUI

The WUI became even more enigmatic in the 1930s. Already set on a reformist course, it was to be a Dublin – or a Dublin and Bray – union too. Appeals for affiliation from places like Bagenalstown, Castlecomer, Derry, and Kilrush, among others, were marked 'read' by the executive.[5] The period since 1925 had been traumatic. Subscriptions declined to £4,072 in 1928, and the union's deficit, though falling, amounted to £1,450. In 1930, an assessment of the WUI by Seán Murray and Young Jim detected a 'tendency towards the right', manifest

> first in a lack of faith in the militancy of the workers, secondly in the tendency to place immediate and sectional interests before the interests of the class struggle as a whole; thirdly, a tendency to utilise negotiations in order to avoid struggles even at a cost to the workers, and fourthly in a reluctance to risk struggles because of their financial effects on the Union.

Noting the parlous fiscal state of the WUI in 1929, it added that finances had since improved 'although the leadership is still greatly concerned with its position and are inclined to place too great an emphasis on this aspect of its activities'.[6] 1930 was the last year of deficit. On paper, the WUI held its own in the 1930s, registering a very stable membership – 16,909 in 1930 and 16,408 in 1939 – throughout the decade, though unions underwent a difficult time of demands for wage cuts and continued decline in the early 1930s, and then enjoyed a growth in membership with the industrialisation drive of the Fianna Fáil government after 1932. Income rose fairly steadily from £7,811 in 1930 to £10,996 in 1939.[7]

In a decade of general trade union advance, when ITGWU affiliation rose by about 150 per cent, the WUI nearly doubled its membership, to some 10,000 by 1939.[8] Apart from 1937, the year of a lengthy building dispute, the union avoided heavy spending on strikes. Annual strike pay over the decade averaged £2,100, or 23 per cent of income, a little less than the comparable percentage for the ITGWU.[9] At the same time, unlike the ITGWU, the WUI did not accumulate a strategic war chest. Its credit balance accrued slowly, to a very modest £6,000 in 1940. Inexplicably – as by all accounts, Larkin worked from a bare office, beneath a bare lightbulb, in a crumbling Unity Hall – the financial returns indicate unusually high expenditure on goods, furniture, and house property. One possible and partial explanation is that the WUI had no political fund before 1952, and it would be surprising – given Larkin's history – if revenue was not diverted to subvent electioneering, or the *Irish*

Worker. Larkin intended to create a fund in 1935, until notified that the procedure required a ballot of members.[10] The union also provided an important source of political patronage. Loans to members sometimes swallowed 25 per cent of annual income, and up to half of this debt was written off.[11] On Sunday mornings Larkin would receive long queues of suppliant members or their wives or mothers. Purged of its dissidents, the union became more of a family for him.[12]

The mid-1930s amounted to a purgatory for Larkin, in which he had turned his back on radicalism, without yet acquiring trust in any quarter. The setbacks deepened his reclusion. His response to the Blueshirts was less than distinguished. After months of relative quiet, he led a counter-demonstration to the joint ITUC-Labour Party rally against fascism at College Green on 6 May 1934, in which he denounced the Labour Party as the real fascist organisation.[13] If the WUI was no longer an outcast in industrial relations, it remained so in the Labour movement; and William O'Brien was determined to keep it that way. In September 1934, he warned that the ITGWU would disaffiliate should Dublin trades council admit the WUI; a threat all the more potent for the recent amalgamation of the rival trades councils in 1928. The council rejected the WUI's application by 95–36 votes, and in October resolved that affiliates should not co-operate or go into conference with unions not in affiliation.[14]

Larkin soaked up the humiliation. Following the outbreak of the Spanish Civil War, he seized upon the prevailing climate to extirpate communism from the WUI. In what must rank as the shabbiest deed of his career, he 'permitted' the WUI executive to ban officials from speaking on any but a union platform. Carney, who had spoken for Republican Spain, regarded the move as an excuse to remove him. Having served his hero through thick and thin for a quarter of a century, he packed his bags for London and freelance journalism. From 1941 to his death he would live, with Mina, in a flat in Fleet Street. Jack Carney surmised that with the return of Young Jim from Moscow, Big Jim wished to let him go. This is a more plausible explanation than that Big Jim feared the political repercussions of association with the Spanish Republic, but the implication that the concern was to curb the WUI's staff costs is less credible. The WUI spent £3,329 on staff in 1930, £3,072 in 1936, and £4,210 in 1939, about twice the equivalent proportions in the ITGWU. Family matters may have been the tipping point. Carney's relations with Young Jim contained an element of rivalry and mutual resentment; he loathed Delia, and didn't think much of Denis.[15] His friendship with Big Jim had survived many a heated moment over politics, and despite Jim's belief that blood was thicker than water, it would continue. Carney was well aware that his unswerving devotion, not to mention Big Jim himself, puzzled their critics in Ireland, America, and Russia. 'At sixteen years of age,' he explained:

I was working 84 hours per week, wearing a gas mask, for the sum of 18s per week. My dreams were smashed, and I had not one single hope in life . . . until one Sunday I heard 'Jim' Larkin speaking . . . Disagreements with him, partings, bitter words . . . but always to me he will be the big-hearted champion of his class – incorruptible and unpurchaseable. Crucified he will be, nailed to the Cross of a misunderstanding people . . . but 'Jim' has left his mark on his people . . . they are better men and women because of his coming.[16]

They maintained regular contact, with Big Jim sending him butter and bacon during the world war.[17] Around this time too, Young Jim ceased to be active in the CPI.[18] His father's abhorrence of fascism had not abated, or his readiness to champion causes like freedom for Frank Ryan, the only soldier of the Connolly Column still imprisoned by Franco. Big Jim had long admired Ryan, and his persistence got the 1939 ITUC in Waterford to pass an emergency motion for Ryan's release. Earlier, when R. S. Anthony, a former Labour TD, criticised a motion against fascism, saying 'I would prefer Fascism to a dictatorship of the proletariat', Big Jim scribbled to a colleague 'I propose we exchange Anthony for Ryan'.[19] Both Larkins also shared the national outrage at the execution of Peter Barnes and James McCormack in February 1940 for their indirect role in an IRA bombing at Coventry.[20]

REHABILITATION

The quarantine began to be lifted in the mid-1930s. Larkin proved to be an amenable colleague on the Dublin bakery workers joint committee, which included an ITGWU delegate.[21] In July 1936, Dublin trades council overrode O'Brien's objections, and Larkin attended the next monthly meeting, saying 'he had come back to work with them, and he hoped there would be no more working against each other'. In 1937, he was elected to the council executive, on which he would remain until his death. Now it was O'Brien's turn to tread the path of isolation and disruption. Also an executive member, he suffered Larkin's presence on a few occasions, but gradually withdrew from the council, and the ITGWU disaffiliated in 1941.[22] Fearing a similar development, the ITUC rejected the WUI's application for membership in 1935. After a fresh application in 1937, the Congress executive met Larkin and asked, in language echoing the toxic diplomacy of contemporary Europe, if he would confine the WUI 'to the <u>de facto</u> position it now occupies', ie. Dublin city and county. When Larkin claimed the union had provincial branches, the executive said it would consider these 'new facts'. Larkin attended annual Congresses from 1937 to 1942 as a Dublin trades council nominee, appealing regularly and in vain against the continuing procrastination about the WUI's admittance. He tried to make a splash at the 1937 ITUC in Dundalk, arguing at length against his union's exclusion, and later walking out because the table cloths in the hall were foreign made. The delegates were unimpressed, and he finished last in the poll for the Congress executive. Despite a more collegial style at subsequent Congresses, he took another drubbing in the elections to the standing orders committee in 1939, and did not stand again for the executive until 1941. At the 1938 Congress a motion to restrict delegates to affiliated unions was moved by the Post Office Workers' Union – of which Labour Party leader William Norton was general secretary – and defeated by 78–52 votes.[23]

Aside from personal memories of Larkinite disruption, the 1930s was a decade of inter-union friction, and feeling against breakaways in the union leaderships ran deep. Trades councils were not represented at the ITUC special conference in 1939 on trade union restructuring – itself an attempt to end the suicidal sectionalism – where O'Brien intended to present a plan for industrial unionism. Indeed in its report to the conference, the commission on restructuring insisted that the 'facility with which a "break-away" Union can secure affiliation to the local Trades Council must be checked', and recommended that trades councils admitting non-Congress unions be debarred from the ITUC.[24] If it is incredible that Big Jim would have made common cause with his unforgiving enemy, his exclusion from the ill-fated conference was ironic. He too was an old advocate of industrial unionism, Young Jim had urged the CPI in 1935 to champion a similar project, and father and son would have endorsed O'Brien's view of the British-based unions as an obstacle to progress.[25] Divisions between Irish unions allowed the British to frustrate O'Brien's plan, leaving him even more intolerant of his rivals.

The personal transformation was limited of course. Larkin loved to dominate proceedings on Dublin trades council, he could be awkward to work with, and never lost his disregard for formalities. He rarely replied to correspondence, and would often deny receiving them. More than once John Swift challenged him on this. In response, Larkin would lift a bundle of letters out of his pocket, sort them on the table, and snarl 'I got no letter from you, Swift'. Swift learned not to argue with him, and wondered how on earth it was possible to run a union on that basis.[26]

James T. Farrell provided an insightful portrait from a visit to Dublin in August 1938. Farrell found him dressed in a crumpled blue suit, swinging a sledgehammer as he re-arranged Unity Hall. Delighted to have an American writer to reminisce with, Larkin drove Farrell about the city, showing him the slums and new housing, Howth of the gunrunning and the secret memorial to the Invincibles in the Phoenix Park, before taking him to Delia's where he scrambled eggs for them both. Introducing Farrell to Young Jim, he warned his son humorously that the American was a Trotskyist. Leon Trotsky had been expelled from Soviet Russia in 1929, and become a rallying point for minor but mounting communist opposition to Stalinism. His plight aroused some sympathy in Ireland, Trotsky and V. I. Lenin having been widely acclaimed during 'the red flag times' of 1917–23. William O'Brien asked the government to grant him asylum in 1930, and Nora Connolly O'Brien wrote to him in April 1936, 'only to establish contact'. Trotsky sent a brief, comradely reply.[27] The first of the show-trials of alleged Trotskyists in Russia took place in August of that year. It was not a subject on which Big Jim wished to be drawn. 'I spoke of the Moscow trials,' wrote Farrell:

> He didn't commit himself, other than to say: 'the trouble with Trotsky is that he doesn't know how to work with anyone.' This criticism was often and justly made of Larkin himself. He spoke warmly of Bukharin, and remarked that he had told Bukharin once that Trotsky was unable to work with any one. This was just about the substance of what he had to say of international affairs and politics.

The reticence on Nikolai Bukharin was curious. Not only had he been one of the friendliest of Comintern officials towards Larkin, but Bukharin's recent show-trial in March 1938, with its chilling juxtaposition of 'confessions' and protestations of subservience to Stalin, had had a particularly shocking impact on intellectuals in the west. Seen as illustrating the insidious psychology of totalitarianism, it inspired people like Bert Wolfe and Arthur Koestler to break with communism, and Koestler to write *Darkness at Noon* (1940). So much a dissident on domestic issues, Larkin stayed silent to Soviet Russia, partly out of loyalty to the 'first workers' state', the 'socialist sixth of the earth', but also because he was never comfortable speaking on international and theoretical questions. We can only speculate on whether he felt inhibited by his lack of formal education. Farrell thought him 'garrulous, human and humane, witty, vindictive, vituperative' and very Irish, but ultimately disappointed.

> All men have weaknesses, but all men are not the victims of their weaknesses. Jim Larkin is a victim of his own weaknesses, and his own temperament. Now, he is embittered and envenomed. He feels that the Irish working class has sold him out.

On returning to New York, and still an admirer of Big Jim, Farrell despatched a lengthy report on Larkin to Trotsky in Mexico.[28]

POLITICS

In politics too, Larkin enjoyed a recovery, albeit one based more on assiduous clientelism than a radical programme. He regained his city council seat in electoral area no 2 in July 1936 with a solid vote of 2,559 first preferences, 63 per cent of the quota, putting him third behind Lord Mayor Alfie Byrne and Mrs Tom Clarke in the first count. Alderman Byrne had won a staggering 14,297 votes. Frank Ryan, standing as a 'Republican', was well down the field with 418 votes.[29] Dublin had recently begun to tackle its appalling slum problem – some 60 per cent of families in the city lived in one room accommodation – and Larkin made housing the focus of his public representation. Following his re-election in 1939, he was elected chairman of the housing committee, a position he held until his death. During the six-month building strike of 1937, he persuaded the Corporation and the building unions to back a direct labour scheme in Ellenfield. He had choice words for the 35 per cent of workers who forsook the job for the private sector after the strike. He was also to the fore in pressing the Corporation to request a government enquiry into housing in Dublin in 1939–40, and took a robust interest in the enquiry's deliberations.[30] Like most other councillors, he strongly opposed the extension of the management system to all local authorities and the transfer of council executive powers to the new city managers.[31]

In 1937 Larkin defied the odds to win a Dáil seat in North East Dublin. Carved out of the old eight seat North Dublin, the new constituency was a three seater, and Byrne's bailiwick. Larkin scraped home, without reaching the quota, with 5,970 votes.[32] He petitioned the High Court to be discharged as a bankrupt, but no attempt was made to debar him on that ground.[33] He had little to say over most of his first term in Dáil Éireann. Only a wish to be part of the historic occasion prompted his maiden speech on 29 April 1938, on the Anglo-Irish Trade Agreement that had ended the Economic War and repatriated the 'Treaty' ports. In a very ambivalent set of desultory observations, he welcomed the Agreement, and yet was the only deputy to vote against it, because the payment to Britain of £10 million in final settlement of the land annuities question compromised the principle behind the retention of the annuities.[34] Having broken the ice, he spoke frequently in May – on specific industrial or constituency matters. His speeches had lost none of their verbosity or proclivity for digression, but undoubtedly revealed a mellowing character. Even an unprovoked taunt from William O'Brien, then a Labour TD, that he 'ran away to America when there was danger', received the placatory reply: 'As long as you and ex-Senator Foran were there to take my place everything was safe in this country.'[35] Like the Labour Party, Larkin normally supported the minority Fianna Fáil government, a position that was more than tactical.

'Honest' was his favourite epithet for de Valera, and he stressed his belief in the Fianna Fáil tripos of economic self-sufficiency, an end to partition, and the restoration of the Irish language. Language was fundamental to the nation, he told an election meeting, and if he was too busy to learn Irish, he thought in Irish.[36] On 25 May Labour joined Fine Gael in a division over an arbitration scheme for the civil service. Larkin abstained, and the government was defeated by a single vote. With the Anglo-Irish diplomatic triumph under his belt, de Valera seized the opportunity to go to the country for an overall majority. In the circumstances, Larkin did well to win 4,859 votes, but lost his seat.[37]

Larkin's admiration for de Valera was mutual. The Taoiseach name-checked him four times in his speech on the 1938 Anglo-Irish Trade Agreement, and nominated him as one of four Labour members of the 25-person Commission on Vocational Organization in January 1939, implicitly granting him recognition on a par with other Labour nominees, Louie Bennett, Senator Thomas Foran, and Senator Seán Campbell, treasurer of the Dublin Typographical Provident Society.[38] Foran resigned on 17 April 1939 and was replaced by Luke J. Duffy, general secretary of the Labour Party.

Devolving public policy making powers to elected councils within the various sectors of the economy was an old syndicalist idea; Larkin had expressed an interest in one variant, guild socialism, after the 1913 Lockout. The concept had since been abused by fascist dictatorships, and was associated with the Blueshirts and Fine Gael, but given its commendation by Pope Pius XI in *Quadragesimo Anno* and by Irish Catholic actionists, Fianna Fáil deemed it politic to make a gesture. J. J. Lee has suggested that the Commission, which included two bishops and two priests, offered Catholic action a fool's paradise, and that in de Valera's Machiavellian design a disposition to dispute was a recommendation for appointment.[39] Larkin certainly was an enigmatic commissioner. He had avowed vocationalism during the 1938 election campaign, deriding Dáil Éireann as a 'gas house', full of empty talk about the past, and was 'very, very friendly' with the Commission's chairman, Dr Michael Browne, Bishop of Galway. One of his most curious requests was to Seán O'Casey for an autographed edition of his works as a present for Bishop Browne.[40] Unlike some of his clerical colleagues, Browne was a firm opponent of all forms of totalitarianism. Yet Larkin was strongly critical of the Commission, and its fascist potential, at the 1939 ITUC. 'Some here today,' he warned, 'had eulogised the teachings of university professors. To my knowledge, some of the people of this type who are on the commission are dangerous individuals.'[41] There were two professors on the Commission: Alfred O'Rahilly of University College, Cork, a bumptious Catholic actionist, and Michael Tierney of University College, Dublin, one of the prime movers of the project and a resolute Fine Gaeler. In 1940 the WUI made a substantial submission to the Commission, written by Young Jim, which declared a conviction in the vocationalism of syndicalist vintage, in the OBU and industrial unionism.[42] Big Jim attended only 46 of the Commission's 312 sessions – whereas the average attendance of the commissioners was high – and, like Duffy, he did not sign the final report in 1943. Swift thought he regarded the Commission 'with more or less silent contempt'; the silence rendering the contempt worthless in Swift's cold judgement. By contrast, Duffy 'ridiculed the recommendations, in spoken and written comment'.[43] A clash with Congress in 1942 may have dictated Big Jim's refusal to join Bennett and Campbell in including a formal reservation in the report, warning against its use for fascist ends and deploring its call for an end to 'externally controlled unions' as an encroachment on the remit of the ITUC.[44] His old antipathy to Bennett softened in the 1940s, when she supported the admission of Big Jim and Young Jim to the Labour Party and their candidature for Dáil Éireann.[45] The government's view of the Commission was as cynical and self-serving as Big Jim's. Nothing was done to implement vocationalism.

During the 1930s Larkin grasped the measure of himself and learned to live within his capabilities. After the awkward disengagement from communism from 1929 to 1932, and a deeper isolation, came a progressive rehabilitation with mainstream Labour from 1936. In putting the pain of overreaching ambition behind him, he settled into a quieter, more conciliatory temperament, though still given to sudden outbursts of rage and fits of pique. He had, in the process, reneged on the most heroic and intense phase of communist agitation in Irish history, on anti-fascism and the Republican Congress; all for the inevitable reasons of jealousy and self-centredness. He continued to use the WUI as a fief. Yet he commanded more respect towards the close of the decade. In 1930, his irrational political vandalism was becoming obvious to those not privy to his relations with Moscow. By 1940, Labour had moved to the right and revolutionary politics had faded into insignificance, leaving Larkin looking like a flickering candle of traditional socialist values in the descending gloom of the post-revolutionary twilight.

NOTES

1   ILHA, ITUC, *Annual Report* (1942), p. 119.

2   Donal Nevin, 'Larkin and the Workers' Union of Ireland', in Donal Nevin (ed.), *James Larkin: Lion of the Fold* (Dublin, 1998), p. 352.

3   Donal Nevin, 'On Larkin: a miscellany', in Nevin (ed.), *James Larkin*, p. 486; Mary Muldowney with Ida Milne (eds), *100 Years Later: The Legacy of the 1913 Lockout* (Dublin, 1913), p. 81; NLI, Seán O'Casey papers, Carney to O'Casey, 9 June 1928, 37989.

4   James Plunkett, 'Big Jim: a loaf on the table, a flower in the vase', in Nevin (ed.), *James Larkin*, pp. 111–12; Donal Nevin, 'Larkin in literature and art', in Nevin (ed.), *James Larkin*, p. 406; John de Courcy Ireland, 'As I remember Big Jim', in Nevin (ed.), *James Larkin*, p. 446.

5   Francis Devine, *Organising History: A Centenary of SIPTU, 1909–2009* (Dublin, 2009), p. 261.

6   RGASPI, joint report on WUI, S. Murray and J. Larkin Jr, 2 August 1930, 495/89/63–19/27.

7   NA, Registry of Friendly Societies, WUI file, 369T.

8   Emmet O'Connor, *A Labour History of Ireland, 1824–2000* (Dublin, 2011), p. 135; NA, based on WUI file, 369T.

9   NLI, ITGWU, *Annual Reports.*

10 NA, Registry of Friendly Societies to Larkin, 8 January 1936, WUI file, 369T, B.

11 NLI, William O'Brien papers, 13958.

12 Plunkett, 'Big Jim: a loaf on the table, a flower in the vase', pp. 111–12; Nevin, 'Larkin in literature and art', p. 406; de Courcy Ireland, 'As I remember Big Jim', p. 446.

13 *Irish Times*, 7 May 1934.

14 NLI, William O'Brien papers, 15676(1), part 7; Séamus Cody, John O'Dowd, and Peter Rigney, *The Parliament of Labour: 100 Years of the Dublin Council of Trade Unions* (Dublin, 1986), p. 155.

15 Nevin, 'Larkin and the Workers' Union of Ireland', p. 351; Emmet Larkin, *James Larkin: Irish Labour Leader, 1876–1947* (London, 1965), p. 298; Jack Carney memoir on Larkin, written for Emmet Larkin and kindly passed on to the author, p. 11; Devine, *Organising History*, p. 287; David Krause (ed.), *The Letters of Seán O'Casey, Volume II, 1942–1954* (New York, 1980), p. 6, fn. 1; I am obliged to James Curry for information on Carney.

16 *Irish Worker*, 21 November 1931.

17 NLI, Seán O'Casey papers, Carney to O'Casey, 19 February 1940, 37989.

18 RGASPI, meeting on Irish question, 23 May 1937, 495/14/339–31.

19 *Irish Worker*, 5 September 1931; Emmet O'Connor, *A Labour History of Waterford* (Waterford, 1989), p. 249; NLI, ITUC, *Annual Report* (1939), pp. 160, 181, 186–7.

20 NLI, Seán O'Casey papers, Carney to O'Casey, 9 February 1940, 37989.

21 John Swift, 'Learning to work with Jim Larkin', *Irish Socialist*, June 1984.

22 Cody, O'Dowd, and Rigney, *The Parliament of Labour*, p. 155, 186; John P. Swift, *John Swift: An Irish Dissident* (Dublin, 1991), p. 112.

23 ILHA, ITUC, *Annual Report* (1937), pp. 107–15, 121–2; ITUC, *Annual Report* (1938), pp. 143–5.

24 NLI, ITUC, *Annual Report* (1939), pp. 13–14.

25 RGASPI, report of the conference of the CPI, 5–6 October 1935, 495/14/337–19/20.

26 Swift, *John Swift*, p. 137.

27 workersliberty.org/story/2009/03/25/comrade-otrotsky-trotskys-attempt-get-irish-visa (accessed 29 June 2015); Nora Connolly O'Brien to Leon Trotsky, 28 April 1936, and reply from Leon Trotsky, 6 June 1936, marxists.org/history/etol/document/ireland-fi/norac.htm #nora (accessed 30 June 2015).

28 James T. Farrell, 'Jim Larkin, Irish Labour leader', *New International*, 13 March 1947; Farrell to Leon Trotsky, 11 December 1938, hworkersrepublic.org/Pages/Ireland/Trotskyism/farrelltotrotsky. html (accessed via Arguments for a Workers' Republic, 8 February 2006).

29 *Irish Times*, 2 July 1936.

30 ILHA, *Dublin Housing Inquiry, 1939: Verbatim Report of Proceedings* (Dublin, 1946).

31 ILHA, ITUC, *Annual Report* (1939).

32 *Irish Times*, 1–2 July 1937.

33 NLI, William O'Brien papers, 15679(6); NA, DT files, S11778A.

34 *Díosbóireachtaí Pairliminte, Dáil Éireann, Vol.71*, 29 April 1938, pp. 403–18, 456.

35 Ibid., 24 May 1938, p. 1594.

36   *Irish Times*, 9 June 1938.

37   Ibid., 20 June 1938.

38   *Díosbóireachtaí Pairliminte, Dáil Éireann, Vol. 71*, 29 April 1938, pp. 428–56; Commission on Vocational Organization, *Report* (Dublin, 1943), p. 1.

39   Joseph Lee, 'Aspects of corporatist thought in Ireland: the Commission on Vocational organization, 1939–43', in Art Cosgrove and Donal McCartney (eds), *Studies in Irish History* (Dublin, 1979), pp. 324–46.

40   NLI, Seán O'Casey papers, Carney to O'Casey, 21 February 1940, 37989.

41   NLI, ITUC, *Annual Report* (1939), p. 158.

42   *Irish Times*, 9 June 1938; NLI, submissions to the Commission on Vocational Organization, 1939–43, vol. 18, doc. 136.

43   Commission on Vocational Organization, *Report*, p. 489; John Swift, 'Report of the Commission on Vocational Organization (and its times, 1930s–40s)', *Saothar* 1 (1975), p. 55; Swift, *John Swift*, p. 55, 92.

44   Commission on Vocational Organization, *Report*, pp. 478–80.

45   Rosemary Cullen Owens, *Louie Bennett* (Cork, 2001), p. 107.

SIXTEEN

EVENING STAR, 1941–7

I must say I was very favourably impressed with his whole attitude . . . He did not
monopolise the discussion as one might expect but gave everyone a chance to speak.
Helen Chenevix on Larkin as chairman of the Dublin Corporation Housing Committee[1]

———

Those who came to know James Larkin in the 1940s often recall a kindness, generosity, and self-effacement almost unrecognisable to a biographer of his earlier life.[2] The manner was characteristic of Larkin's last years, when he was conscious of his reputation for domineering and anxious to make amends. Of course, he still wanted to be a chief, and the protests against the Wages Standstill Order and the Trade Union Act (1941) enabled him to find a niche as a second string leader of Dublin Labour. The protests were just part of a wider confrontation between militant Labour and a wartime state determined to apply severe austerity policies. Battered and bruised, the Dublin working class called out for a man like Big Jim. If not national recognition, it was a consolation. Alert and active almost to the end, he enjoyed a more productive life, distinguished by renewed trade union campaigning, constructive work on Dublin Corporation, and re-election to Dáil Éireann.

In the WUI he delegated more responsibility to Young Jim, whose emerging reputation as an able union official and visionary politician without his father's more irritating characteristics – or his oratorical power – did Big Jim no harm. While Big Jim's relations with other trade unionists improved, the reconciliation was not total. His past and self-regard were against him. So too were union leaders anxious to quash rank-and-file dissent from Congress efforts to reach an accommodation with the increasingly interventionist wartime state. The ITUC contrived to have him excluded from Congress after 1942, and his adoption as a Labour Party candidate in the 1943 general election provoked a shattering riposte from the ITGWU. But it was William O'Brien who over-reached himself in splitting the Labour Party and the Congress, leaving his old antagonist looking more like injured innocence. Once O'Brien had walked out of the ITUC, the WUI walked in, sealing its admittance to the fold, and giving Big Jim another platform for reconciliation. The end was timely. The happy warrior was still in harness and had more to say. Equally, he had said his piece and made his peace, passed the baton to Young Jim, and was unsettled by the recent death of Elizabeth. He could hardly have staged a better exit.

WITH THE COUNCIL OF ACTION

The prelude to Larkin's last great moment in history began on 6 May 1941, when Dublin trades council condemned the Trade Union bill. The bill originated as a reaction to strikes, as workers struggled to keep wages abreast of prices. Over the Emergency years, wages rose by one third, whereas the cost of living rose by two thirds. Poverty, unemployment, and, above all, the inequality of wartime social hardship were already leading to a sharpening of class tensions. In mid-1940, O'Brien simultaneously warned against anti-strike legislation, and confidentially invited the Department of Industry and Commerce to consider the reform proposals he had wanted to put to the ITUC in 1939. Following secret discussions with O'Brien, the government shifted the content of its legislation from strikes to rationalising trade unions; aiming to eliminate union multiplicity by granting one or more unions exclusive rights to negotiate for a category of workers, where that union, or unions, represented a majority of those workers. Congress was briefed on the principles of the proposed bill in October, and expressed no reservations. Nor did observers detect any unease in Labour circles when the bill was published on 30 April 1941.[3]

Dublin trades council's stand, and the untimely promulgation of the Wages Standstill Order, which introduced an absolute wage freeze from 7 May, started a snowball of rank-and-file opposition to what was seen as a concerted attack on workers' rights. O'Brien balked at a public defence of the government, and the ITUC felt obliged to oppose the bill as well as the Standstill Order, though it invited the Labour Party to lead the resistance. O'Brien kept Larkin isolated by ensuring that trades councils were excluded from the ITUC deliberations on the bill, but Dublin trades council organised its own campaign. At a special council meeting on 20 May, Larkin proposed that a Council of Action be formed, and Young Jim was appointed secretary.[4] On 22 June, members of 53 trade unions marched to College Green, where some estimates put the crowd at 20,000 people. There were repeated calls for Larkin, who was not listed among the speakers. When he rose to speak at the end of the meeting, the Garda reporter could hardly hear him above the shouts and cheers. After denouncing the 'rotten fascist government' he swept a match from his pocket and torched a copy of the bill. Owen Sheehy Skeffington afterwards enquired if the trick was not a little risky? 'No fear of that,' said Larkin, 'with ten matches tied together, sandpaper on the seat of the trousers, and the paper well soaked in paraffin.'[5] 'I never felt so lifted up as I was that day in Dublin', he would tell the 1941 Congress.[6] It was the climax of the campaign.

The Council of Action's continuing efforts embarrassed Congress, and O'Brien was not alone in his irritation with Larkin's complaints of the ITUC's half-hearted commitment. Shaken by the popular reaction, the government amended the bill to make compliance easier for small unions, and more difficult for British unions. In these circumstances, some union leaders moderated their hostility; and with a rift deepening between Irish and British affiliates, others concluded that Congress unity required a more diplomatic response and thought it irresponsible of Larkin to be acting the gadfly. Larkin insisted on going close to the bone, telling the 1941 Congress that he had heard from Seán MacEntee, Minister for Industry and Commerce – what many suspected – that the bill was prompted by certain union leaders 'and they ought to have the courage to get up and say that'. On the campaign against the bill, he treated delegates to a traditional riff:

> They had got a bit ashamed of using the word 'class'. They had allowed themselves to become such respectable people because they had fairly decent salaries as trade union officials that they had lost touch with the common rank and file. Was it not time to return to where they started from, no matter what their differences might be? I thank the government for introducing these measures. I believe it will result in the bringing together of elements that have been diverse and antagonistic into a common fold. I think it will lead to the building up and foundation of a real Labour movement in the thirty-two counties.[7]

If the reprimand contained a truth, he was naïve to behave as if his own history of disruption or support for Fianna Fáil was water under the bridge. The rhetorical radicalism also camouflaged Larkin's continuing drift back to the establishment. He lavished praise on the right-wing Labour deputy Michael Keyes for his opposition to the bill and agreed that there were 'as good Irishmen in the English unions as in any other' and they should not be asked to leave them. For the first time since 1937 he stood for the executive, and missed a seat by three votes.[8]

The retaliation came at the 1942 Congress, when the executive departed from its usual obfuscation to reject the WUI's application for affiliation for

> its record as a cause of disruptive action within the Trade Union movement and a promoter of libels against officers of affiliated Unions and of Congress itself [which] would make its admission a disintegrating instead of a harmonising element within Congress.[9]

Larkin replied with restraint until goaded by O'Brien into blundering over one of the libels – both of which had been settled in 1925. The basis of O'Brien's smug confidence became evident when Sam Kyle of the Amalgamated Transport and General Workers' Union spoke for the executive. Kyle had formerly seemed sympathetic, and Larkin was particularly hurt by his intervention. And the grief was not over. Evidently more concerned to sustain his union's recent rapprochement with the ITGWU, Kyle seconded a proposal from Bill Norton's union, the Post Office Workers – clearly directed at Larkin despite the transparent excuses – that in future all delegates would have to belong to ITUC affiliates. Again, Larkin made an equable, if long-winded and self-regarding, plea for fair play, going over his own history in the movement and tendering a roundabout apology for the libel of Denis Cullen. Again O'Brien tricked him into losing his temper. He ended up calling O'Brien 'an unmitigated liar'. The motion was carried by 107–60 votes.[10]

Larkin had the consolation of support from Dublin trades council, which elected him president in 1943 and stood by him despite a deterioration in its relations with the ITUC. Congress made arrangements for that year's Connolly Day without consulting the council, as Larkin might otherwise have chaired the events, and censured the council for a trivial breach of protocol by the WUI during a parade against wage control in October 1942. Regardless, Larkin presided over the council's executive meetings until 1945 after his own fashion, his elbows sprawled across the top of the table, leaving P. T. Daly to 'nudge' for room for his secretarial papers.[11]

> Larkin's usual sign to start the meetings was the raising of his hooked stemmed pipe in the style of a conductor's baton. The meticulous Daly . . . passed his carefully prepared agenda towards Larkin who, more often than not, swept it aside and started talking about himself. A typical Larkin discourse consisted of an exposition of his views on world affairs, coupled with reminiscences of some of his more dramatic experiences.[12]

The ITUC's muted response to the Trade Union Act, coupled with the Labour Party's forthright opposition, politicised workers. Extending its agenda to unemployment, housing, prices, blackmarketeering, and food and fuel supplies, Dublin trades council's Council of Action pitched into a hectic round of public meetings. The invaluable input of Big Jim as speaker and Young Jim as organiser, and their collaboration with the Labour Party, led to their admission to the party in December.[13] In February 1942 they joined with ex-communists in the formation of a Dublin Central branch. Rather than confront the consensus for neutrality, the CPI had 'suspended' its solitary branch in Éire following the Nazi invasion of the Soviet Union. Barney

Larkin led the opposition to the decision, which was passed by 11–9 votes in the Dublin branch. Communists were instructed to 'tear up their membership cards' and enter the Labour Party and work for a Labour-Fianna Fáil coalition that would carry Éire into the war.[14] Young Jim was close to the ex-CPI circle. He had been consulted on the dissolution – advising against – and in January 1943 led the formation of the Dublin Labour Party executive, which became dominated by communists.[15] A government informer afterwards alleged that he belonged to the 'Johnny Nolan group', but one member of this secret hub of communist activity, John de Courcy Ireland, was emphatic that he knew nothing of its existence.[16]

Big Jim never renewed any special association with the communists, content to play a supportive role in the Labour Party and devote himself primarily to municipal politics. Indicative of his mellowing was a rapport he struck up with Archbishop John Charles McQuaid. McQuaid paid a courtesy call to Unity Hall before his consecration in 1940. On that occasion Larkin harangued him about Dublin's social conditions.[17] Evidently impressed with the response, Larkin joined other city councillors after the consecration in visiting the Archbishop's palace to present an address of congratulation, and in 1942 he told His Grace that 'they were particularly blessed that they had an Archbishop who was in such intimately close touch with the people's needs'.[18] During the 1940s the two often sat together on industrial or civic committees.

Larkin was re-elected to the Corporation in August 1942, when Labour became the biggest group on the council with 13 of the 35 seats. Continuing his work on the housing committee, he championed causes like the employment of direct labour, the relocation of Dublin's cattle mart and abattoir, and preference in new housing allocation for newlyweds – the optimal way, he argued, of breaking the corrupting influence of the slums on tomorrow's families. On his initiative the Corporation purchased St Anne's estate, Clontarf, and his wish that it be divided equally between dwellings and playing fields, a park, and gardens was realised, in timeworn municipal tradition, some years after his demise.[19]

There remained the unyielding enmity of the ITGWU. In April 1943, union delegates helped to have Larkin rejected as a general election candidate by Dublin Labour's selection convention. Efforts to have the decision overturned drove the normally composed O'Brien to occasional fits of fury, and overshadowed meetings of Labour's Administrative Council for the next nine months.[20] Norton tried to mediate an accord. On 14 May, Larkin assured the Labour leader that he was 'willing to work loyally with any member of the Party regardless of previous personal differences and antagonisms and to put aside all divisions and conflicts . . .'[21] When the ITGWU complained that the undertaking nowhere 'expressed regret for his part in the earlier conflict with the Union', Norton prevailed on Larkin to tender an apology. Though apologies

were becoming almost a habit for him in the 1940s, it was with some difficulty
that he wrote:

> if in the heat of past conflicts statements were made by me, I regret having made
> such statements if those statements today appear as obstacles in the way of a united
> effort by all members of the Party at the present moment.[22]

It was not enough for the ITGWU. The Administrative Council, on which
the union controlled eight of the 17 seats, rejected Larkin's nomination by 8–7
votes. With the ITGWU isolated, the party preparing for a big electoral
breakthrough, and activists enthusiastic for Larkin, Norton pressed on. When
Labour opened its election campaign on 27 May, he declared that Larkin
would stand, nominated by the Dublin Labour Party executive, a body with
no right to overrule the Administrative Council.[23]

The general election boosted the Labour vote from ten per cent in 1938 to
15.7 per cent; and 6.7 per cent to 16.2 per cent in Dublin. For Larkin, it was a
summer of recognition and reconciliation. He was returned in North East
Dublin with 5,896 votes, and touched that Tom Johnson – latterly a friend and
admirer of Young Jim – spoke during his campaign.[24] He had too the satisfaction of seeing his favourite son elected in South Dublin. Subsequently, he
addressed an ILP summer school in England, where he was eulogised by
another legend, Red Clydeside's James Maxton, MP. His largely autobiograph-
ical speech defended neutrality – 'it was not reasonable to expect Ireland to fight
for Britain' – while sympathising with the British people. Maxton and the
Scottish ILP had opposed the war. Larkin went on to assert that Labour in both
countries would end partition and that Irish workers would seize economic
power and break their dependency on British capital: 'what the Bolsheviks did
in Russia, socialist led workers would do in Ireland one day.' The summer
school announced that he was to be presented with a certificate as a founder
member of the ILP, and Larkin described the ILP – which had dwindled to a
small far left group since cutting its ties with the British Labour Party in 1932 –
as 'nearer to his idea, maybe, than any other Party'.[25] At home, he was appointed
by Seán Lemass to the Commission on Youth Unemployment, and his buoyancy was evident over the following year in frequent, lively contributions to Dáil
debates, demonstrating remarkable stamina and command of factual detail for
a 70-year-old.[26] On one occasion, MacEntee – a none too chivalrous hammer of
the left – extended a dry compliment:

> Those of us who have listened to Deputy Larkin (Senior) for the past hour will
> agree that he is a very difficult man to please and a very difficult man to follow in
> the wide range of his imagination, and the mighty spate of his oratory.[27]

THE LAST SPLITS

The dispute over Larkin's candidature continued to hang fire. The ITGWU opposed his admission to the parliamentary Labour Party, and moved that the Administrative Council expel the Dublin Labour Party executive's chairman, Young Jim, and secretary for breaching the party's constitution. With Norton making every effort to defuse the crisis, the controversy dragged on until 3 December, when the Administrative Council defeated the expulsion motion 8–9.[28] On 7 January 1944, the ITGWU disaffiliated from the Labour Party, and on 15th, O'Brien circularised branches with a defence, citing Larkin's ancient enmity to the union, and arguing that his acceptance into the Labour Party was facilitated by communists. Five of the eight ITGWU members in the parliamentary Labour Party resigned. Norton countered with accusations that the roots of the split lay in the ITGWU's secret backing for the Trade Union Act, and that the union was acting from 'a thirst for revenge' against Larkin, and 'without any reference to their own members'.[29] These charges were widely believed, and the schism was perceived as an illustration of how far O'Brien was ready to take his private war against Larkin; even within the ITGWU, officials shook their head in disbelief at Labour being nobbled for an old man's spite, and counselled restraint.[30] O'Brien hastily reshuffled his arraignment. Revising and emphasising what had been presented originally as a secondary reason for disaffiliation, he now purported that his real concern lay with a communist conspiracy to control Dublin Labour.[31] The claim was echoed by the five ITGWU deputies who sealed the political split in forming the National Labour Party. O'Brien added a second coat of camouflage to his vindictiveness by conniving with Alfred O'Rahilly, correspondent of the Catholic weekly, the *Standard*, in prosecuting an anti-communist witch hunt over the next five months.[32] Norton tried to limit the damage by convening an enquiry into communist entryism. Seventeen members were summoned before the enquiry and six were expelled for attending a CPI conference in Belfast in October 1943. Both Larkins were investigated, but not expelled. Norton refused to regard previous membership of any organisation as a ground for expulsion, though he did have the Central branch and the Dublin executive dissolved.[33] When de Valera called a snap election in May, the Labour vote plummeted to 8.8 per cent of the poll. Big Jim's tally slipped to 4,489 and he lost his seat; Young Jim held his.[34]

Young Jim's increasing input into the WUI is reflected in the convergence of figures for membership and income in the union's annual returns after 1940. Membership was put at 12,500 in 1941; it then declined to a low of 8,800 in 1944, and climbed to 10,000 in 1946. The severe restrictions on strikes during the Emergency allowed many unions to fatten their coffers substantially, but the WUI's credit balance showed only a marginal improvement. The union moved to a new headquarters in 5a College Street in 1942, named Thomas Ashe Hall after a poet and friend during the 1913 Lockout and, in 1917, the first republican prisoner to die on hunger strike. There was too an ironic personal connection with 1913: following the infamous baton charge in O'Connell Street, Big Jim had been held in a cell in the building, then a DMP barracks.[35] In 1943 the WUI began recruiting farm labourers in County Dublin, extending the work to neighbouring counties in 1944.[36] The wartime demand for rural labour raised the possibility of a general re-organisation of the sector, which would transform the WUI into a national union. Another door opened for the WUI in April 1945, when O'Brien pushed the divisions in Congress to their conclusion, and led the formation of the rival Congress of Irish Unions. In 1944, the ITUC had been treated to a lengthy presidential address which reviewed the struggles of 1907 and 1913 without mentioning Larkin's name! With O'Brien gone, the WUI was welcomed in without further ado. Big Jim had played no part in the split, and he was happy to forget his misgivings about British-based unions, and endorse the 'internationalism' of the ITUC against the Congress of Irish Union's insistence on an exclusively Irish movement. At the 1945 ITUC he moved an emergency resolution calling on Irish workers in Britain to vote Labour in the forthcoming elections. As the polling was on the following day, it is questionable if the initiative had any rationale other than broadcasting to all and sundry that the new sunny Jim was no longer anti-amalgamated.

> I am still proud of my association with the Union, amongst others, represented by the chairman [the Amalgamated Transport and General Workers' Union, which had absorbed the NUDL] . . . Those people who talk about representing Irish Unions and about 1913 do not tell you of the help given by the British workers. I was in London a short time ago. I do not think there was ever a working class like the London working class – magnificent men, women and little children. How they stood up to that bloody, murderous attack upon them![37]

However the summer of 1945 brought a series of setbacks. Big Jim refused to call off a hopeless strike of the union's beef and pork sections for a fortnight's holidays, until, after three months, with the union's reserves reduced by half, he turned a blind eye to Young Jim's intervention.[38] In the autumn of 1945, the WUI concluded that organising farm labourers was beyond its resources. In early 1946, it requested the ITUC to consider the project, and in May the Congress sponsored the foundation of the Federation of Rural Workers, with Young Jim as president. Four thousand members were transferred from the WUI to the Federation. More difficulties arose in 1946 in the gas workers' section, and 400 members defected to the Seamen and Port

Workers' Union.[39] The WUI nonetheless continued to modernise and appointed its first full-time general president in 1946.[40]

The 'limited liability' strategy implicit in the creation of the Federation of Rural Workers bore the hallmark of Young Jim's prudence. The contrast between himself and his father remained subdued by deference to 'the Big Fella', but was obvious nonetheless. Nothing captured more the passing of Big Jim's style of trade unionism, and his lack of vision in his declining years, than the suspicion he cast on Congress-government discussions on the Industrial Relations bill at the 1946 ITUC, while his son welcomed consultation with government *per se*. Young Jim subsequently combined pride in his father's legacy, with implicit reservations about his management of the WUI. 'Those of us who know the full story,' he said in 1959, 'were doubtful that the union would last another 12 months. We had less than £5,000 and of that we owed at least half.'[41] His succession as general secretary brought fundamental changes, and he emphasised that henceforth the union would be guided by teamwork, procedure, and practicality rather than sentiment. One of his first acts as general secretary was to write a rulebook.

The WUI's admission to the ITUC came too late for Big Jim to resume a role on the national stage. He did however hope to crown his municipal career with a term as Lord Mayor of Dublin. A bid in 1943 failed to secure the backing of the Labour Party, to the relief of some old comrades who felt the largely ceremonial office would be a sad end for an old rebel who had always scorned pomposity.[42] But following re-election to the Corporation in 1945, the Labour councillors proposed him for the post. Fine Gael was willing to back a Labour candidate, but last minute instructions arrived from the party to make an exception of Jim Larkin. Jim promptly denounced the Fine Gael leader Richard Mulcahy, withdrew his nomination, and walked out of the council to sit reproachfully in the public gallery, much to the embarrassment of the remaining Labour group. Larkin at least enjoyed the vicarious honour, in March 1946, of moving that the freedom of the city be conferred on George Bernard Shaw. Shaw, who was averse to honours, rounded off a letter of thanks with customary wit:

> My dear Jim, Nothing could have pleased me more in this Freedom Honour than its being initiated by you nor made it surer of acceptance. You have been a leader and a martyr while I have never had a day's discomfort . . . Horoo for Libertee! Says the Shaw Van Vocht.[43]

Larkin of course was no stranger to acclaim from literati great and small. In addition to labour songs, poems, and stories, he had inspired the stage heroes of Patrick Wilson's *The Slough*, and Daniel Corkery's *The Labour*

Leader, the socialist, Culainn, in AE's *The Interpreters*, published in 1922; and
the poems 'To Jim Larkin', written by Lola Ridge after his jail sentence in
1920, and 'Homage to Jim Larkin' by Frank O'Connor in 1944. His greatest
admirer was Seán O'Casey. O'Casey's Larkin was forever the poetic champion
of 1913 vintage, a visionary and giant among the little clerkly men who ran the
trade union movement. When Larkin visited O'Casey in Devon in the summer
of 1939 'he and Seán, who was overcome with emotion at seeing him, sat in the
kitchen to eat their meal and to talk over the past in a racing torrent of words'.
O'Casey had just finished *The Star Turns Red*. A play on the 'red star' had been
in his head since 1922, and Larkin's visit to Soviet Russia in 1924 provided the
title. The *Star* remained a 'nebula' for years, but O'Casey was determined to
write a homage to Big Jim, in itself remarkable as the perverse playwright otherwise depicted his socialist characters negatively. The Russian dimension was
probably a factor too, as O'Casey became steadily more pro-Soviet in the 1930s.
The finished product is set in the future and draws heavily on the author's view
of the 1923 split in the ITGWU. Though written during his hero's most
timorous hour, the play features a secondary character, 'Red Jim' – egotistical,
compassionate, and fearless – defying a conspiracy of fascists, reactionaries,
and penny-pinching, self-seeking union bureaucrats to spark a workers' revolt.[44]
The revival of Larkin's contact with O'Casey was strengthened by the presence
of their mutual friend, Jack Carney, in London. Mina Carney ran their flat in
Fleet Street as a salon for literati and was close to Eileen O'Casey.

It says something for Jim's bond with Elizabeth that his own health deter-
iorated not long after her death. She had contracted a serious lung infection in
November 1945 and went to stay at Young Jim's home, 'Gweedore', Putland
Road, Bray, where it was hoped the sea-air would do her good. After three
weeks, on 1 December, she died suddenly of heart failure. She was buried on 3
December following a small, private funeral at Mount Jerome. The enigmatic
relationship persisted into eternity. In death, as in life, Elizabeth and Jim
would be separated, she lying on Dublin's south side, and he on the north side.
Yet, Big Jim paid £14.13s for the plot, and her sons erected a headstone
inscribed 'beloved wife of James Larkin, TC'.[45] On 10 January, O'Casey wrote
cryptically to Jack Carney following a visit from Big Jim:

> Of course Jim was always religious – in the good sense of the word. I don't think he
> acted quite justly to Mrs L . . . Of course, he would dream about her, for his mind
> is full of her now: and all associations would come into the dreams . . .[46]

'I am going down to the grave rapidly,' Larkin told the ITUC congress in July.
Many dismissed it as standard hyperbole. He made frequent and lengthy contributions to the debates and was chosen as one of the ITUC's two fraternal

delegates to the Scottish TUC in 1947. But he sensed the Styx, and it may have been more than coincidental that in his very last intervention he made a gesture of friendship and apology to ITUC secretary 'Comrade Johnson', affirming that he had never 'in all the years' doubted his 'honesty of purpose and his great gift of conciliation'.[47] Shortly afterwards, John Swift, an affirmed atheist and anti-clerical, learned from Young Jim that he was planning to slip away to Liverpool to avoid clerical concern for his spiritual welfare.[48] In all likelihood, Young Jim wanted to give his father a 'red funeral', as his father had given his uncle Peter. As usual, when caught between the devil and the deep blue sea, Big Jim let things drift.

Carney, O'Casey, and Peadar O'Donnell, among others, were meanwhile pressing Larkin to write his memoirs. 'I am conscious of my obligations,' he explained humorously to O'Casey in September 1946, 'that if anything in "Mein Kampf" would be helpful to the present or the future generation I would be compelled to accept . . . but I am in a very diffident mood for the last few months and I am not in the humour for trivial matters.' In December he asked Carney to help. Carney had started 'a life' in 1927, but the manuscript was 'captured' by 'the Polish Government'.[49] He agreed to the latest request on condition Larkin would dictate the memoir in London. A cabin had been booked on the B&I boat when events intervened. Young Jim proposed a biography to Carney in 1948, only to cancel the project on Delia's insistence. Delia reckoned that Carney had a low opinion of her, and if she imagined he could be subjective and bitter, she was right on both counts.[50] The beginning of the end came in December 1946. When supervising repairs in Thomas Ashe Hall, Big Jim fell through the floor and suffered internal injuries. He insisted on continuing with the work, but was eventually admitted to the Meath Hospital. Coincidentally or not, the Meath was perceived as a Protestant hospital.[51]

ON HIS KNEES?

The ambiguity of Larkin's attitude to the Catholic Church is corroborated by the Franciscan, Fr Cormac Daly, who explains how the clergy finally got to him.

> I knew Jim well. Many a time we discussed the theatre and films together. When I heard he was ill on January 24th . . . I decided to call on Jim. He was in a private room. The nurses said he did not wish to see any clergyman, but I mentioned that I knew he would see me. He said 'yes', so I went in and in spite of his condition, I received a warm welcome. He joked [with] me about my chaplaincy of the Stage Guild and we continued to talk of the theatre.

I asked him how he was and he said he was very low and had no hope. I remember asking him if he was prepared for the journey and he answered 'no'. I said I could help him and he appreciated the gesture; but first, he emphasised, that he would like, in sympathy with James Connolly, to see the priest who attended him in his last moments. He said he did not know the Capuchin Father well, but I could arrange it for him. If he couldn't come, I was to come back again. I contacted Gabriel Fallon and Fr Counihan, SJ, who were members of the Commission on Youth Unemployment at the time. Jim and Fr Aloysius OFM Cap., were also members.[52]

On Monday 28 January, Fr Aloysius Travers, who had given the last rites to Patrick Pearse and James Connolly, left his own sick bed for the Meath Hospital. Larkin still resisted. 'Now Jim, what about number one?' said Fr Aloysius. 'Time enough at the end of the week,' Larkin replied. But that night Fr Aloysius persuaded him to make his confession and, with his permission, contacted Archbishop John Charles McQuaid, who hastened to seal his 'most treasured conversion' the next day.[53] There are two versions of the scene at the deathbed. In one, McQuaid was anxious for the soul of a good man he had come to respect, and wished to say sorry for past enmities – which was more than many Labour men would ever do.

[McQuaid] found the big man propped up in bed with a tiny prayer-book held in his left hand, at arm's length, as he prepared for the Viaticum. Larkin greeted him with a gruff kindliness and, characteristically, with some vivid adjectives told him what he thought of a group that had then declared strike action. Dr McQuaid calmed him and spoke of other things for he had little time left on this earth. At the end he said: 'Now put your whole trust in the Mother of God.' To the Archbishop's amazement, he got this clear answer: 'I never did anything else.'[54]

Extreme unction was then administered by the hospital chaplain.[55]

In the other version, held by some in the Labour movement, the Church was insensitively intent on securing a show conversion. Reportedly, McQuaid pleaded, with consummate subtlety: 'You've being doing God's work all your life Jim, don't deny Him now.'[56] Young Jim asked Swift, as a family friend and president of the ITUC, to deliver the graveside oration. Embarrassed, Swift pleaded that he was not sufficiently gifted in oratory. He would later say that the religious ceremony 'of sycophants who had maligned and despised him' did not commemorate the man he knew, and that Big Jim had 'died on his knees'.[57] The last WUI comrade to see Big Jim was Barney Conway, to whom he gave his gold-rimmed glasses, saying 'Here you are, Barney, I won't be needing these any more.' He had a habit of borrowing Conway's glasses when he forgot his own.[58]

At 6.30 am on Wednesday 30 January 1947 Larkin was found to have died in his sleep. Dressed in the brown habit and scapular of St Francis, his hands wrapped in a rosary given to him by the Archbishop the evening before his death, his remains were taken from the Meath Hospital to lie in state for two days in Thomas Ashe Hall, between an old Starry Plough at his feet and a huge crucifix at his head, surrounded by a guard of honour drawn from Citizen Army veterans and the WUI. On Saturday, he was received at his parish church, St Mary's, Haddington Road, by Dr Wall, titular Bishop of Thasos. McQuaid presided at the requiem mass in St Mary's on Monday morning, with the President, Taoiseach, and cabinet in attendance.[59] Outside, it was blizzardous, a heavy fall of snow covering the ground. Carney wrote with solemn emotion to O'Casey:

> Then we moved off. The crowd was increasing in size. The Old Guard and Citizen Army led the way. Glasnevin was a long way off. We moved along Haddington Road and over Mount Street Bridge along Lower Mount Street. The streets of Dublin belonged to Jim on this sad day. Not a wheel turned but that of the procession cars. Through Merrion Square and sharp [?] along Westland Row. Then sharp left along Pearse Street. Then we all stood outside the WUI headquarters. The band played the Dead March. Off again along Westmoreland Street and over O'Connell Street Bridge and then sharp right along Eden Quay. And to my great but happy surprise, the procession halted outside of Liberty Hall. No sign of mourning on the Hall. The band again played the Dead March. Two things I remember: a crate hanging in midair over the Liffey. The crane driver had left his crane to pay his last tribute to Jim and a coalie with his face begrimed and his tears copiously flowing. Beresford Place was crowded. We then moved off to Abbey Street and turned into Marlborough Street and again we stood outside Unity Hall where the band again played. Then off through Cathal Brugha Street, where often Jim had spoken to thousands of people. Then past Parnell's statue and on to Glasnevin. The tail end of the procession had not reached Parnell's statue in O'Connell Street as the procession entered Glasnevin. I checked up by timing. At the cemetery the advance guard stood to attention to allow the coffin through. The old men who had known Jim since the beginning stood in the shivering cold. Tears flowed unashamedly. More priests. Father Aloysius again appeared and recited the rosary in Irish. Then pulled out a special vial of holy water to sprinkle over Jim's grave.

He was laid beside Pete. Norton delivered the graveside oration.[60] Delia would join her brothers in the same plot in 1949. She died after a prolonged heart trouble and had been 'particularly affected' by her elder brother's death.[61]

Big Jim Larkin left £4.10s, the balance of his weekly wages; and a personal estate to the gross value of £16.2s 6d.[62]

NOTES

1 Quoted in R. M. Fox, *Jim Larkin: The Rise of the Underman* (London, 1957), p. 165.

2 Ibid., p. 172; interview with Joe Deasy, 10 September 2000.

3 For the backdrop, see Emmet O'Connor, *A Labour History of Ireland, 1824–2000* (Dublin, 2011), pp. 151–64.

4 John P. Swift, *John Swift: An Irish Dissident* (Dublin, 1991), p. 113.

5 Ibid., pp. 113–14; Donal Nevin, 'On Larkin: a miscellany', in Donal Nevin (ed.), *James Larkin: Lion of the Fold* (Dublin, 1998) pp. 476–7; *Irish Times*, 23 June 1941.

6 NLI, ITUC, *Annual Report* (1941), p. 112.

7 Ibid.

8 Ibid., p. 121.

9 ILHA, ITUC, *Annual Report* (1942), p. 22.

10 Ibid., p. 84, 126, 128.

11 'John Swift remembers Larkin', *Irish Socialist*, August 1984.

12 Swift, *John Swift*, p. 118.

13 Séamus Cody, John O'Dowd, and Peter Rigney, *The Parliament of Labour: 100 Years of the Dublin Council of Trade Unions* (Dublin, 1986), p. 172.

14 Mike Milotte, *Communism in Modern Ireland: The Pursuit of the Workers' Republic since 1916* (Dublin, 1984), pp. 191–8. Communist policy is evident from the party paper, *Irish Workers' Weekly*, which continued until 1 November 1941; interview with Mick Barry, Waterford, 30 June 2000.

15 UCDA, 'UCD party history lecture, 9 January 1975', uncatalogued papers, Communist Party of Ireland; Seán MacEntee papers, 'Dublin Executive of Labour Party', P67/537(2).

16 UCDA, Seán MacEntee papers, P/67/522(4); letter to the author from John de Courcy Ireland, 5 April 1995.

17 Roland Burke Savage, 'The Church in Dublin, 1940–1965: a study of the episcopate of the Most Rev. John Charles McQuaid, D.D.', *Studies* (winter 1965), p. 314.

18 *Standard*, 17 January 1941, 20 February 1942.

19 John P. Swift, 'The last years', in Nevin (ed.), *James Larkin*, p. 86; Joe Deasy, 'As I remember Big Jim', in Nevin (ed.), *James Larkin*, pp. 457–9; Fox, *Jim Larkin*, pp. 165–66.

20 J. Anthony Gaughan, *Thomas Johnson, 1872–1963: First Leader of the Labour Party in Dáil Éireann* (Dublin, 1980), p. 378; Niamh Puirséal, *The Irish Labour Party, 1922–73* (Dublin, 2007), pp. 91–105.

21 Emmet Larkin, *James Larkin: Irish Labour Leader, 1876–1947* (London, 1965), p. 300.

22 Ibid.

23 Ibid., pp. 300–1; Gaughan, *Thomas Johnson*, p. 377.

24 *Irish Times*, 24 June 1943; Gaughan, *Thomas Johnson*, p. 378.

25 *New Leader*, 14 August 1943.

26 Nevin, 'On Larkin: a miscellany', p. 477.

27 *Díosbóireachtaí Páirliminte, Dáil Éireann, Vol. 91*, 18 November 1943, p. 2460.

28 Swift, 'The last years', p. 89; Gaughan, *Thomas Johnson*, pp. 377–8.

29 UCDA, Seán MacEntee papers, P/67/535(7), P67/535(12).

30 NLI, William O'Brien and Thomas Kennedy papers, 33718/I(272).

31 UCDA, Seán MacEntee papers, P67/535(12).

32 NLI, William O'Brien papers, 13960.

33 Milotte, *Communism in Modern Ireland*, p. 199.

34   *Irish Times*, 1 June 1944.

35   Swift, 'The last years', p. 88.

36   Dan Bradley, *Farm Labourers: Irish Struggle, 1900–1976* (Belfast, 1988), pp. 74–82.

37   NLI, ITUC, *Annual Report* (1945), pp. 116–7; Terry Cradden, *Trade Unionism, Socialism, and Partition: The Labour Movement in Northern Ireland, 1939–53* (Belfast, 1993), p. 114.

38   Breda Cardiff, 'As I remember Big Jim', in Nevin (ed.), *James Larkin*, p. 456.

39   UCDA, Seán MacEntee papers, 'Communism in Ireland', P67/548(1).

40   Donal Nevin, 'Larkin and the Workers' Union of Ireland', in Nevin (ed.), *James Larkin*, p. 347.

41   Ibid.

42   John Swift, 'Larkin's new clothes', *Irish Socialist*, December 1984.

43   Fox, *Jim Larkin*, pp. 178–9.

44   Donal Nevin, 'Larkin in literature and art', in Nevin (ed.), *James Larkin*, pp. 406–9, and Nevin, 'On Larkin: a miscellany', p. 482; Garry O'Connor, *Seán O'Casey: A Life* (London, 1988), p. 318.

45   Dublin City Archive and Library, Mount Jerome Register of Perpetuities, 3 December 1945, cited in James Curry, 'Elizabeth Brown and the marriage of James Larkin', unpublished paper.

46   Nevin, 'On Larkin: a miscellany', in Nevin (ed.), *James Larkin*, pp. 486–7.

47   ILHA, ITUC, *Annual Report* (1946), p. 136, 160, 215.

48   Swift, *John Swift*, p. 133.

49   *Irish Worker*, 21 November 1931.

50   NLI, Seán O'Casey papers, Larkin to O'Casey, 16 September 1946, 37994; Carney to O'Casey, 10 September 1946, 27 July 1948, 37989.

51   Daphne Deacon, a nurse in the Adelaide Hospital (later merged with the Meath) from 1962, recalled that Meath Hospital nurses were mainly Catholic and the doctors were mainly Protestant.

52   Letter from Fr Cormac Daly, OFM to Francis McManus, 27 February 1965, *History Ireland* (March/April 2014), p. 13.

53   Nevin, 'On Larkin: a miscellany', p. 477; Swift, *John Swift*, p. 133; John Cooney, *John Charles McQuaid: Ruler of Catholic Ireland* (Dublin, 1999), p. 211.

54   Burke Savage, 'The Church in Dublin, 1940–1965: a study of the episcopate of the Most Rev. John Charles McQuaid, D.D.', pp. 314–15.

55   *Standard*, 7 February 1947.

56   I am obliged to Joe Deasy for this anecdote, told to him by his father, Richard Deasy.

57   Swift, 'Larkin's new clothes'; 'How Larkin died on his knees', *Irish Socialist*, January 1985.

58   NLI, Seán O'Casey papers, Carney to O'Casey, 5 February 1947, 37989.

59   Ibid.

60   Swift, 'The last years', pp. 91–2, and Nevin, 'On Larkin: a miscellany', p. 477; Swift, *John Swift*, pp. 133–4; NLI, Seán O'Casey papers, Carney to O'Casey, 5 February 1947, 37989.

61   NLI, Seán O'Casey papers, Jim Larkin Jr to Seán O'Casey, 28 October 1949, 37994.

62   James Plunkett, 'Big Jim: a loaf on the table, a flower in the vase', in Nevin (ed.), *James Larkin*, p. 115, and Nevin, 'On Larkin: a miscellany', p. 478.

WIRKUNGSGESCHICHTE

*Don't submit your minds to any one man. Think these problems out for yourselves. A
leader who can lead you out of the wilderness can lead you back again. If there is a
thinking, intelligent movement, no leader can mislead you.*
Larkin at the ITGWU's adjourned delegate conference, 14 May 1923[1]

———

Greats defy death through Wirkungsgeschichte, or historical impact – the
English word 'afterlife' is too vague and misleading. After his burial and the
customary eulogies, James Larkin lay quietly. As the divided Congresses edged
towards unity in the 1950s, there was a reluctance to re-open old wounds by
celebrating the ITGWU's *bête noire*. The souvenir *Fifty Years of Liberty Hall:
The Golden Jubilee of the Irish Transport and General Workers' Union, 1909-1959*,
edited by Cathal O'Shannon, featured a chapter on James Connolly, but none
on Larkin. He was not even cited in William O'Brien's chapter 'Nineteen-
thirteen – its significance'. At the same time, it is a tribute to the power of the
name that the chapter on the 1923-4 split referred repeatedly to 'the General
Secretary' before admitting who 'the General Secretary' actually was.

The fiftieth anniversary of the lockout marked the rebirth of the legend.
Acknowledging the lockout as the foundation myth of the Labour movement
in the public memory, the ITGWU supported Dublin trades council in
mounting an exhibition and commissioning a pageant 'Let freedom ring: a
masque of 1913-16', written by Donagh MacDonagh. O'Brien's successors
were also realistic enough to accept that the lockout could not be severed from
Larkin. Nonetheless, the commemoration diminished the Larkin and class
struggle dimension by linking 1913 to 1916 and integrating the lockout into a
narrative of state-building, the fruits of which were now ripening under Seán
Lemass's programmes for economic expansion. The message was that 1913
was the bad old days, and they were over, thanks to the better relations of trade
unions, employers, and government. Tellingly, the commemoration is forgotten
apart from MacDonagh's rousing Larkinite ballad 'Dublin 1913'.[2] It fell to the
WUI to hail the golden jubilee in print, and restore a more class – and
Larkin – centred perspective through the publication of *1913: Jim Larkin and
the Dublin Lockout*, with material compiled by Donal Nevin, research officer
for the Irish Congress of Trade Unions.[3] The self-effacing, non-triumphalist

style of Nevin and Young Jim's WUI fostered a consensus on how Big Jim and 1913 should be remembered. The agreed solution was to celebrate both in a way that dwelt narrowly on the cult of Big Jim and his mighty efforts for Dublin's underclass. The Larkin legend was rehabilitated, but confined to the pre-1914 years, a discreet veil being drawn over his subsequent career and his antagonism towards the amalgamateds.

The process was enhanced by literary admirers, notably James Plunkett, and the treatment of the lockout in art and the media. As a producer with Radio Éireann from 1955, Plunkett was well placed to promote interest in Larkin. Radio Éireann marked the golden jubilee of the lockout with lectures, interviews, and a documentary. Newspapers commissioned special features. And, unusually for the time, Radio Éireann devoted a Thomas Davis lecture series to 'leaders and workers' in 1966, with Larkin covered by Plunkett himself. Over half the lecture was on 1913. About five per cent deals with the post 1923 years.[4] Between Plunkett and Nevin, Larkin's memory was in safe hands, and the guardian angels came together when Plunkett's play *The Risen People* was chosen as the motif of Congress's centenary celebrations in 1994.

More influential again was Plunkett's fiction, above all *Strumpet City*. *Strumpet City* became the *Uncle Tom's Cabin* of the Irish Labour movement. The powerful, graphic imagery of the slums displaced the complexities of syndicalism and the contentious issue of sympathetic action, or secondary picketing as one version of it became known in the 1980s before being made illegal. The novel's exclusion of the European industrial unrest, of which Larkinism was an echo, complimented the idea of pre-1960s Ireland as backward and intellectually isolated. With Plunkett sharing Seán O'Casey's view of nationalism as a distraction from class consciousness, *Strumpet City* further simplified the Larkin myth, and made it more palatable to a people terrified of the Northern violence spilling across the border, by ignoring Larkin's republicanism, excluding Connolly, and repeatedly reminding readers that William Martin Murphy refused a knighthood.[5] Today, trade unions would like to remember 1913 as a protest against slumdom for the right to join a union. That Larkinism began in Belfast, where housing was good, or that joining a union is not the most obvious way to improve one's housing, are problems rarely posed.

Larkin has benefited from the public image of the lockout and been peculiarly spancelled to it. Attempts to widen his relevance have never enjoyed more than marginal or ephemeral success. He has always been regarded as the ultimate trade unionist and internationalist; Ireland's one great embodiment of pure class struggle, unadulterated with nationalism. Yet efforts by Eoghan Harris and Sinn Féin/the Workers' Party to capitalise on that during the height of historiographical 'revisionism' in the 1980s, and counterpose Larkin to Connolly, as O'Casey liked to do, failed to gain traction.[6] The preferred Larkin was not republican, but neither did the public want him to be anti-nationalist. In the 1990s, the Services, Industrial, Professional, and Technical Union (SIPTU) – formed from the merger of the two unions which he was popularly believed to have founded – made a virtue of necessity by projecting him as an icon of unity. Old Transport Union veterans were not convinced. SIPTU's centenary history dispensed with the pieties to present a warts and all account of its father figure in his war with O'Brien.[7] Other aspects of Larkinism, such as his syndicalism or republicanism, have been left well alone. Still others, such as his love of theatre or belief in the importance of culture as a weapon, were remembered in initiatives such as the Jim Larkin Theatre Group and the WUI Dramatic Society without acquiring the centre-stage status they deserved. Larkin is the lockout. The lockout is Larkin.

The centenary of the lockout confirmed its centrality to Labour's public history and Larkin's centrality to the lockout. The centenary was itself stitched into 'the decade of centenaries', patently a device of the *bien pensants* to manage problems of commemoration during the one-hundredth anniversaries of the revolutionary period. The traditional focus on 1916–23 was extended to 1912–23 in order to bring Redmondites and Unionists into the frame and celebrate their moments of glory in the Home Rule crisis and World War I. The logic of inclusion unlocked the idea that all should have their place in the sun, workers and women being the most obvious of the hitherto marginalised people, and 1913 was the ideal candidate for Labour's year in the decade. The idea was embraced by the Northern Ireland regime as well as the Republic.[8] Moreover, the rationale of state-sponsored commemorations being to 'kill with kindness', the treatment of the lockout was more blandly celebratory than it otherwise might have been. Some consideration was given to the position of strikebreakers and the paternal and entrepreneurial side of Murphy in television programmes and in oral history, but the employers' perspective was generally left to reactionaries and contrarians, and there was no public enthusiasm for doubts about Larkin's leadership.[9]

As with Irish Labour generally, academic scholarship on Larkin evolved slowly before gathering pace from the 1980s. It began with the lockout. Aware that 1913 would echo down the ages, employers took the rare step of commissioning an apologia, Arnold Wright's *Disturbed Dublin*. Another substantial monograph on the conflict would not appear until Pádraig Yeates's *Lockout*. Before the 1970s, references to the lockout in general histories were normally terse and of note only in being the sole acknowledgement of Labour. Subsequent surveys have been more willing to recognise the importance of class.[10] R. F. Foster's *Modern Ireland, 1600–1972* marked a step-change, and Diarmaid Ferriter's *A Nation and Not a Rabble: The Irish Revolution, 1913–1923* a coming of age in the way they dealt with Labour as a player rather than one of the extras to be covered in the supernumerary sentences, inserted to insure the author against charges of neglect.[11]

Studies of the lockout invariably address some or other of four elements in the making of the dispute – Larkin, Murphy, the slums, and the course of industrial relations. Larkin has become by far the most central and controversial of these for historians, and for his early biographers he in turn was defined by the lockout. R. M. Fox and Emmet Larkin presented him as a charismatic revolutionary rousing the downtrodden masses of a decrepit city. Dermot Keogh and Kenneth Brown were sceptical about his revolutionary credentials, and placed greater emphasis on social inequality as an explanation of Dublin's class war. More recent research is breaking down the traditional resistance of academics to the possibility that industrial militancy in Ireland was subject to more or less the same influences as militancy in Britain and elsewhere. John Newsinger's *Rebel City: Larkin, Connolly, and the Dublin Labour Movement* is an unabashed, engagé salute to Larkinism, progressive in its consideration of the wider context, regressive in that it repeats many of the jaded old misrepresentations of Larkin's personality and politics of those who refuse to accept him as anything other than a pure class hero. Yeates's more objective and exhaustive *Lockout*, while definitive on events, is essentially a reportage, and revises the conventional view of events only in placing a greater weight on the context of industrial unrest throughout the UK from 1911. Yeates's Larkin is both towering and 'peculiarly perverse', and all the more credible for that.[12] Surprisingly, *A Capital in Conflict: Dublin City and the 1913 Lockout*, an edited collection, was the only substantial academic publication to appear on the lockout in the centenary year, and it was commissioned by Dublin City Council as the first in a series on the decade of commemoration. *A Capital in Conflict* also signposted a fresh field of enquiry in challenging Yeates's thesis that the lockout was the outcome of the immaturity of Irish industrial conciliation machinery and asking if long-term stability is possible in industrial relations; a question prompted by the post-Keynesian assault on trade unions and one which demonstrates the enduring relevance of 1913 and its endless capacity to be re-interpreted in the light of the present.[13]

In the debate generated by the centenary, such as it was, Larkin got off lightly. With the lens on the lockout, controversy focused on his wisdom in picking up the gauntlet thrown down by Murphy, on the alienation of the BTUC in the way he pursued the Fiery Cross, and on whether sympathetic action could have won the day. Obviously the decision to take on Murphy turned out to be a colossal misjudgement, but the verdict of history is that the cause was just, Larkin did what he could to avoid confrontation, and if the ITGWU stood back from every militant employer it would never have gotten very far. By contrast, the attacks on the BTUC leaders illustrate how Larkin would throw caution to the wind in the heat of battle. No one would defend the attacks. Whether they contained a core of validity or were responsible for the BTUC's overwhelming rejection of sympathetic action is another matter. The greatest contention is over cross-channel sympathetic action. Yeates has argued that major, sustained, official action would not have happened, or been effective if it had. John Newsinger and Paul Smith have maintained that it could and would have been a trump card. Perhaps Larkin is a winner either way. If Yeates is right, or, to put it more accurately as we will never know, deemed to have the more plausible case, then the rhetorical extremes of the Fiery Cross made no difference.[14]

Looking beyond the lockout, publications in the 1970s and 1980s broadened the importance of Larkin to the 1907–23 period, and the centenary of the lockout saw a deepening of research on the 1911–13 years and on sidelights of Larkin's life, such as the *Irish Worker* and Liberty Hall and his relations with Delia and Elizabeth. There were also attempts to project the lockout as a microcosm of a hidden history, a glimpse of a counterfactual history focused on class rather than nation, or a motif for the exclusion of the working class from power and from historiography.[15] The liberalisation of access to the Comintern archives after the collapse of the Soviet Union encouraged more critical appraisal of Larkin's career in the 1920s.[16] In short, historians these days have more time for labour, a growing interest in Larkin, and a willingness to consider him as a less than stainless hero, but there remains a reluctance to tackle the big picture or grapple with the essential Larkin, the syndicalist and the republican.

The mystery of Larkin is that he achieved so much for trade unionism, but the key to understanding him is to grasp that he was, more often than not, a reluctant trade unionist and therefore an inferior union leader. That is not to fault Larkin*ism* or say that Larkin was never a great leader. It was the nub of an enduring frustration that he wanted to be something more, but lacked the application to achieve it. An endemic problem of self-discipline surfaced once he became his own boss. After an outstanding record with the NUDL, his command of the ITGWU from 1909 to 1911 was an anti-climax. He took little interest in the backstage grind of union building, and showed himself to be egocentric, jealous, dictatorial, and hyper-sensitive to criticism. His thirst for fame and restless mind began to draw him to a lengthy quest for a more glamorous role – in journalism, political agitation, public speaking, and cultural, social, and commercial projects. Fortuitously, the growth of trade union membership between 1911 and 1913 allowed union work and Larkin's creativity to synergise gloriously. Again, as in 1907–8, but this time on a grander scale, he transformed the spirit of the working class, and brought to trade unionism a dynamism, a charisma, a theatrical flair, and a moral and cultural vision unmatched by any of his colleagues or critics. Moreover, his achievements were not ephemeral. He revolutionised trade unionism in two respects. In developing the ITGWU he delivered a terminal blow to the crippling policy of dependence on British Labour, and laid the basis of the modern Irish Labour movement. In industrial relations, he introduced a method of struggle which made possible the unionisation of unskilled workers, without whom Labour could not have become a force of significance. He then made the method heroic and enduring by embedding it in a set of moral values. The spectacular success and popularity he enjoyed exacerbated his personality problems, with disastrous results. The 1913 Lockout arose from a reasonable attempt to win union rights for the tramwaymen. The Fiery Cross campaign was based on the astute conclusion that only sympathetic action in Britain could defeat the lockout, and only rank-and-file pressure would compel the British labour leaders to act. But the conduct of the campaign showed that Larkin put himself before anything else. The lockout was the turning point in his life. Even beforehand, he was suffering from stress and bouts of depression, and invariably his gut reaction to defeat was to walk away.

Larkin never had the same appetite for union work again. He wanted out by December 1913, and eventually embarked on an intended world speaking tour with an open mind on coming back. In the US, where he grew accustomed to self-indulgence, he spent no more than a few weeks as a union organiser, and on his return to Ireland he hoped that Soviet Russia would retain him as its commercial agent in the Free State. By now, his egotism had degenerated into a self-destructive egomania. Hubris and jealousy caused him to split the ITGWU. Intolerance and mistrust precluded him from forming a communist party; his only chance of securing substantial Russian assistance. He was left with little choice but to lead the WUI, and coped with its chronic internal wrangling only by quashing all dissent. For his admirers, he still had his charms. It was a rare thing for a union leader to be a magnificent orator, a socialist, an intellectual, and, above all, so passionate about injustice, so accessible, and so close to his people.

One of the consistencies in Larkin's politics was nationalism, and from 1908 he incorporated nationalism into his trade unionism. He established the ITGWU on the principle that Irish workers should belong to Irish unions, and held that view at least until the 1940s. There was no difference between himself and Connolly on the national question, except that Larkin's nationalism was more sentimental and he was willing to wear it on his sleeve. He opposed an insurrection during his absence in the US, but his private reservations about Connolly's involvement with Easter Week sprang from jealousy of the status given posthumously to Connolly. It was particularly galling for him to find Connolly celebrated as the hero of the union he had founded. Larkin's republicanism deepened after his return from America. It was no less possible for Larkin, than for Connolly, to reconcile nationalism with internationalism or socialist revolutionism. As an ILP'er, he came to understand socialism as a humanist religion. Though normally too insecure to be a relentless or reckless militant, from 1910 he became attracted to the syndicalist idea of trade unionism as the place to make the socialist world in embryo, and its goal of a society run by, not for, the working class, and organised on industrial unionist, or guild, or vocational lines. Bolshevism, for Larkin, was simply the latest form of revolutionism and a way of identifying with the first workers' state. He never subscribed to its theory or tactics.

The break with communism was a blessed release – not least for the communists – from the most tortuous phase of his life. He was fortunate in being able to come to terms with himself in his final years. If he made a selective input into the Labour movement after 1932, it was at least a largely positive and well-intentioned one. The last ten years of his life were relatively productive and happy for him, when he enjoyed some degree of official recognition from his peers, and a measure of reconciliation with old adversaries. For the first time since coming to Ireland, he was no longer driven, by himself or his enemies, and he realised a contentment simply in being of service.

Larkin deserves to be remembered as a hero for his titanic achievements between 1907 and 1913. It was he who founded the modern Irish Labour movement. It is unfortunate for his reputation that the story cannot be frozen in time. Even Napoleon wished he had died in Moscow. Equally, what Larkin did achieve can never be taken away from him. He remains the greatest of Irish Labour leaders.

NOTES

1   ITGWU, *The Attempt to Smash the Irish Transport and General Workers' Union* (Dublin, 1924), p. 148.

2   John Cunningham, 'From *Disturbed Dublin* to *Strumpet City*: the 1913 "history wars", 1914–1908', in Francis Devine (ed.), *A Capital in Conflict: Dublin City and the 1913 Lockout* (Dublin, 2013), pp. 353–77, provides an excellent historiography of the lockout.

3   ITGWU, *Fifty Years of Liberty Hall: The Golden Jubilee of the Irish Transport and General Workers' Union, 1909–1959* (Dublin, 1959), pp. 34–9.

4   J. W. Boyle (ed.), *Leaders and Workers* (Cork, 1966), pp. 77–86.

5   For critiques see Lawrence Wilde, 'Making myth: the image of "Big Jim" Larkin in Plunkett's *Strumpet City*', *Journal of European Studies* 41 (2011), pp. 63–75; and, wonderfully concise and incisive, D. R. O'Connor Lysaght, 'Would it have been like this? James Plunkett and *Strumpet City*', *History Ireland* (winter 2004), p. 9.

6   Cunningham, 'From *Disturbed Dublin* to *Strumpet City*', p. 374.

7   See especially the illustrations on the 1923–4 split in Francis Devine, *Organising History: A Centenary of SIPTU, 1909–2009* (Dublin, 2009), pp. 304–5.

8   See, for example, Seán McGeown (comp), 'Perspectives on: Dublin lockout and the rise of the Labour movement' (Northern Ireland Assembly, Belfast, 2013).

9   See Mary Muldowney with Ida Milne (eds), *100 Years Later: The Legacy of the 1913 Lockout* (Dublin, 1913), pp. 3–15; Kevin Myers, 'The union cult of Larkin is built on factually baseless myths', *Irish Independent*, 19 February 2013; and 'Crushing Larkin: the tycoon who saved Dublin from anarchy', *Business Plus*, September 2013.

10   Fergus A. D'Arcy, 'Larkin and the historians', in Donal Nevin (ed.), *James Larkin: Lion of the Fold* (Dublin, 1998), pp. 371–8.

11   R. F. Foster, *Modern Ireland, 1600–1972* (London, 1988); Diarmaid Ferriter, *A Nation and Not a Rabble: The Irish Revolution, 1913–1923* (London, 2015).

12   Pádraig Yeates, *Lockout: Dublin 1913* (Dublin, 2000), p. xi.

13   Colin Whitston, 'The 1913 Dublin lockout and the British and international Labour movements', in Devine (ed.), *A Capital in Conflict*, pp. 47–51.

14   Pádraig Yeates, 'Larkin – his own worst enemy?', unpublished paper; John Newsinger, *Jim Larkin and the Great Dublin Lockout of 1913* (London, 2013); Paul Smith, review of *Lockout* in *Historical Studies in Industrial Relations* 17 (spring 2004), pp. 147–50.

15   David Convery (ed.), *Locked Out: A Century of Irish Working-Class Life* (Dublin, 2013); James Curry, 'Andrew Patrick Wilson and the *Irish Worker*, 1912–13', in Convery (ed.), *Locked Out*, pp. 39–55; Theresa Moriarty, 'Delia Larkin: relative obscurity', in Nevin (ed.), *James Larkin*, pp. 428–38; James Curry, 'Delia Larkin: "More harm to the big fellow than any of the employers"?', *Saothar* 36 (2011), pp. 19–25; James Curry and Francis Devine (eds), *'Merry May Your Xmas be & 1913 Free From Care': The* Irish Worker *1912 Christmas Number* (Dublin, 2012).

16   Matt Treacy, *The Communist Party of Ireland, 1921–2011: Vol. 1, 1921–1969* (Dublin, 2012), is particularly cynical.

Bibliography

PRIVATE PAPERS AND COLLECTIONS

Cathal O'Shannon, ILHA
Charlotte Despard, PRONI
Desmond Fitzgerald, UCDA
Donal O'Reilly, NLI
Ellen Grimley, NLI
Hanna Sheehy Skeffington, NLI
ITGWU, NLI
Joseph McGarrity, NLI
Poole photographic collection, NLI
Séamus McGowan papers, UCDA
Seán MacEntee, UCDA
Seán O'Casey, NLI
Thomas Johnson, NLI
William O'Brien, NLI and UUMC
William O'Brien and Thomas Kennedy, NLI

PUBLIC RECORDS

British House of Commons debates, vols 119, 121 (1919); vol. 188 (1925); vol. 245 (1930)
Census, 1881, 1891, 1911
Díosbóireachtaí Páirliminte Dáil Éireann, vol. 71 (1938), vol. 91 (1943)
Federal Bureau of Investigation file, James Larkin, 62–312 Section 1

British Parliamentary Papers
Factories and Workshops. Annual Report of the Chief Inspector of Factories and Workshops for the Year 1899 (Cd.223, 1900)
Reports on Strikes and Lockouts, 1907-12 (Cd.4254, Cd.4680, Cd.5325, Cd.5850, Cd.6472, Cd.7089)
The Industrial Council. Minutes of Evidence Taken before the Industrial Council in Connection with Their Enquiry into Industrial Agreements (Cd.6953, 1913)
Report of the Dublin Disturbances Commission (Cd.7269, 1914)
Communist Papers: Documents Selected from Those Obtained on the Arrest of the Communist Leaders on October 14, 21, 1925, Cmd.2682 (1926)

Irish Labour History Archives
Dublin Housing Inquiry, 1939: Verbatim Report of Proceedings (1946)
ITGWU, 'Draft Rules for the ITGWU', 1923
ITUC national executive minute book, 1917
ITUC, reports, 1937, 1942, 1946

Irish Railway Record Society Archive, Dublin
Great Southern and Western Railway, files 1019, 1069

Law Library, Dublin
The Irish Reports (1925)

Library of the Northern Ireland Assembly
Seán McGeown (comp), 'Perspectives on: Dublin lockout-out and the rise of the labour
    movement' (2013)

National Archives of Ireland
Department of Foreign Affairs papers
Department of Justice files
Department of the Taoiseach files
Registry of Friendly Society files on the WUI

National Archives of the United Kingdom
Cabinet papers
Colonial Office papers
Foreign Office papers
Home Office files
Metropolitan Police reports
Ministry of Labour reports on strikes and lockouts
Security Service records

National Library of Ireland
Reports of the ITUC, 1925, 1938–9, 1941, 1945
Submissions to the Commission on Vocational Organization, 1939–43, vol. 18, doc.136

Public Record Office of Northern Ireland
Cabinet papers
Interviews of Sam Hanna Bell with veterans of the 1907 strikes in the 1950s, D3358/1

RGASPI fondi
17, Central Committee, VKP(b)
495, ECCI
515, CPUSA
534, Profintern
538, WIR
539, ICWPA

University of Ulster, Magee College
Belfast trades council minutes, 1904, 1907, 1911
Dublin trades council minutes, 1907–14
Reports of the ITUC, 1907–14, 1919, 1923

Waterford Chamber of Commerce
Minutes, 1911

NEWSPAPERS

Altoona Tribune, 1920
Arkansas City Daily Traveler, 1920
Atlanta Constitution, 1916
Belfast Labour Chronicle, 1905
Belvidere Daily Republican, 1914, 1916
Bismarck Tribune, 1915
Blast (San Francisco), 1917
Boston Post, 1916, 1920
Brooklyn Daily Eagle, 1917, 1919–20, 1922–3
Brooklyn Times, 1914
Business Plus, 2013
Call (New York), 1920
Charlotte News, 1920
Chicago Daily Tribune, 1914
Chronicle-Telegram, 1919
Cincinnati Enquirer, 1922
Communist International, 1928
Connacht Tribune, 1911
Co-operative News (Everett, WA), 1918
Cork Examiner, 1909
Daily Free Press (Carbondale 11), 1917
Daily Herald, 1913–14
Daily Messenger, 1922
Day Book (Chicago), 1914
Derry Journal, 1891, 1896, 1907, 1909, 1911–14
Dublin Saturday Post, 1913
Dunkirk Evening News, 1934
Durham Chronicle, 1914
Eau Clair Leader, 1915
Evening Herald, 1914, 1929
Evening Telegraph, 1908, 1910, 1918–19
Evening World, 1919
Fitchburg Sentinel, 18 April 1923
Forward (Glasgow), 1910

Freeman's Journal, 1907–8, 1912–13, 1923
Gaelic American, 1914–15, 1923
Gettysburg Times, 1934
Greensboro Daily News, 1916
Harp, 1910
Harrisburg Telegraph, 1916, 1919–20
Huntingdon Press, 1920
Indianapolis Star, 1914
Industrial Syndicalist, 1910
Irish Democrat, 1980
Irish Hammer and Plough, 1926
Irish Independent, 1911–13, 1919, 1923, 1927, 1929, 2013
Irish Labour Journal, 1909
Irish News and Belfast Morning News, 1907
Irish People (Chicago), 1923–4
Irish Socialist, 1984
Irish Times, 1908, 1911–14, 1925, 1930, 1933–9, 1941–4, 1956, 1983, 2012
Irish Worker, 1911–14, 1923–5, 1930–2
(Irish) Workers' Voice, 1930–1, 1933
Irish Workers' Weekly, 1941
Labour Leader, 1908
Lawrence Daily Journal-World, 1920
Leader, 1910
Lincoln Evening Journal, 1919
Liverpool Forward, 1914
Londonderry Sentinel, 1907, 1920
Manchester Guardian, 1913, 1923
Montana Socialist, 1915
Muskogee Times-Democrat, 1920
Nenagh Guardian, 1924
New Leader, 1943
New Witness, 1913
New York American, 1914
New York Sun, 1914, 1934
New York Times, 1913, 1916, 1919–23
New York Tribune, 1914–15
Northern Whig, 1907
Northwest Worker, 1915, 1917
Ogden Standard-Examiner, 1920, 1922–3
Oneonta Star, 1922
Oshkosh Daily Northwestern, 1917
Ottawa Journal, 1914
Peasant, 1908
Reading Times, 1917
San Bernardino County Sun, 1934

San Francisco Chronicle, 1920

Santa Cruz Evening News, 1915

Saoirse na h-Éireann: Irish Freedom, 1911

Socialist (Glasgow), 1920

Standard, 1941–2, 1947

The Times, 1914, 1919

Times-Herald, 1922

Truth That Is News, 1933

Voice of Labour, 1919, 1922, 1924–5

Washington Post, 1916, 1919, 1922

Waterford News, 1908

Weekly Record, 1913

Wilmington News-Journal, 18 July 1927

Winnipeg Tribune, 1916, 1922

Workers' Republic, 1915, 1923, 1927

PUBLISHED CONTEMPORARY SOURCES AND PUBLICATIONS
OF LARKIN'S CONTEMPORARIES

Askwith, Lord, *Industrial Problems and Disputes* (Brighton, 1974)

Bower, Fred, *Rolling Stonemason: An Autobiography* (London, 1936)

Briscoe, Robert, with Alden Hatch, *For the Life of Me* (London, 1959)

British and Irish Communist Organization, *The American Trial of Big Jim Larkin, 1920*
    (Belfast, 1976)

Cardiff, Breda, 'As I remember Big Jim', in Donal Nevin (ed.), *James Larkin: Lion of the
    Fold* (Dublin, 1998)

Chaplin, Charles, *My Autobiography* (London, 1964)

Clarkson, J. D., *Labour and Nationalism in Ireland* (New York, 1970, first edn New York,
    1926)

Cohen, Maximilien, 'Long live the Communist Party! 2,500 seized in raids', *Communist
    World*, 15 November 1919

Collins, Séamus, 'The situation in Ireland', *Communist International*, 1 February 1928

Commission on Vocational Organization, *Report* (Dublin, 1943)

Connolly, James, *The Axe to the Root and Old Wine in New Bottles* (Dublin, 1934)

——, *Collected Works, Volume Two* (Dublin, 1988)

Connolly O'Brien, Nora, *Portrait of a Rebel Father* (Dublin, 1935)

Cork Workers' Club, *Convict No. 50945: Jim Larkin, Irish Labour Leader*, Historical Reprints
    no 12 (Cork, *n.d.*)

Corkery, Daniel, *The Labour Leader: A Play in Three Acts* (Dublin, 1920)

Dallas, George, 'Larkin's life history', in Donal Nevin (ed.), *James Larkin: Lion of the Fold*
    (Dublin, 1998)

Daly, Fr Cormac, OFM, correspondence, *History Ireland* 22:2 (2014)

Dangerfield, George, *The Strange Death of Liberal England* (London, 1983 edn) de Courcy Ireland, John, 'As I remember Big Jim', in Donal Nevin (ed.), *James Larkin: Lion of the Fold* (Dublin, 1998)

Deasy, Joe, 'As I remember Big Jim', in Donal Nevin (ed.), *James Larkin: Lion of the Fold* (Dublin, 1998)

Degras, Jane (ed.), *The Communist International, 1919–1943: Documents, Volume 2, 1923–1928* (London, 1971)

Eglington, John, *A Memoir of AE, George William Russell* (London, 1937)

Fanning, Ronan, Michael Kennedy, Dermot Keogh, and Eunan O'Halpin (eds), *Documents on Irish Foreign Policy, Vol. II, 1923–1926* (Dublin, 2000)

——, *Documents on Irish Foreign Policy, Vol. III, 1926–1932* (Dublin, 2002)

Farrell, James T., 'Jim Larkin, Irish Labour leader', *New International*, 13 (March 1947)

Fox, R. M., *Jim Larkin: The Rise of the Underman* (London, 1957)

Gitlow, Benjamin, *The Whole of Their Lives: Communism in America – A Personal History and Intimate Portrayal of Its Leaders* (London, 1948)

Gosling, Harry, *Up and Down Stream* (London, 1927)

Gurley Flynn, Elizabeth, *The Rebel Girl, an Autobiography: My First Life (1906–1926)* (New York, 1986)

Haywood, William D., *Bill Haywood's Book: The Autobiography of William D. Haywood* (New York, 1929)

Industrial Council, *Report of the Industrial Council of the British Board of Trade on Its Inquiry into Industrial Agreements: August 18, 1913* (1913, reprinted Memphis, TN, 2010)

ITGWU, *The Attempt to Smash the Irish Transport and General Workers' Union* (Dublin, 1924)

——, *Fifty Years of Liberty Hall: The Golden Jubilee of the Irish Transport and General Workers' Union, 1909–1959* (Dublin, 1959)

Krause, David (ed.), *The Letters of Seán O'Casey, Volume I, 1910–1941* (London, 1975)

——, *The letters of Seán O'Casey, Volume II, 1942–1954* (New York, 1980)

——, *The Letters of Seán O'Casey, Volume III, 1955–58* (Washington, DC, 1989)

Larkin Release Committee, *James Larkin: A Labour Leader and an Honest Man* (Liverpool, 1910)

MacDonnell, J. M., *The Story of Irish Labour* (1921, Cork Workers' Club reprint)

MacLiammóir, Micheál, *All for Hecuba: An Irish Theatrical Autobiography* (London, 1946)

Mann, Tom, *Tom Mann's Memoirs* (London, 1923)

Montefiore, Dora B., *From a Victorian to a Modern* (London, 1917)

Murphy, J. T., *New Horizons* (London, 1941)

O'Brien, William *Forth the Banners Go: The Reminiscences of William O'Brien as Told to Edward MacLysaght, D.Litt* (Dublin, 1969)

O'Casey, Seán, *Autobiography Book 3: Drums under the Windows* (London, 1972)

——, *The Story of the Irish Citizen Army* (London, 1980)

Ó Cathasaigh, Aindrias (ed.), *The Life and Times of Gilbert Lynch* (Dublin, 2011)

Ó Ciosáin, Éamon, *An t-Éireannach, 1934–37: Páipéar Sóisialach Gaeltachta* (Dublin, 1993)

O'Connor, Emmet and Trevor Parkhill (eds), *Loyalism and Labour in Belfast: The Autobiography of Robert McElborough, 1884–1952* (Cork, 2002)

Ó Duinnín, Eoghan, *La Nina Bonita agus an Róisín Dubh; Cuimhní Cinn ar Chogadh na Spáinne* (Dublin, 1986)

Orpen, Sir William, 'Larkin at Liberty Hall', in Donal Nevin (ed.), *James Larkin: Lion of the Fold* (Dublin, 1998)

Pataud, Emile and Emile Pouget, *How Shall We Bring about the Revolution: Syndicalism and the Co-operative Commonwealth* (London, 1990, first edn France, 1909, British edn 1913)

Penty, Arthur J., *The Restoration of the Gild System* (London, 1906)

Plunkett, James, 'Big Jim: a loaf on the table, a flower in the vase', in Donal Nevin (ed.), *James Larkin: Lion of the Fold* (Dublin, 1998)

Robbins, Frank, *Under the Starry Plough: Recollections of the Irish Citizen Army* (Dublin, 1977)

Ryan, W. P., *The Irish Labour Movement from the 'Twenties to Our Own Day* (Dublin, 1919)

——, 'The struggle of 1913', in WUI, *1913: Jim Larkin and the Dublin Lock-Out* (Dublin, 1964)

Sexton, James, *The Riot Act: A Play in Three Acts* (London, 1915)

——, *Sir James Sexton, Agitator: The Life of the Dockers' MP. An Autobiography* (London, 1936)

Stewart, Bob, *Breaking the Fetters: The Memoirs of Bob Stewart* (London, 1967)

Swift, John, 'Report of the Commission on Vocational Organization (and its times, 1930s–40s)', *Saothar* 1 (1975)

——, 'Learning to work with Jim Larkin', *Irish Socialist*, June 1984

——, 'John Swift remembers Larkin', *Irish Socialist*, August 1984

——, 'Larkin's new clothes', *Irish Socialist*, December 1984

——, 'How Larkin died on his knees', *Irish Socialist*, January 1985

——, 'The last years', in Donal Nevin (ed.), *James Larkin: Lion of the Fold* (Dublin, 1998)

Thom's Directory, 1931 (Dublin)

White, Jack, *Misfit* (London, 1930)

Wicks, Harry, *Keeping My Head: The Memoirs of a British Bolshevik* (London, 1992)

Wolfe, Bertram D., *Strange Communists I Have Known* (New York, 1982)

Wright, Arnold, *Disturbed Dublin: The Story of the Great Strike of 1913–14, with a Description of the Industries of the Irish Capital* (London, 1914)

BOOKS, ARTICLES, AND PAMPHLETS

Alderman, Geoffrey, 'The National Free Labour Association: a case-study of organised strike-breaking in the late nineteenth and early twentieth centuries', *International Review of Social History* 26 (1976)

Allen, Kieran, *Fianna Fáil and Irish Labour: 1926 to the Present* (London, 1997)

Barrington, Ruth, *Health, Medicine, and Politics in Ireland, 1900–1970* (Dublin, 1987)

Bowman, Terence, *People's Champion: The Life of Alexander Bowman, Pioneer of Labour Politics in Ireland* (Belfast, 1997)

Boyle, J. W., 'The Belfast Protestant Association and the Independent Orange Order, 1901–10', *Irish Historical Studies* 13:50 (1962)

——, (ed.), *Leaders and Workers* (Cork, 1966)

——, *The Irish Labor Movement in the Nineteenth Century* (Washington, DC, 1989)

Bradley, Dan, *Farm Labourers: Irish Struggle, 1900–1976* (Belfast, 1988)

Brommel, Bernard, *Eugene V. Debs: Spokesman for Labor and Socialism* (Chicago, 1978)

Brown, Ken, *The English Labour Movement, 1700–1951* (Dublin, 1982)

Brundage, David, 'American Labour and the Irish question, 1916–23', *Saothar* 24 (1999)

Burch, Steven Dedalus, *Andrew P. Wilson and the Early Irish and Scottish National Theatres, 1911–1950* (New York, 2008)

Burke Savage, Roland, 'The Church in Dublin, 1940–1965: a study of the episcopate of the Most Rev. John Charles McQuaid, D.D.', *Studies* (winter 1965)

Calhoun, Daniel F., *The United Front: The TUC and the Russians, 1923–1928* (Cambridge, 1976)

Campaign for Labour Representation in Northern Ireland, *The Forgotten Conference* (Belfast, 1982)

Carroll, Denis, *They Have Fooled You Again: Michael O'Flanagan (1876–1942), Priest, Republican, Social Critic* (Dublin, 1993)

Chubb, Basil (ed.), *Federation of Irish Employers, 1942–1992* (Dublin, 1992)

Clarkson, L. A., 'Population change and urbanization, 1821–1911', in Liam Kennedy and Philip Ollerenshaw (eds), *An Economic History of Ulster, 1820–1939* (Manchester, 1985)

Coates, Ken and Tony Topham, *The History of the Transport and General Workers' Union: Vol. I, Part I, 1870–1911: From Forerunners to Federation* (Oxford, 1991)

——, *The History of the Transport and General Workers' Union: Vol. I, Part II, 1912–1922: From Federation to Amalgamation* (Oxford, 1991)

Cody, Séamus, 'The remarkable Patrick Daly', *Obair* 2 (1985)

Cody, Séamus, John O'Dowd, and Peter Rigney, *The Parliament of Labour: 100 Years of the Dublin Council of Trade Unions* (Dublin, 1986)

Conradi, Peter, *Hitler's Piano Player: The Rise and Fall of Ernst Hanfstaengle, Confidante of Hitler, Ally of FDR* (New York, 2004)

Cooney, John, *John Charles McQuaid: Ruler of Catholic Ireland* (Dublin, 1999)

Convery, David (ed.), *Locked Out: A Century of Irish Working-Class Life* (Dublin, 2013)

Cousins, Mel, 'The creation of association: the National Insurance Act, 1911 and approved societies in Ireland', in Jennifer Kelly and R. V. Comerford (eds), *Associational Culture in Ireland and Abroad* (Dublin, 2010)

CPI, *Communist Party of Ireland: Outline History* (Dublin, 1975)

Cradden, Terry, *Trade Unionism, Socialism, and Partition: The Labour Movement in Northern Ireland, 1939–53* (Belfast, 1993)

Cullen, L. M., *An Economic History of Ireland Since 1660* (London, 1987)

Cullen Owens, Rosemary, *Louie Bennett* (Cork, 2001)

Culleton, Claire A., 'James Larkin and J. Edgar Hoover: Irish politics and an American conspiracy', *Éire-Ireland* 35 (fall/winter 2000–01)

Cunningham, John, *Labour in the West of Ireland: Working Life and Struggle, 1890–1914* (Belfast, 1995)

——, 'From *Disturbed Dublin* to *Strumpet City*: the 1913 "history wars", 1914–1908', in Francis Devine (ed.), *A Capital in Conflict: Dublin City and the 1913 Lockout* (Dublin, 2013)

Curriculum Development Unit, *Dublin 1913: A Divided City* (Dublin, 1984)

Curry, James, 'Delia Larkin: "More harm to the big fellow than any of the employers"?', *Saothar* 36 (2011)

——, 'Andrew Patrick Wilson and the *Irish Worker*, 1912–13', in David Convery (ed.), *Locked Out: A Century of Irish Working-Class Life* (Dublin, 2013)

——, 'Elizabeth Brown and the marriage of James Larkin', unpublished paper

Curry, James and Francis Devine (eds), *'Merry May Your Xmas Be & 1913 Free From Care': The* Irish Worker *1912 Christmas Number* (Dublin, 2012)

D'Arcy, Fergus A., 'Larkin and the historians', in Donal Nevin (ed.), *James Larkin: Lion of the Fold* (Dublin, 1998)

Dallas, Kenneth G., correspondence, *Saothar* 6 (1980)

de Wiel, Jerome aan, *The Irish Factor, 1988–1919: Ireland's Strategic and Diplomatic Importance for Foreign Powers* (Dublin, 2009)

Devine, Francis, *Organising History: A Centenary of SIPTU, 1909–2009* (Dublin, 2009)

Diggle, G. E., *A History of Widnes* (Widnes, 1961)

Dorgan, Theo, 'Larkin through the eyes of writers', in Donal Nevin (ed.), *James Larkin: Lion of the Fold* (Dublin, 1998)

Draper, Theodore, *American Communism and Soviet Russia* (New York, 2003)

Emmons, David M., *The Butte Irish: Class and Ethnicity in an American Mining Town, 1875–1925* (Chicago, 1990)

Enright, Michael, *Men of Iron: Wexford Foundry Disputes 1890 & 1911* (Wexford, 1987)

Farrell, Michael, *Northern Ireland: The Orange State* (London, 1976)

——, 'Anti-communist frenzy', *Irish Times*, 28 March 1983

Ferriter, Diarmaid, *A Nation and Not a Rabble: The Irish Revolution, 1913–1923* (London, 2015)

Foster, R. F., *Modern Ireland, 1600–1972* (London, 1988)

Gallagher, Michael, *Political Parties in the Republic of Ireland* (Manchester, 1985)

Gaughan, J. Anthony, *Thomas Johnson, 1872–1963: First Leader of the Labour Party in Dáil Éireann* (Dublin, 1980)

Geraghty, Hugh, *William Patrick Partridge and His Times (1874–1917)* (Dublin, 2003)

Gibbons, Luke, 'Labour and local history: the case of Jim Gralton, 1886–1945, *Saothar* 14 (1980)

Golway, Terry, *Irish Rebel: John Devoy and America's Fight for Ireland's Freedom* (New York, 1999)

Gotovitch, José and Mikhail Narinski et al (eds), *Komintern, L'Histoire et les Hommes: Dictionnaire Biographique de l'Internationale Communiste en France, en Belgique, au Luxembourg, en Suisse et a Moscou (1919–1943)* (Paris, 2001)

Gray, John, *City in Revolt: James Larkin and the Belfast Dock Strike of 1907* (Belfast, 1985)

Greaves, C. Desmond, *The Life and Times of James Connolly* (London, 1961)

——, *Liam Mellows and the Irish Revolution* (London, 1971)

——, *Seán O'Casey: Politics and Art* (London, 1979)

——, 'Jim Larkin's earliest years', *Irish Democrat*, September 1980

——, *The Irish Transport and General Workers' Union: The Formative Years, 1909–1923* (Dublin, 1982)

Halevy, Elie, *A History of the English People in the Nineteenth Century, VI: The Rule of Democracy, 1905–1914 (Book II)* (London, 1952)

Hanley, Brian, *The IRA, 1926–36* (Dublin, 2002)

Haverty, Anne, *Constance Markievicz: An Independent Life* (London, 1988)

Hepburn, A. C., 'Work, class, and religion in Belfast, 1871–1911', *Irish Economic and Social History* 10 (1983)

——, *Catholic Belfast and Nationalist Ireland in the Era of Joe Devlin, 1871–1934* (Oxford, 2008)

Herbert, Michael, *The Wearing of the Green: A Political History of the Irish in Manchester* (London, 1991)

Holton, Bob, *British Syndicalism, 1900–1914: Myths and Realities* (London, 1976)

Howell, David, *A Lost Left: Three Studies in Socialism and Nationalism* (Manchester, 1986)

Hudelson, Richard, 'Jack Carney and the *Truth* in Duluth', *Saothar* 19 (1994)

Hutt, Allen, *British Trade Unionism: A Short History* (London, 1975)

Hyman, Richard, *The Workers' Union* (Oxford, 1971)

Hyslop, Jonathon, *The Notorious Syndicalist: J. T. Bain; a Scottish Rebel in Colonial Africa* (Johannesburg, 2004)

Jones, Mary, *These Obstreperous Lassies: A History of the Irish Women Workers' Union* (Dublin, 1988)

Kenefick, William, *'Rebellious and Contrary': The Glasgow Dockers, c.1853 to 1932* (East Linton, 2000)

Keogh, Dermot, *The Rise of the Irish Working Class: The Dublin Trade Union Movement and Labour Leadership, 1890–1914* (Belfast, 1982)

Landau, Captain Henry, *The Enemy within: The inside Story of German Sabotage in America* (New York, 1937)

Lane, Leann, 'George Russell and James Stephens: class and cultural discourse, Dublin 1913', in Francis Devine (ed.), *A Capital in Conflict: Dublin City and the 1913 Lockout* (Dublin, 2013)

Lane, Padraig G., 'Daniel Corkery and the Cork working class', *Saothar* 28 (2013)

Larkin, Emmet, *James Larkin: Irish Labour Leader, 1876–1947* (London, 1965)

——, 'Socialism and Catholicism in Ireland', *Studies* (spring 1985)

——, 'James Larkin, labour leader', in Donal Nevin (ed.), *James Larkin: Lion of the Fold* (Dublin, 1998)

Larkin, Jim, *In the Footsteps of Big Jim: A Family Biography* (Dublin, 1995)

Lee, Joseph, 'Aspects of corporatist thought in Ireland: the Commission on Vocational organization, 1939–43', in Art Cosgrove and Donal McCartney (eds), *Studies in Irish History* (Dublin, 1979)

Lowery, R. G., 'Seán O'Casey and the *Irish Worker*', in R. G. Lowery (ed.), *O'Casey Annual No. 3* (London, 1984)

Lynch, Patrick, 'Larkin in history', in Nevin (ed.), *James Larkin: Lion of the Fold* (Dublin, 1998)

MacMahon, Joseph A, OFM, 'The Catholic clergy and the social question in Ireland, 1891–1916', *Studies* 70:280 (winter 1981)

McCabe, Conor, 'The context and course of the Irish railway disputes of 1911', *Saothar* 30 (2005)

——, '"Your only God is profit": Irish class relations and the 1913 lockout', in David Convery (ed.), *Locked Out: A Century of Irish Working-Class Life* (Dublin, 2013)

McCamley, Bill, *The Third James: James Fearon, 1874–1924, an Unsung Hero of Our Struggle* (Dublin, 2000)

McGuire, Charlie, *Seán McLoughlin: Ireland's Forgotten Revolutionary* (Pontypool, 2011)

McLoughlin, Barry, 'Proletarian academics or party functionaries? Irish communists at the International Lenin School', *Saothar* 22 (1997)

——, *Left to the Wolves: Irish Victims of Stalinist Terror* (Dublin, 2007)

Maume, Patrick, 'Arthur Trew', *Dictionary of Irish Biography* 9 (Cambridge, 2009)

Miller, James A., Susan D. Pennybacker, and Eve Rosenhaft, 'Mother Ada Wright and the international campaign to free the Scottsboro Boys, 1931–1934', *American Historical Review* 106:2 (April 2001)

Millman, Chad, *The Detonators: The Secret Plot to Destroy America and an Epic Hunt for Justice* (New York, 2006)

Milotte, Mike, *Communism in Modern Ireland: The Pursuit of the Workers' Republic since 1916* (Dublin, 1984)

Mitchell, Arthur, *Labour in Irish Politics, 1890–1930: The Irish Labour Movement in an Age of Revolution* (Dublin, 1974)

Morgan, Austen, *James Connolly: A Political Biography* (Manchester, 1988)

——, *Labour and Partition: The Belfast Working Class, 1905–23* (London, 1991)

Morgan, Kevin, *Bolshevism and the British Left, Part Three: Bolshevism, Syndicalism, and the General Strike: The Lost International World of A. A. Purcell* (London, 2013)

Moriarty, Theresa, 'Delia Larkin: relative obscurity', in Donal Nevin (ed.), *James Larkin: Lion of the Fold* (Dublin, 1998)

Morrissey, SJ, Thomas J., *A Man Called Hughes: The Life and Times of Seamus Hughes, 1881–1943* (Dublin, 1991)

——, *William Martin Murphy* (Dundalk, 1997)

——, *William O'Brien, 1881–1968: Socialist, Republican, Dáil Deputy, Editor and Trade Union Leader* (Dublin, 2007)

Muldowney, Mary with Ida Milne (eds), *100 Years Later: The Legacy of the 1913 Lockout* (Dublin, 1913)

Murray, Christopher, *Seán O'Casey: Writer at Work, a Biography* (Dublin, 2004)

Murray, Peter, 'Electoral politics and the Dublin working class before the First World War', *Saothar* 6 (1980)

Myers, Kevin, 'The union cult of Larkin is built on factually baseless myths', *Irish Independent*, 19 February 2013

Nevin, Donal (ed.), *Trade Union Century* (Cork, 1994)

—— (ed.), *James Larkin: Lion of the Fold* (Dublin, 1998)

——, *James Connolly: 'A Full Life'* (Dublin, 2006)

—— (ed.), *Between Comrades: James Connolly, Letters and Correspondence 1889–1916* (Dublin, 2007)

Newsinger, John, 'A lamp to guide your feet: Jim Larkin, the *Irish Worker*, and the Dublin working class', *European History Quarterly* 20 (1990)

——, *Rebel City: Larkin, Connolly and the Dublin Labour Movement* (London, 2004)

——, *Jim Larkin and the Great Dublin Lockout of 1913* (London, 2013)

Noonan, Alan J. M., '"Real Irish patriots would scorn to recognise the likes of you": Larkin and Irish-America', in David Convery (ed.), *Locked Out: A Century of Irish Working-Class Life* (Dublin, 2013)

O'Connor, Emmet, *Syndicalism in Ireland, 1917–23* (Cork, 1988)

——, *A Labour History of Waterford* (Waterford, 1989)

——, 'Jim Larkin and the Communist Internationals, 1923–9', *Irish Historical Studies* 31:123 (May 1999)

——, *A Labour History of Ireland, 1824–2000* (Dublin, 2011)

——, 'Anti-communism in twentieth century Ireland', *Twentieth Century Communism: A Journal of International History* 6 (2014)

O'Connor, Garry, *Seán O'Casey: A Life* (London, 1988)

O'Connor Lysaght, D. R., 'Would it have been like this? James Plunkett and *Strumpet City*', *History Ireland* (winter 2004)

Ó Drisceoil, Dónal, *Peadar O'Donnell* (Cork, 2001)

O'Riordan, Manus, 'Larkin in America: the road to Sing Sing', in Donal Nevin (ed.), *James Larkin: Lion of the Fold* (Dublin, 1998)

——, 'From Sing Sing to sing and sing: the 1934 Larkin affidavit', *Irish Political Review* (October, December 2011)

Patterson, Henry, 'Independent Orangeism and class conflict in Edwardian Belfast', *Proceedings of the Royal Irish Academy*, 80, section C, 1 (1980)

——, *Class Conflict and Sectarianism: The Protestant Working Class and the Belfast Labour Movement, 1868–1920* (Belfast, 1980)

Pelling, Henry, *A History of British Trade Unionism* (Harmondsworth, 1974)

Phillips, G. A., 'James Sexton', *Oxford Dictionary of National Biography*, online

Puirséal, Niamh, *The Irish Labour Party, 1922–73* (Dublin, 2007)

Rhodes, Anthony, *The Vatican in the Age of Dictators, 1922–45* (London, 1973)

Ripley, B. J., and J. McHugh, *John Maclean* (Manchester, 1989)

Smith, Paul, review of *Lockout* in *Historical Studies in Industrial Relations* 17 (spring 2004)

Stanley, John L., *From Georges Sorel: Essays in Socialism and Philosophy* (New Brunswick, NJ, 1987)

Swift, John P., *John Swift: An Irish Dissident* (Dublin, 1991)

Taplin, Eric, *The Dockers' Union: A Study of the National Union of Dock Labourers, 1889–1922* (Leicester, 1986)

——, 'Liverpool: the apprenticeship of a revolutionary', in Donal Nevin (ed.), *James Larkin; Lion of the Fold* (Dublin, 1998)

Treacy, Matt, *The Communist Party of Ireland, 1921–2011: Vol.1, 1921–1969* (Dublin, 2012)

Waller, P. J., *Democracy and Sectarianism: A Political and Social History of Liverpool 1868–1939* (Liverpool, 1981)

Whitston, Colin, 'The 1913 Dublin lockout and the British and international labour movements', in Francis Devine (ed.), *A Capital in Conflict: Dublin City and the 1913 Lockout* (Dublin, 2013)

Wilde, Lawrence, 'Making myth: the image of "Big Jim" Larkin in Plunkett's *Strumpet City*', *Journal of European Studies* 41 (2011)

Woggon, Helga, 'Landscapes of James Connolly, 1916–2016: from re-interpretation to reconquest?', *Socialist History* (forthcoming 2016)

WUI, *1913: Jim Larkin and the Dublin Lock-Out* (Dublin, 1964)

Yeates, Pádraig, *Lockout: Dublin 1913* (Dublin, 2000)

——, 'Craft workers during the Irish revolution, 1919–22', *Saothar* 33 (2008)

——, 'Larkin – his own worst enemy?', unpublished paper

Zumoff, Jacob A., *The Communist International and US Communism, 1919–1929* (Leiden, 2015)

DISSERTATIONS

Banta, Mary M., 'The red scare in the Irish Free State, 1939–37' (MA, UCD, 1982)

Coe, W., 'The economic history of the engineering industry in the north of Ireland (PhD, Queen's University, Belfast, 1961)

Collins, Peter Gerard, 'Belfast trades council, 1881–1921' (D.Phil, University of Ulster, 1988)

Hall, Fred S., 'Sympathetic strikes and sympathetic lockouts', *Studies in History, Economics and Public Law* (PhD, New York, 1898–9)

McDermott, Daniel V., 'The British Labour movement and Ireland, 1905–25' (MA, University College, Galway, 1979)

Pimley, Adrian, 'A history of the Irish Citizen Army from 1913 to 1916 (M.Soc.Sc, University of Birmingham, 1982)

ONLINE

Independent Labour Party, *Report of the Sixteenth Annual Conference* (London, 1908)

Kenefick, William, 'James O'Connor Kessack', *Oxford Dictionary of National Biography*

White, Lawrence William, 'Jack Carney', *Dictionary of Irish Biography*

workersrepublic.org/Pages/Ireland/Trotskyism/farrelltotrotsky.html (accessed 8 February 2006)

workersliberty.org/story/2009/03/25/comrade-otrotsky-trotskys-attempt-get-irish-visa (accessed 29 June 2015)

marxists.org/history/etol/document/ireland-fi/norac.htm#nora (accessed 30 June 2015).

Index

Index